THE SWORDBEARERS

THE

Supreme Comman

SWORDBEARERS

in the First World War

Correlli Barnett

INDIANA UNIVERSITY PRESS

Bloomington

Copyright © 1963 by Correlli Barnett
Published in Great Britain in 1963
First published in the United States in 1964 by William Morrow
& Company
First Indiana University Press editions published by arrangement with
William Morrow & Company, 1975.

Manufactured in the United States of America

Library of Congress Cataloging in Publication Data
Barnett, Correlli.
The swordbearers.
Reprint of the 1964 ed. published by Morrow, New
York.
Bibliography
1. European War, 1914-1918—Campaigns. 2. European
War, 1914-1918—Biography. I. Title.
[D530.B26 1975]   940.4'14'0922   74-19057
ISBN 0-253-35584-2
ISBN 0-253-20175-6 pbk.
3 4 5 6 7 8 87 86 85 84 83 82

FOR CLARE AND HILARY

Contents

AUTHOR'S PREFACE «XV»
AUTHOR'S NOTE «xvii»

I
THE TRAGIC DELUSION
Colonel-General Helmuth von Moltke «3»

II
SAILOR WITH A FLAWED CUTLASS
Admiral Sir John Jellicoe «101»

III
TRAVAIL, FAMILLE, PATRIE
General Philippe Pétain «193»

IV
FULL CIRCLE
General Erich Ludendorff «269»

APPENDIX: Organisation of Armies in 1914 «363»
BIBLIOGRAPHY «365»
ACKNOWLEDGEMENTS «371»
INDEX «373»

Illustrations

I. FACING PAGE 78

1   Colonel-General von Moltke
2   The Kaiser and Moltke at pre-war manoeuvres
3   The Reichs Chancellor, Theobald von Bethmann-Hollweg
4   The outbreak of war: cheering crowds in the Odeonplatz, Munich. Adolf
      Hitler is circled.
5   General Joffre
6   Colonel-General von Kluck (taken in 1916)
7   Field-Marshal Sir John French
8   Colonel-General von Bülow
9   General von Hausen
10 Lieutenant-Colonel Hentsch
11 The battle of the Marne: French troops passing through a village
12 The battle of the Marne: a retrospective propaganda picture

II. FACING PAGE 142

13 Admiral Sir John Jellicoe
14 Vice-Admiral Reinhard Scheer
15 Vice-Admiral Sir David Beatty
16 Vice-Admiral Franz Hipper
17 Jutland: the battle cruiser *Lion* being hit on a turret
18 The battle-cruiser action: *Queen Mary* blows up
19 The German battle cruiser *Seydlitz* on fire
20 Commodore Goodenough

21   Vice-Admiral Sir Charles Madden

22   Kaiser Wilhelm II, in Grand Admiral's uniform, talking to a dockyard worker

III.   FACING PAGE 206

23   General Philippe Pétain
24   General Robert Nivelle
25   Paul Painlevé

Living quarters:

26   The Château de Beaurepaire, occupied by the British C-in-C from March 1916 to April 1919

27   A dugout near Miraumont, occupied by the Royal Artillery, March 1917

28   French troops deserting during the mutinies of 1917

29   The Passchendaele campaign, 1917: a canal and bridge destroyed in the fighting

30   Albert Thomas, Haig, Joffre and Lloyd George
31   General Sir Henry Wilson
32   Field-Marshal von Hindenburg

IV.   FACING PAGE 270

33   General Erich Ludendorff

Commanders in the March offensive, 1918:

34   General Otto von Below
35   General von der Marwitz
36   General Oskar von Hutier
37   General Sir Hubert Gough

The March offensive:

38   German troops attacking
39   German field artillery advancing
40   British heavy artillery retreating
41   A German 5.9-inch howitzer

42   Field-Marshal Sir Douglas Haig
43   Marshal Ferdinand Foch
44   Crown Prince Rupprecht of Bavaria
45   General Sir Julian Byng
46   Foch shakes hands with the United States C-in-C, General John J. Pershing

Acknowledgements are due to the Imperial War Museum for plates 4, 6, 7, 14, 15, 16, 17, 18, 19, 20, 22, 23, 26, 27, 29, 30, 34, 35, 36, 37, 39, 40, 41, 42, 43, 44, and 45; to the Radio Times Hulton Picture Library for plates 2, 3, 5, 11, 12, 21, 24, 25, 28, 31, 32, 38, and 46; to the Bibliothek für Zeitgeschichte at Stuttgart for plates 1, 8, 9, 10, and 33; and to Lady Jellicoe for plate 13, for the letter reproduced on page 104 and the sketches on pages 153 and 162.

Maps

Europe in 1914
The western front, 1914-18

I

1 The Schlieffen Plan, 1905 «23»
2 August 1914: deployment of the armies «28»
3 1st Army's march through the Liége bottleneck «32»
4 Plan 17 and the battles of Morhange-Sarrebourg «38»
5 Kluck's failure to drive the Belgians from Antwerp «40»
6 The German opportunity on August 20 «42»
7 The French offensive in the Ardennes «47»
8 The battle of Mons «54»
9 The German chance on August 24 «56»
10 Moltke's alteration of the Schlieffen Plan «65»
11 Axes of advance of German right-wing armies,
    August-September 1914 «67»
12 The Marne campaign: main rail routes «71»
13 Joffre's plan for the battle of the Marne «80»
14 The battle of the Marne «82»
15 Kluck's march to the Ourcq «83»

II

16 The North Sea «111»
17 Jutland: the approach to battle «124»
18 The battle cruisers make contact «137»
19 The opening of the battle-cruiser action «139»
20 The battle-cruiser action «141»

21 The battle fleet action: eve of deployment «148»

22 The Grand Fleet's deployment «152»

23 Scheer's battle-turn away «161»

24 The second battle fleet encounter «165»

25 The third encounter «170»

26 Fleet movements, May 31, 1916: 6 P.M. till dusk «172»

27 Scheer's alternative escape routes «174»

28 Jutland: the night action «175»

III

29 Nivelle's plans «200»

30 Nivelle's offensive, April 1917 «202»

31 The Passchendaele campaign, 1917 «238»

32 Verdun, August 23, 1917 «254»

33 Malmaison, October 23, 1917 «256»

IV

34 Alternative offensives considered by Ludendorff «286-287»

35 Ludendorff's final plan for the March 1918 offensive «288»

36 Ludendorff's orders of March 23 «316»

37 Ludendorff's orders of March 26 «329»

38 The *Georgette* offensive, April 1918 «332»

39 The Chemin des Dames offensive, May 1918 «334»

40 Marneschütze-Reims, July 1918 «338»

41 The western front, July-November 1918 «341»

42 German defence systems, 1918 «348»

All the maps were drawn by W. H. Bromage

AUTHOR'S PREFACE

The theme of this book is the decisive effect of individual human character on history. The background, in sharpest contrast, is a sudden and violent transition to mass collectivised life—to twentieth-century industrial civilisation. The principal actors are four national commanders-in-chief: two German, one Frenchman, one Englishman. Theirs was the novel task of directing these new and terrifying forces of mass power in battle. Each had been born and bred in the last age; each belonged to a highly conservative profession. Their abilities and defects reflected and illustrated those of their countries. For the historian, with his priceless gift of hindsight, it is moving and fascinating, therefore, to study these men locked in struggle with events greater than themselves; to see their moments of clarity and prophecy, of optimistic self-delusion, of uncertainty, of despair. Each in turn, as commander-in-chief, bore his nation's sword at a period when the course of the war pivoted on his judgement and will: four actors in a continental tragedy of death and rebirth.

The supporting cast is large: subordinates, enemy commanders, politicians, colleagues and allies. The periods of command of the four chiefs together span the war years and give an almost continuous history of the struggle on the western front, including the single encounter at sea that might have broken the deadlock. In 1914 Colonel-General von Moltke led the German army in its gamble to make it a short war by totally defeating France in six weeks. He failed, yet still succeeded in giving Germany the strategic advantage in the trench warfare that followed for the next three years. By 1916 the German front was too strong to be broken by assault; it could be outflanked only at sea. At the battle of Jutland, Admiral Sir John Jellicoe had the chance of transforming the war by destroying the German High Sea Fleet. He commanded the force to which Great Britain had given the best her technology and great wealth could produce; for the Grand Fleet, not the improvised "New Army," was her equivalent of the German army. Jutland was indecisive; the stalemate in the west was confirmed. In 1917 the crushing failure of the French army's final effort to break the stalemate by an offensive led to the appointment of General Pétain, a patient realist whose policy was to await the arrival of the Americans in 1918. However, in the summer of 1917 the French army mutinied, and Pétain's qualities as a commander depended on whether the French were still in the field when the Americans arrived. Meanwhile the collapse of Russia gave Germany once again a brief and slender superiority of numbers. General Ludendorff decided to use it to win a great victory in the west in 1918. The war thus ended as it began with a titanic German offensive and its failure.

Lengthening distance changes the shape and significance of the First World War. Historians of 1919-39 could not know that it was but the first of two episodes in the same conflict, in the same painful sequence of social and political transition. At this distance, it is easier to see the war in terms of the birth of our own civilisation rather than of the death of the Victorian age; easier to relate each nation's war effort to the whole pattern of its peacetime life and history, rather than narrate the conflict in strictly military or political terms. For war is the great auditor of institutions. The First World War, for example, pitilessly reveals French economic and social obsolescence, the gulf between German technological sophistication and political primitiveness, British industrial decay. It ended by displaying the dwarfishness of even the strongest of European powers when scaled against America.

For the European of the present day, the First World War has a fascination beyond the historical insights it gives. It is the fascination of events, of sentiments, as near as one's father's youth and yet as remote as the crusades: lances of the *Garde Ulanen* scratching the summer sky of 1914; guns of Jellicoe's thirty-four capital ships firing the valedictory salute to British sea power into the mists of Jutland; horizon blue and field grey; the Motherland, the Fatherland, *La Patrie*.

CORRELLI BARNETT

East Carleton, Norfolk
April 1963

AUTHOR'S NOTE

References in footnotes: Where only one work by an author is referred to as a source, only the name of the author is given. The full title of the work can be found in the Bibliography where it is marked with an asterisk. Where two or more works by the same author are referred to, a short title of the work is given as well as the name of the author. Where more than one book by the same author is cited in the Bibliography but only one is referred to in the footnotes, that one is marked in the Bibliography with an asterisk. In the case of a work by different authors a short title only is given: e.g. *British Official History.*

EUROPE
1914

Boundaries
Central Powers
Boundaries·1933

NO

SCOTLAND
Edinburgh

JUTLAND
DENMARK

IRELAND

Dublin   Liverpool

ENGLAND
LONDON

HOLLAND
Amsterdam

S'hampton

le Havre

BELGIUM
Brussels

Cologne

Rhine

G

Somme
Seine   Amiens

PARIS

Loire

F R A N C E

SWITZ.D

Lyon

Milan

Bordeaux   Garonne

Rhône

Marseilles

PORTUGAL

Douro

Madrid

Tagus

Ebro

Lisbon

S P A I N

M E D I

Gibraltar

N O R T H   A F R I C A

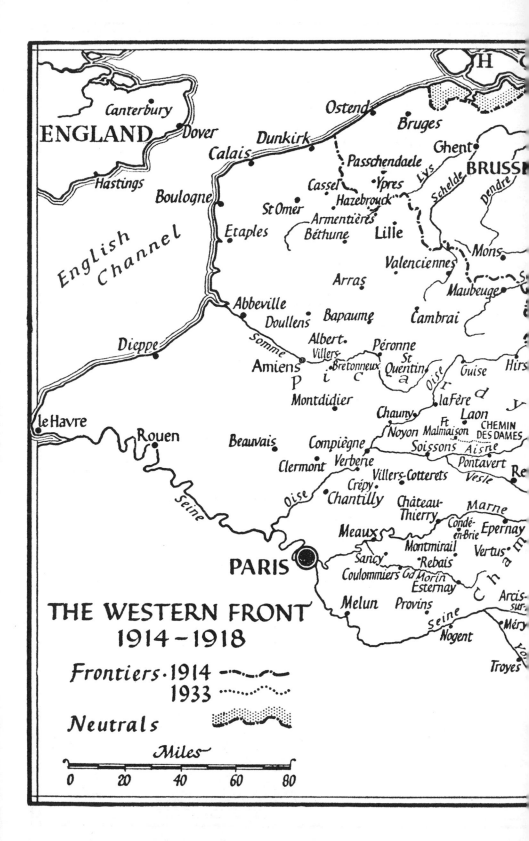

THE WESTERN FRONT
1914–1918

Frontiers·1914

1933

Neutrals

Miles

0   20   40   60   80

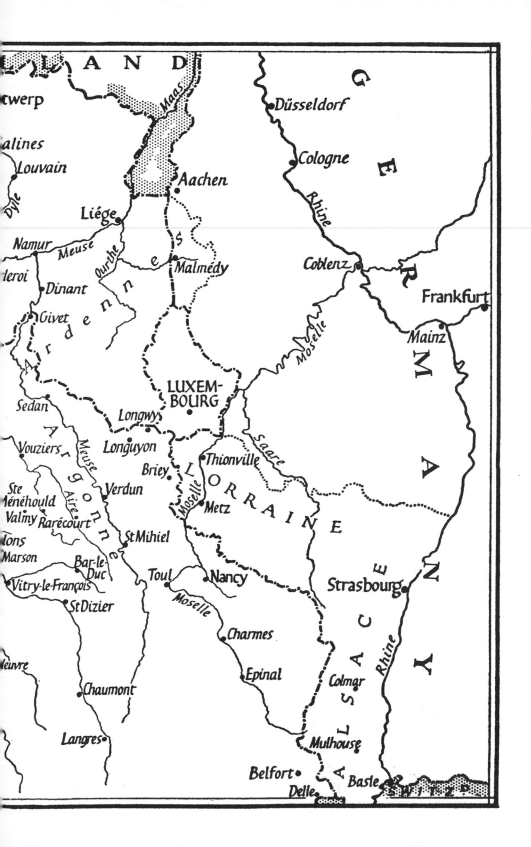

THE SWORDBEARERS

I

THE TRAGIC DELUSION

Colonel-General Helmuth Johannes Ludwig von Moltke

Thus conscience does make cowards of us all,
And thus the native hue of resolution
Is sicklied o'er with the pale cast of thought,
And enterprises of great pith and moment
With this regard their currents turn awry
And lose the name of action. . . .

SHAKESPEARE. *Hamlet* III. i.

1

In the late afternoon of August 1, 1914, Colonel-General von Moltke, Chief of the General Staff and *de facto* Commander-in-Chief of the Field Army of the German Empire, drove back from the Berliner Schloss, the Kaiser's palace, to the general staff building in the Königsplatz to carry out the assignment for which he had been preparing nine years and which he had dreaded even longer. At 12 noon Germany's ultimatum to Russia requiring her to cease mobilisation had expired; the countries were now at war. At 5 P.M. the Kaiser had signed the order for general mobilisation; it would start tomorrow. That the order to mobilise had been given one day later than the Russian order and no earlier than the French was a fact that added fresh weight to the anxieties pressing on von Moltke's sensitive and introspective mind.

For in speed lay Germany's best hope—indeed her only hope—of defeating the combination of enemies surrounding her. If there was to be war, Germany must strike first, with all her strength and against France, while Russia's slow and clumsy mobilisation was still going on. In May Moltke had told Conrad, Chief of the Austrian General Staff, that within six weeks of mobilisation the French would be so reduced to rout that the main body of the German army could be transferred to the east to smash Russia in her turn. This perfected deployment and campaign plan, first sketched by Count Schlieffen in 1905 and now embodied in a complicated mass of unit orders, railway timetables, loading tables, route plans and supply arrangements, sought victory in a wide flank march past the dense and powerful French fortress system between Verdun and Belfort. Such a march, of course, obliged Germany to violate Belgian and Luxembourg neutrality, with incalculable effects on Great Britain, who was otherwise not involved by formal alliance in European quarrels.

Yet faced with the possibility of war on two fronts against the apparently superior power—once deployed—of France and Russia, the German government and General Staff overrode or neglected these wider consequences for the sake of exploiting that brief opportunity when German organisation would have placed her mobilised army in the field before both her principal enemies were ready.

This opportunity was a matter of days, of hours. For Moltke's peace of mind, therefore, the mobilisation was already dangerously late, held up by the hapless efforts of the Kaiser and the Imperial Chancellor to preserve peace at the last moment. And even without this hounding pressure of time, the German campaign plan against France remained an audacious gamble. Partial successes in return for partial risks were not enough; the plan embodied Schlieffen's belief in staking the entire German resources on one throw, with the total annihilation of the French as the reward.

Now, as Moltke drove back to his headquarters through the streets of Berlin, whose people were already manifesting that horrifying and extraordinary outburst of tribal emotion common to belligerent nations in 1914 (in the Odeonplatz in Munich one of the elated crowd was Adolf Hitler), he was about to lead this gamble upon which the survival of his country depended. It was a professional task greater by far than those so brilliantly carried out by his great uncle and namesake in 1866 and 1870; Bismarck's diplomacy had brought Prussia into conflict only with isolated and poorly prepared enemies. Would Moltke be equal to it? When he had known in 1905 that the Kaiser was likely to choose him as Count Schlieffen's successor as Chief of the General Staff, he had confessed his doubts to Prince Bülow: "I lack the power of rapid decision. I am too reflective, too scrupulous, and, if you like, too conscientious for such a post. I lack the capacity for risking all on a single throw, that capacity which made the greatness of such born commanders as Napoleon, or our own Frederick II, or my uncle." [1]

[1] Bülow, II, 176.

At that time he had been in his fifty-seventh year; now he was sixty-six.

Before Moltke could reach his headquarters, a messenger intercepted his car: the Kaiser wanted him back at the Schloss, urgently and immediately. Once again Moltke passed through the gates of the Schloss, into the courtyard that lay beyond the sombre baroque façade whose blank windows stared out over the Lustgarten. In the magnificence of the Star Hall he found the Kaiser, General Erich von Falkenhayn (Secretary of State for War), Grand Admiral von Tirpitz and Admiral von Müller, General Freiherr von Lyncker (Adjutant-General to the Kaiser, and Chief of the Military Cabinet), von Bethmann-Hollweg (Imperial Chancellor) and von Jagow (Secretary of State for Foreign Affairs).

These men comprised the grand strategical brain of the most powerful and modern power outside America. Both individually and as a group they were as ill-equipped to lead this great machine as a seventeenth-century coachman would be to drive a Mercedes-Benz. The Kaiser was constitutionally an absolute monarch, but his bombast concealed a neurotic weakness and instability; instead of continuous dictatorship he provided sudden and alarming bouts of self-assertion alternating with reliance on his Chancellor. In his state and private correspondence, humanity and good sense equally mingled with wild and childish romanticising. Wilhelm II was a man haunted by his congenitally withered arm and by brutal treatment as a child; with tragic aptness his own sense of inferiority vis-à-vis his British royal relatives reflected that of the *arriviste* German Empire towards the British Empire.

Theobald von Bethmann-Hollweg, the Imperial Chancellor, was appointed by the Kaiser and responsible to him; he also had to retain the support of the Reichstag if he could. His position was that of a late Stuart chief minister in Britain, just as the German constitution, in action, lay at the uneasy halfway mark between absolutism and parliamentary government. Bethmann-Hollweg himself was a devoted, humane man, but whereas the European situation demanded greatness, he was only mediocre. As a personality in that gathering, earnest and undistinguished in his frock coat, he was outweighed by the men in uniform—von Falkenhayn, with his cruel and almost feminine elegance; von Tirpitz, the fork-bearded and formidable creator of the German High Seas Fleet.

Moltke himself was a tall, portly man who carried well the tight grey uniform with the carmine trouser stripes and collar tabs of the Great General Staff. Beneath a balding forehead his face was soft and plump, with quick intelligent eyes. There was a memory there, amid the flesh and sagging lines of late middle age, of a handsome and splendid young officer; the clipped, short grey moustache added a hard military feature to a face otherwise lacking in hardness and strength. He came in now, the senior soldier of a military empire. All the others present showed the faces of men who have heard marvellous news, a curious thing on such a day.

The Chancellor, von Bethmann-Hollweg, explained in his quick stuttering voice that a despatch had just arrived from Prince Lichnowsky, German Ambassador in London. Sir Edward Grey, the British Foreign Secretary, had promised Lichnowsky that Great Britain would guarantee that France would not enter the war against Germany, if Germany would undertake to carry out no acts of aggression against France.

The delight on Bethmann-Hollweg's trimly bearded face at this news was to Moltke's consternation clearly shared by everybody else in the room. In fact, earlier the Kaiser had called for celebratory champagne. The Kaiser, in this final crisis as ever before hysterically veering between belligerency and conciliation, hope and pessimism, now displayed that facile skating-over of reality that Moltke had always distrusted. When Bethmann-Hollweg finished speaking, he said to Moltke: "Now we need only wage war against Russia! So we simply advance with the whole army in the east!"

For Moltke, personally, in this incredible pronouncement by his sovereign and titular Commander-in-Chief lay the decisive moment of the 1914 campaign. He was far too intelligent and perceptive a man not to have appreciated during nine years of close association the dangerous inconsistencies and instabilities of Wilhelm II's character, but, in the words of his wife, "it had always been his opinion that if a really serious situation arose, the personalities that mattered would have the best brought out in them."[2] Instead Moltke found himself faced with a childlike flight from reality. He began now to fight his first and most exhausting battle.

"I answered His Majesty," he wrote later, "that this was impossible. The deployment of an army a million strong was not a thing to be im-

[2] Moltke, Introduction.

provised, it was the product of a whole year's hard work and once planned could not be changed. If His Majesty were to insist on directing the whole army to the east, he would not have an army prepared for the attack but a barren heap of armed men disorganised and without supplies." [3]

Jolted out of his facile delight, the Kaiser swung swiftly to mortification and personal abuse. "Your uncle would have given me a different answer," he told Moltke. Thrown out without thought by a baulked monarch, this comparison with the great field-marshal was perhaps the most deeply wounding thing that could have been said to Moltke. The Kaiser followed it by insisting on giving the order for deployment in the east.

Yet pressing even more sharply on Moltke's mind than this general question of reversing the national deployment was the fact that the offensive plan against France depended on immediate seizure of the Luxembourg railways. "Our patrols," he told the Kaiser, "are already in Luxembourg and the Trier (16th) Division is following them." [4]

As the argument became general, tempers rose under the stress of crisis. In Moltke's words, "I stood there quite alone. . . . Of the fact that it was bound to lead to catastrophe for us if we were to march into Russia with a mobilised France at our backs, of this no one seemed to think. Even assuming good will on her part, how could England ever have prevented France from stabbing us in the back?" [5]

All this was true. Moltke was forced to put out all his strength of argument and will power against a hostile circle led by his sovereign. Bethmann-Hollweg went on to declare that the occupation of Luxembourg by the 16th Division under existing orders must in no circumstances take place; it was a direct threat to France and would wreck the British guarantee. Moltke, "in a mood of almost complete despair," [6] tried to point out to the unbelieving politicians that the entire complicated campaign rested on initial moves planned to the minute.

Now, ignoring Moltke, the Kaiser turned aside to his Orderly-Adjutant-General, von Plessen, and ordered him to signal the 16th Division in

[3] *ibid*, 18-19.
[4] Müller, 11.
[5] Moltke, 18-19.
[6] *ibid*, 21.

Trier not to advance. Moltke's agony and humiliation were obvious to the others in the room. In desperation, he told the meeting that unless the army deployed against France according to plan, he would not accept responsibility for the outcome of the war. Bethmann-Hollweg, equally out of control, replied: "And I can take no responsibility unless we accept the English offer." [7]

The conference dragged on, the argument revolved. Finally Moltke succeeded in convincing the Kaiser that the deployment of the bulk of the army in the west, with a weak screen only against Russia, must take place according to plan if Germany's strength were not to be paralysed in chaos. Once deployment was completed, it would be possible to switch forces to the east. However, the Kaiser remained immovably obstinate over the advance of the 16th Division to occupy the Luxembourg railways. "I was shrugged off," wrote Moltke, "with the remark that I might care to use some other railway instead." [8]

When the meeting finally broke up after the drafting of suitable telegrams to the British government and to the King of England, Moltke had been intellectually and emotionally sucked dry; his self-confidence and will power ruptured by the appalling display of imperial and governmental inadequacy in the Star Hall. Back at his headquarters, in the quiet of his office, in the loneliness of supreme command, he wept in despair. Later, Lieutenant-Colonel von Tappen, the arrogant and unpopular Chief of the Operations Section of the General Staff, brought in, for him to sign, the confirming order to the 16th Division not to move. It contradicted in black and white an essential part of the deployment plan and gave the subordinate formation a clear proof of indecision in Berlin, and indeed of Moltke's inability to dominate his sovereign and the politicians even on a military question; as he read the order, horror and mortification flooded up in him. He flung his pen back on to the desk.

"Do what you like with the order," he told Tappen. "I'll not sign it."

He sat on in his room until eleven o'clock in the evening, in a trance of complete exhaustion and paralysis of will: the still centre round which spun the European catastrophe. Then came another summons from the Kaiser to go to the Schloss. What now, at so late an hour?

[7] Müller, 11.
[8] Moltke, 21.

When Moltke was shown into one of the Kaiser's private apartments he saw his sovereign before him in vest and underpants, with a mantle thrown over his shoulders and withered arm; saw once more that too familiar face, neurotically handsome, the upswept moustache making a brave attempt at martial and masculine strength, but the weak jaw line and mouth already flaccid with middle age. It was so nearly a fine face, and yet it revealed the uncertainty and lack of ease that robbed the Kaiser of effective personal charm and dominance. He had evidently been roused hastily from his bed, and the reason had plainly upset him badly. With his sound arm, he handed Moltke a sheet of paper. It was a telegram from George V in answer to the Kaiser's afternoon cable.

As he read it, Moltke felt "overwhelmed by the sensation of standing on the brink of a gulf . . . as though he would have an apoplectic fit." [9] The King informed the Kaiser that Lichnowsky had quite misunderstood Sir Edward Grey; there was no question of a British guarantee of French neutrality.

Unspoken between the "very agitated" Kaiser and his distracted Chief of the General Staff was the realisation that the dreadful conference at the Schloss that afternoon and the consequent delay and dislocation (whose results none could measure) to the German deployment had been based on a fiction.

"Now you can do what you like," remarked the Kaiser helpfully in dismissal.

The effects of this day on Moltke's personality and powers of leadership were deep and permanent. In his own words: "That was my first experience in this war. I am convinced that the Kaiser would not even have signed the order to mobilise if Prince Lichnowsky's despatch had arrived half an hour earlier. I have not [in 1915] been able to overcome the impressions made by this experience; something was destroyed in me that was not to be rebuilt; faith and confidence were shattered." [10]

His wife noted that "after these hours, Moltke was a changed man. The relationship of trust between him and the Kaiser was destroyed." [11]

To Moltke, however, from that hour forwards fell the command of the largest army in history in the greatest battle yet fought.

[9] Quoted Bülow, II, 168.
[10] Moltke, 21.
[11] *ibid*, Introduction.

The flurry caused by Prince Lichnowsky's misleading telegram illustrates the inconsistency, the want of character and good sense in the governing circle of the German Empire that had contributed largely to the European crisis which Moltke was now to try to resolve by force. It also showed the helplessness of the Kaiser, the executive political head of the Empire, and of the Imperial Chancellor in the face of military requirements.

It was inevitable that an initially land-locked state like Prussia, without natural frontiers, should have depended on her army to preserve and extend her territory; natural that continual wars against powerful neighbours should have made the state machinery and Prussian society serve and reflect the needs of the army. In 1866 and 1870 it was the guns of the army that had at last unified Germany, not the ideals, aspirations and political capacities of patriotic democrats. All nation states were simply organisations for power. By its growth from Mark Brandenburg to a German Empire dominating Europe, Prussia (and her army) illustrated this with a naked frankness distasteful perhaps to older powers who had learned to disguise with altruistic ideals the source of their independence.

However, Frederick the Great had been as competent a statesman as he had been a soldier; Bismarck's grasp of policy and force of character had towered above even the elder Moltke's professional capacity. The army, as Clausewitz insisted should always be so, had been the instrument of policy; its military plans had served, and formed a part of, a national grand strategy laid down by civilians.

Between the dismissal of Bismarck in 1890 and the present European crisis, political control had been represented by a hysterical and militaristic monarch, a succession of chancellors and favourites of limited ability and a rubber-stamp Reichstag. It had faded away before the great prestige of the army and the superb organisation and technical ability of its Great General Staff. It was a measure of German political ineptitude that the deployment plan conceived by Schlieffen and now under way, with its tremendous political implications and consequences, had never in the nine years since it was first drafted been the subject of a general conference by the German government, *never* been the subject of formal approval by Kaiser, Chancellor and Foreign Secretary.

Equally the plan itself was the result of the failures of German foreign policy; it was the desperate solution of a strategic problem posed by having both France and Russia as probable enemies. With the German annexation of Alsace-Lorraine in 1871, it was likely enough that in a future war France would be an enemy, fighting to retrieve her lost provinces. So long as she was alone, however, she was helpless. But supposing she ever found powerful allies—Russia, for instance? In 1887 Bismarck renewed the treaty of friendship with Russia "purchasing the neutrality of Russia in a war provoked by France by promising neutrality to Russia in a war provoked by Austria."[12] This treaty was allowed to lapse by Bismarck's vain and midget successors. Two things followed, from which an unbroken line runs to the summer catastrophe of 1914. Firstly, Germany was reduced to absolute dependence on Austria-Hungary, the only great power that was still her friend, but now far gone in the humiliating weaknesses and dangerous vanities of senile decay. Secondly, in the event of war, Germany might have to fight on two fronts against France and Russia. This became certain in 1894 when France and Russia signed a treaty of alliance and military assistance.

Yet Europe was then far from war. It was the curious German inability to read other people's minds, a restless wish to dominate their neighbours rather than live with them, the crude diplomacy that regarded threats and unreal bribes as subtle instruments of persuasion, these were the things that helped to create European uneasiness and apprehension. The European sense of community, so strong in the days of Metternich and even of Bismarck, disappeared in favour of the defensive alliances of two great camps, both armed sincerely only in defence, staring across a psychological no man's land of fear and suspicion. These alliances made it certain that, if all the parties honoured their obligations, a local war would swiftly become general. A peculiar danger was thus given, for example, to Russian and Austrian rivalries in the Balkans.

However, Germany was neither wholly nor principally responsible for the war; certainly not "guilty." The crisis of 1914 was, as a human event, the result of many complex elements: economic rivalry, violent national and racial feeling, and particular international problems insoluble in a world of sovereign powers except by war.

There were other deeper forces, moving to broader rhythms, that made it very probable that the antique frame of the old Europe would ex-

[12] Gooch, 140.

plode. Since the last European war in 1870 technology had made gigantic changes in the pattern of life and social organisation, and mostly so in Germany, lying across the heart of Europe. No other European country —certainly not Great Britain, clinging to the faded liberal dream of free trade, small-scale enterprise and private social initiative—had such an elaborate modern social and industrial machine. What small country could emulate this long-striding march into the twentieth century? What future reality lay in national independence when to the power of great states were added the recent world-shrinking inventions of radio, aircraft, the telephone, the motorcar? Yet between 1870 and 1914 there was beating against the confining channels of social and technological reality a boiling tide of national and racial feeling, a tide welling perhaps from the profound unreadiness of man to accept a collectivised and highly organised life. For there had been greater changes in the life of European man in the century since Waterloo than in the previous fifty.

Of these great movements beneath the surface, the statesmen and generals of the old Europe—privileged, cynical—were insufficiently aware. They travelled about in their *trains de luxe* between one glittering slum-strewn capital and another, playing the shallow game of Talleyrand and Metternich, Frederick the Great and Marlborough, without once making contact with the new realities. Ignorant of the gigantic force of modern social organisation and modern industry once harnessed to war, they engaged in power rivalries with the insouciance of men who believed that war, should it come, would be a matter of six weeks' autumn manoeuvres with live ammunition.

By 1914 the elements of catastrophe had all been collected together: the connecting alliances, the intense mutual hatred of the nationalist masses, leaders hopelessly inadequate for the situation, the armaments, the Schlieffen Plan.

Austrian senility was the immediate cause of the death of old Europe. A supranational state in an age of neurotic nationalism, of low governmental vitality and falling prestige, she faced, as all knew, eventual collapse and disintegration. Of the various national movements working to break up this great state, none was more dangerous than that which wished to unite all Austria-Hungary's south-Slav dominions into a great Serbia. The Serbian government, itself permeated by the Black Hand terrorist society, backed the movement, and Russia backed Serbia. When the Austrian Archduke Francis Ferdinand and his wife were assassinated on June 28, 1914, by a member of the Black Hand, this was regarded by Count Berchtold, the Austrian Chancellor, as a final opportunity to humiliate Serbia and restore Austrian prestige. Vienna was the first capital in 1914 to witness the hysteria of street mobs braying for war and vengeance. Only Germany could have held the Austrians back; but Austria was her only friend and Germany dared not let her down. Nor at first did she wish to. The Kaiser was at this stage in a mood of childlike belligerence. Austria was left a free hand. Although the likelihood of a general war might depend upon the terms of the Austrian ultimatum to Serbia, Germany did not even express a wish to see it before it was despatched.

This ultimatum gave Serbia forty-eight hours in which to accept eleven conditions, several of which infringed Serbian sovereignty. In particular Austria demanded that her own officials and police should take part in Serbian investigations of anti-Austrian agitation. Since the Serbian government and police were deeply involved in the Black Hand, this demand was logical. But politically it meant that Serbia would certainly reject the ultimatum if Russia backed her—as she must. And this in turn meant that Austria would mobilise against Serbia.

On July 28, in Berlin, Moltke had analysed the situation in a General Staff memorandum. In his view the conflict between Austria and Serbia would have remained private and local if Russia had not interfered. Indeed, Austria had only mobilised eight army corps—sufficient for the Serbian operation. Nevertheless Russia was preparing to mobilise twelve corps: Austria would be forced in turn to mobilise her entire army to guard her rear while she marched into Serbia. This would mean war between Russia and Austria. Germany would have to aid her ally; Russia would then mobilise all her forces and call for French aid. "It cannot be denied," wrote Moltke, "that the whole thing is a masterly piece of staging on the part of Russia." [13]

Apart from the slander on Russia this was, so far as it went, an accurate forecast. It left out the two elements that turned the crisis into a four-year catastrophe—Britain and the Schlieffen Plan.

[13] Moltke, 3-7.

It is sometimes said that in 1914 the two armed camps were balanced. This is not true. The Dual Alliance of France and Russia faced the Triple Alliance of Germany, Austria and Italy (except that Italy defaulted on her obligations). Had the war involved only these countries it is very probable that Germany and her allies would have won. It was Britain that enabled the Dual Alliance to survive until the Americans arrived in 1917-18. Yet Britain was in no way obliged by treaty to go to war. The only link between Britain and France was the Entente of 1904, which was not a military alliance but a settlement of various questions that stood in the way of friendship. It was true that as a result of the Entente military conversations had taken place between the British and French staffs. It was true that the military heads had agreed on joint deployment plans whereby the British mobilisation should be simultaneous with the French and the British Expeditionary Force would assemble round Maubeuge on the French left flank. It was also true that the detailed joint plans for this British deployment had been worked out. But the British government was not contracted to implement any of it, even if it felt morally obliged to do so. Indeed the Foreign Office, which had authorised the staff talks, was largely unaware of their results. These military agreements had been negotiated without Cabinet sanction or even knowledge. More than this, British public opinion and the majority (Liberal) parliamentary party did not consider Britain's interests to be necessarily involved in a European war. As the crisis deepened into August it was therefore Sir Edward Grey's task either to point out to the French that, since there was no formal alliance and since British opinion was not in favour of war against Germany, the French could expect no help from Britain, or to manœuvre Parliament and public opinion round behind a declaration of war.

July-August 1914 was not the most glorious moment of British foreign policy; its shifts and hesitations marked the bankruptcy of her policy. She believed in a balance of power, but she was not prepared to go to any trouble in peacetime to preserve it. The basic fact of European life since 1870 was the dominance of Germany and German technology. Until 1894 this dominance was overwhelming and thus a factor conducive to peace. As the German political (though not technological) ascendancy lessened after 1894, as France found allies, and power in Europe began to move again towards a balance, so the danger of general war, the sense of insecurity grew. The British attitude was characteristic of the national evasion of the new challenges of the twentieth century, of the refusal even to recognise them until they were absolutely inescapable. Britain disliked German dominance in Europe, disliked still more her navy and her world ambitions. To stop this dominance, to swing the balance permanently against Germany, Britain had merely to ally herself with France and Russia and agree to place a large army (perhaps conscript) at the side of the French. Such a policy was politically impossible—as was rearmament and firmness towards Hitler in the 1930's. The British people (or the British Foreign Office) wanted an impossibility. Where Germany stood, they wanted a power vacuum and one that they were not prepared to fill themselves.

In 1914 therefore the British were forced for the first time in the century to decide in haste and in the least advantageous circumstances whether they were in fact part of Europe or whether they should leave Europe to a domination they had done nothing hitherto to prevent.

Without Count Schlieffen it is questionable whether Sir Edward Grey would have succeeded in foisting war on Britain. Without Count Schlieffen it is even possible that war would not have spread beyond the Balkans.

The statesmen of Europe, except for Berchtold, the Austrian Chancellor, made frantic and genuine efforts in July to claw away from the slide into general war. It was all illusion; they had no free will. Once Austria declared war on Serbia, Europe moved helplessly according to a determinist fate; and that fate lay in the military timetables of each nation, above all of Germany's.

When the young men of Europe swarmed into the depots and, in new uniforms, marched out again into the shambles, gaily singing, the man most responsible had been dead two years; but it is not melodramatic to say that in August 1914 the ghost of this fanatical theorist, with the cold staring eyes and the icy distinction, walked more potently than the living.

Schlieffen had become Chief of the Great General Staff in 1891. At that time the German deployment plan in the event of a two-front war provided for a defensive against France while Russia was paralysed by an offensive with limited objectives. The basic conception was strategically defensive, without any intention or hope of total victory on either front. Almost immediately Schlieffen's mind moved towards a reversal of this plan—a deployment first against France, possibly with a wide turning movement through Belgium. In December 1905 he embodied the final development of this thinking in a great memorandum which he handed to his successor, Colonel-General von Moltke. This memorandum was "the Schlieffen Plan." It reflected entirely the narrow militarism, the ruthless and rigid theorising of Schlieffen's mind and personality.

For a campaign of limited objectives, he substituted the goal of total victory over France by annihilation. This was to be achieved by speed and audacity, by the use of nearly three-quarters of the national army in a wheel through Holland and Belgium, down past Amiens, across the lower Seine west of Paris and then round to the southeast, pressing the outflanked French back, with their front reversed, against Switzerland and their own frontier defences. Schlieffen's appreciation of the effects of these violations of neutrality shows with clarity the limitations of the specialist mind, however good. To outflank the French as far as Dunkirk, he wrote, "the neutrality of Luxembourg, Belgium and the Netherlands must be violated. The violation of Luxembourg neutrality will have no important consequences other than protests. The Netherlands regard England allied to France no less as an enemy than does Germany. It will be possible to come to an agreement with them. Belgium will probably offer resistance." [14]

The 1905 memorandum is entirely concerned with the attack on France; and indeed Schlieffen wrote it at a time when Russia had been enfeebled by the unsuccessful 1905 revolution. However, Russian weakness was not in Schlieffen's mind. His plans for a two-front war left the attack in the west almost unaltered: 62 divisions against France, only 10 against Russia.

Although the military details of the plan were amended by Moltke (as will be seen) it was nevertheless Schlieffen's conception of swift total victory that the Germans on August 1, 1914, were about to attempt. Moltke, with his broader mind and wider education, saw some of the dangers of violating three neutralities. Without Belgium and Luxembourg, of course, the offensive was impossible; but careful staff work could enable the Germans to avoid violating the neutrality of Holland. In 1911 Moltke wrote:

[14] Ritter, 136-7.

I cannot agree that the envelopment demands the violation of Dutch neutrality in addition to Belgium. A hostile Holland at our back could have disastrous consequences for the advance of the German army to the west. . . . Furthermore it will be very important to have in Holland a country whose neutrality enables us to have imports and supplies. She must be the windpipe that enables us to breathe.[15]

It was a tragedy that in fact this exclusion of Holland actually sharpened the crisis of July-August 1914. For it now became essential to the advance that the Belgian fortress of Liége, covering vital routes, be seized by a surprise blow immediately war was declared, a fortnight before the main forces moved.

Thus the consequences of the Schlieffen Plan, as amended by Moltke, were that an Austrian quarrel with Russia meant automatically a swift and gigantic onslaught on Belgium, Luxembourg and France. No subsequent diplomacy could affect this unsteerable, irreversible, unstoppable machine. And German troops in Belgium, immediately after the mobilisation order and while declarations of war were still being traded, were exactly what Sir Edward Grey needed.

August 2, first day of German mobilisation, was a Sunday; the day that on each side saw families united now saw them sundered, in so many cases forever. The streets of every town were filled with men shopping for essentials they needed for their kit, with women already in tears. This swarming, formless bustle from Königsberg to Metz, from Schleswig-Holstein to Bavaria was all that could be seen of the vast, intricate, exquisitely worked out mobilisation plan which placed an army of a million and a half men in battle array, with all its artillery and supply services, on the French and Belgian frontiers in thirteen days. In France there were similar scenes, similar efficiency; in Austria and Russia confusion was real as well as apparent. In the afternoon Vice-Admiral Jellicoe, Commander-in-Chief designate of the Grand Fleet, arrived in Scapa Flow with secret Admiralty orders in a sealed envelope. Major-General Ludendorff, thirsting for action, joined the 2nd Army at Aachen that evening, having travelled all day with his horses from Strasbourg. He was to be Deputy Chief of the 2nd Army Staff. Colonel Pétain, 58 years old and near retirement, joined Lanrezac's 5th Army on mobilisation in acting command of a brigade.

[15] *ibid*, 166.

In Stettin, Colonel-General von Kluck, Commander of the German 1st Army, which was to be the outermost army in the German wheel through Belgium, held his first conference with his Chief of Staff, General von Kuhl.

In Berlin, Moltke was happy to learn that, after all, the 16th Division had succeeded in occupying the Luxembourg railways.

All Europe was swarming with men abandoning the secure, perhaps monotonous rhythms of peacetime and private life and preparing themselves to kill each other. Why? It is the fact that this question cannot be rationally answered that gives to these August days of 1914 their tragedy and their horror. The First World War had causes but no objectives.

Of all the powers, only Austria entered the war with a positive policy. Not one other had an intelligible, formulated war aim. Germany, for example, who hoped to break France in six weeks, had no peace or armistice terms in mind; indeed until July 26 she had not even drafted the ultimatum to Belgium that must precede the onslaught. As was characteristic of the political feebleness at the summit of the German Empire, the hasty drafting of the ultimatum had been left to Moltke, the Chief of the General Staff. The Austrians had not yet declared war on Russia; the German government therefore summoned them to fulfil their treaty obligations. The Austrians, never in a hurry, waited until the 6th. The Italians, similarly summoned, declared their neutrality.

The lurching run into war continued. In England on August 2 Sir Edward Grey, with icy English correctitude, was fending off French appeals for help. He went so far, however, as to assure the French Ambassador that if the German fleet came into the channel to attack the French coast or shipping, the British fleet would intervene.

At 7:20 that evening Moltke's ultimatum, under seal in the hands of the German Ambassador since July 29, was presented in Brussels; it gave the Belgians twelve hours to give Germany free passage for her troops through Belgium.

Next day the final political acts dictated by the Schlieffen Plan were carried out; war was declared on France on pretexts ("frontier violation") so ridiculous that one wonders what belated shame induced the German government to put them in. Since Belgium had announced that she would fight all comers, war was declared on her as well. Sir Edward Grey was thus at last enabled to make a moving and high-principled speech to the House of Commons about the necessity of defending Belgian neutrality; he made much of "honour" but not less of Britain's "interest." This talk of "honour" under the Great Powers' guarantee of Belgian neutrality was in fact cant. In 1887, when there had been a brief danger of war between France and Germany, the British government had told the Belgians not to expect British help if Belgian neutrality were violated. Sir Edward Grey was in fact leading Britain into war to aid France in smashing Germany. This was her "interest"; Belgium was useful as a legal excuse for war and as a cry for public opinion. The British declaration of war and order for general mobilisation followed on August 4. On August 6 Austria declared war. Jellicoe, now Commander-in-Chief, had already taken the Grand Fleet to sea.

It had begun. It was now the task of Moltke and his army to bring back that quick victory for which such a heavy political price had already been paid. Vast historical consequences depended on Moltke's qualities as a man and as a commander in the next few weeks. For he alone of all the sanguine generals of 1914 enjoyed a genuine chance of making it a short, old-fashioned war.

But how much of a chance?

2

In 1913 Moltke had reckoned that, once their forces were mobilised and deployed, the enemies of Germany and Austria would have a superiority of twelve army corps.[1] Since the Russian army was in the course of re-organisation and re-equipment and the French had adopted a three-year period of conscription, this superiority would increase. Moltke did not count on the Austrians for much: he appreciated that "Austria-Hungary's offensive capability would not last long."[2] With the help of his then Chief of Operations Section, Colonel Ludendorff, he therefore tried hard in the winter of 1913-14 to persuade the Imperial Government to create three extra army corps and to build up the insufficient ammunition reserves. The government refused, and Ludendorff was posted to the command of a regiment as a reward for trying. Thus the German plan of campaign was not at all an aggression plotted by a general staff conscious of great power, but a desperate sally by men haunted by numerical weakness. Apart from the 9th Reserve Corps in Schleswig-Holstein (to guard against a British landing) and only five and a half corps to guard the eastern frontiers against Russia, all the German field forces were now deploying against France in seven armies between the area north of Aachen and the Swiss frontier near Basle. These armies numbered 1,485,000 men.

They faced five French armies with a total strength of 1,071,000 plus two extra groups of three and four reserve divisions, the Belgians with

[1] See the list of military establishments in Appendix.
[2] Koeltz, 95.

three major fortresses (Liége, Namur and Antwerp) and 117,000 men, and the British Expeditionary Force of 100,000. Since the French fortress line on their eastern frontier could enable them, if they wished, to thin out greatly their troops there, and since, as Schlieffen himself had recognised, the power of the offensive would wane the further it progressed, the German numerical superiority in the west was slender. Nor could the Germans compensate for want of numbers by revolutionary techniques as they were to do in 1940, although Schlieffen had assumed without much reason that the German troops would significantly outperform their opponents. It is therefore not surprising that even the memorandum of 1905, embodying Schlieffen's enticing and gigantic vision, is curiously marked by undertones of doubt and pessimism. And indeed the strategic problem was baffling.

The French common frontier with Germany was covered by extremely powerful and well-sited fortifications in difficult hill country, running from Verdun to Épinal and from Toul to Belfort. Between Toul and Épinal had been left a deliberate gap of forty miles—in fact a trap. The length of this front—some two hundred and seventy kilometres—was not great enough to allow Germany to deploy her superior numbers. Schlieffen concluded, and Moltke did not dispute it, that "the sector Belfort-Verdun is almost impregnable." [3] But, he added: "The sector Mézières-Maubeuge-Lille-Dunkirk is only fortified in parts and at the moment [1905] almost unoccupied." [4] Therefore the German army should appear by surprise on this line—the French frontier with Belgium—in great strength, constantly attacking and outflanking the French left wing.

> By attacks on their left flank [wrote Schlieffen] we must try at all costs to drive the French eastward against their Moselle fortresses, against the Jura and Switzerland. The French army must be annihilated.
>
> It is essential to form a strong right wing, to win the battle with its help, to pursue the enemy relentlessly with this strong wing, forcing him to retreat again and again.
>
> If the right wing is to be made very strong, this can only be at the expense of the left. . . .[5]

[3] Ritter, 144.
[4] loc. cit.
[5] Schlieffen, Text B; quoted Ritter, 145.

Here is the core of Schlieffen's operational plan. To the right wing, north of Metz, he allotted thirty-six corps—the majority of them along the Belgian and Dutch frontiers. South of Metz he allotted only five corps. With characteristic theoretical elaboration Schlieffen traced out in detail the course of the campaign, dealing with all possible French reactions. He concluded that the great fortress of Paris, which would form the western corner post of a French final stand on the Oise and Aisne, must itself be outflanked by another enormous wheeling movement to the south. Schlieffen allotted no less than thirteen corps for the masking and envelopment of Paris, eight of which did not exist in his time, but which he assumed in his grand way would be provided by the government.

Schlieffen's conception of the technique of command in the coming war was equally remote and rigid: sitting at his ease in an office full of telephones, the supreme commander would control the advance of the vast and distant array "like battalion drill."

When Moltke inherited this paan in 1906, he did not question the basic assumption that Germany's best hope lay in a concentrated assault on France, nor that it should be based on a strong right wing moving wide through the Belgian plain, but he was never happy about it. For it reflected a mind utterly uncongenial to his own. As Moltke put it, "One could not imagine a greater contrast than our two ways of looking at things." [6] In place of Schlieffen's rigid theoretical prophecies, Moltke had doubts about the nature of future war. As he had told the Kaiser even before his appointment:

> In my opinion it is in any case very difficult, if not impossible, to picture now what form a modern war in Europe would take. We have at present a period of over thirty years of peace behind us and I believe that in our outlook we have become very unwarlike in many ways. How, if at all, it will be possible to lead as a unit the immense armies we shall create, no man, I think, can know in advance. . . . It will become a war between peoples which is not to be concluded with a single battle but which will be a long, weary struggle with a country that will not acknowledge defeat until the whole strength of its people is broken; a war that even if we should be the victors will push our own people, too, to the limits of exhaustion.[7]

[6] Ritter, 292.
[7] Recounted by Moltke to his wife, 29.1.05.

Of decisive importance to the campaign plan, as even Schlieffen had recognised, was French action and reaction. The contrast between Schlieffen's temperament and mode of thought and those of his successor was illuminated by their treatment of this problem.

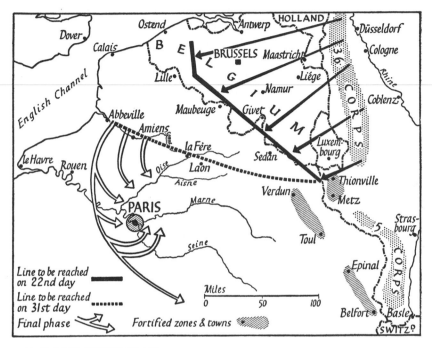

I. THE SCHLIEFFEN PLAN, 1905

Schlieffen's allotment of forces left the Germans in Alsace-Lorraine dangerously weak. Since the French might well wish to use their army to retake their lost provinces, what would be the consequence of a powerful French offensive against the German left while the German right was still wheeling across Belgium? In his great memorandum Schlieffen comfortably predicted: "If the Germans persevere in their operations [on the right] they can be sure that the French will hastily turn back . . . in the direction whence the greatest danger threatens." [8]

Indeed he would have been happy to entice the French well to the east into a great area of field fortifications based on Metz. Moltke, and

[8] Ritter, 147-8.

Ludendorff, his pre-war Chief of the Operations Section, could not accept that the pressure of the German right wing, together with the defensive strength of Metz, would prevent serious danger to the feeble German screen in Alsace-Lorraine. On the contrary, they feared that a successful French offensive in Lorraine would get across German communications before the German right wing had completed its long semicircular sweep to the French rear. The German swinging arm would be dislocated at the joint—as was to happen in reverse to the French in 1940. There was another consideration: if there was nothing solid to grip the French in Alsace-Lorraine, the French could strip their front to meet the danger of encirclement.

Therefore as extra troops became available, Moltke allotted them to the left wing, while leaving the offensive group at the strength planned by Schlieffen: thirty-six corps. These were in any event the maximum that could be deployed, moved and supplied by available communications. Moltke had other doubts about rigidly carrying out the Schlieffen Plan without regard to opportunities presented in the course of battle. As his writings show, he was a profound admirer of his uncle's generalship—he recorded with glee the day he beat him at chess—and the elder Moltke had epitomised his own strategy by saying that no plan survives contact with the enemy. Would not a French advance in Lorraine therefore present a splendid opening for taking them in flank by a southward switch of the strong German right wing? In one of his staff rides Schlieffen himself had agreed that it would; but his final conclusion nevertheless remained that "I believe *in reality* the French would not carry out their plan." [9] Moltke, however, in a staff ride of 1912 told his officers:

> From the moment when it is known that the mass of the French army is taking the offensive between Metz and the Vosges, the movement of the German right wing across Belgium becomes without object. The manœuvre should be planned as follows: while the German left wing stands on the defensive against the French offensive, all forces not necessary to contain the Belgians and English should march southwest in order to attack on a line passing through the fortress of Metz and west of that fortress.[10]

[9] Förster, 65. Throughout Part I the work by Förster referred to is *Le Comte Schlieffen et la Guerre Mondiale: La Stratégie allemande pendant la Guerre de 1914-1918.*
[10] *ibid*, 66.

Thus, though apparently committed to the Schlieffen Plan, Moltke's mind remained open; a fine quality in a great commander, but often a fatal ambiguousness in a second-rater.

Whatever misgivings or qualifications about the Schlieffen Plan existed in Moltke's mind, the great deployment (*"Aufmarsch"*) between August 2 and 16, 1914, remained based upon it. By four trunk railways (Green: Stettin, Berlin, Hanover and Aachen. Blue: Schneidemühl, Berlin, Cassel and Cologne. Brown: Posen, Frankfurt am Main, Thionville. Red: Lissa, Dresden and Strasbourg) the packed trains rolled gently at nineteen miles per hour at fixed intervals towards the west, 180 trains to each army corps. At night the arc lights flared high over remote village stations as the troops detrained in their assembly areas; by day the industrial towns of the Ruhr blazed with flags, rang with cheers, and effervesced with patriotic enthusiasm. That great tract of country that lies between the Rhine and Holland and Belgium was filled with troops breaking in stiff new jack boots on the march, learning again to bear the weight of full kit with its creaking new leather. And after each day's training there were the first of the war's atrocity stories to be read in the newspapers: accounts of the terrible things done to German advance guards by Belgian troops and, worse, civilians.

In Berlin the Great General Staff was metamorphosed into a Supreme Headquarters[11] without making a scrap of difference, since the same organisation and the same officers continued to work in the same building. But the shooting war reached Moltke in his headquarters a fortnight before it reached the deploying western armies and their commanders: from August 5 onwards Moltke waited for news of the fall of Liége with an anxiety that he was unable to hide.

Liége, with its circle of subterranean reinforced concrete forts, commanded the close defile through which von Kluck's 1st Army of 320,000 had to pass in order to deploy on the Belgian plain. It had been Moltke's idea (or so he claimed)—a daringly unorthodox one by the standards of his time—to seize the town of Liége by a sudden assault immediately on the outbreak of war. This assault, to be carried out by General von Emmich and a force maintained on a war footing in peacetime, had been planned (and perhaps invented) by Colonel Ludendorff when Chief of

[11] OHL = *Oberste Heeresleitung.*

the Operations Section. Liége was the essential key to the development of the offensive, and the fact that the General Staff had at this moment less work to occupy it than in peacetime added to the atmosphere of tension that preceded the fall of the fortress.

> The first reports were good [wrote Colonel Bauer, of Section 2—Operations]. But these were followed by hair-raising reports, each one wilder than the first. General von Emmich and his headquarters seemed to have been wiped out, most of the attacking columns repulsed, and of two of them —including Ludendorff's [now on the staff of the 2nd Army]—there was no news of any kind. Fear that the attack had gone wrong grew and Moltke's face wore a look of heavy care.[12]

Moltke's worries were not diminished by the Kaiser who, when Moltke on the evening of August 5 reported the apparent failure of the assault, rounded on his Chief of the General Staff and said: "I knew it. This affair against Belgium has brought war with England down on my head." [13] Next day, however, Moltke found himself "showered with kisses" from his sovereign, for the town of Liége was in German hands, thanks to the fine personal leadership of Major-General Ludendorff in an early display of his restless attacking spirit. The forts still held out; but one by one they were crushed like beetles by enormous shells from 42 cm. howitzers. The last of them was taken on August 16, the day that the German mobilisation and deployment were completed; Liége would not hold up the German advance a single day. The Belgians had made the first of all the uncountable mistakes of the war: instead of fighting with their field army alongside the forts and thus keeping the big howitzers out of range, they concentrated their field forces well back from Liége, behind the Gette, and left the forts unsupported. In view of the extreme delicacy and difficulty of the German advance through the Liége defile, this Belgian failure to impose a serious check was regrettable.

Now the seven German armies, together more vast than any that had ever marched, were ready for the general advance: from right to left lay the 1st Army (von Kluck: 320,000 men), under temporary command of 2nd Army (von Bülow: 260,000), 3rd Saxon Army (Baron von Hau-

12 Bauer, 38-9.
13 Moltke, 23.

sen: 180,000), 4th Army (Duke Albrecht of Württemberg: 200,000), 5th Army (Imperial Crown Prince: 200,000), 6th Army (Crown Prince Rupprecht of Bavaria: 220,000) and 7th Army (von Heeringen: 125,000). The first five armies were designated for the great wheel. Not one of the generals had over conducted a larger operation of war than a regimental action. After nearly half a century, even the memories of some of them of 1870-71 could not have been very fresh.

The French peacetime deployment plan was based on a strategy that in fact made the Schlieffen Plan in its full rigour unnecessary, for the French were going to make the offensive in Lorraine that had figured so much as a contingency on German pre-war staff rides. The plan (Plan 17—the seventeenth revision) consisted of an offensive by four French armies in two groups advancing on either side of Metz. It was hoped that this would separate the two German wings. The French 5th Army on the extreme left wing (Lanrezac: 254,000) was to concentrate between Verdun and Mézières with a detachment east of the Muese; then came the 3rd Army (Ruffey: 168,000) round Verdun, 2nd (de Castelnau) round Nancy and 1st Army (Dubail) round Epinal. In general reserve in the region Ste. Ménéhould-Commercy was to lie the 4th Army (de Langle de Cary: 193,000), and on either flank groups of reserve divisions: four round Belfort and three (General Valabrègue) round Vervins.

However, the German capture of Liége and the ominous massing of German troops in Belgium led to modifications of the French deployment, although the basic plan of an offensive remained intact. The French army was actually deployed as follows: Lanrezac now sidestepped westwards to Hirson-Sedan; de Langle de Cary was astride the Meuse between Sedan and Montmédy; Ruffey northeast of Verdun; de Castelnau east of Nancy and Dubail east of Lunéville.

Except in the crucial matter of morale the French army of 1914 was little better prepared for the realities of the campaign ahead than in 1940. In the first place Plan 17 was based on a complete misreading of German intentions, as its opening breath-catching paragraphs indicate:

> From a careful study of information obtained it is probable that a great part of the German forces will be concentrated on the common frontier. . . .

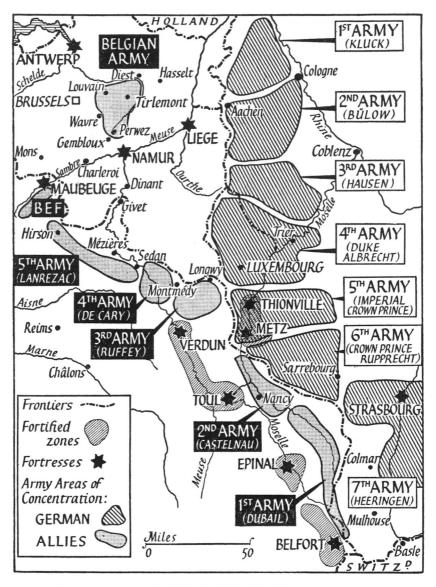

2. AUGUST 1914: DEPLOYMENT OF THE ARMIES

Whatever the circumstances [author's italics], it is the C.-in-C.'s intention to advance, all forces united, to the attack of the German armies. . . .[14]

Secondly, French tactical doctrine was based not on careful analysis of recent wars but on myth and abstract thought. Myths are essential to the morale of field troops; every army has them. Between the defeats of 1870-71 and 1914 a myth therefore was woven of the *Furia Francese,* of the irresistibility of massed Frenchmen dashing forward to the *pas de charge,* bugles squealing, colours streaming, of the glorious memories of Marengo and Austerlitz (and more dubiously Wagram), of the supposed *récipé* for success of Napoleon I. The myth admirably restored the French soldiers' morale. However, the French leadership became a victim of its own public relations: its strategy, its military organisation and equipment and its tactical doctrine were influenced by the myth. Hence the offensive, *whatever the circumstances.* But this was not to be based on the careful use of ground or on the fire power of modern rifles and machine guns, or on modern artillery preparation; it was merely an abstract idea. *Elan* and *cran* ("guts") would do it all by a succession of charges—by attack pushed "body to body."

The *Règlement* of 1913 (*Service des Armées en Campagne*) contained no discussion of the difference between a strategic and a tactical offensive, no distinction between pure defensive and the defensive offensive. It took no account of the tremendous progress of modern fire power, particularly of the high casualties caused by artillery in the Balkan War of 1912. "It is today recognised," asserted the *Règlement*,[15] "that the essential role of artillery is to support attacks . . . artillery no longer prepares attacks, it supports them." As a result the French had no medium artillery at all with divisions or corps, whereas the Germans had eighteen 105 mm. light howitzers (a highly mobile weapon, fast firing and with a curved trajectory useful in hilly country) per division and sixteen 150 mm. heavy howitzers per corps. In all the French had only three hundred heavy guns to oppose two thousand German heavy howitzers and other heavy guns, and one thousand five hundred light howitzers. The French depended almost entirely on their 75 mm. field gun, an excellent gun that fired faster, further and more accurately than the Ger-

[14] *French Official History,* Tome I, i, 54.
[15] p. 15.

man 77 mm., and of which a French corps had a hundred and twenty against a hundred and eight 77's in a German corps. Nevertheless the French threw away the advantage of the superior range of the 75 by training their gunners not to fire above 5,000 metres—less than the range of the 77.

The French infantry were not, of course, trained in field fortification. The current official instruction on this topic (dating from 1906) was out of date in regard to the effects of modern weapons. In the words of a French artillery general, "They reasoned as if the German artillery ought not to exist." [16] Nor were the French infantry trained to use their own fire power, which indeed rested on a clumsy rifle, the Lebel. It had no magazine, eight bullets being held in a tube beneath the barrel. It could not be reloaded by clip but only by one bullet at a time. In action it was therefore easier and faster to load and fire single bullets. The French attitude to modern war was summarised by this remark made in 1913 at a General Staff conference: "Imprudence in an offensive is the best of securities." [17]

However, the unreadiness of the French for the realities of modern combat and the crudity of their tactics are not to be attributed solely to the doctrines of Colonel de Grandmaison, the pre-war Chief of the Operations Section of the General Staff who had laid such emphasis on the offensive. Rather it was owing to a general decadence in the French army since the demoralising Dreyfus affair, which had led to a poor quality of junior and noncommissioned officer and to confused and amateurish ideas on tactics. In the words of the official report on the French army manœuvres of 1913: "The troops are neither trained nor disciplined . . . the junior officers and N.C.O.'s [regular] display an inexperience that would have fatal consequences in a real campaign . . . the command does not follow through the achievement of its given tasks with the activity, the energy essential for success." [18]

German field tactics and training were much more realistic than the French and were based on the fire power of their rifles and machine guns and of their light and medium artillery. They were skilled in and well-equipped for field fortification. Yet they also had failed to read the true

[16] Gascouin, 71 fn.
[17] *ibid*, 56.
[18] de Gaulle, 219.

lesson of the Balkan War and Russo-Japanese war of 1904; their tactics depended too much on mass rushes, indeed on a supposed *furor teutoni-cus*. Their troops were commanded by men who, if they had experienced war at all, had done so in the last of the "parade-ground" battles of history in 1870-71 and who since then had commanded only in peacetime evolutions. The Germans never achieved in peacetime the loose extended net of fire power now practicable.

However, the German army was built round 115,000 intelligent, highly-trained and resourceful N.C.O.'s. It was capable of great supple-ness and initiative therefore in tactical combat. Nor was German training, as the British and French believed, of a brutally rigid and parade-ground nature. "We entertain in France," wrote Colonel Serret, the French mili-tary attaché in Berlin, "false ideas about German discipline; it is believed to be extremely rough when in fact the soldiers are treated without harsh-ness." [19]

The British Expeditionary Force was in quality of its field troops best of all, but of course fractional in quantity. Its superb musketry was the result of the experiences of the Boer War. Yet it, too, had resounding in-adequacies: "almost wholly deficient in heavy guns and howitzers, trench mortars, high-explosive shell and trench-warfare equipment," [20] and with a shortage of really good staff officers. The main body of the B.E.F. disembarked in France on August 16; its concentration area was to be around Maubeuge, on the left of Lanrezac's 5th Army.

This was also the day that Moltke and his staff—with the Kaiser and his entourage as unwelcome fellow travellers—moved from Berlin to Coblenz on the Rhine. It was a splendid summer's day, and on the special train, after breakfast, Moltke displayed "fabulous confidence," [21] jubi-lant over the fate of the last Liége forts. Everywhere on their route they passed garlands of flowers; in Germany as in Britain and France the popu-lace in their naïveté could not distinguish between war and a national holiday.

Next day Kluck and Bülow and their chiefs of staff held a conference in Liége. The essential preliminaries to the great advance had been com-pleted: in particular, the 1st Army, by a brilliant feat of staff work, had

[19] H. Contamine, 148.
[20] *British Official History,* Vol. I, 11.
[21] Müller, 24.

passed through the Aachen-Visé-Herstal defile by three roads in columns thirty to forty-five miles long. At 4.30 P.M. Kluck and Bülow received this order from Moltke:

> The 1st and 2nd Armies and the 2nd Cavalry Corps (General von der Marwitz) will be under the orders of the commander of the 2nd Army during the advance north of the Meuse. This advance will begin on August 18. It is important that the enemy's forces reported to be in a position between Diest-Tirlemont-Wavre should be shouldered away from Antwerp. It is intended to initiate further operations of both armies from the line Brussels-Namur, and measures must be taken to secure their flank against Antwerp.[22]

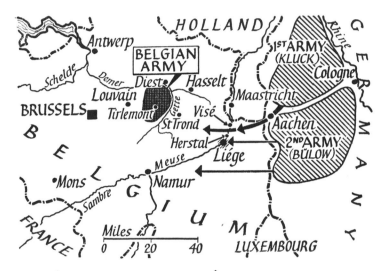

3. IST ARMY'S MARCH THROUGH THE LIÉGE BOTTLENECK

This amplified Moltke's general instruction:

> The main forces of the German army are to advance through Belgium and Luxembourg into France. Their advance is to be regarded as a wheel pivoting on the area Thionville-Metz . . . its [the 1st Army's] advance, together with that of the 2nd Army, will regulate the pace of the general wheel.[23]

[22] Kluck, 21.
[23] Kluck, 9-10.

At 11.15 P.M. on August 17, Kluck issued his own orders for the eighteenth:

The army will attack tomorrow and envelop the enemy's left wing, driving him away from Antwerp.

Thus at last the ponderous and clumsy machine, product of so much thought and care over so many years, was ready to trundle forward across the long horizons of Belgium and northern France—a machine constructed of more than a million men, their individuality drowned in field grey and spiked helmet, disciplined, obedient, yet believing that their own happiness and that of their families depended on what they were about to do; believing even more in the manner common to their fellows in all armies, that "Kaiser and Fatherland" (or its equivalent) was a reality worth death or mutilation. On jack-booted feet ringing down the *pavé,* on grinding steel-tyred wheels, on hoofs along a trail marked by fresh dung, on solid rubber automobile tyres, the vast mass would flood and trickle its way through the roads and lanes, always onwards, without rest or pause, westwards and south to Paris and victory.

But no one, from Moltke to reservist, had any idea of what it would really be like. It was a journey into the unknown—into unknown problems of mass organisation and control, of technology, of electrical and human communication. Suddenly and awfully Europe had plunged into the twentieth century.

3

Since his appointment as Chief of the General Staff in 1905, Moltke had been only too aware of this unknown quality in a future great war—only too conscious of the speculative character of all their plans and rehearsals. Trapped between a nagging sense of duty and profound self-doubt and introspection, he had worried away for nine years at preparing himself and his army for the conflict. Extreme conscientiousness even gave him the moral courage to oppose the Kaiser—as when he insisted that the imperial manoeuvres should be realistic and not merely a rigged pageant in which the Kaiser's side always won. This was more than Schlieffen had cared to do.

Yet Moltke was devoid of ambition: his appointment as Chief of the General Staff had been as unexpected as it was unwelcome. For a soldier of his epoch, he was unexpectedly sophisticated in his intellectual and emotional life. Here was neither narrow-minded professional absorption nor the rather boyish ingenuousness and simplicity that are so often the qualities of even the most distinguished commanders. These traits contrasted sharply with the ignorance (in the larger sense) of his own predecessor, Schlieffen, and with the crude peasant earthiness of his opponent Joffre, in whose mind there often appeared to be no other thought than of his next meal. Moltke had been a soldier since he was twenty-two; an excellent staff officer, and between 1902 and 1904 commander of the 1st Division of the Guards Corps. Perhaps, however, there had been too much of the Court and "social" soldiering about his career.

To wide military experience and education Moltke added a vague in-
tellectualism characteristic of his period in Germany, but not of a Prussian officer. He took a Darwinian view of nations: "This war we are now
waging is an unavoidable part of 'world evolution.' Nations are subject
to the laws of their evolution in the same way as individuals." [1]

Now it was Germany's turn to be the dominant nation:

> The Romance peoples have already passed the summit of their develop-
> ment. . . . The Slav people, and principally Russia, are still too far behind
> in their culture to be able to take over the leadership of the human race.
> Under its rod of iron, Europe would be driven back into the state of mental
> barbarity. England is only concerned with material aims. Germany is the
> only possibility for the further spiritual development of Man. [2]

Fashionable philosophers—Nietzsche, for example—interested Moltke,
but although his Swedish wife was something of a religious crank and
mystic, he remained an interested sceptic over religion. He always ques-
tioned blind faith but regretted that he lacked the gift of it. His wide-
ranging reading and interests brought him no solid convictions, no simple
basis for action, and only enhanced this floating quality in his mind
which was reflected by a dreaming sentimentality over the arts. Music
moved him greatly—especially Mendelssohn and Bach—and he himself
played the 'cello; in his letters he linked the emotional experience of
music with a vague religious sentiment.

Moltke's interests and habits of mind were thus curiously unsoldierly,
not so much in themselves as in their vague and indecisive pattern. The
commander's will must rest on iron faith; faith in God, in his cause, or in
himself. The toughness of mind of great commanders shows itself even
in intimate or trivial letters; Moltke's displayed only a softness that his
extreme conscientiousness could only exacerbate.

Nor was Moltke able to conceal this softness—reflected in his tall,
flabby figure and plump face—from his subordinates. Frau Ludendorff
recounted, for example, the impression made on her husband before
the war by his chief during the struggle to increase the size of the army:
"One day after a stormy meeting, Ludendorff came home visibly exhausted. He showed how seriously he regarded the situation. 'I have,' he

[1] Moltke, 13.
[2] Moltke, 14.

said, 'to make Moltke stand his ground by gripping him like a vice, otherwise I think his weakness would bring him to utter ruin.' " [3]

Colonel Bauer, of Section 2 of the General Staff, wrote: "General von Moltke was a highly cultured, clever man of unimpeachable character. In spite of outward coldness, he was a man of strong feelings, perhaps too much so." [4]

Moltke's physical constitution was not made of steel either. From 1911 onwards he had suffered from heart trouble and shortness of breath, which his physician attributed to an infection carried in the blood stream from inflamed tonsils. In 1913 his heart murmur had been louder, and the width of the heart had increased. When his physician had given him these findings, Moltke had replied:

"I am not so sick as you believe."

"Your Excellency," had answered Dr. Hermann, "is nevertheless much more seriously sick than *you* believe."

But Moltke had sharply challenged him: "According to your view, Doctor, I cannot continue as Chief of the General Staff." [5]

Although Moltke's wife claims he was perfectly healthy at the outbreak of war, it is clear that this was not so. Moltke was an elderly man; severe strain would soon expose his chronic unfitness.

Even before the move to Coblenz for the battle of France on August 16, the nerve-stretching period of inaction and waiting had given way to intense pressure: of work, of events difficult to evaluate, of cumulative anxiety. For all over Europe the armies were lurching and blundering into each other. On August 11 the French had attacked near Mulhouse in Alsace, in strength too weak for an offensive and too strong for reconnaissance. They had been thrown back. On August 14 had come news that powerful French forces were across the frontier of the Reichsland (their lost provinces of Alsace-Lorraine) on a wide front south of Metz facing the 6th Army (Crown Prince Rupprecht). The German forces were held well back in their prepared defences, and the French had to pick their way forward under a sweltering sun through thick woodland, up and down steep hill slopes, their progress broken or de-

[3] Frau Ludendorff, 18.
[4] Bauer, 33-5.
[5] "How von Moltke Died," *American Medical Association Journal*, 26.5.28.

flected by streams or marshes, cursing and stumbling in their long Second Empire *capotes* and heavy packs.

It was clear to Moltke that the French were after all committing themselves to a major offensive in Lorraine and that battle would be joined there before his own advance in Belgium, not due to start before August 18, reached the French left flank. The pre-war solution had been clear:

"From the moment when it is known that the mass of the French army is taking the offensive between Metz and the Vosges, the movement of the German right wing across Belgium becomes without object."

Moltke now became aware of the difference between the abstract, weightless decisions of the staff ride and similar decisions in war loaded with great consequences and with the heavy inertia of pre-set plans already in motion in Belgium. If the French continued to advance, passing Metz on their left, they could be stopped by the German field defences and attacked in both flanks. There was for Moltke the tempting vision of a decisive victory on his left wing before the right wing, on its long march, could even make contact with the French. He therefore considered stopping the 5th Army's forward march (and even for a moment that of the 4th) and throwing them astride Metz and the Nied into the French left rear. He actually ordered six ersatz divisions, promised to the Austrians, to go to Lorraine. However, while Moltke was still making up his mind, it became clear from the cautiousness of the French pursuit of Rupprecht that there could be no decisive encounter before August 18, when the great advance of the right wing had to begin. German strategy remained unaltered after all.

On August 14 Moltke had also been concerned with the safety of East Prussia; he had ordered General von Prittwitz und Gaffron, commanding the 8th Army, that "if the Russians come, there must be no defensive, but an offensive defensive." This order was timely: on August 17 the Russians, carrying out loyally their promises to their French allies, crossed the East Prussian frontier in force and beat the Germans in a brisk action at Stallupönen. This was truly bad news. The appearance of so powerful a Russian force at so early a date entirely wrecked Schlieffen's and Moltke's calculations for a two-front war.

When, therefore, the western advance was unleashed on August 18, the danger in the east was already pressing on Moltke's mind. It narrowed to virtually nothing that margin of time which was the basic calculation of the western deployment. From now on the necessity for a speedy decision in France dominated all thought. The developing situation in Lor-

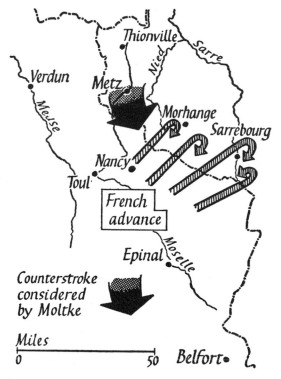

4. PLAN 17 AND THE BATTLES OF MORHANGE-SARREBOURG

raine was also distracting Moltke from his own great attack. Yet this was the moment, as the army marched away from him into the west, that saw the first marginal thoughts of Schlieffen twenty-three years ago at last turned into the reality of over a million men implementing the most grandiose, the most rigidly classical work of strategic architecture ever designed.

Away through red-brick Belgian villages, past the glowering stares of Belgian civilians, and on through the summer dust the long grey columns tramped. From time to time the smouldering ruins of a house sullenly brought home to the troops, innocent yet, that war is violence. For the twentieth-century cycle of hatred and atrocity was beginning to spin. Already, before the army battle was joined, the horrors of a people's war were loosening moral restraint. Kluck's own headquarters had to be guarded against guerrillas by a battalion of infantry with a machine gun and a 77. He and his staff carried rifles. The Germans had retaliated against the guerrillas by not very discriminate shootings and house burnings.

All that day and the next Kluck's 320,000 men pressed on in the first of the campaign's wide flanking movements to the right, striving to get between the Belgian field army on the Gette and their rallying point in the fortress of Antwerp. It was important to succeed, for if the Belgians could fall back into Antwerp, with its double perimeter of forts, they would constitute a perpetual menace to the communications of the German right wing: a menace requiring a flank guard deducted from the wing's attacking strength.

Outnumbered five to one, the Belgians fought it out for a day on the Gette; then as Kluck's massive columns began to press round their left, and there was no sign of the British or the French, they fell back in good time towards Antwerp. Kluck's troops marched dourly on, through Louvain, its spires glowing gold in the afternoon sun, and into Brussels, where the sounds of a passing army echoed hollowly through the streets. It was August 20, and the Belgians were now safe in Antwerp. It was the Germans' first failure, and it had immediate effects. In Kluck's words: "As the Belgian army had neither been dispersed nor forced away from Antwerp, in spite of the rapid advance of the 1st Army, it became of the utmost importance for the latter to protect the right flank of the German armies, not only against Antwerp, but also against the coast and the coastal provinces of Northern France." [6] So the 3rd and 4th Reserve Corps dropped out of the advance to mask Antwerp. Already, before the main encounter with the French and British, the outflankers were concerned about their own flank.

It was now the twentieth day of mobilisation and still the great armies had not collided; to the puzzled troops, war appeared to consist of endless route marches in the tropical heat of the last summer of the Golden

[6] Kluck, 35.

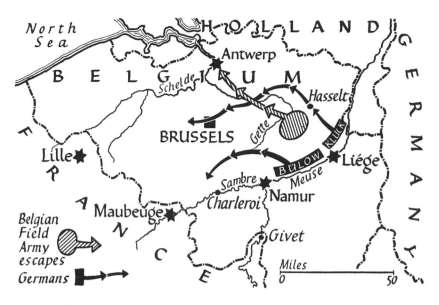

5. KLUCK'S FAILURE TO DRIVE THE BELGIANS FROM ANTWERP

Age. And yet August 20 was one of the days upon whose decisions the campaign was to turn.

On Moltke's right flank Bülow and Kluck were up to a line Brussels-Gembloux, Hausen (3rd Saxon Army) was on the Meuse, running between its steep cliffs between Givet and Namur (invested by two reserve corps and bombarded on the 19th); the 4th Army (Duke Albrecht of Württemberg) linked Hausen to the 5th (Imperial Crown Prince) which was pushing through the close wooded country of the Ardennes to reach the line Etalle-Thionville. Lieutenant-Colonel Hentsch, Moltke's Chief of the Foreign Armies Section of the General Staff (Intelligence Section), estimated that west of the Meuse between Namur and Mézières there were now four French corps, four reserve divisions, a Moroccan division and three cavalry divisions. The British, whose strength was put at four infantry divisions and a cavalry division, were reckoned to be still disembarking at Boulogne; only advanced guards were thought to be in the field—round Lille.

By these calculations the thirty-two infantry divisions and five cavalry divisions of the German 1st, 2nd and 3rd Armies were about to fall upon twenty-one allied infantry divisions and four cavalry divisions (including Belgians still fit to fight). In the centre, Hentsch estimated that the 4th Army had a superiority of five corps to four over the 4th French Army and that the 5th Army, northeast of Verdun, enjoyed an even greater margin over the 3rd French Army—five corps and four cavalry corps, against three corps, three reserve divisions and one cavalry division.

The first stage of the plan had therefore gone well; the Germans were on and beyond the French left flank in crushing strength. Yet time—the key to Schlieffen's calculations—was already working for the French. Although Joffre, the French Commander-in-Chief, remained obsessed with his own offensive in Lorraine, the German ultimatum to Belgium had induced him as early as August 2 to alter Plan 17 and to extend his flank by side-stepping Lanrezac's 5th Army to the left and bringing up de Langle de Cary's 4th Army (hitherto in reserve) between Lanrezac and the 3rd Army. The dwindling element of surprise in the German manoeuvre—surprise of time, weight and place—was eroded still further by Hentsch's crashing error over the B.E.F. which, far from still filing down the gangways was, even as he wrote his appreciation, assembled near Maubeuge and ready for battle.

The allied left flank, although much weaker than its opponents, could now if necessary extend solidly as far as Valenciennes. By a French G.Q.G.[7] order of August 18, General d'Amade, commanding French reserve divisions round Lille, was "to establish a barrier between Dunkirk and Maubeuge in order to protect the railway communications from possible raids by enemy cavalry." This was only a screen as yet, but it was the first shadow thrown by Joffre's progressive redeployment of the French forces. And, as if to make sure that Kluck remained blind to the B.E.F.'s presence, Moltke took away most of Marwitz's cavalry corps from 1st Army for use by 2nd Army.

Yet the ingredients were still there for a decisive German victory, for Lanrezac's 5th French Army, now lining the right angle of the Sambre and Meuse, could be cut off by Hausen's 3rd Army attacking from the east, while Bülow's 2nd Army held it to the ground by a frontal assault. At the same time Kluck could use his prodigious superiority of numbers to curl round the British left flank and drive them back against Lanrezac. A concerted attack by three German armies could lead to a double en-

[7] G.Q.G. = *Grand Quartier Général.*

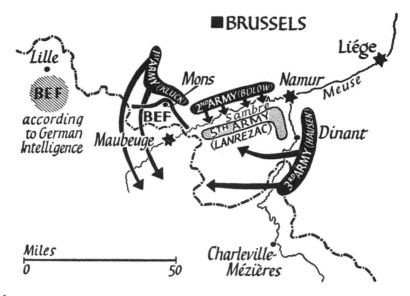

6. THE GERMAN OPPORTUNITY ON AUGUST 20

velopment of the allied left wing. The first question, however, was: who should do the concerting? It was a novel problem in 1914, although it is clear enough now—it was clear enough a few months later—that Moltke should have appointed an army group commander to direct the right wing throughout the campaign. As it was, there was no command echelon between the armies and O.H.L. Should Moltke therefore have gone forward from Coblenz himself and taken charge?

He was responsible not only for the entire western front but also for the war against Russia. And August 20 was not a day to make Moltke feel free to leave O.H.L. In the first place there was a heavy atmosphere of gloom over the imperial entourage in Coblenz, for the Master of the Horse began the day at 7 A.M. by shooting himself—an early victim of the nervous strains of war. There was bad news from Austria, where two armies had recrossed the river Drina after being savaged by the Serbs. There was worse news from East Prussia, where three German corps had been defeated at Gumbinnen. Many generals have found politicians trying at times of crisis, but a politician who is also sovereign, titular supreme commander, as moody as an adolescent, and on the spot, would be enough to make the strongest nerves creak. The Kaiser did not take the Russian invasion of Prussia lightly; when two of his entourage during a walk fetched a second bench rather than sit with him on a seat too short for three, he asked: "Am I already such a figure of contempt that no one wants to sit next to me?" [8]

At 8:30 P.M. that evening Prittwitz telephoned Moltke from East Prussia in a state of panic to say that he was ordering a general retreat behind the Vistula. There were stouter hearts than his in Coblenz, but Moltke's was not among them, as one of his staff noted: "General von Moltke was deeply shattered when the order to retreat was announced but he did not think of giving a resolute counter-order." [9]

To complete an overcrowded day news had come from Crown Prince Rupprecht of a magnificent victory over the French in Alsace-Lorraine. All that week the French had been pressing on with increasing fatigue into the German trap. On the nineteenth there had been stiff fighting— almost a battle—but the French thought that a last determined attack would overwhelm the German rear guards. As they came on eastwards on the twentieth, long bayonets glittering above the brave red of their trousers, bugles blaring amid the sharp banging of the 75's, the French 1st and 2nd Armies paid with defeat for the decadence and conservatism of French society. Blasted and bemused by the weight of fire from the plentiful German medium artillery accurately directed by aircraft (a German innovation), the French were cut down, broken toys in period uniform, by well-sited machine guns. Not all the *cran* and *élan*, even of so consistent an optimist as Foch, commanding a corps, could take the French further. As orders came through to retire, Foch uttered one of those characteristic phrases that were to sound like bugle calls over so many thousands of dead: "If ever I was tempted to disobey, it is today." [10]

These defeats of Morhange-Sarrebourg were not the swift and dramatic massacre of the first day of the Somme; they were the culminating and deciding moment of a week of steady, small, daily defeats of badly led French by better troops with better officers and staff. The contrast between the chaotic staff work and unrealistic planning on their own side and the deadly fire of the Germans had an overwhelming moral effect

[8] Müller, 22-4.
[9] Bauer, 45.
[10] Falls, *Foch*, 49.

on the French troops in the field. In the words of General de Gaulle: "But the actors, at that moment, had only one thought: 'It's absurd!' " [11]

For Moltke this wrecking of the French offensive was marvellous news. In the words of his quartermaster-general, von Stein,[12] he saw in the counterstroke of the German 6th and 7th Armies the hope of "the great decision of the war," and wished therefore to remain in Coblenz to be in touch with his left flank.

Thus Moltke was not going forward to direct the imminent decisive battle on the Franco-Belgian frontier. His uncle had left the fighting of the battles to the initiative of his army commanders; he would do likewise. In his own words: "The Supreme Command needs to be intelligently helped by the initiative of army commanders. The latter, on their side, should always think in terms of the general situation and try unceasingly to conform to it." [13] On the evening of August 20 Moltke therefore issued a general directive to his right wing, leaving "to the commanders of the 2nd and 3rd Armies the job of coming to a mutual understanding over the co-ordination of the attack which the 2nd Army was to carry out against the enemy forces west of Namur, with the attack which the 3rd Army was to direct against the line of the Meuse between Namur and Givet." [14]

This abdication of Moltke's was a mistake. The method of command applied by his uncle to the separated, so much smaller battles of 1870-1 was quite inappropriate to three armies that must manoeuvre in a single battle as a single unit. Battles directed by a committee are rarely victorious, and never a substitute for a single driving will. And what a committee this was! Alexander von Kluck, a ruthless sixty-eight-year-old hard-marching and recently ennobled careerist, already chafing at being under the control of Bülow, his fellow army commander; Bülow, a cautious aristocrat, also born in 1846, with a great peacetime reputation and a dominating desire to see everybody closed tightly up in mutual support; and Hausen, a lazy, feeble commander, full of Saxon resentment of Prussians, always waiting for orders and making excuses.

Victory lay in the bold use of superior German numbers in a double envelopment of the B.E.F. and Lanrezac's 5th French Army. Kluck, on

[11] de Gaulle, 244.
[12] *Nation*, 1919.
[13] Förster, 29.
[14] Baumgarten–Crusius, 27.

the basis of an intelligence report from O.H.L., expected the B.E.F. to appear from the direction of Lille; he therefore wanted to march wide to the southwest, his left passing Maubeuge. But on August 21, Bülow ordered him to invest the north and northwest front of Maubeuge and support the 2nd Army's coming attack on the Sambre. Kluck, a man of short and violent temper, protested at this feeble use of the largest army in the German line and the one intended to outflank the enemy continuously. Bülow replied in characteristic but unconvincing terms that "otherwise the 1st Army might get too far away and not be able to support and 2nd Army at the right moment."[15] On this day, while his army commander was disputing with Kluck, Major-General Ludendorff was present when the 2nd Guards Division crossed the Sambre west of Namur.

Next day Kluck and Bülow received vague news of the British presence in front of them; but the area towards Lille, west of the Mons-Condé canal, appeared clear. To Kluck, "it seemed . . . all the more important to aim at outflanking the British left wing by keeping the 1st Army well away westward as a strong right wing."[16] Consumed with frustration, he asked O.H.L. if he were to remain under Bülow's command. He was. Kluck then sent a staff officer to argue it out with Bülow. That cautious old man relented over the restrictions of the role of the 1st Army to investing the north and northwest of Maubeuge but refused to allow Kluck to march on Bavay via Mons.

It had been an error on Moltke's part to solve the problem of command by putting one army commander under the control of another, who must always think of his own army first. It was a capital mistake on Bülow's part to prohibit Kluck from swinging wide to the westward according to the spirit of the campaign plan. The 1st Army's new line of march led directly into the B.E.F.; Kluck's original axis would have manoeuvred the B.E.F. out of its positions without a shot. However, Bülow still enjoyed every chance of a great victory over Lanrezac on the Sambre and Meuse—a chance enormously enhanced by another French miscalculation and another shattering French defeat elsewhere.

Joffre was undaunted by the wreck of Plan 17 in Alsace-Lorraine. An engineer with a mostly colonial and not very distinguished career, he

[15] Kluck, 37.
[16] *ibid*, 41.

had been chosen as Commander-in-Chief because he had no strong convictions in either the religious or the military fanaticisms of the French army. It was therefore perhaps his greatest quality that he was not easily daunted. He had on August 21 ordered his centre (the 3rd and 4th Armies) to strike north into the Ardennes in order to break the German centre, get across their lateral communications, and hew off their right wing at the pivot. Since they, the Germans, had proved strong in Alsace-Lorraine (actually 345,000 Germans had defeated 456,000 French), and since they were also strong west of the Meuse, they must surely be weak in their centre. In fact, as Hentsch's appreciation had pointed out, the Germans were stronger here too. Joffre's calculations and strategic thinking were unfortunately based on the French General Staff's underestimation of total German strength against them by no less than four corps—thirty corps and eight cavalry divisions as against the real figure of thirty-four corps and ten cavalry divisions. This was equivalent to an extra army. No wonder Joffre was surprised by the extent of the German deployment.[17]

The battle of the Ardennes on August 22 was Morhange-Sarrebourg all over again. The German cavalry, fighting defensively with infantry and guns in that undramatic but effective way in which their descendants the panzers were to fight in Africa thirty-eight years later, baffled the attempts of the French cavalry, dressed for Waterloo, to launch charges as at Waterloo, or even to reconnoitre, an operation at which the French cavalry were in any case almost useless. In total ignorance of the whereabouts and strength of the Germans before them, the French infantry and guns plunged into the close, broken country of the Ardennes, a romantic landscape full of steep little hills and narrow little valleys, remarkably empty of good roads. Magnificent staff work took a German panzer army through the same country easily in 1940; slapdash French staff work in 1914, and the haphazard brawls of battles that followed, convinced the French for the future that the Ardennes were impassable to an army.

August 22 was another blazing day of that fabulous summer; in the valleys and thick murmurous woodlands no breeze could cool the sweating, struggling soldiers. The roads—what there were of them—became jammed with guns and horsed transport. The 75, with its flat tra-

[17] *German Official History*, I, 69. *French Official History*, Tome I, i, 40.

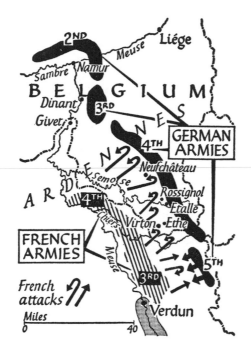

7. THE FRENCH OFFENSIVE IN THE ARDENNES

jectory and lack of manoeuvrability over rough ground, was not at its best in this hill country; the German light and heavy howitzers were. There were close, savage *mêlées* at Ethe, Virton, Rossignol and Neuf-château where the French displayed that driving gallantry in attack that under Napoleon I had borne down so many opponents. But the offensive nevertheless collapsed with fearsome losses. The 3rd and 4th Armies fell back towards the Meuse and Chiers in confusion, leaving Lanrezac, an intelligent but gloomy man, growing gloomier, without support on his right and desperately outnumbered.

No situation could have been more favourable for the imminent general assault of the German right-wing armies.

Bülow had arranged with Hausen (3rd Saxon Army) that their attacks on Lanrezac on the Sambre and the Meuse should start simultaneously in the morning of August 23. However, at midday on the twenty-second, Bülow, finding that the French in front of him appeared to be only a screen of cavalry with some infantry, decided "to profit from the momentary advantage and cross the extremely difficult line of the Sambre with his left flank that same day, before new enemy reinforcements could come up." [18] In fact, he still faced the French 5th Army in full strength. Nevertheless the 2nd Army began to hammer Lanrezac's line along the Sambre to pieces; at the end of the day it was actually across the river.

Unfortunately Bülow, in the fever of hasty decision, had forgotten to tell Hausen that he was about to attack a whole day earlier.

Hausen therefore stayed where he was on the twenty-second except for a few outposts thrown across the Meuse. Under Bülow's frontal pressure, and aware of Hausen's presence on his flank, the sour and sardonic Lanrezac fell back. When Hausen himself crossed the Meuse westwards in force on the twenty-third as arranged, it was too late: Lanrezac had already gone too far to the south. Instead of having an army across his communications, Lanrezac had merely been pushed back, although with some loss and in some confusion.

Meanwhile Kluck, under Bülow's orders, had been fighting the British. For various reasons it is impossible to withhold sympathy from Kluck. In the first place, he was having to carry out a manoeuvre he believed wrong. Secondly, the last information from O.H.L. on the twenty-first about the British had indicated that "large disembarkations had not taken place," when in fact they were assembled, ready for battle. Thirdly, O.H.L. had taken away Marwitz's cavalry corps which Kluck would have employed for his own reconnaissance. The British cavalry division (Major-General Allenby) was the best-trained cavalry of any army for modern war; Kluck's army cavalry was unable to get through Allenby's screen. Therefore the 1st Army Commander had absolutely no idea of the whereabouts or strength of the British. German Intelligence under the charge of Lieutenant-Colonel Hentsch, of the Foreign Armies Section of the General Staff, had proved as incompetent and misleading as the French. On the twenty-second there was a glimmer of light—enough to cast wild distortions into the surrounding darkness. Kluck informed his army at 8:30 P.M.: "A squadron of British cavalry was encountered today at Casteau, northeast of Mons, and a British aircraft, coming from Maubeuge, was shot down near Enghien." [19] Such was

[18] Koeltz, 31.
[19] Kluck, 34.

the basis of the operation orders issued by Kluck for the twenty-third—day of the battle of Mons.

His troops, too, were no less uncertain about the British. They had now marched three hundred and forty kilometres, on some days covering up to forty-five kilometres, trapped by discipline in a cycle of heat, thirst, hunger, fatigue and blistered feet. By day the relentless sun had shone down on their heavy packs, on the glistening napes of their necks, throwing their shadows down into the dust. By night they had marched in silence through sleeping villages, as fires flickered and glowed against the sky. They had outstripped their supplies but lived well enough off the countryside, except for a total lack of bread. This caused much grumbling. A reservist in the Brandenburg Grenadiers noted: "I now learned for the first time what a vitally important part bread plays in the life of the working man." [20]

But where, wondered the 1st Army, was the war? When would they meet the British in their bearskins and scarlet?

At Coblenz, now two hundred and fifty kilometres behind the 1st Army, August 21 and 22 were days of acute tension and critical decisions—or the need to make them—as the German armies fought savagely in East Prussia, in Alsace-Lorraine and in the Ardennes, and the heaviest battle of all was about to explode west of the Meuse. By contrast, hardly a gun had been fired at sea, although Jellicoe had cruised between Norway and the Grand Fleet bases. On August 21 and 22, for example, the Grand Fleet was peacefully carrying out training exercises in the North Sea.

The German General Staff had settled now into their campaign routine, working from 8:30 A.M. to 1 A.M. with two and a half hours for meals in the hotel where they were billeted.

"One ate at small tables, simply but substantially, and a glass of wine was drunk with the food—this was on the Rhine, of course," wrote one of Moltke's staff. "Champagne was prohibited by Moltke as he said it was unfitting when so many men out there were sacrificing their lives and their health." [21] It was characteristic of Moltke's moral awareness.

[20] Bloem, 51.
[21] Bauer, 46.

Every four or five days each O.H.L. officer was on night duty, encoding and decoding reports and instructions and mapping the situation on the basis of the latest information. Already they found their telecommunications net inadequate and old-fashioned; the field armies were receding into a fog of scanty, garbled and hopelessly delayed messages, and the crisis of the campaign was yet to come. The problem of long-distance control was sharply posed by Prittwitz's decision, endorsed by Moltke, to abandon East Prussia. It was a decision so defeatist that the operations section of O.H.L. set out to reverse it by telephoning the staff of each of Prittwitz's corps to see if things were as bad as he made out. From Coblenz to East Prussia lay more than nine hundred kilometres of telephone line without amplifiers. It took long hours of struggle, frustration and shouting into mouthpieces before the operations staff could assemble notes on each corps' situation. Yet the result justified the effort: "All the corps maintained that the position was serious but that the retreat was overhurried," wrote Colonel Bauer. "The matter was put to Stein [Chief Quartermaster-General and Moltke's deputy], then to Moltke, and lo and behold, with success! Ludendorff was confirmed as chief for the east and Hindenburg named as Prittwitz's successor." [22] Meanwhile Hoffmann, Prittwitz's chief of staff, had already persuaded Prittwitz to accept his proposals for a counterstroke: the proposals that later made the reputation of Hindenburg and Ludendorff.

Nevertheless, such initiative by relatively junior officers at O.H.L. indicated how far Moltke's resolution and self-mastery had already been submerged; how obvious to his staff the effects of strain, ever screwed even tighter, on his oversensitive mind and nerves. East Prussia still haunted him. Hindenburg and Ludendorff, the hero of Liége, might supply the spirit Prittwitz had lacked, but they would still face odds of nine divisions to twenty-two. It was essential to send them reinforcements as soon as possible; but how soon would it be before they could be spared from the west?

On August 22 there was wonderfully cheering news. Namur had fallen. The French had been thrown out of the Ardennes, back behind the Meuse and the Chiers. And from Crown Prince Rupprecht came jubilant reports of his shattering victories at Morhange-Sarrebourg and of

[22] *ibid,* 45.

the advance of the 6th and 7th Armies to Lunéville and the upper Vezouse.

To Rupprecht the French appeared to be a disordered, defeated and retreating mass which might be utterly destroyed by a relentless advance. He sought Moltke's sanction. Once again Moltke juggled with the terrible imponderables of war. The present line of the 6th and 7th Armies was short and excellent for defence, should he decide to halt his left wing, according to the Schlieffen Plan, while the right wing made its offensive on the Franco-Belgian frontier tomorrow. A halt now would allow him to start switching reinforcements to Kluck and Bülow. In the path of a further advance by Rupprecht lay the strong French frontier fortifications.

Yet on the other hand Rupprecht was on the spot, running the battle, and cogently arguing that a decisive success was possible; Moltke in Coblenz had not the facts, the intuition or the consistency of will to contradict him. Rather, the possibility glittered before him of smashing both French flanks simultaneously. After all, concrete frontier fortifications did not seem so formidable after the easy destruction of Liége. As for reinforcements for Kluck and Bülow, the demolition of the Belgian railways made such transfers in any case impossible: the German wings had been as effectively severed by a few Belgian engineers as they would have been by a French army.

So Moltke once again accepted the views and wishes of his local army commander: Rupprecht was to continue attacking. "If the breakthrough succeeded," wrote von Tappen, Moltke's Chief of Operations Section, "the encirclement of the enemy army would be concerted in a broad way with the movements of the right wing, and the encirclement was expected, if it happened quickly, to bring the end of the war." [23]

Two days later, on August 24, came reports from Kluck, Bülow and Hausen of resounding victories over the French and British. In the words of a Court diarist, Admiral Müller, "News of victories in the west including the repulse of the English cavalry by General von Bülow. Great jubilation." [24] Next day, August 25, the reports from the right wing continued to trumpet victory.

[23] Koeltz, 105.
[24] Müller, 24.

"Bülow is driving the enemy before him," wrote Admiral Müller in his diary. "The 1st Army is already turning the French and English flanks and a great debacle is expected. The Kaiser is radiant!" [25]

Once more Moltke was presented with the appearance of decisive victory. Once more he had to accept it. He could not discuss the victory in person with his army commanders; a bellowed telephone conversation over a bad line was no substitute for the direct contact of minds and personalities and indeed was never tried by Moltke. There remained coded telegrams and radio signals, naturally kept as brief as possible. Moltke and his battle commanders were like deaf men with poor ear trumpets trying to carry out a complex technical discussion. One thing, devoid of nuance or qualification, penetrated: the great battle of the frontiers had taken place and the Germans had won it. Certainly the army commanders believed so. On August 25 (11:50 P.M.) Kluck's orders for the next day were for the "continuation of the pursuit of the beaten enemy." Bülow equally ordered "the pursuit of the beaten enemy in a southwesterly direction with the greatest possible energy."

"The entirely favourable news," wrote Tappen, "that arrived every day from the right wing and which was still arriving at O.H.L. on August 25 created the belief that, together with the great victory in Lorraine of August 20-23, the great decisive battle of the western front had taken place and had been favourable to us." [26]

If this were so, then the desperately needed reinforcements for East Prussia could now be released from the western front, and not a moment too soon, in view of the time necessary to march them to railheads and transfer them right across Europe. Moltke ordered six corps to start this movement: two from the right wing, released by the fall of Namur, two from the centre and two from the left.

Tappen asserts that Moltke made this crucial decision because of his belief that "having won a decisive victory in the west, large forces could be sent to the east to seek a decision there too." [27] Moltke himself afterwards took an opposite view:

"While our right-wing armies made victorious progress beyond the Meuse and the Sambre, events on the eastern front . . . obliged us to

[25] *loc. cit.*
[26] Koeltz, 110.
[27] *loc. cit.*

send reinforcements to this front before a definite decision could be reached over the Franco-English army." [28]

It is possible that Moltke's actual position was somewhere between the two: he believed, with reason, that East Prussia stood in dire need of reinforcements; but he knew that the west was not supposed to be weakened before a decisive victory, and he may have therefore told his staff that he believed that this victory had taken place.

Yet Moltke's assessment of the events on the front of the B.E.F. and the French 5th Army between August 22 and 25, and that of his army commanders, was dangerously remote from the truth; and the truth was that there had been gross tactical bungling, grotesque lapses in coordination, and two missed opportunities for encirclement battles of annihilation; the truth was that the British and French, although retreating, had preserved their cohesion and much of their fighting capacity.

The British Expeditionary Force, under Sir John French, had been advancing on Lanrezac's left in order to take up a position from Binche to Lens, north of Mons, according to Joffre's instructions. On the evening of August 22 they were halted for the night in a dismal region of mining villages, slag heaps and open ground near Mons. While Sir John French and his officers were busy plotting the next day's forward move, a British liaison officer with the French 5th Army brought them news that Lanrezac was not going to advance; on the contrary, he was defending himself with difficulty against violent German attacks. So the night stop at Mons, level with Lanrezac, became a place where the British accepted battle in northern Europe for the first time in ninety-nine years.

In almost every way it was unsuitable for a battle. The area was strewn with red-brick miners' cottages, factories, pit heads and slag heaps, all of which gave splendid cover but limited observation and fields of fire. Mobility and cohesion were further reduced by the Mons-Condé canal, running east to west seven feet deep and sixty-four feet wide, with its sixteen bridges, and by elaborate ditching in the open spaces of this industrial zone.

Such a terrain would have broken up the most cohesive of operations carried out by the most clever and strong-minded leadership. Kluck and Sir John French contributed neither. The latter, a cavalryman who had

[28] Moltke, 434 ff.

made his reputation in the Boer War, was reckoned by one of his corps commanders (Haig) to be unstable in temper and inadequate for his post. Events were to prove this a sound judgement.

As the 1st Army came swinging down from the north in an early-morning drizzle on August 23, they knew the British were somewhere across their path, west of Maubeuge; perhaps a cavalry screen, perhaps an army. A rumour that the British lay to the west, at Tournai, had halted the army for two hours. The "British" turned out to be a French territorial brigade. There was little to see: their march was closed in by hamlets, and the shallow valley in which Mons lay was full of cover. Nor could the British see the 1st Army coming. Since it was a Sunday, and civilians did not know about modern war, the bells were ringing,

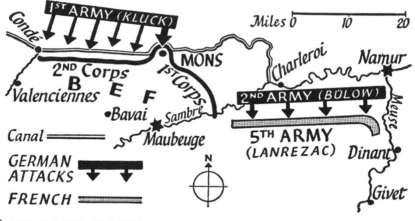

8. THE BATTLE OF MONS

and families were going to church in their best clothes all over the battlefield. This did not aid tactical clarity and cohesion.

The German cavalry stumbled into the British cavalry, then into the main British position. Stopped, the Germans began to pile up, deploy and attack the enemy in front of them. The appearance of the British soldiers proved a surprise: "a man in a grey-brown uniform, no, in a grey-brown golfing suit with a flat-topped cloth cap. Could this be a soldier?" [29] The German corps stumbled into battle one by one as they came up; the

[29] Bloem, 56.

main weight of the German assault fell on the B.E.F.'s right centre round the town of Mons, whereas Kluck would have wished it to fall on its left and beyond, where superior numbers could tell.

For both armies it was a brutal encounter with the reality of modern war. Plumes of dark smoke, earth and rubble jumped into the hot sunshine that had followed the drizzle. Little white clouds suddenly appeared above the troops, rained down shrapnel, drifted and evaporated. The noise of guns filled the battlefield with violence, unexpected in its stupendous impact on ears and nerves. Through the roar of artillery pierced the scaly churning of machine guns and the irregular rattle of the British volley firing. There was the smell of explosive, the sight of friends dead and insulted by grotesque injuries. The British punished the badly organised German attacks with terrible casualties.

The 1st Army was profoundly shocked by its first battle. In the words of the official German history of the battle: "Well entrenched and completely hidden, the enemy opened a murderous fire . . . the casualties increased . . . the rushes became shorter, and finally the whole advance stopped . . . with bloody losses the attack gradually came to an end." [30]

However, the Germans had at least one surprise for the British: the devastating fire of their light and heavy howitzers, which plunged down behind all cover, ploughing up dead ground with an accuracy that convinced its victims that spies were at work. This was a tribute to the German aircraft spotters, an innovation the British had yet to copy. As the day faded, the German bugles blew "Cease Fire" down their line, a sad and beautiful anachronism, and two British divisions (only Smith-Dorrien's 2nd Corps had been engaged) had stopped six German without losing much ground. Such was the battle of Mons. Its result was to delay Kluck's advance by twenty-four hours, and it is thus militarily without great significance in the campaign of 1914—certainly not more significant than Lanrezac's fight on the Sambre, and less significant than Joffre's two miscarried offensives. But it was the first battle fought in northern Europe by the British since Waterloo; it expressed in blood Britain's inevitable yet so long evaded commitment to the continent. Above all, it was the place where Anglo-German rivalry became, to paraphrase Clausewitz, extended by other means—the collision of armies.

[30] *Die Schlacht bei Mons*, 37.

At last, after a wasted day and futile casualties, Kluck began to grip his battle. He guessed (wrongly) that after such a successful defence the British would fight again on the morrow on the high ground south of Mons. He therefore resolved to continue the attack the next day enveloping the left flank, with the intention of cutting off the enemy's retreat to the west. In other words, Kluck's plan for the twenty-fourth was what he *would* have planned for the twenty-third, had it not been for Bülow and his own resoundingly poor intelligence service.

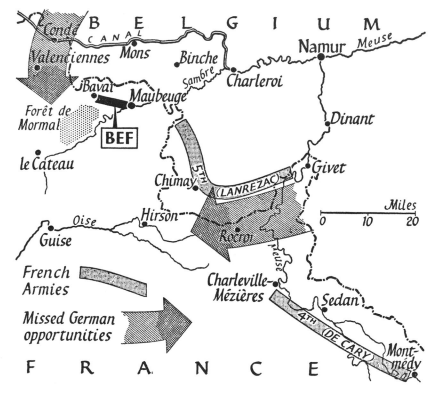

9. THE GERMAN CHANCE ON AUGUST 24

He was too late. The British slipped away during the night. They went because Lanrezac was going; and Lanrezac was going because de Langle de Cary's retreat out of the Ardennes to Montmédy—Sedan—Mézières had opened a gap on his right. The need for an army group commander over the three armies on the allied left wing was just as imperative as it was for their opponents.

Thus, on August 24 these armies came wavering back, in poor cohesion and in places badly shaken and disorganised, pushed by the weight of German superiority. Now the Germans were given a second chance of a great victory of encirclement on the frontier. For, as Kluck felt for French's left flank, French was in fact struggling against the temptation to march his exhausted and outnumbered army into the fortress of Maubeuge. On the Meuse, south of Givet, lay the gap between Lanrezac and de Langle de Cary; if Hausen's 3rd Army attacked vigorously southwestwards through it on the axis Rocroi-Hirson, Lanrezac and French would find themselves cut off and surrounded by three German armies. Hausen was aware of this gap and had signalled its existence to O.H.L. However, it was only at 8:25 in the morning of the twenty-third, when Hausen was already committed to his westward attack round Dinant, that he had received a characteristically permissive signal from Moltke, characteristically too late to fit the situation that day: "It is recommended that available forces of the 3rd Army should push beyond the Meuse, south of Givet, to cut off the retreat of the enemy forces opposite it." [31]

Nevertheless, as Lanrezac came stumbling south with Bülow after him, Hausen proposed to carry out this attack the next day. Once more Bülow's caution saved the French. Impressed by a vigorous counterattack by Lanrezac's 18th Corps against his left, Bülow called for help from Hausen. This signal, couched in urgent language, reached Hausen's headquarters at four in the morning of the twenty-fourth. Hausen abandoned his projected advance across Lanrezac's line of retreat and prepared directly to support Bülow. As he put it later: "One after all had the right to suppose that a commander so experienced and of such a reputation as that at the head of the 2nd Army would only ask for immediate help in the case of absolute necessity." [32]

Hausen's supposition was wrong; a few hours later Bülow's alarm had passed, as his own army continued to push Lanrezac back. The 3rd Army had lost precious hours, however, and Hausen was not the man to make them up, especially as he could blame Bülow for failure. In the

[31] Baumgarten–Crusius, 31.
[32] *ibid*, 31.

action on the Meuse against Hausen, Pétain's brigade fought so skilfully that its commander, at fifty-eight, was marked as a coming man.

On the other side of Bülow, Kluck was still attempting to carry out his own plans as far as possible and Bülow's instructions as little as possible. Bülow wanted him to press closely round the south of Maubeuge against Lanrezac's flank; Kluck began that series of swings at the B.E.F.'s left flank that were to continue for a week and imposed tremendous marching performances on his already tired troops. It was Kluck's belief that the British wanted to retreat westwards to the Channel ports, and his first care, therefore, was to employ (and wear out) Marwitz's cavalry corps (which had been returned to him) in cutting this retreat. In fact Sir John French, having overcome the temptation to shelter in Maubeuge, was retreating southwards, linked by cavalry to Lanrezac.

On the twenty-fifth Bülow shed a corps to mask Maubeuge. For an old-fashioned fortress, this detachment was excessive.

On the twenty-sixth Kluck was given a superb chance of destroying one of the B.E.F.'s two corps. Astride the B.E.F.'s line of retreat lay the dense Forest of Mormal. The known roads ran north-south on either side of it. Sir John French was obliged to split his army by sending 2nd Corps (Smith-Dorrien) down the west of the forest; 1st Corps (Haig) down the east. At Le Cateau Smith-Dorrien found his troops so tired and Kluck so close that it was better to fight than retreat. Sir John French and his staff had nothing to do with the decision to accept battle. It was another close-fought defensive action that hurt the Germans enough to give Smith-Dorrien time to slip away next day. But Kluck reported to Moltke that he had defeated not three but nine British divisions. The gap between truth and fantasy widened rather than narrowed as the campaign progressed.

Le Cateau was only possible because the B.E.F. was organised in two corps. Yet this had never been intended by the British; two corps headquarters had been set up to conform with French practice.

Now the great battles of the frontier flowed into a general fighting pursuit. The allied forces, depressed by retreat, struggled back along roads full of trucks, horse wagons, ambulances and refugees crawling south, and more convoys struggling north against the stream with essential supplies and ammunition for the fighting troops. The Germans, once more endlessly swinging from one boot to another down the long roads of France, had no rest days, no time even to wash or dry their stiff and reeking socks. Behind them, demolished railways, guerrillas, and damaged or sabotaged telephone lines created a gulf over which it was more and more difficult to pass food, ammunition, or information. Both sides were drugged with exhaustion, moving on through the chaos like automatons, responsive only to the whistles and shouts of officers. At least the German fighting troops enjoyed hot food without personal effort from their mobile field cookers. The French had to cook their own soup over their own fires, as if this were the campaign of 1814.

Although the battle of the frontiers had apparently ended with a German victory, in fact it was a deeply significant failure. The German armies of the right wing had smashed into the allies at their maximum deployed strength; thirty-four divisions against twenty. They had already produced their single strategic surprise—the extension of their front from the Meuse to Mons. From now on, as Schlieffen had foreseen, their strength would wane, the effects of surprise evaporate, the enemy grow stronger. Only by a crushing victory on the frontier, with the destruction of one or more allied armies, with hundreds of thousands of prisoners, could the allies have been so decisively weakened as to prevent this process. In 1940, after ten days of offensive battle, the Germans reached the sea at Abbeville, thus cutting the French army completely in two. In 1914, after ten days' attacking, the Germans achieved only frontal victories that did not decisively weaken the allied armies and produced in them only tactical loss of cohesion. Never again would Moltke have so fine an opportunity; on the contrary, German superiority was already so slender (and diminishing continuously) that, while victory was still possible, there remained no margin at all for error.

Nor was the German right wing well placed to carry out the second stage of the Schlieffen Plan—the march round Paris and eastwards. There was no general reserve behind it. Pulled about by the tactical demands of the frontier battles, the wing now extended only as far as Cambrai instead of to the coast. The army commanders tried now to correct this crowding to the left. Bülow's orders for August 27 were for pursuit in a "sharp southwesterly direction . . . as sufficient elbow room had to be obtained for the great wheel of the 3rd, 4th and 5th Armies round Verdun." [33] On the same day Kluck was at last set free by Moltke and began

[33] Koeltz, 38.

to veer wide to the west again. But the magnificent stride, the perfect staff work of the march through Belgium was not repeatable. Like a racing eight that loses its length and begins to struggle, the German army's advance became marked by a desperate haste, a snatching at fleeting opportunities, a loosening cohesion. Already on August 27 there was a gap of thirty kilometres between the 2nd and 3rd Armies astride Hirson.

Yet despite Moltke's passive command and crumbling personality, despite Bülow's mishandling of the battle of the frontiers, the fundamental mistakes had been Schlieffen's. Up till now his plan of 1905 had been carried out virtually without modification so far as the direction of advance was concerned. Neither Moltke's preoccupation with Alsace-Lorraine nor his removal of two corps from the right wing for the east had as yet affected operations. Schlieffen's plan had now placed the German armies in a gigantic arc from Picardy to Switzerland. This arc was without lateral rail communications except by immense detours through Aachen (even in September one corps was to take sixteen days for the move). In the case of lines from Germany to the front, the great attacking wing was so far away that it could barely be supplied, certainly not reinforced. The French armies, on the other hand, now formed the periphery of a web whose centre was Paris and whose radiating filaments were first-class railways. Every step taken by the Germans worsened their own communications and improved the French. As if to demonstrate Schlieffen's failure, Joffre on a visit to Sir John French on August 27 told him that a new army (the 6th: General Maunoury) was being formed round Amiens, on French's left, and *outside* Kluck's right. Troops from Belfort were already detraining. Joffre, far from being bent helplessly to the German will, was, in his patient and stolid way, beginning to evolve a counterstroke that would fall on the German right rear. In any case, he hoped to stand and fight on a line Verdun-Laon-Amiens-Abbeville.

On the same day Moltke also sensed that a new and decisive phase of the campaign had opened and that his army commanders needed another general directive. But whereas Joffre was taking the pulse of his army by conferences with his army commanders on the spot, forming his own direct opinions of their morale and capacity (for example, Lanrezac's corroding pessimism), inspiring them with his own crude strength, Moltke sat beside the lovely Rhine amid the gardens and peaceful sunshine of Coblenz, remote from his struggling armies and the reality of their situation, a prey to all the agonies of a man outside the fight, who waits in uncertainty and ignorance for news of distant developments. At the same time Moltke had to endure the Kaiser and the Court, with their hysterical glee at good news, their melodramatic gloom at bad. He knew he must lay down firm lines for the consummation of victory; the basis of his decisions lay in the decoded reports of his army commanders. He knew what he must do—he had foreseen it all before the war:

> The Supreme Command's heavy task will consist in making a picture of the general situation with the aid of scanty and inaccurate information. How much intuition, what gift of prophecy will it need in order not to make mistakes! [34]

He could not run every German battle—he must leave that to his army commanders. Yet equally he must not let the campaign as a whole escape him:

> The Supreme Command can and must have a great aim, followed logically . . . only in this way can mind and will-power conquer matter. But if the inevitably separate battles of different armies lead to general loss of cohesion because each army follows its own objectives instead of working together, then the Supreme Command will have let the reins fall from its hands, it will not have known how to create the basic unity in the battles and manoeuvres of separate groups.[35]

Yet the directive that he sent off to his army commanders that day displayed instead of these qualities an absence of clear strategic design, an incapacity to choose and reject possibilities equally enticing on the surface, and the abandonment of the fundamental campaign plan under the attraction of apparent local successes. In knowing so clearly what he should do, in knowing equally clearly that he had not the character to do it, and in finally failing to do it, lay Moltke's tragedy and the cause of his developing personal collapse.

Within the next ten days this unhappy, intelligent and devoted man was to involve Germany and Europe in his own ruin.

[34] Förster, 31.
[35] *loc. cit.*

4

Schlieffen (and Moltke himself before the war) had intended the second phase of the offensive to consist of a further wheel to the south by the right wing, dressed in a straight line pivoting on Metz-Thionville. Only short advances, therefore, were demanded of the inner armies of the wing, the 4th and 5th, with their slender superiority over the French. After the line Metz-Verdun-Laon had been reached, the advance was to be continued only from Laon to the sea, swinging south, then southeast and east against the Oise and round Paris. The weight of the offensive was to fall more and more on the extreme French left.

However, on the basis of reports on August 26-7, 1914, this development appeared no longer adequate. Not only had the 1st, 2nd and 3rd Armies won a great victory, but so had the centre (the 4th and 5th Armies), and indeed the left, where Rupprecht had pressed the French back into their frontier line. Everywhere the French seemed to be struggling, wavering, melting, reeling back. In Moltke's words: "The French —at least their northern and centre groups—are in full retreat to the west and southwest; therefore on Paris. It is likely that they will offer a new and energetic resistance. All information coming from France confirms that the French army is fighting to gain time and that it is a matter of holding on its front the largest part of the German forces so as to help the Russian armies' offensive." [1]

Would it not be wiser to hit them everywhere, give them no place or time to recover their breath, rather than carry out the partial advance

[1] Baumgarten-Crusius, 47.

planned before the war? Would not the early capture of Paris break the back of French resistance? Would not general pursuit rather than deliberate operations lead to French wastage at a faster rate than German?

Moltke concluded that, "It is the task of the German army, by advancing rapidly on Paris, to deny the French army the time to reorganise itself, to prevent the creation of new units and to take away from France all possible means of resistance." [2]

Moltke's General Directive thus opted for a general offensive on the entire front. The great sweep from southwest through south to east was abandoned: the right-wing armies were all given directions of march to the southwest, and instead of short advances round the hinge, the 4th and 5th Armies were given the distant objectives of Epernay and Vitry-le-François. The effect of these operations, if successful, would be to drive the French off their frontier fortifications while these were breached in front by Rupprecht—a collapse of the French *right* wing, instead of the left.

> The 1st Army will advance. [wrote Moltke] to the lower Seine, marching on the west of the Oise. It should be ready to take part in the 2nd Army's battle. Its task, above all, is to cover the right flank of the armies.
>
> The 2nd Army . . . will cross the line La Fère-Laon and march on Paris.
>
> The 3rd Army, crossing the line Laon-Guignicourt, will continue its advance on Château-Thierry.
>
> The 4th Army will march through Reims on Epernay . . .
>
> The 5th Army will take the line Châlons-Vitry-le-François. By echeloning itself to the left and rear it will cover the left flank of the army until such time as the 6th Army can take over this role of flank guard on the left bank of the Meuse. Verdun will be invested.
>
> The 6th Army . . . will have first and foremost the task of opposing an enemy advance in Alsace-Lorraine. If the enemy falls back, the 6th Army will cross the Moselle between Toul and Epinal and advance in the general direction of Neufchâteau.
>
> The 7th Army will remain at first under the orders of the 6th. . . . Its task will be to prevent an enemy break-through between Epinal and the Swiss frontier.
>
> If the enemy strongly resists on the Aisne and later on the Marne

[2] *ibid*, 87.

[Moltke added], it may be necessary to abandon the southwesterly direction, and wheel the army to the south.

Schlieffen had thus become a qualifying afterthought. The directive was concluded by a paragraph that conveyed something of Moltke's desperate sense of haste, of his feeling that victory was indeed there, but just beyond his finger tips:

"It is a matter of urgency that the army advances swiftly, so as not to give the French time to regroup and organise serious resistance."

There are two particularly interesting aspects of this directive of August 27. In the first place, the new roles and axes of advance given to the right wing (except for Kluck) would bring it to the northern perimeter of Paris, and east of Paris along the Marne, whereas Schlieffen had limited it to the lines of the Aisne and the Oise. The directive was thus an essential cause of the battle of the Marne. Secondly, if the 3rd, 4th and 5th Armies could take their allotted objectives and drive on further, they would cut, one after another, the great railway lines that linked Paris to the east and southeast of France. Schlieffen's plan, on the other hand, would have brought the Germans across these lines only after that tremendous peripheral march round Paris and at a much later stage of the campaign. Above all, these orders of August 27 marked the decisive modification of the Schlieffen Plan, in favour of an advance *southwestwards,* three days earlier than the alteration *southeastwards* by Kluck usually taken as the moment of abandonment by Schlieffen.

Moltke's directive took twelve hours to reach Kluck and Bülow; German communications were now sliding from inadequacy into collapse. Kluck's idea of his army's future line of march was very different from Moltke's; it relied on the assumption that the B.E.F., which Kluck's intelligence staff had completely lost since Le Cateau, was no longer battleworthy and could be ignored; it took no account of Maunoury. It embodied his ceaseless obsession with outflanking the French and swinging in eastwards behind them. In the words of a 1st Army appreciation of August 28: "It appears to be of decisive importance to find the flank of this force . . . drive it away from Paris and outflank it." [3]

At midday on August 28, before receiving Moltke's directive but not

[3] Kluck, 75.

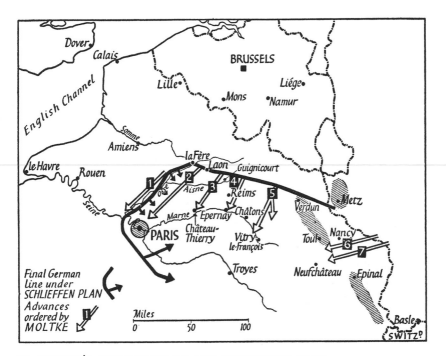

10. MOLTKE'S ALTERATION OF THE SCHLIEFFEN PLAN

before it was written, Kluck had suggested to Bülow that both their armies should wheel inwards against the Oise, on a line through Chauny to Compiègne.

For O.H.L. was so distant now; the supreme commander was no longer a person, a will power, an immediate and insistent reality, but a name at the end of infrequent and tardy signals. It would not require much of an excuse for the bullheaded Kluck to swing eastwards out of the axis of advance prescribed by Moltke.

Lanrezac's French 5th Army provided that excuse on August 29 by striking back strongly at Bülow round Guise—an attack driven forward by Joffre's massive authority against the wishes of the pessimistic Lanrezac. It was like a blow on a man's left shoulder, spinning him round leftwards. Bülow, stopped and momentarily shaken, called as usual for help; and Kluck was only too happy to supply it by swerving to the left. At

7:05 P.M. on August 30 Bülow heard from Kluck by radio: "Right wing of the 1st Army has thrown the enemy over the Avre. Will advance tomorrow against the Oise, section Chauny-Compiègne."

This was the decision taken without consultation with Moltke, that apparently swung the German right-wing advance from a southwest axis to southeast. It was also tactically unnecessary, for Lanrezac, abandoned by the British, whose retreat was at this stage of an impressive rapidity, and having struck his dislocating blow, now fell swiftly back. Bülow, once again emerging from his moment of alarm, signalled Kluck by radio at 5:55 P.M. on the thirtieth: "Enemy decisively beaten today; strong forces retiring on La Fère. The British, who were barring the Oise southwest of La Fère, are also retreating in a southerly, and some in a southeasterly direction." [4]

He therefore wished Kluck to consummate his "victory" by the very turn inwards already intended by Kluck, which would now be too late to catch Lanrezac. Thus Kluck, instead of continuing to trample over various units of Maunoury's French 6th Army and to move outside the B.E.F.'s left flank, was now leaving Maunoury undisturbed to the west, while converging again on the B.E.F. and passing southeast across the British front. It was now almost certain, unless Kluck swerved yet again, that his army would pass northeast of Paris, not west and south of it.

When Moltke received the signal notifying him of this manoeuvre at a time when it was already under way, he could only, once more, give his blessing: "The movements carried out by the 1st Army conform to the intentions of O.H.L." [5]

Nothing could have been more untrue. Because Kluck's initiative was the occasion of the radical alteration in his and Bülow's line of march, he has shared the blame with Moltke for the heresy of abandoning the Schlieffen Plan and for opening the way to the disaster on the Marne. Yet if Bülow was to have been helped in time at Guise, Kluck could not possibly have waited for Moltke's sanction, because with the final great battle still to be fought even deeper into France, the German armies for operational purposes had now become utterly cut off from their supreme commander.

[4] *ibid*, 83.
[5] Baumgarten-Crusius, 55.

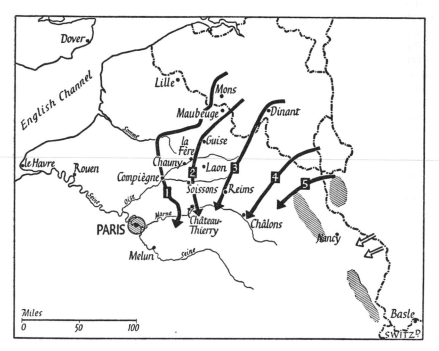

II. AXES OF ADVANCE OF GERMAN RIGHT-WING ARMIES,
AUGUST-SEPTEMBER 1914

The field telephone system, short of cable and equipment, constantly cut by sabotage and accidental damage, ill-adapted to rapid manoeuvre, was useless over long distances and little used. Radio provided the only link, but it was a link so slight and overloaded that no more than the briefest and most important of signals dared be sent. O.H.L. had only a single receiving set; the 1st Army had just two transmitters, of which one alone could communicate with Coblenz. The primitive radio equipment had so short a range that intermediate stations were required at little greater intervals than mechanical semaphore stations. Allowing for coding and decoding, messages of critical operational urgency could take up to twenty-four hours to arrive and be so garbled by retransmission as to be useless. Communications between the armies themselves were little better. The French, on the other hand, could rely on their own permanent civilian telephone network as well as on field telecommunications.

« 67 »

Kluck therefore had to make his own decision, with its heavy consequences. Yet the 90° turn of the German advance round to the southeast would in fact have happened without Kluck and his opportunism;
for the Germans no longer had the strength to carry out Moltke's unrealistic orders of August 28; their line was so stretched that the armies were
being pulled apart in gaps that could be dangerous if ever the enemy recovered the initiative. Hausen's 3rd Army, for example, was like a man
on a rack: when Bülow made his customary request for help in the
battle of Guise, Hausen had already had to swing part of his army in the
opposite direction to aid the 4th Army (Duke Albrecht of Württemberg). For the French 4th and 3rd Armies had recovered from their Ardennes defeat, stopping the Germans in the deep valley of the Meuse on
August 27 and 28, and giving ground only slowly in bitter fighting.

From Metz westwards the German armies were being forced inexo-
rably to close on their left and turn south and east; Kluck's initiative
merely coincided with and hastened this process. Neither Kluck nor
Moltke in fact *caused* the abandonment of the Schlieffen Plan; it was the
physical balance on the battlefield that did so.

So over the wide, spreading landscape of northern France, with its
great skies, plentiful rivers and streams, vast open fields and army-
concealing forests laid on the countryside like green rugs, the armies
floundered towards the crisis. On both sides cohesion was loosening,
fatigue was overwhelming. Behind the fragmentary and always shifting
line of contact—where men deployed on the edge of a wood, behind a
stream, or along a railway, fired their rifles at anonymous movement
and listened to the banging of the guns—along every road sprawled un-
deployed columns on the march, dust-covered, stinking, bewildered,
obedient men, and all the horses and cars and wagons. Precise control
over so many elements moving so rapidly was impossible by field telephone, primitive wireless and by order-bearers in cars or on horseback.
The armies were blundering dinosaurs, with huge muscular and primitive nervous systems. From private to army commander each man was
wrapped and insulated in his own cocoon of ignorance and rumour. Only
the pilots, drifting over that noble landscape in their clattering kites,
could really place in perspective the blind gropings and toilings of the
millions of insect-men. In this essentially nineteenth-century campaign,
they, and automobiles on the ground, were visitants from the future. One

such primitive aircraft in terms of reconnaissance was worth all the twenty thousand splendid horsemen of a cavalry corps.

One thing, however, was clear to both sides, and it was a fact of enormous moral importance. The Germans were advancing and the allies retiring. The diminishing kilometres on the signposts to Paris inspired the Germans to wring impossible marching performances out of raw feet and painful legs; only discipline and fear of capture kept the British and French going through defeat and discouragement.

On the twenty-ninth Moltke moved his headquarters forward to Luxembourg, seventy kilometres behind his centre, but more than two hundred from Kluck. O.H.L. was uncomfortably housed in a girls' school with only kerosene lighting, but the officers lived without hardship in the Hôtel de Cologne. Luxembourg had one advantage over Coblenz—Court and O.H.L. were separated, the Kaiser living in the German Embassy. Indeed the train journey from Coblenz to Luxembourg had displayed the Kaiser at his worst. As an eyewitness wrote in his diary: "The Kaiser—as he has often done recently—positively revelled in blood: 'Piles of corpses 6 ft. high . . . a sergeant killed 27 Frenchmen with 45 bullets, etc.' appalling! Moltke, who was sitting beside him, was undergoing tortures." [6]

To Moltke, with his perhaps excessive sensibility, these displays were as wearing as the strain of command. That day he confided to his wife by letter: "I am glad to be on my own and not at Court. I become quite ill whenever I hear the talk there. It is heartbreaking how little idea the Supreme Commander [the Kaiser] has of the seriousness of the situation." [7]

However, it was a day of good news—Hindenburg and Ludendorff had won a colossal victory over the Russians at Ortelsburg-Neidenburg (which the Kaiser named "Tannenberg" in revenge for the Poles' victory five hundred years ago). It was the battle that did most to make Ludendorff's reputation for brilliant strategy and vigorous leadership. Actually the basic plan had been evolved before his arrival at 8th Army. There was also good news from Bülow who reported that he had utterly beaten a French force of five and a half corps near St. Quentin (the battle of Guise).

September opened on a surging tide of optimism, therefore, although

[6] Müller, 26.
[7] Moltke, 382.

Moltke was careful to tell Admiral Müller that "we have driven the French back but they're not defeated yet. We still have to do that."[8] From Verdun to the Oise the German armies were still marching on down roads littered with abandoned French equipment that suggested increasing French moral and physical disintegration. And indeed the initiative was still firmly in German hands: that day (September 1), as Soissons fell, Joffre ordered his armies back to the line Verdun-Bar-le-Duc-Vitry-le-François-Arcis-sur-Aube and the Seine through Nogent, with the British at Melun. Despite his splendidly stolid and unhurried leadership and his unshakeable will, Joffre stood at last on the brink of catastrophe. For a retreat to this line would leave the French only three lateral railways from Paris to the armies of the centre and right: Neufchâteau-Nancy, Sens-Dijon-Epinal and Belfort, Orléans-Bourges-Nevers-Chagny-Dijon. The first would be too near the front line, too vulnerable to a further German advance. Including those already abandoned in the retreat, the French, under Joffre's new orders, would lose half their army supply stations. They would find their war production limited only to the factories round Lyon and in the centre of France. Indeed, in the words of a French railway expert, the total result of Joffre's order would be this: "In a short time we should have been placed in the impossibility of keeping our armies alive and giving them the means to fight."[9] If the Germans took Melun from the British, thus getting across the line from Paris to Dijon, France would in fact be cut in half.

On September 2 the French government left Paris. It was another day of suffocating heat. Kluck turned south again after the British, failed again to grip them, covered ten miles to reach a line Longpont-Villers-Cotterets-Crépy-Verberie, with one corps well back behind his right flank. He was now a day's march ahead of Bülow, who had reached the Aisne from Pontavert to Soissons, with advanced guards on the Vesle. Hausen, pressed by signals from Moltke, was approaching Reims. The 4th and 5th Armies continued to make slow and painful progress.

In Luxembourg Moltke weighed the continued disintegration and retreat of the French in front of Kluck and Bülow with reports of heavy rail traffic from the French right wing to the left through Paris. His solution was a compromise. "The intention is," he told Kluck in a signal re-

[8] Müller, 26.
[9] Henaffe, 19.

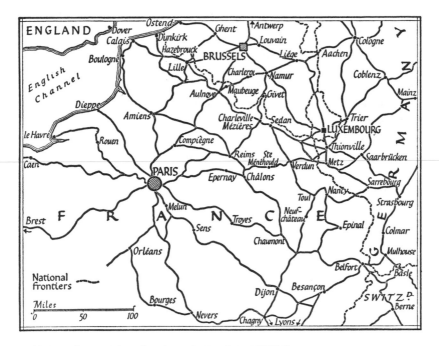

12. THE MARNE CAMPAIGN: MAIN RAIL ROUTES

ceived during the night of September 2-3, "to drive the French in a south-easterly direction from Paris. The 1st Army will follow in echelon behind the 2nd Army and will be responsible for the flank protection of the armies." [10]

Since Kluck was ahead of Bülow, this would make it necessary for the 1st Army to halt for two days. This Kluck could not stomach, especially at a moment when the campaign apparently needed only another brisk pursuit to crown it with victory. "It was therefore," wrote Kluck after-wards of his momentous disobedience, "fully in keeping with the spirit of the often-mentioned radio order for the 1st Army to continue the pursuit across the Marne." [11]

This he did, marching south-southeast between the Marne and the Petit Morin, whose pastoral loveliness, tranquil in the evening light, struck the observant and sensitive in his army. However, British and

[10] Kluck, 94.
[11] *ibid*, 97.

French aircraft had been watching Kluck's long columns turn away to the southeast; air power, which had been two years old when Schlieffen wrote his great memorandum, supplied Joffre with the priceless information he needed. From his campaign onwards there would be no hidden "other side of the hill" to any commander with control of the air.

Meanwhile Bülow crossed the Marne from Condé-en-Brie-Epernay on Kluck's left rear, and Hausen advanced to that river at Châlons and further west. The 4th Army reached Marson-Valmy and the 5th was fighting a savage and claustrophobic battle in the Argonne Forest on a line Ste. Ménéhould-Clermont-Rarécourt. Crown Prince Rupprecht, after repeated attacks in Alsace-Lorraine since August 25, failed again to make any impression on the Grand Couronné, covering Nancy.

Victory seemed so terribly near. The troops, in fact, would not be able to fight or march much further for it. "It was no pleasure," wrote a reserve officer in Kluck's army, "to look at the inflamed heels, soles and toes of my wretched young lads, whole patches of skin rubbed off to the raw flesh." [12]

"Scarcely a single pair (of the Company's boots) that hadn't a nail sticking through the soles which were as thin as paper. A few more days and my grenadiers would be marching barefoot." [13]

In every army of the right wing the constant zigzagging of the line of march according to tactical needs and supposed opportunities had added to the exhaustion of men and horses. The 1st Army signalled O.H.L. on September 4 that "the 1st Army . . . has reached the limit of its endurance." [14]

Despite the perpetual advances and continual victories, despite the signs of enemy collapse, a curious and electric unease now ran through the German army. The troops sensed that something was wrong even in that moment of final victory.

> At the time [wrote the same reservist], we just swam, as it were, in midstream of the flood of events in blissful ignorance, except, perhaps, for these occasional uncanny feelings of general uneasiness, for no special reason other than such as losing touch with Bülow's 2nd Army, or the apparent

[12] Bloem, 110.
[13] *ibid*, 148.
[14] Kluck, 99.

complete absence of communications behind, or the news gradually trickling through to us that our artillery were running short of ammunition.[15]

The same unease was gripping Moltke's stomach too. Helfferich, the German Foreign Secretary, describes an interview with Moltke on the fourth:

> I found Colonel-General von Moltke by no means in a cheerful mood inspired by victory; he was serious and depressed. He confirmed that our advanced troops were only thirty miles from Paris, "but," he added, "we've hardly a horse in the army that can go out of a walk." After a short pause, he continued: "We must not deceive ourselves. We have had successes, but we have not yet had victory. Victory means annihilation of the enemy's powers of resistance. When armies of millions of men are opposed, the victor has prisoners. Where are ours? There were some 20,000 taken in the Lorraine fighting, another 10,000 here and perhaps another 10,000 there. Besides, the relatively small number of captured guns shows me that the French have withdrawn in good order and according to plan. The hardest work is still to be done." [16]

Amid the stark furniture and schoolroom smell of chalk dust of O.H.L., Moltke studied the reports, trying to form a true picture by reason and intuition out of "facts" that might or might not be correct, out of subordinates' judgements that might or might not be sound. The map of France, so long pored over in war games, did not show him a pattern of victory.

There were his armies marching every day more deeply into a vast salient between the two fortresses of Paris and Verdun, growing every day weaker in supplies and effectives. Within the great fortified perimeter of Paris and in that region of extensive forests and wide-open horizons to its north and west, he knew French troops were gathering: troops that Rupprecht had failed to hold by his attacks east of Nancy; troops whose numbers and fighting capacity he was unable to judge, but which were certainly much stronger than the single army corps that Kluck was using as a flank guard.

It was like a war-game problem. The war-game answer was clear enough: his attempt to outflank the French and drive them away from

15 Bloem, 140.
16 Helfferich, II, 17-18.

Paris had failed, and instead the French were threatening his own flank. Therefore it logically followed that he must protect his flank, according to the rules of the game, by stopping Kluck and Bülow and swinging them to face Paris. This meant the collapse of his right-wing offensive. But his inner-wing armies—the 3rd to 5th—were getting close behind the French facing Rupprecht. A double attack from east and northwest by all these armies could still smash the French right wing that stretched in a salient from Châlons, round Verdun and down to Toul, and perhaps drive it against the Swiss frontier.

Therefore at 7:45 P.M. (German time) on September 4, he issued a general memorandum (and accompanying orders in similar terms) by radio and by liaison officers in cars. It was the directive that lost the Germans the campaign. It read:

> TO ALL ARMIES:
> The enemy has evaded the enveloping attack of the 1st and 2nd Armies and a part of his forces has joined up with those about Paris. From reports and other information, it appears that the enemy is moving troops westwards from the front Toul-Belfort, and is also taking them from the front of the 3rd, 4th and 5th Armies. The attempt to force the whole French army back in a southeasterly direction is thus rendered impracticable, and the new situation to be appreciated shows that the enemy is bringing up new formations and concentrating superior forces in the neighbourhood of Paris, to protect the capital and threaten the right flank of the German army.
>
> The 1st and 2nd Armies must therefore *remain* [author's italics] facing the east front of Paris.

The orders added:

> The 1st Army between the Oise and the Marne, occupying the Marne crossings west of Château-Thierry; the 2nd Army between the Marne and the Seine, occupying the Seine crossings between Nogent and Méry inclusive. . . . Their task is to act against any operations of the enemy from the neighbourhood of Paris. . . .
>
> The 4th and 5th Armies . . . must maintain constant pressure to force (the enemy) southeastwards, and by this means open a passage for the 6th Army over the Moselle between Toul and Epinal. . . .
>
> The 6th and 7th Armies . . . will take the offensive as soon as possible against the line of Moselle between Toul and Epinal. . . .
>
> The 3rd Army will march in the direction Troyes-Vendeuvre. It will be

employed, as the situation demands, either to the west to support the cross-ing of the 1st and 2nd Armies over the Seine, or to the south and southeast to co-operate in the fighting of our armies on the left wing.

This directive was an astonishing document. In the first place Moltke seemed to have a better idea of the enemy's dispositions than his own. To *remain* where Moltke ordered meant a retreat of two or three days for Kluck. Thus Moltke's map exercises did not even correspond with the reality of the armies' situation on the ground. However, in any case the essence of his orders was to hand the strategic initiative to the French by stopping his attacking right wing and placing it on the defensive.

It was a curious thing that within half an hour of Moltke's sending these orders, Joffre issued his own instructions for the seizure of that initiative by a counterstroke to be made on September 6 against both sides of the German salient. For on September 3 both British and French aircraft had reported that Kluck was marching east of Paris. These re-ports were a decisive ingredient of the German failure, a critical interven-tion by a new instrument of war that was better utilised by the allies than by the Germans, who actually had more aircraft.

Both generals read the facts alike. But whereas Joffre first asked his army commanders if their men were up to a counterstroke, Moltke was utterly out of touch and feel with the moral and physical state of his troops. He himself, the supreme commander, had never stepped out of peacetime—never heard the thunderous weight of the light and heavy howitzers crushing French attacks, seen that splendid German infantry swinging down, eyes shut with fatigue, into the heart of France; never, like Ludendorff at Liége, felt the reality of leadership in inspiring and driving men on through the death and muddle of a battle; never been in-spired himself by close comradeship with his soldiers in the field. Rather he had been demoralised by inactivity and by the atmosphere of the Kaiser's court. His directive of September 4 was that of an intelligent staff officer reading a map on a staff ride.

Now as the German armies marched into the supreme battle crisis they needed an inflexible driving will—moral courage amounting to faith. This is the core of generalship. Instead, far behind them lay an old and desperately tired man, his physical and mental powers spent by a month of crisis and of responsibility heavier than that of any other soldier, shat-tered in his innermost confidence by that terrible interview in the Star

Hall on the day before mobilisation. His plump features pallid with
fatigue and unstrung nerves, Moltke could barely drive his own body
through the daily round of duty, let alone drive his armies through catastrophic danger into victory. This, even more than alterations to Schlieffen's plan, Kluck's vagaries, and the brilliance of Joffre and Galliéni,
was the essential cause of the German failure in 1914.

For the real balance of physical and moral forces between the two
armies was such as to make the map situation meaningless to a resolute
commander. The Germans held absolute moral dominance over the defeated, retreating allies *so long as they continued to hold the initiative.*
The numerical superiority that Joffre had built up on his left could not
be decisive while his troops declined in cohesion and fighting quality with
every mile they fell back.

Bülow's impression of French dissolution was far from unreal. The
condition of the troops of the French 5th Army, sapped by Lanrezac's
defeatism, was, as even their aggressive new commander, Franchet d'Espérey, admitted, "not brilliant," though he thought the army could still
fight. The 9th Army (Foch) was to be defeated during the Marne
battle. The 6th Army (Maunoury) was a scratch force containing four
reserve divisions, which in the French army were of indifferent quality. It
too was to be beaten in the Marne battle. The B.E.F., although a professional army, had also suffered in morale during the long retreat.

"They were very glum," wrote a staff officer of the British; "they
marched silently, doggedly, never a whistle or a song, or even a ribald
jest, to help weary feet along the road. Staff officers moving up and down
the line with orders were glared at gloomily." [17] By August 30, Sir
John French had in fact given up the campaign altogether and wished to
take his army to the nearest port. He was kept in Joffre's line by government instruction.

Therefore if Moltke had been resolute and pressed on, the moral
balance would have dropped still further against the allies. By ceding
Joffre the initiative without a fight, he brought the balance level again,
for the allied troops took instant heart from turning their faces towards
the enemy, and his own soldiers were shaken and discouraged by a halt
without victory.

And for Moltke on September 4 victory was neither impossible nor

[17] Terraine, *Mons*, 211.

distant. Kluck's troops lay only forty-five kilometres from Melun on the last direct lateral rail routes from Paris to the 5th, 9th, 4th, 3rd, 2nd and 1st French Armies and on the direct route to Lyon and the south. Nothing behind Kluck's flank was of equivalent importance, nearness and sensitivity. A blow against the B.E.F. towards Melun on September 5 and 6 might have paralysed the coming French counterstroke by breaking France's back. No further German advance would have been needed; they could have dug and wired themselves in with their artillery (as they were to do on the Aisne).

There were two reasons why Moltke ignored this real and decisive opportunity. In the first place, he did not realise Kluck's troops were so far south. Secondly, he did not think operationally in terms of railways. Nor had Schlieffen. Nor had his uncle. The aristocrats, rich and poor, who created and developed the Great General Staff in the nineteenth century were intelligent, curious and open-minded enough to use the technological revolution to serve the army. The German railway system had indeed been planned by the General Staff. But the *Junker* General Staff *used* modern technology; they were not *of* it. Fundamentally their military thought was based on Clausewitz and Napoleon and on their battlefields. The army was mobilised, deployed and afterwards supplied by railway; but it fought its campaign on foot and hoof in the old-fashioned way, manoeuvring for the enemy *army's* flank, not for his vital rail communications. In Schlieffen's drafts and memoranda there is no mention of French railways as an objective of his great wheeling movement.

As Moltke's new directive painfully made its way to them, Kluck and Bülow were still blazing with optimism. Kluck's operation orders of the evening of September 3 asserted that "there are signs of the beginnings of great disorder among the retreating enemy columns." [18] Twenty-four hours later a signal of Bülow reported that "the enemy in front is hastening back, utterly disorganised, to the south of the Marne." [19]

At 9:30 that evening, September 4, two hours and forty-five minutes *after* Moltke had despatched his new directive halting them and swinging them to the west, the army commanders therefore issued orders for further pursuit to the southeast. Kluck aimed to reach Esternay-Sancy—

[18] Kluck, 100-1.
[19] Kluck, 102.

south of Coulommiers, with cavalry riding out towards Provins, only about six miles from the great lateral railway Paris-Troyes-Nancy. In his haste to smash the British, reported south of Coulommiers, and drive in the flank of the French 5th Army, Kluck was now crowding across the front of Bülow; the left-wing corps of the 1st Army was blocking the advance of the 2nd Army's right-wing corps. Selfishness and ill-concealed bad feeling thus completed what a lack of co-ordinating command machinery had begun. Because of this, and because Hausen was not yet up level with him, Bülow ordered for September 5 only a short march to the line Montmirail-Vertus.

At 7:15 A.M. on the fifth, when the troops were already committed to the day's pursuit, Moltke's orders reached Kluck and Bülow by radio. Moltke had slammed on the brakes; but the army rolled on for another twenty-four hours without slackening speed.

Now, as the army marched its last few miles into France and found not victory but a crisis at the end of its 540-kilometre advance, there began in the German command a dense traffic of protests, signals, visits, conferences and finally recriminations. Kluck and his Chief of Staff, von Kuhl, began it after reading Moltke's signal in their headquarters at la Ferté-Milon in the bright early morning of September 5. Their own command—their own intelligence service especially—had not so far been brilliant, but neither lacked resolution. Moltke's weak orders, his ignorance of their geographical situation, although signalled to him, alike were infuriating. Kluck—"big, majestic . . . a face razed and ravaged, hard features, a terrifying glance" [20]—signalled Moltke that he considered "breaking contact of thoroughly battle-fit field army and shifting of the 1st and 2nd Armies is undesirable. I propose instead: pursuit to be continued to the Seine and then investment of Paris." [21]

Bülow, of course, obeyed Moltke without protest. He was always for caution. That evening Kluck's troops had reached Rebais-Montmirail. A patrol made its way to the country road that leads down from Villiers St. Georges to Provins. From their cover they saw a good sight: "Columns of the enemy were marching along it southwestwards in dis-

[20] Fabre, quoted Hanotaux, VIII, 158.
[21] Kuhl, 128 ff.

1. Colonel-General von Moltke

2. The Kaiser and Moltke at prewar maneuvers

3. The Reichs Chancellor,
   Theobald von Bethmann-Hollweg

4. The outbreak of war: cheering crowds in the Odeonplatz, Munich. Adolf
   Hitler is circled.

5. General Joffre

6. Colonel-General von Kluck

7. Field-Marshal Sir John French

8. Colonel-General von Bülow

9. General von Hausen

10. Lieutenant-Colonel Hentsch

11. The battle of the Marne: French troops passing through a village

12. The battle of the Marne: a retrospective propaganda picture

order." [22] No Germans would advance further into France until June 1940.

In the evening Lieutenant-Colonel Hentsch, head of the Foreign Armies Section of the General Staff, arrived at Kluck's headquarters by car from Luxembourg, stiff and dusty and carrying O.H.L.'s gloom into a fighting headquarters. He handed Kluck Moltke's full written orders, of which the morning's signal had been only a summary, and they discussed the battle situation with Kuhl, an old colleague of Hentsch's, and Lieutenant-Colonel Grautoff, senior General Staff officer.

Hentsch was a senior staff officer (his post could have been a Major-General's in the British service) personally trusted by Moltke. However, as a plenipotentiary of the supreme commander during a desperate battle crisis he was to prove a disastrous choice. Although, in the words of a colleague, "a very clever, conscientious man, hard-working, well-versed in his job," the effect he had "was not inspiring but crippling." For "it would have been as well if [he] had been more firmly decisive, capable of differentiating false from true intuitively. But he was not, and as reports on the enemy are always exaggerated and generally sound disheartening, it was no wonder that he developed more and more into a pessimist." [23]

Although this conference was held when the allied armies were already moving into their battle stations for Joffre's counterstroke next morning, "Neither O.H.L. nor the 1st Army staff had the remotest idea that an immediate offensive of the whole French Army was imminent." [24] It was merely that, in Hentsch's phrase, the situation was "dubious." When Hentsch was told that the 1st Army would carry out Moltke's orders for the 5th on the 6th, Hentsch replied that this would comply with O.H.L.'s wishes "and that the movement could be made at leisure; no special haste was necessary." [25]

However, late that night, after Kluck's order had gone out, came more urgent news—Kluck's right flank guard, north of Paris, General von Gronau's 4th Reserve Corps, had fought a brisk and successful action near St. Soupplets during the afternoon against strong enemy forces. For

[22] Bloem, 149.
[23] Bauer, 36.
[24] Kuhl, 128.
[25] *loc. cit.*

Maunoury's 6th Army had struck a day earlier than the rest of the allied army. The German troops in the rest of the front line uneasily felt the gathering of strength in front of them, beyond the low hills, in the shelter of the dark French forests and steep river valleys, almost as the white pioneers in America must have felt, from small signs, the presence of massed Indians near them moving into ambush.

Joffre's plan was simple but grandiose: while the two French armies

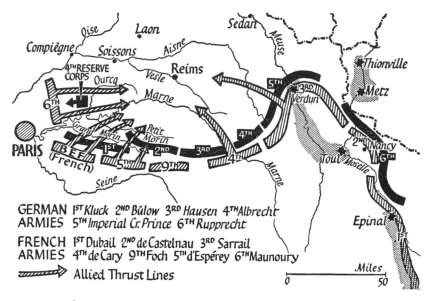

GERMAN 1ST Kluck 2ND Bülow 3RD Hausen 4TH Albrecht
ARMIES 5TH Imperial Cr. Prince 6TH Rupprecht
FRENCH 1ST Dubail 2ND de Castelnau 3RD Sarrail
ARMIES 4TH de Cary 9TH Foch 5TH d'Espérey 6TH Maunoury
▭▭▭▷ Allied Thrust Lines

13. JOFFRE'S PLAN FOR THE BATTLE OF THE MARNE

round the southern curve of the German salient (Foch's 9th and de Langle de Cary's 4th) stood firm, the flank armies near Paris and Verdun would drive in the salient's sides. If these flank armies could get deep into the chaotic German net of road communications before the Germans could regroup, there was a possibility not merely of stopping the German invasion but destroying it.

On the sixth both sides began simultaneously to carry out their new orders. It was a day of sporadic and muddled fighting from the Forest of Compiègne through the dense, hot thickets and steep slopes south of the Marne to the Argonne, as in cumbrous, sluggish response to their commanders-in-chief the armies marched and countermarched.

In the north, Maunoury and his mixture of good divisions and doubtful reservists struck eastwards beyond Meaux at Kluck's communications. He was stopped with heavy losses by Kluck, who was in the middle of performing one of the most brilliant feats of agility and faultless staff work seen in the campaign. While part of the 1st Army and Marwitz's cavalry corps remained south of the Grand Morin in touch with Bülow, three of his corps were making forced marches northwards by day and night up and down the steep valleys and winding roads to the line of the Ourcq. In effect Kluck was reversing his army and pivoting it 90° to the west to face Maunoury. As the troops were slogging out this march, Gronau's 4th Reserve Corps fought a splendid battle with Maunoury's army, holding it back as the German reinforcements came up unit by unit.[26]

On the Grand Morin front of the 1st Army and on Bülow's front, the allied counterstroke made little progress. The bulk of the British were not yet in the field; Franchet d'Espérey's 5th Army dug itself in after a short advance "to resist any new attack no matter the cost." In this battle Pétain was now commanding the 6th Infantry Division. Its attacks, it was noted, were always preceded by careful artillery bombardment. A month later he would be commanding a corps. Foch, who had characteristically attacked in defiance of orders, had been characteristically flung back, outflanked, by Bülow to the south of the St. Gond marshes. West of Verdun, on the other side of the German salient, the French pressure never became in the least dangerous or strategically significant.

The most important effect of the day had been moral. German spirit had already sunk: "Why? we were all asking—why were we going back?"[27] On the allied side, the British, for example, lost all their gloom when they realised they were going forward again. "The happiest day in my life; we marched towards the morning sun," wrote Colonel Seely in his diary. The troops went off with songs and cheers.

September 7 went not unfavourably for the Germans. Maubeuge fell, releasing the 7th Reserve Corps. Kluck's troops came up to the Ourcq in every kind of confusion and wrong order but were formed quickly and effectively into three battle groups. It was a tribute to the German talent for swift, flexible reorganisation in the heat of battle, for which Schlief-

[26] See below, Map 15, p. 83.
[27] Bloem, 168.

fen had allowed no scope in his planning. Kluck, although at times in a mood of haste near to panic, had brought his army successfully out of one danger and was now intent on bludgeoning Maunoury into Paris by outflanking him from the north. For he stopped Maunoury in the morning and drove him back in the afternoon. Only his southern groups had had to be pulled back slightly. The British were still a threat, not a fact. It took the British all day to drive Marwitz (reinforced now by Kraewel's group of infantry and guns) back from the steep, narrow valley of

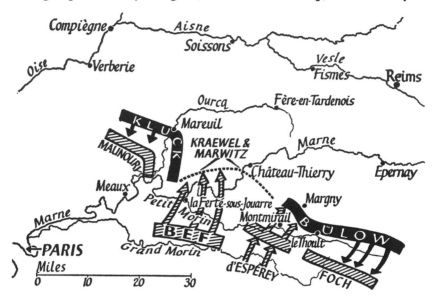

14. THE BATTLE OF THE MARNE

the Petit Morin, which was in the words of the *British Official History*[28] "most skilfully and gallantly defended." D'Espérey's 5th Army had made some progress on its left but on the right had had to send help to Foch.

There was one single gaping flaw in this picture of a slow, smouldering, sputtering allied counterstroke stopped by German guns: in stripping his front on the Grand Morin of troops to face Maunoury on the Ourcq, Kluck had left only Marwitz's cavalry corps and Kraewel's group to face the B.E.F. He had also forgotten to tell Bülow about his swing to

[28] *British Official History*, I, 286.

the Ourcq, and Bülow only learned by accident that there was no longer an army on his right flank, but a twenty-one-mile gap screened by cavalry and half a division of infantry and towards which air reconnaissance told him the B.E.F. was slowly plodding.

In Luxembourg, Moltke could only wait helplessly for news of the battle he could not influence because he had no reserves. The days were full of torment; his bodily health and nerves were crumbling together, his sick heart unable to give his brain the oxygen it needed for clear thought and energetic action. He found relief from mental terror in confiding to his wife in daily letters.

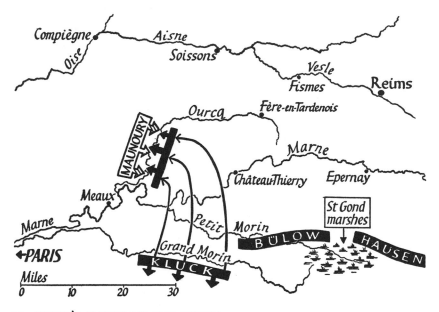

15. KLUCK'S MARCH TO THE OURCQ

That day, September 7, he wrote:

Today our armies are fighting all the way from Paris to upper Alsace. I would give my life, as thousands have done, for victory. How much blood has been spilled and how much misery has come upon numberless innocent people whose houses have been burned and razed to the ground.

Terror often overcomes me when I think about this, and the feeling I have is as if I must answer for this horror, and yet I could not act otherwise than as I have.[29]

Yet September 8 also brought the French no nearer decisive successes; none of the German commanders was thinking in terms of retreat, but rather of holding their ground or attacking. A German brigade from Brussels had arrived north of Maunoury at Verberie, on his flank; the remainder of Kluck's marching corps would be on the Ourcq during the day. Late that evening Kluck moved his headquarters to La Ferté-Milon. As the H.Q. cars were approaching a nearby airfield it was attacked by French dragoons, glorious in brass and horsehair helmets, like firemen on cart horses. Kluck and his staff seized rifles and carbines and formed a firing line. "The dusky red and clouded evening sky," wrote Kluck, "shed a weird light on this quaint little force . . . the gigantic flashes of the heavy guns lit up the deep shadows of the approaching night." [30] On September 9 Kluck proposed to drive the shaken and despondent Maunoury westwards. Maunoury's 6th Army, that overrated cause of the "miracle of the Marne," was now defeated. Maunoury reported to Joffre that he had suffered heavy losses, and if Kluck attacked him again, he would retire his left.[31] Maunoury in fact went further and issued secret conditional orders for the conduct of a retreat.[32] In the south Marwitz's cavalry and Kraewel's infantry and guns fought a skilful rear-guard action in the intricate, wooded and stream-cut country south of the Marne. The British, in overwhelming force and roasting heat, followed hesitantly, cautiously, over the Grand Morin. Bülow advanced along most of his front.

Meanwhile Rupprecht had been pegging away at the French frontier fortifications in the hills east of Nancy, where Moltke still retained that persistent hope of a decisive victory on the left flank. Despite the capture of the isolated fort of Moronvilliers, the attacks had broken down with heavy losses. On the eighth Rupprecht tried again, and apparently failed again. Moltke ordered him to cease his attacks and at last release reserves for the right wing. Moltke's lack of resolution, his inability to drive Rupprecht on, possibly cost him a victory, for de Castelnau, Rupprecht's French opponent, was already so shaken by the German attacks

[29] Moltke, 384.
[30] Kluck, 33.
[31] *French Official History,* Tome I, III, 156.
[32] *French Official History,* Tome I, III, Annexe II, 114.

that Joffre had had to order him categorically to stand his ground. Certainly Moltke's preoccupation with the left wing was not as stupid or unrealistic as some critics have alleged.

The French countermove on the Marne was now three days old; it had proved not a smashing blow, but a slow, fumbling, confused forward movement that in several places had been stopped and thrown back with discouraging losses. There was in fact only one dangerous development—that gap on the Marne on Bülow's right, where Marwitz and Kraewel, reinforced now by one infantry division and part of another, were retreating slowly before the B.E.F. Joffre had spotted this gap between the German 1st and 2nd Armies; he ordered the B.E.F. to advance into it across Kluck's rear and crush Kluck against Maunoury. Open flanks had always been Bülow's nightmare; when he read the air reconnaissance reports of dense British columns moving towards his own open flank, he swung his right protectively back to Margny-le-Thoult. Thus, while Kluck was preparing to attack westwards, Bülow's nearest troops were going away from him to the northeast. In the present crisis of the war, as in the offensive battles earlier, mistakes owing to excessive caution were Bülow's sombre speciality. Bülow, like Moltke, was old, steeped in war gaming, impressed by the consequences on the map of being outflanked. He also was exhausted by the strains of the weeks' campaigning.

Thus the battle of France, absorbing the last energies of exhausted armies, was still smouldering slowly away without a decision on the battlefield. Perhaps the real, and for Germany, the most dangerous competition was taking place in the two general headquarters, between Joffre, that huge, ruthless, self-confident, perhaps complacent man, and Moltke, visibly prostrate with worry, with his almost hallucinatory awareness of all the moral and general issues at stake.

It mattered nothing now, in the crude business of leadership in war, that Joffre was an intellectual pigmy. Men trembled when his great nostrils flared and the eyes blazed with fury; and this was the engine that had kept the French going through catastrophe, was keeping them going now. Equally it mattered nothing that Moltke had a first-class intelligence and a brilliant staff record; he could no longer control his army for he had lost control of himself. About this time a staff officer found Moltke "sitting hunched up over his table, his face buried in both hands. Moltke

looked up and turned a pale and tear-stained face on the officer." [33]
With each hour of this battle he worsened; now on September 8, at the
height of the crisis, he had reached the stage when terror surges in the
throat like vomit:

> The weight of responsibility has borne me down in the last few days
> [he wrote to his wife]. For still our army is struggling on and there has
> been no decision. It would be frightful if there is nothing to show for the
> blood that has been spilt. The suspense, with the absence of news from the
> far distant armies, almost goes beyond what human strength can stand,
> when one knows the issues involved.[34]

Helplessness, with all his plans failed and no new forces to throw in,
brought despair: "The terrible difficulty of our situation often stands like
a black wall in front of me, seeming quite impenetrable." [35]

Although a great commander must have an almost feminine sensitivity and intuition about the enemy and his intentions, he must also be
able to screen all the impressions crowding on his consciousness, so that
their emotional reality is blocked and only neutral factors of calculation
are allowed into the mind. No man could command with Moltke's extreme and unselective sensitivity, no matter how strong his basic resolution. Now, on September 8, 1914, the battle crisis and the crisis at O.H.L.
came together. Since his orders of September 5, Moltke had made no intervention at all in the complicated and nicely balanced operations between Compiègne and Verdun, although the threat he had feared from
Paris had become a general French offensive. Now, however, the reports
from the front, scanty, contradictory and vague though they might be,
suggested that the 1st and 2nd Armies were desperately in danger, with
powerful forces smashing north across the Marne through the gap between them. Bülow's reports were particularly disquieting. What was the
true situation? What should be done to exorcise the danger?

Moltke and his staff held a conference to answer these questions. It
was a tense gathering, the officers' tight uniforms of field-grey with the
carmine-red tabs and broad trouser stripes of the staff contrasting with
the inappropriate surroundings of genteel feminine education. Moltke,
sick and spent, presided.

[33] Bülow, II, 169.
[34] Moltke, 384.
[35] *loc. cit.*

Much now depended on the quality and character of his staff officers. They were, *in toto,* no better than could be expected of the Wilhelmian empire and its pervading favouritism and sycophantism. Lieutenant-General von Stein, Moltke's Chief Quartermaster-General (his deputy), and responsible for the army's administration, was a rough, even coarse, kindly man, clear-headed and tireless at his administrative work; however, in a strategic crisis like this, a curious underlying diffidence prevented him from showing leadership. Lieutenant-Colonel Tappen, Chief of the Operations Section, was, wrote a colleague, "a man of unusually strong will, good nerves and a power of quick decision." [36] He was a vigorous military conservative, meeting unpopular opinions with bitter sarcasm. Despite his strong character, no one was going to rally to him: "He made a cold impression everywhere and acted like a brake, and seldom was any officer so much hated by subordinates." And then there was the pessimistic Hentsch, a Saxon among Prussians, head of the Foreign Armies Section, personally favoured by Moltke, and the only officer in the room who had been near the front.

The gap between Bülow and Kluck—that was the real problem. If Kluck was forced away from the rest of the army, surrounded and destroyed, a major catastrophe would follow: at best a long general retreat, at worst the loss of the war. Kluck and Bülow must bring their armies together again—and in desperate haste. If Kluck could fall back on Bülow quickly enough, perhaps the line of the Marne could be held and the corps at last in transit from Rupprecht used to mount a fresh offensive round Maunoury's 6th French Army.

If there was no chance of holding the Marne, the junction would have to take place further back—on the Vesle. This meant a limited but general retreat. Perhaps this retreat was already in progress. It was essential that the movements of the armies should be so regulated that the retreat would in fact bring them together. Yet all this depended on the actual situation at the front—what Kluck and Bülow could actually do—and the situation *now,* not as revealed in reports twelve hours stale.

So it was resolved to send Hentsch again round the army headquarters. Because of the tremendous consequences of his mission, there has been bitter dispute about the exact instructions and powers given to Hentsch, as in the heat and haste of this conference his verbal orders were not con-

[36] Bauer, 34-5.

firmed in writing. Tappen wrote afterwards: "The officer sent on this mission had not . . . received any kind of full powers to order or approve retreats on the part of these armies . . . O.H.L had not given any order laying down rearward movements. . . ."[37]

In May 1917, in reply to questions put to him by O.H.L., Hentsch on the other hand asserted: "Colonel-General von Moltke and Lieutenant-General Tappen formally gave me full powers to act on my own initiative. The reason is that O.H.L. was only in touch with the 1st Army and as far as I recollect with the 2nd Army, by radio"[38]—that is, at twelve hours' or more delay.

It seems almost certain that Hentsch was speaking the truth and that at no time during his mission did he go beyond his instructions. For in view of the desperate nature of the situation, the absolute necessity for speed, what could have been the point of sending him on a mere fact-finding tour (supposing, that is, the army commanders had not yet issued their own orders for retreat) and postponing the strategic decision until another O.H.L. conference in two days' time? Anyone who went to the front at such a time must have had powers to make decisions on the spot on predetermined lines, or waste his petrol. Hentsch, a senior and able staff officer enjoying Moltke's trust and accustomed to such missions, was the obvious choice, being less involved in urgent routine work than Stein or Tappen. Moltke himself could not of course be away and isolated from the centre of the war for forty-eight hours or more.

Hentsch was clear as to his instructions:

> They [the conference] expressed first of all the hope that the crisis would be mastered and that it would not be necessary to retreat. But in case such a retreat proved essential, they pointed out to me the line Ste. Ménéhould-Reims-Fismes-Soissons as a general direction for the mass of the German army. I am certain that these four places were repeated to me by Colonel-General von Moltke and Lieutenant-General Tappen.[39]

So Hentsch climbed up into his staff car and rattled away on a 400-mile tour of the front. Unfortunately he began with the armies nearest Luxembourg—4th and 5th—and worked his way westwards to Kluck.

[37] Tappen; quoted Baumgarten-Crusius, 166.
[38] *ibid*, 174.
[39] Baumgarten-Crusius, 179.

This meant that his first call on the Marne battlefield would be upon the gloomy Bülow. His tour began promisingly: the 4th and 5th Armies were fighting hard and happy. At the 3rd Army at Châlons he found his fellow Saxons also moderately full of cheer, having attacked along most of their front and taken ground, including La Fère-Champenoise.

It was yet another suffocatingly thick and hot afternoon as Hentsch was driven west along the dusty shimmering roads to Bülow's head-quarters. These were comfortably placed in a country house with a name of ill omen—le Château de Montmort, thirteen miles northeast of Mont-mirail. Hentsch reached the château when the day had cooled slightly into a golden evening. At 8 o'clock he rounded out a full day of conferences and long-distance motoring on the horsehair seat of a toughly-sprung car by discussing the battle situation with Bülow, General von Lauenstein (Chief of Staff, 2nd Army) and Lieutenant-Colonel Matthes.

Hentsch found morale at Montmort to be "calm and entirely confi-dent." This appreciation by such a pessimistic man is not entirely reas-suring, for retreat was the main topic. They discussed all the possibilities of avoiding retreat, went to bed, and began again at 6:30 in the morning on the basis of the night's situation reports. The conclusion was clear. Because Kluck had taken his main body from the Marne to the Ourcq, "there rested no other possibility but retreat at once behind the Marne. The 2nd Army *could* and *wanted* to hold on along this river" [40] if the 1st Army could restore its flank guard and stop the British crossing the river west of the 2nd Army. Bülow and Lauenstein took a glum view of the general tactical situation of their own troops—a view later sharply at-tacked by lower commanders as unjustified, but just the sort of thing to chime in with Hentsch's own temperament. They had an equally grim impression of Kluck's situation; they appeared unaware that that iron man was bent on attacking. Hentsch left Bülow convinced that the situa-tion was indeed sombre and that only swift action could avoid a catastro-phe.

Nothing he saw with his inexperienced peacetime eye along the roads behind Bülow's and Kluck's armies awakened optimism. His driver had to manoeuvre the heavy car past convoys of cavalry-division supply echelons "falling back in all haste" towards Fère-en-Tardenois. "Groups of wounded [a novelty to an O.H.L. officer] flowed in the same direc-

[40] Baumgarten-Crusius, 176.

tion; they were afraid of being cut off." At Neuilly-St. Front, Hentsch was much impressed by an experience that would have been banal to the fighting troops and their comrades on either side.

"Different columns were bottled up in a jam: an air attack had caused a complete panic. I had to get out of my car several times to clear a way by force." [41]

It took him seven hours to cover the sixty miles to Kluck's headquarters at Mareuil. Here at midday in the main street of the grey and shuttered little place, amid groups of soldiers, he was met by General von Kuhl, Kluck's Chief of Staff, whose greeting was: "Well, if the 2nd Army's going back, we can't stay here either." [42]

For in the seven hours that Hentsch had been on the road nourishing his defeatism the battle situation had developed fast. In Bülow's words: "When in the morning (after Hentsch's departure) of September 9 the enemy in numerous columns crossed the Marne between La Ferté-sous-Jouarre-Château-Thierry, I had no further doubt that the 1st Army's retreat had been made inevitable by the strategic and tactical situation and that, so far as the 2nd Army was concerned, it found itself obliged to retreat to avoid being completely outflanked on its right." [43]

Bülow had therefore issued orders for his own army's retirement and signalled the news to Kluck and O.H.L. With a fine diplomacy he told O.H.L. that the purpose of his retreat was to "support the 1st Army north of the Marne."

Though present at his headquarters, Kluck did not take part in the conference. He pretended for some reason in his memoirs that he did not know of Hentsch's presence, which was not true, and it was left to Kuhl to preside at the conference. It began beneath the shadow of the first, fatal slipping into retreat. Despite Kuhl's laconic greeting, the 1st Army did not want to retreat and saw no need for it. Kuhl pointed out to Hentsch that the 1st Army's own attack on Maunoury's 6th Army was going well and that retreat would be more hazardous than attack when units were so mixed together. Hentsch was more passionately aware of the weakness of the 1st Army's situation than Kuhl, particularly that

[41] *ibid*, 177.
[42] *ibid*, 178.
[43] Koeltz, 66.

Kluck's southern group was already in retreat north of the Marne and that the northern group's chances of a decision against Maunoury were doubtful.

The only hope of avoiding a general retreat, it seemed to Hentsch, lay in Kluck being able *immediately* to support Bülow north of the Marne. Hentsch therefore asked Kuhl "if the 1st Army would be in a position to support the 2nd Army tomorrow with all its forces if it beat Maunoury that day." Kuhl had to admit that this would be impossible.

For Hentsch this was the clinching factor. His stay with Bülow, Bülow's orders to retreat and his own temperament had brought him to the point where only a general retreat seemed possible. In his own words:

"As there was no possibility of giving immediate help to the 2nd Army, I therefore gave the 1st Army the order to retreat, basing my action on the full powers given me, because it was only in this way one could bring it once more into co-operation with the 2nd Army." [44]

Hentsch went to Kuhl's battle map and marked on it with crayon the line to be reached by the 1st Army's retreat, Soissons-Fère-en-Tardenois.

Joffre had won the battle of the Marne.

It is a comment on the limited immediate effect of sea power on a land campaign that on the following day Jellicoe took the Grand Fleet to the Heligoland Bight on yet another sweep and met nothing.

In considering Hentsch's role in the conferences at O.H.L. and at the 2nd and 1st Armies, it would be wrong to see him as a minor staff officer among generals, resting in the last resort self-importantly on his "full powers." On the contrary, a factor impossible to evaluate but of unquestionable significance in all the crisis was his strong personality and persuasiveness. Kuhl's opinion of him was: "a well-balanced officer, very circumspect, particularly versed in major questions of strategy. You could put your trust in him without reserve." [45] An old comrade of Hentsch's on the staff and at the staff college wrote: "One must always point out with what lucidity and force of persuasion Hentsch could unfold his views. He was thus able to influence not only his colleagues, but also his superiors. Moltke had great confidence in him." [46]

[44] Baumgarten-Crusius, 174.
[45] *ibid*, 173.
[46] Colonel B. Schwertfeger. *Deutsche Allgemeine Zeitung*, 5.9.20.

Did Bülow influence Hentsch, Hentsch Bülow or both mutually? Did Kuhl agree to retreat only because Hentsch made it an order, or because Hentsch convinced him it was necessary?

There has been much discussion of whether Hentsch and Bülow were justified in their pessimism. The gap on Bülow's flank unquestionably existed, and despite the most gallant and resolute fighting by Marwitz and Kraewel, the B.E.F. was now north of the Marne and well into the gap. Logically and theoretically it followed that the B.E.F. and Espérey's 5th Army would drive energetically into the gap and across either Kluck's rear or Bülow's. There were in Bülow's view no immediate reserves to throw in. Yet the B.E.F. performance in the battle so far had been paralytically sluggish, and Franchet d'Espérey was nearer defeat than victory. Was there *real* ground for assuming that the B.E.F. constituted an instant desperate threat? Why should Bülow take it that the B.E.F. was aware of the gap?

In fact, although the British knew of the gap, there is evidence that they were apprehensive that it was a trap. Sir John French, in particular, was intensely nervous of hazarding his army in any way.

Thus all depended on the nerves and wills of the opposing commanders. If Kluck on September 9-10 had wheeled his northern groups slightly southwest, as he had intended, to punch Maunoury, and had brought his southern groups eastwards on one shoulder of the gap, if Bülow had stood firm on the other and fought aggressively, a commander as jumpy as Sir John French would have been very unlikely to put his head into a hole with two hard-fighting armies on either side of it. All turns on the length of time Bülow and Kluck would have had to hold on before reinforcements arrived to help Marwitz and Kraewel plug the hole. Maubeuge had surrendered on September 7, releasing the 7th Reserve Corps. It was first ordered to clear the British off the Flanders coast, then on September 10 to La Fère to become the nucleus of a new 7th Army. On September 12 it was ordered to Laon and covered forty miles in twenty-four hours. Since the railway through Maubeuge was open on September 8 as far as Noyon, only some fifty miles from the Marne, the Seventh Reserve Corps could, had O.H.L. wished, have been deployed between Kluck and Bülow by the afternoon of September 9; the fact of its being on its way and later the fact of its presence might have reassured Bülow. However, as it was, the German command made the capital mistake of not rushing all nearby and available forces to the decisive battlefield; and Hentsch's entire mission was carried through on the false basis that there were no troops to fill the gap on the Marne.

Yet even on that basis retreat was not inevitable; the armies had yet to fight it out for a decision. In the words of General de Gaulle: "There were in the line on September 8 eighty French and British divisions, against eighty-one better German. From the material point of view, nothing ordered the enemy to retreat." [47]

In fact, therefore, the battle of the Marne was decided not by the brilliant generalship of Joffre and/or Galliéni, nor by the German change of direction to the east of Paris, nor by the ineluctable circumstances of the battlefield. Indeed there was no real *battle* of the Marne. Before such a battle could be joined, the victory was handed to the French and British by an unjustifiable failure of nerve and resolution on the part of the German command.

At last to Moltke in Luxembourg, after hours of waiting and of churning thoughts, came Hentsch's news of a general retreat. That night when Moltke sat down in his loneliness to try to make reassuring contact with his wife through his pen, his elegant, formal letter style had disappeared in short, incoherent sentences that fell like sobs across the paper.

It is going badly. The battles to the east of Paris will go against us. One of our armies must withdraw [Bülow's?], the others will have to follow. The opening of the war, so hopefully begun, will turn into the opposite—I must bear whatever befalls and shall stand or fall with my country. We must suffocate in the fight against east and west—how different it was when we opened the campaign a few weeks ago—the bitter disillusionment now follows. And we shall have to pay for everything that is destroyed. The campaign is not lost, no more than it was until now for the French, but French spirit, which was on the point of being extinguished, will now flare up tremendously and I am afraid that our nation in its headlong careering towards victory will scarcely be able to bear this misfortune—how burdensome this becomes to me no one but you, who live completely in my soul, can better measure.[48]

Between September 9 and 13, in painful, depressing marches, often in heavy rain, always in apparent confusion, Kluck and Bülow's troops

[47] de Gaulle, 248.
[48] Moltke, 385.

fell back to the Aisne, Hausen keeping station with them. It could have been a time of great danger, but good staff work on the German side and limp leadership and sheer exhaustion on the allied meant that the armies were only intermittently in contact. There was no relentless, spoiling pursuit. Back from Paris and the Marne the grey masses ebbed, marching at night like ghosts through the dense wreathing mists, through dead, echoing villages, "no jokes, no complaints, but just a bitter indifference." [49]

On September 12, Moltke ordered his armies to entrench themselves north of the Aisne, while he organised a new offensive group round St. Quentin (for hope was to be as persistent as a weed in this war). On September 13 and 14, the allies came up and attacked the German positions. It was a different kind of battle from the Marne: fought in thick, wet weather, it was a savage *mêlée,* company to company, in which both sides discovered that the Germans in their primitive trenches, backed by their field guns and howitzers, could fire their rifles and machine guns more accurately than could attacking troops on the move or while lying in temporary shelter trembling with exertion. Meanwhile Hindenburg and Ludendorff were celebrating their second great victory over the Russians in the battle of the Masurian Lakes.

At O.H.L., Moltke's condition was now pitiable: "Moltke had broken down completely. He sat in front of the map, pale and apathetic." [50]

Yet he still remained supreme commander. It was left to junior members of the General Staff to argue to Stein that he must be replaced. Stein agreed and went to see Lyncker, Chief of the Kaiser's Military Cabinet.

On September 13, Moltke was asked to see the Kaiser privately after dinner. "I must admit," wrote Moltke, "that my nerves were very bad as a result of everything I had undergone and that I very likely gave the impression of being a sick man." [51] This was only a prelude.

> On September 14, in the afternoon, General von Lyncker appeared at the office and told me the Kaiser had asked him to say that His Majesty had gained the impression that I was too ill to conduct operations further. His

[49] Bloem, 151.
[50] Bauer, 57-8.
[51] Moltke, 23.

Majesty had commanded that I should report sick and travel back to Berlin. General von Falkenhayn was to take over operations.[52]

In this bleak final moment of failure Moltke now showed that, for all his lack of a commander's gifts, he could be as brave in self-sacrifice as any of his soldiers:

> I told the Kaiser I believed it would not make a good impression in the army abroad if I were to be dismissed immediately after the retreat of the army. . . . At this the Kaiser said Falkenhayn should act as chief quarter-master and I should remain "pro forma". . . . So I stayed at headquarters while everything was taken out of my hands and I stood there as a spectator. . . . I took this martyrdom upon myself and lent my name to the operations that followed for the sake of the country.

Release only came with a telegram from the Kaiser on November 3, 1914:

> As a result of your illness I have, to my greatest regret, found myself under the necessity of placing the post of Chief of the General Staff in other hands . . . with all my heart I wish you a speedy recovery. . . .

Moltke lived on until 1916; he saw the war pass beyond the scope of mere armies, however big. People's war, with hate and fear instead of policy, and total national wealth as an instrument, had been born out of his failure to wield Germany's sword in a single killing stroke.

In this failure the battle of the Marne has enjoyed excessive emphasis, for all can spot the moment when an army ceases to advance and begins to retreat. But the Marne was only the last phase, just as the recoil of the Old Guard at Waterloo was the last phase, but not the decisive one, of that action. Retreat is the fruit of victory, not the moment of decision. Nor often is there a fixed moment of decision, but rather a slow and complex accumulation of small decisions. In the battle of France in 1914 the Germans began with a certain fixed stock of advantages—speed, surprise and numerical superiority. The failure to destroy the Belgians began the dwindling of this stock. The failure in the frontier battles, when the situation was so very advantageous, is a factor at least equal in importance to the Marne battle in the total decision of the campaign; after it the German stock of advantages was indeed slender. At the Marne the

[52] *loc. cit.*

stock had disappeared; the two sides were at rough parity of physical and moral forces.

Discussion of Moltke's or Kluck's culpability in wheeling inside Paris is irrelevant, because there were no longer the forces to do otherwise. Far more important is the failure of the German planners to perceive and exploit in their advance the French dependence on their railway network. The Schlieffen Plan was always hazy in its strategic hopes; railways would have provided a clear, attainable and decisive objective. Without apparently being aware of it, the Germans on September 6 had stumbled within thirty miles of victory.

It was a curious and unnecessary failure that Germany, the nation with the largest and most advanced electrical industry in Europe, should have equipped its army with a signals net inferior in quality and quantity of equipment, and in efficiency, to that of the British.

Perhaps a decisive factor in the German failure lay in the lack of operational experience; this explains so many of the small muddles and blunders that accumulated into disaster. In 1870 they had had the Austrian campaign of 1866 recently behind them; in 1940 they were to have Poland.

So much critical attention has been focussed on the failure of Schlieffen's great plan to end the war in six weeks that it is sometimes forgotten that nevertheless the Germans had achieved a colossal success that was to influence the whole course of the war; the French by contrast had seen their own offensives utterly crushed and the north of their country occupied. Because the Germans lay deep in French territory, they now could afford to adopt the defensive; the French and their allies, however, were forced to attack again and again, despite their lack of guns and shells. No position in war is stronger than a strategic offensive coupled with a tactical defensive. This the Germans enjoyed until 1918. For all his faults, it was under Moltke's planning and control that Germany achieved this commanding position.

One delusion fades, but for those who find delusions more comfortable than reality, there is always a new one. Victory in six weeks became victory next year—and when 1915 had arrived, *this* year. Neuve Chapelle, Artois, Champagne—without enough heavy guns or trench mortars, the French and the British generals pitted their inadequate techniques and the courage of their soldiers against German wire, machine guns and artillery. The ranks thinned, the cemeteries filled; the year ended in failure. Yet the Germans still lay across northern France. The allies were not discouraged. *Next* year would see the new mass British armies deployed in France with plenty of heavy guns and ammunition; the tactical mistakes that had just robbed Joffre and French of a great victory would be avoided. Victory was therefore scheduled for 1916.

In truth, the politicians and soldiers of the First World War were gamblers; not, however, in the sense of risk, but of obsession. They began with a system: the first stake and the first play would therefore make their fortunes. They lost. The *next* play, with a higher stake to compensate for losses and perhaps a new system, would see success. Gradually they were drawn further into the game, staking more and more of their people's lives and prosperity, obsessed by the search for a winning system, by the belief each time that they had found it, and that the next play would give them the bank. As with a gambler, the concentration on each current play mentally obscured the total extent of mounting losses, prevented any sober and detached assessment of the total cost of further continued losses. So they went on, deeper into the blood, the lies and the hatred. Yet the truth was—a truth that could and should have been perceived—that once the temporary disequilibrium that the Schlieffen Plan tried to exploit was over, the central powers and the allies were in a state of balance in terms of military and industrial power. Along the trenches of the western front this balance expressed itself in mutual paralysis. In the vast spaces of eastern Europe it oscillated violently as each side, with a temporary local superiority, achieved spectacular local successes; yet here too there was no decision: the great offensives ended always in a restored balance. Surprise could win a brief advantage, as at Gallipoli, but a fresh balance of strength quickly followed, and with it, paralysis. The origins of the balance lay in the long and roughly equal preparations of each side for war. There is here a sharp contrast with the Second World War, where there was only momentarily equilibrium. Up to 1942 Germany was decisively stronger, and after 1942 the United Nations; the result was a war of continual movement, of sweeping successes and great defeats.

Thus in 1915-16 the politicians and generals struggled to find by means of military ingenuity a method by which evenly balanced weights could be moved out of equilibrium without the introduction of extra weight. The soldiers in the ranks paid for the failure of the experiment.

Yet there was one area, on the grey-green seas beyond the Belgian sand dunes where the trenches and barbed wire petered out at the high-tide mark, in which there was no balance, no paralysis. It was here that Great Britain, Motherland of the Empire, had planned and prepared for ten years to make her war effort. The great armies, raised by Kitchener and now in spring 1916 massing in Picardy under General Sir Douglas Haig, were an afterthought—a prodigious feat of improvisation.

Britain's major, long-matured preparations had gone elsewhere—into the Royal Navy. To the Royal Navy Britain gave her pride, her love, her money, the best her technology could invent and produce. Not on the raw armies of the western front but on the all-professional long-service navy is British performance in the First World War fairly to be judged. The Royal Navy was the symbol as well as the shield of the British maritime empire, her global trade and finance, and of the technology that Britons believed to be the best in the world. And by 1916 the sea was the only open flank; only here was there no balance, because the Royal Navy outnumbered the German High Seas Fleet by forty-two modern capital ships to twenty-three. In the spring and summer of 1916 the future course of the war turned on the quality of the Royal Navy's Grand Fleet and on the leadership of the Commander-in-Chief, Admiral Sir John Jellicoe.

II

SAILOR WITH A FLAWED CUTLASS

Admiral Sir John R. Jellicoe

G.C.B., K.C.V.O.

. . . It is highly dangerous to consider that our ships as a whole are superior or even equal fighting machines.

VICE-ADMIRAL SIR JOHN JELLICOE,
July 14, 1914

. . . there seems to be something wrong with our bloody ships today.

VICE-ADMIRAL SIR DAVID BEATTY,
May 31, 1916

5

Ten years before the outbreak of the First World War the gunnery of the Royal Navy, in its own estimation the finest as well as the largest fleet in the world, was not much better than that of the dilapidated Russian ships that Rodjestvensky sailed round the world to destruction at Tsushima.[1] This was the result of the long Victorian peace and of the near-monopoly of the navy's officer corps by the aristocracy and gentry. For the navy was no longer a deadly functional instrument of policy: it was an exclusive yacht club. Yet by August 1914, in ten years, it had been dragged into the twentieth century, redeployed, given modern ships of a revolutionary pattern, and had its educational system reformed. It had been transformed once more into a fighting service. The credit belonged to Admiral-of-the-Fleet Sir John Fisher, as First Sea Lord from 1904 to 1910.

Long before 1914 he had chosen the man who would lead this great fleet to victory over the new German High Seas Fleet. In 1889 when Fisher had been Director of Naval Ordnance, he had chosen as his assistant Lieutenant John Jellicoe. Jellicoe impressed him deeply. "By far the best officer in my opinion and that of the Captain of the *Excellent* [Jellicoe's appointment at the time] is Lieutenant J. R. Jellicoe," Fisher wrote in a Minute of June 6, 1889, and went on to refer to Jellicoe's "very great abilities and the very high praise he has received from all his captains." [2]

[1] Dewar, 72.
[2] Jellicoe, Private Papers.

In a service dominated by social life, Jellicoe was a keen and clever professional; in a service that truly regarded guns as objects that made ships dirty when they fired, he was profoundly knowledgeable on gunnery and shells. Jellicoe was the modest son of a master of the merchant marine. His mind was a well-ordered filing system of detail, reflected by his small neat person, the tight mouth, and the watchful, calm brown eyes that looked out steadily past the prominent nose. His manner was cool, controlled and always polite. This self-containment rested on profound self-confidence. Above all, like Fisher, he believed in the supreme importance of big guns. In 1904 Captain Jellicoe was a member of the committee that drew up the general specification for *Dreadnought,* the first of the world's all-big-gun capital ships. The completion of this ship in 1906 made all existing battleships obsolete; such ships became known as "pre-*Dreadnoughts.*" In 1908-11 Jellicoe was Naval Controller under Fisher as First Sea Lord, responsible for developments in ship design, armour, guns and shells. Then he went to sea again, appointed as Second-in-Command of the Channel Fleet. Fisher had tested him and groomed him, and now, in Fisher's judgement, he was ready. As Fisher expressed it in a letter of Christmas Eve, 1911: "My sole object was to procure Jellicoe to be C.-in-C. of the Home Fleet on 17th December 1913: and that is being done by his being Second-in-Command, and he will automatically be C.-in-C. in two years from that date. All the recent changes revolve round Jellicoe and NO ONE sees it."

Next year Fisher defined Jellicoe's role in his new navy even more closely. He wrote on April 2, 1912: "If war comes before 1914 then Jellicoe will be Nelson at the Battle of St. Vincent. If it comes in 1915 he will be Nelson at Trafalgar." [3]

Fisher had unrolled the carpet; Jellicoe stepped neatly along it. Early in 1914, when Jellicoe was Second Sea Lord, he was appointed C.-in-C. designate of the Home Fleet and could hoist his flag in December, when the term of old Admiral Sir George Callaghan expired. However, the July crisis upset the deliberate rhythm of Fisher's designs; Churchill, the First Lord, told Jellicoe that he was to join Callaghan immediately as Second-in-Command. On July 31, with war probable any day, Jellicoe's Fisher-made destiny was telescoped; at a meeting with Churchill and the

[3] Bacon, 197.

Marquis of Milford Haven (who had replaced Fisher as First Sea Lord) Jellicoe was told that "in certain circumstances" he would instantly succeed Sir George Callaghan. Suddenly Jellicoe was faced with the imminent responsibility for the most powerful fleet ever built, for the maintenance of British maritime supremacy in a great war of a kind for which there were no precedents. His reaction to this unexpected news illuminates his character in a curious way at the very outset of his great command.

"This intimation," he wrote later, "came upon me as a great surprise, and I protested against such an appointment being made on what might possibly be the very eve of war." [4]

Churchill and Milford Haven being unmoved by his protests, however, he set off to join Callaghan. That evening, as the papers rang with news of impending war, when Jellicoe had settled in his first-class compartment at King's Cross for the long night journey to Wick, nearest mainland station to the fleet's anchorage at Scapa Flow, an officer handed him a long envelope with a red Admiralty seal, all over the front of which a bold hand had written that it was only to be opened from instructions from the Admiralty. In view of the afternoon's interview, the envelope's contents were not much of a mystery.

Through the long, tedious hours, when a night train becomes a world of its own, cut off from the past and the future, Jellicoe faced the implications of sudden supreme command and also the painful personal problem of relieving Callaghan at the very moment when the old admiral would most want to remain in command. Although ambitious, Jellicoe had never been ruthless; and in any event his sense of order, of respect for his seniors, amounting sometimes to excessive conformism, gave the precipitate relief of Callaghan the character of outrage, in which he, Jellicoe, would be the main actor. The Royal Navy was an institution of legendary violent personalities and resounding quarrels; but Jellicoe, in his neat, methodical, quiet and polite way, had always steered a course clear of controversy. Now it could not be avoided. Jellicoe dreaded the coming scene with Callaghan and its effect on the fleet. As soon as the train reached Wick, in a grey depressing mist that delayed his departure for Scapa, he began despatching a series of telegrams to the Admiralty re-

[4] Jellicoe, 3.

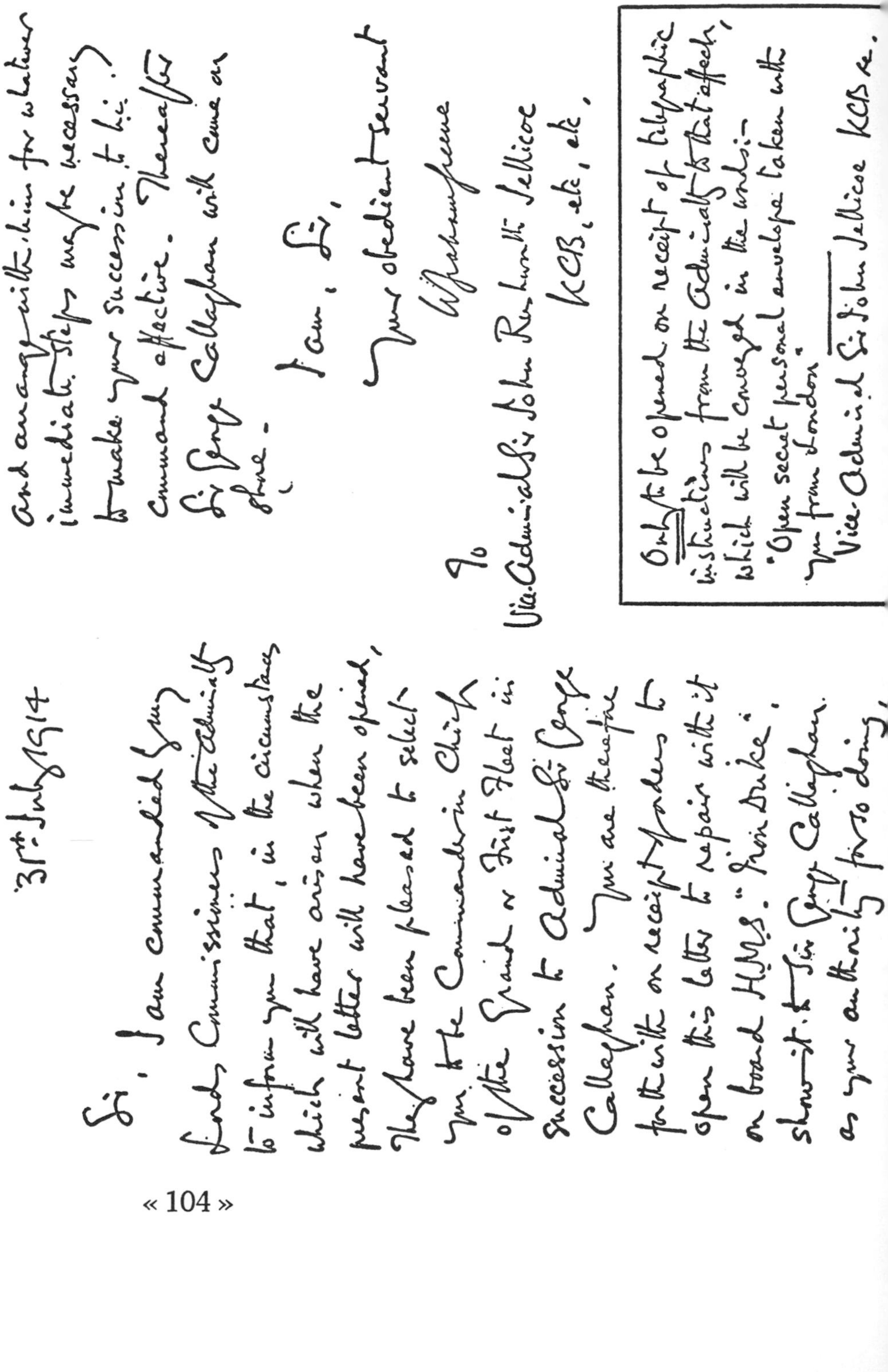

31st July 1914

Sir, I am commanded by your Lords Commissioners of the Admiralty to inform you that, in the circumstances which will have arisen when the present letter will have been opened, They have been pleased to select you the Commander in Chief of the Grand or First Fleet in succession to Admiral Sir George Callaghan. You are therefore forthwith on receipt of orders to open this letter to repair with it on board H.M.S. "Iron Duke", show it to Sir George Callaghan, as your authority forthwith first to dismiss,

and arrange with him for whatever immediate steps may be necessary to make your succession to his command effective. Thereafter Sir George Callaghan will come on shore.

I am, Sir,

Your obedient servant

W. Graham Greene

To
Vice-Admiral Sir John Rushworth Jellicoe
KCB, etc, etc.

Only to be opened on receipt of telegraphic instructions from the Admiralty to that effect, which will be conveyed in the words—
"Open secret personal envelope taken with you from London"
Vice-Admiral Sir John Jellicoe KCB &c.

markable for a man who knew he was about to achieve the summit of a naval officer's ambition. To Churchill:

> 10 P.M. Saturday August 1st 1914.
> Detained Wick by fog. Am firmly convinced after consideration that the step you mentioned to me is fraught with gravest danger at this juncture and might easily be disastrous owing to the extreme difficulty of getting into touch with everything at short notice. The transfer even if carried out cannot be accomplished safely for some time. I beg earnestly that you will give the matter further consideration with First Sea Lord before you take steps.

To Milford Haven, a similar message, with this addition:

> You will understand my motive in wiring is to do my best for Country, not personal considerations.[5]

Next day Jellicoe reached the flat waters of Scapa Flow and the dismal low islands that partly sheltered it, passed between the dark grey ships he knew he was about to command in war. As the pipes shrilled, he came aboard the flagship, *Iron Duke;* alert and active, an impassive weather-brown face under the old-fashioned, small-crowned uniform cap. There was something of a bird about him: in the neatness, the alacrity, the calm brown eyes deep-set amid wrinkles, the big-nosed face. As he came over the side, fingers to the peak of his cap, the interview in Callaghan's cabin he had been dreading for three days was only minutes away. It fully lived up to expectations, being "both embarrassing and painful, as I could see he had no knowledge of the possibility of his leaving the fleet, and obviously I could not tell him." [6]

That day Jellicoe fired another salvo of even more overwrought telegrams.

> Scapa Sunday Aug 2:
> To First Lord and First Sea Lord.
> Reference my personal telegram last night, am more than ever convinced of vital importance of making no change. Personal feelings are entirely ignored in reaching this conclusion.

At 8:30 in the evening came the reply:

[5] Bacon, 199-200.
[6] Jellicoe, 4.

I can give you 48 hours after joining you must be ready then.[7]

It is reasonable that a commander-in-chief designate who believed that an instant change in command would be against the interest of the service might send a single signal to the Admiralty setting out his views. Yet despite this definite negative to his first three telegrams, Jellicoe now sent off another three telegrams whose language reveals a sense of urgent personal involvement, a desperate wish to be saved at the last moment from replacing Callaghan.

> Scapa. 1130 A.M. 3rd August 1914. Personal to First Lord and First Sea Lord:
>
> Yours of Second. Can only reply am certain step contemplated is most dangerous beg that it may not be carried out. Am perfectly willing to act on board Fleet Flagship as assistant if required to be in direct communication. Hard to believe it is realised what grave difficulties change Commander-in-Chief involves at this moment. Do not forget long experience of Commander-in-Chief.[8]

Next day at 9:15 A.M., as the Germans advanced on Liége and in Luxembourg, and most of Europe had declared war, Jellicoe sent another personal telegram to the First Lord and First Sea Lord, in reply to their brief message giving him forty-eight hours to be ready:

> Quite impossible to be ready at such notice. Feel it my duty to warn you emphatically you court disaster if you carry out intention of changing before I have thorough grip of fleet and situation. Am sure Hamilton, Madden or any admiral recently Home Fleet will be of my opinion.

Two hours later he added:

> Add to my last message. Fleet is imbued with feelings of extreme admiration and loyalty for C.-in-C. This is a very strong factor.

All this use of the telegraph was vain; back came an inflexible reply from the First Sea Lord:

> Expeditionary force [B.E.F. to France] will not leave at present and therefore fleet movements with it will not be immediately required. I am sending Madden tonight to be at your side. I am telegraphing Commander-in-Chief directing him to transfer command to you at earliest moment suit-

[7] Bacon, 199.
[8] *loc. cit.*

able to the interests of the Service. I rely on him and you to effect this change quickly and smoothly, personal feelings cannot count now only what is best for us all. You should consult him frankly.[9]

When Jellicoe and Callaghan met on board Callaghan's flagship at 8:30 A.M. on August 8, after Jellicoe had opened his sealed letter ordering him to take command and Callaghan had received Churchill's signal, the interview was in every way as gruesome as Jellicoe feared. Three days later Jellicoe wrote of it to the Second Sea Lord:

> I hope never to live again through such a time as I had from Friday to Monday. My position was horrible. I did my best but could not stop what I feel is a great error . . . the tragedy of the news to the C.-in-C. was past belief, and it was almost worse for me.[10]

Jellicoe was a kindly man, obsessed by correctitude and exactness, and by a wish always to do the proper thing. For these reasons his share in the hasty and wounding manner in which Callaghan's career was terminated was to nag away at his conscience for four and a half years until the day when Callaghan presented him with a gold christening cup for his son on behalf of flag officers. Jellicoe made a point of drawing Callaghan aside to show him the papers that proved how hard he had tried to avoid the supercession.

Yet there was surely more to this series of telegrams than Jellicoe's horror at a painful personal ordeal and at being the principal actor in upsetting the navy's due method and decorum. There was the surprise, the jolt of taking up this great command immediately, and with war in the offing, instead of at the time which he had expected and to which he was psychologically attuned. Like Moltke, Jellicoe began his war command with a personally upsetting interview; unlike the German commander, Jellicoe had two years to go before he became involved in decisive battle. Nevertheless, in his own characteristically uncoloured and deliberate words, the next fourteen days were "a period of great strain and anxiety." [11] "To assume so heavy a responsibility as the Command of the Grand Fleet at such short notice on the eve of war was in itself not to be taken lightly." [12]

9 *Ibid,* 200.
10 Hamilton, MSS; quoted Marder, *From the Dreadnought,* I, 434.
11 Jellicoe, 6.
12 *loc. cit.*

There was also something else. No officer of his seniority had closer knowledge of the navy's ten years of modernisation. No officer had so profound and detailed an awareness of the Grand Fleet's strength, but also of its hidden and serious weaknesses. Perhaps there were moments between London and Scapa when Jellicoe saw himself cast not as Nelson, according to Fisher's scenario, but as Villeneuve, a part no man would be keen to play.

Now he was Commander-in-Chief, *Iron Duke* was his home and his headquarters. That day, however, he was still the new tenant in what had been so recently Callaghan's home—a stranger to the spacious fore cabin where he would mess with his staff at a round table placed on the centre line, the war room below the conning tower which served as fleet headquarters, the spotless deck where he and his officers were to keep fit with hard games of deck hockey, or physical exercises under the direction of Surgeon-Commander Digby Bell, the 13.5-inch guns, the admiral's cabin with its homely chintz curtains and its stern walk. Jellicoe was the only commander-in-chief in the war (except for his opponent in the High Seas Fleet) who would have to lead his command personally into battle, who would bear equal risks of death or mutilation with his men. He was personally brave: as a junior officer he had jumped overboard into heavy seas to save a man, and he had been badly wounded in the Boxer Rebellion of 1900.

Jellicoe needed courage and cool nerves, for he faced gigantic problems unrealised by the public who had counted fifty-seven ships of the line steaming past George V at the Spithead Review in July 1914, and whose view of the navy and naval strategy was a blend of Nelson according to schoolbooks and Fisher's new battleships. Although Germany had been recognised as the principal naval enemy as long ago as 1904, and Fisher's battle fleet had been designed and built expressly to fight the High Seas Fleet, Jellicoe found himself without a properly protected fleet base on the North Sea containing docking and repairing facilities capable of handling his big ships. Rosyth, on the Forth, had been designated the main fleet base against Germany in 1903, but in 1914 its docks were not completed, nor were there enough mines (a weapon the British had neglected as unseamanlike) to protect sufficient water to contain the whole of the Grand Fleet. Fisher, in any event, had preferred Cromarty.

As late as 1912 Scapa Flow had been intended as the base of only light forces and therefore remained without defences. In 1914 and 1915 the Grand Fleet was to spend much time at sea, not because it was carrying out valuable strategic tasks, but because the open sea was safer than its bases.

Anti-submarine nets, shore batteries, canteens, recreational facilities—all had to be improvised by Jellicoe, after the outbreak of war, on the naked, treeless islands and bleak waters of Scapa. Had it not been for a floating dock that he had initiated when Controller and which as Commander-in-Chief he had had towed up to Invergordon in the Cromarty Firth, the fleet would have had no nearer naval dockyard than Chatham. The Germans, by contrast, had well equipped and defended naval bases, which Jellicoe had himself seen before the war, and he was surprised that the Germans did not make vigorous submarine attacks inside his exposed deep-water anchorages. His explanation of the German failure is a sardonic comment on the British and German methods of preparation: "It may have seemed impossible to the German mind that we should place our Fleet, on which the Empire depended for its very existence, in a position where it was open to submarine or destroyer attack." [13]

Nevertheless Jellicoe's fleet had a marked superiority of numbers in modern capital ships over the German—twenty-four to sixteen—although the superiority was slender in light forces.

Because until 1912 there had been no Admiralty staff and no naval staff college, there had been no systematic study of strategy in the Royal Navy, and in 1914 there was thus no operational war plan. Instead there were the personal and vehement prejudices of the men at the top. Fisher, who had been obsessed by the power aspects of big, fast ships and big guns, had little knowledge of strategy, which was the art of using them. As late as 1912 he advocated the capture of Heligoland and even a seaborne landing on the German Baltic coast, operations that the German navy, plentifully supplied with mines, submarines and impregnable bases, would have welcomed. Because the Royal Navy did not *study* history, but copied it, the idea was briefly reconsidered as late as 1912 of mounting a close blockade of German ports in the style of 1798. Yet one thing seemed clear to all: that it was the Grand Fleet's task to keep the

[13] Jellicoe, 31.

High Seas Fleet out of the world sea lanes. Therefore when it dawned that the range of modern guns and torpedoes and the short steaming range of modern battleships made a close blockade impossible, it was decided to block the passages between Scotland and Iceland and Iceland and Greenland, from the base at Scapa.

This was a strange decision, eloquent of the strategical confusion, want of staff training and of high intellectual calibre to be found in the red-brick Admiralty building beneath the wireless mast that now connected it to ships all over the world. In the first place, the British enjoyed the same decisive strategic advantage over Germany that they had enjoyed over the Dutch—the island of Britain lay between the German ports and the world seaways. This in itself would have made it impossible for the Germans to sail their fleet into the Atlantic except at the daunting risk of having their retreat to their ports cut and being forced to face a battle of annihilation—as happened to the *Bismarck* in the Second World War. In the second place, the retirement of the Grand Fleet to Scapa meant that Britain no longer controlled the North Sea. Throughout the war it was a disputed zone, where the Germans were always free and able to make dangerous sallies. Indeed, the Grand Fleet could not and did not protect the crossings of the B.E.F. to France; the transports that passed, as myth has it, under the invisible protection of British sea power, could have been sunk by the High Seas Fleet before the British fleet could have reached the Channel. Jellicoe himself says so: "Our main Fleet was based, as he must have been aware, far away to the northward; he could have stood a good chance of making the attack and returning to his base before that Fleet could intervene." [14]

And throughout the war, therefore, British military deployment abroad was affected by the presumed danger of invasion at home.

Jellicoe therefore had to extemporise his own naval strategy after the outbreak of war. This was based on four conceptions: making sure of unimpeded British use of the sea, essential for an island that was not self-sufficient; compelling the enemy to accept peace by starving him of food and raw materials; covering the passage and protecting the communications of a British army sent overseas; and preventing invasion of Britain or her dominions. It is fair to say that these conceptions are too general to constitute a plan of war. Unlike Moltke the elder, Jellicoe had not been

[14] Jellicoe, 22-3.

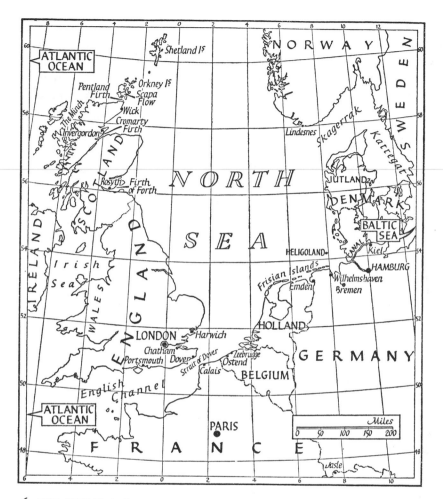

16. THE NORTH SEA

principally trained or enjoyed experience as a strategist. Except as an officer at sea, his career had been entirely concerned with material equipment and administrative detail. Neither he nor any senior officer of the fleet had received any staff training or a high education in strategic studies; he had never served on a proper professional staff and never made use of one. Jellicoe himself had never had an advanced general education. The fact that the Royal Navy had no corporate brain meant that

« 111 »

its training, equipment and technical design were unrelated to one another or to coherent basic principles. Admiral Lord Charles Beresford had quarrelled violently and publicly with Fisher over the questions of war plans and naval staff in 1910. Fisher, the technical revolutionary and extreme individualist, was against the creation of a naval general staff, partly because he, too, was a prisoner of the navy's tradition and believed that admirals, by themselves, did all the thinking necessary in the fleet, and partly because a corporate brain like a general staff would curb his personal rule. There was a cabinet committee to consider Beresford's charges, and the last paragraph of its report portrayed a situation that the next four years did little to alter:

"The Committee have been impressed with the difference of opinion amongst officers of high rank and professional attainments, regarding important principles of naval strategy and tactics. . . ." [15]

Such was the situation in the high command; it was similar throughout the body of the fleet, for there was no naval equivalent of the Army's Field Service Regulations and therefore no standard tactical and operational procedures and training. In their arrogant assumption of superiority, British naval officers were unaware of their service's glaring weaknesses. A few observers, however, saw clearly enough the dry rot in the stately edifice of British sea power. A Japanese officer explained to a British officer why his navy had given up British tuition: "He told me they were not satisfied with our methods of command and training. He said we possessed no *system* in the true sense of the word and that our methods were based purely on custom and not any intelligent principles. He also expressed the opinion that owing to the lack of a modern staff system our Navy might prove a collection of units without any directing brain." [16]

Douglas Haig, in a confidential paper of 1913 to Winston Churchill about the Report of the Committee on the organisation and training of the naval war college, wrote: "On its own report, the navy stands condemned as inefficiently trained in the art of war."

Of the project in the Report for a naval staff course, Haig wrote: "Some time must elapse before its influence can begin to be felt—and in

[15] Bellairs, 30.
[16] Dewar, 84.

the meantime we should, presumably, be careful to steer clear of any wars." [17]

It was Jellicoe, after the war had begun, who created a Grand Fleet staff on proper principles. When his brother-in-law, Rear-Admiral Sir Charles Madden, joined him as Chief of Staff, he divided the existing staff into two distinct sections—Operations and Administration. Such a division had been for sixty years the essential feature of the Prussian General Staff and the more recently created general staffs of the French and British armies, but not of the two-year-old Naval War Staff at the Admiralty (still only "advisory"). Jellicoe's new double staff created another problem: there was inadequate room for it in a fleet flagship never designed to accommodate a fleet headquarters.

Despite his creation of a fleet staff based on proper principles Jellicoe, like Fisher, was himself a mental prisoner of the habits of the unreformed navy. He had no outside standards or experience by which to judge these habits and his own character did not help him to step outside the old navy's pattern. He could never delegate and rest happy in his mind. This was noted before the war by Admiral Bridgeman, Commander-in-Chief of the Channel Fleet, when Jellicoe was his second-in-command in 1911: "He has had no experience of fleet work on a big scale, and is so extremely anxious about the work in it, that he really does too much. . . . He must trust his staff and captains. . . ." [18]

Jellicoe's obsession over detail, his tidy distaste for the uncertain and his temperamental inability to delegate were enshrined in the Grand Fleet battle orders, drawn up in 1914. He strove to think of every eventuality that could possibly happen and then lay down exactly in the Battle Orders the manoeuvre that would meet it. The tragedy was that he *wished* and *intended* to do as Nelson had done; indeed he constantly discussed battle tactics with his subordinates, played them out in war games, and practised his fleet at them. His Battle Orders specified that although the Commander-in-Chief would control the movements of the fleet before and on deployment, there would be afterwards a need for wide decentralisation of command. The tradition that only the Commander-in-Chief has a brain was too strong for both Jellicoe and his subordinates:

[17] *Haig Papers* (unpublished).
[18] Letter to Fisher; quoted Marder, *Fear God*, II, 416.

the Battle Orders were a huge and complicated volume of foolscap sheets, not a summary of principles, and admirals and captains continued to wait for the flagship's signals.

If nothing in Jellicoe's experience or knowledge equipped him to judge the weaknesses of command and staff in the British system, on the other hand he was as great an expert as any officer in any navy on the technical aspects of ships and guns, mines and torpedoes. By the end of 1914 operational experience, added to his pre-war work at the Admiralty, showed him that in quality and variety of equipment the Grand Fleet was dangerously inferior to the German High Seas Fleet. "My knowledge of the German navy, which was considerable," he wrote, "left me under no delusions as to his character. I had made it my business to keep myself very fully acquainted with German progress . . . touch on many occasions with the German Fleet had convinced me that in *matériel* the Germans were ahead of us. . . ." [19]

German submarines could cruise further and keep the sea better than the British. German cruisers were faster and were equipped for mine laying; the Germans had all the mines they wanted and of excellent design. The British at first lacked them altogether; when they did get them, they had, in Jellicoe's words, "defects in the pattern." Fear of submarines and mines forced the Grand Fleet to abandon its base and Scapa Flow for a time and retreat to Lough Swilly in Ireland—a German victory without the High Seas Fleet firing a shot. Fast, big German destroyers outnumbered similar British ships in August 1914 by ninety-six to seventy-six. They carried more torpedo tubes than the British, and the Germans had a better torpedo. Whereas Fisher had sacrificed weight in armour to weight in gunpowder and speed in his capital ships, the Germans, as Jellicoe would himself have preferred, had given their ships thicker and more extensive armoured belts. British gunnery, which had only been practised about 12,000 yards in 1913, suffered in wartime from a lack of safe practise grounds. Its quality varied greatly from ship to ship, instead of being of a consistent standard. Of German gunnery Jellicoe wrote: "I knew, perhaps better than most of our officers, how efficient was the gunnery and torpedo work of the High Seas Fleet." [20]

As for the British battleships as ships, some classes displayed crass

[19] Jellicoe, 62.
[20] *ibid*, 62.

errors of design. Jellicoe's own flagship, *Iron Duke,* had her 6-inch batteries so low-placed that all the gun ports had to be unshipped, as the sea washed them away in rough weather. The result was that the sea entered the ship between the gunshields and the ship's side, allowing three to four inches of water into the crew's living quarters. A partial bulkhead had to be fitted behind the guns, and a rubber joint between the gunshields and the ship's side. Similar alterations had to be made with the *Queen Elizabeth* class of battleships and the battle cruiser *Tiger.* The two after 6-inch guns in *Iron Duke* were completely removed, because as Jellicoe drily put it, "It was apparent that these guns could never be worked at sea, being only a few feet above the water line." [21]

Jellicoe also suffered from chronic engineering breakdowns. In 1914 five of his battleships had to have condensers replaced: "It will be realised," he wrote, "that such wholesale breakdowns caused me uneasiness." [22] It was a curious coincidence that it was the small-tube boilers on the German warships, so economical in weight for a given horsepower, that enabled the Germans to devote more weight to armour. Before the end of 1914 serious defects were discovered in the boilers of the *Liverpool,* defects common to every ship in this class of light cruiser. At the end of January 1915 no less than four battleships were out of service, as well as the battle cruiser *Indomitable,* which was being refitted after a fire caused by a defective electrical circuit. Since it was Jellicoe's cold and sober assessment that British command of the sea depended not, as it should, on quality but on a slender numerical superiority, the effects of the bad design and poor engineering of the British ships were critical.

Nor was Jellicoe happy about the quality of British shells. As Controller in 1910 he had presided over extensive experiments with armour-piercing shells. The results showed that the standard British shell was excellent at a 90° angle—that is, at the flat trajectory, close-range firing that had been so far the navy's custom—but that a new armour-piercing shell should be designed that could penetrate armour at an oblique angle—that is, long-range, plunging fire—and in a state fit for bursting. Jellicoe asked for this new shell to be produced but two months later went to sea. Somewhere in the bureaucracy of the Admiralty the project died. The British explosive, lyddite, was also highly unstable, espe-

21 Jellicoe, 175.
22 *ibid,* 168.

cially in hot conditions; at least two ships that mysteriously blew up and sank in harbour before 1916 owed their destruction to their own ammunition.

On July 14, 1914, while still Second Sea Lord, Jellicoe had summarised the relative quality of British and German battleships in a memorandum to the First Lord: "The inferiority of the protection of the British ships of 1909-1911 classes against guns and torpedoes is very striking. This is undoubtedly a weak point in the design of our ships."

Jellicoe then gave a detailed comparison of British and German vessels year by year back from 1913 to 1906 and stated. "It will be seen therefore that far from the British ships showing a superiority in displacement the exact opposite is usually the case and assuming equality in design it is highly dangerous to consider that our ships as a whole are superior or even equal fighting machines." [23]

Such was the fleet that some critics, politicians and historians have expected Jellicoe to lead straight into the High Seas Fleet, with the ruthless aggressiveness of Nelson and St. Vincent. Jellicoe's own ideas on how such a fleet could be best employed in a decisive action, matured through the autumn of 1914, were coldly and soberly realistic. On October 30, 1914, at a time when the western front had already hardened from the sea to Switzerland and General Pétain already had doubts about the likelihood of a successful offensive, Jellicoe wrote a letter of eighteen paragraphs to the Admiralty setting forth his intentions. He began with strategy. The Germans could best use their superiority in submarines, torpedoes and mines in the southern part of the North Sea.

> My object will therefore be to fight the fleet action in the northern portion of the North Sea, which position is incidentally nearer our own bases, giving our wounded ships a chance of reaching them.[24]

Since the German Commander-in-Chief would hardly be rash enough to venture his smaller fleet so far from home, Jellicoe had in fact by this paragraph announced that he was in present circumstances going to avoid a fleet action. Nevertheless he went on to discuss tactics in a battle especially in regard to torpedoes from German submarines and destroyers. He was particularly afraid of a trap:

[23] Jellicoe Papers, II, 48990.
[24] Dewar, 82.

If, for instance, the enemy Battle Fleet were to turn away from an advancing fleet, I should assume that the intention was to lead us over mines and submarines, and should decline to be so drawn.

He went on:

I desire particularly to draw the attention of their Lordships to this point, since it may be deemed a refusal of battle, and, indeed, might possibly result in failure to bring the enemy to action as soon as is expected and hoped.

Such a result would be absolutely repugnant to the feelings of all British officers and men, but with new and untried methods of warfare new tactics must be devised. . . . I feel that such tactics, if not understood, may bring odium upon me, but so long as I have the confidence of their Lordships I intend to pursue what is, in my considered opinion, the proper course to defeat and annihilate the enemy Battle Fleet. . . .

Jellicoe was worried also about submarine attack *before* battle was joined:

The safeguard against submarines will consist in moving the Battle Fleet at very high speed to a flank before deployment takes place as the gun action commences. This will take us off the ground on which the enemy desires to fight, but it may, of course, result in his refusal to follow me.

It is a significant thing that among the eighteen paragraphs of this letter, there is not one that discusses how to grip the enemy so that he might be annihilated. Nevertheless it was a true and honest picture of Jellicoe's cautious intentions, and it received the Admiralty's blessing, in which was presumably included that of Winston Churchill, that aggressive optimist:

I have laid before My Lords Commissioners of the Admiralty [wrote the Secretary of the Admiralty] your letter of the 30th ultimo No. 337/H.F. 0034, and I am commanded by them to inform you that they approve your views, as stated therein, and desire to assure you of their full confidence in your contemplated conduct of the Fleet in action. . . .[25]

Luckily before a fleet battle Jellicoe had another eighteen months in which to train his fleet, rectify its worst deficiences, increase its size and impress his own leadership on officers and men. Few commanders of British armies have been as fortunate.

[25] Dewar, 84-5.

If it was characteristic of the twentieth-century British to produce an instrument of sea power deficient in many particulars, it was equally characteristic of the Germans to make a fundamental mistake of high policy that rendered null all their thorough and clever preparations.

The mistake was enshrined in the preamble to the first German Navy Bill of 1900, by which the new High Seas Fleet was to be big enough to constitute a provocation and a worry to the British, but not big enough to defeat the Royal Navy. The Germans thus drove the British into alliance with their enemies without as a compensation being able to defend German overseas colonies and trade. As soon as war began, German merchant shipping, except for a few and lucky blockade runners, vanished from the sea. When the six-week war lengthened into a struggle measured in years and involving total national economic effort, Germany began to suffer physically from a shortage of food and raw materials and financially from the collapse of her sea-borne export trade. It was in fact true that British sea power could do the Germans great damage (although slow in effect) without ever fighting battles.

The German strategic problem was insoluble. Their North Sea coast was no wider in extent than the British East Anglian coast from London to the Wash. Compared with the 360° flexibility of British coasts and ports, this gave them only a narrow 90° exit, easily watched and masked. Their battle fleet was too inferior in numbers for them to invite and fight a decisive battle fot the command of the sea. And indeed, even if they had built more ships (an impossible burden when added to a huge army) and won a decisive battle, they would still have found the British Isles blocking their commerce routes, a base for submarines and surface raiders. The basic truth about the High Seas Fleet was that it should never have been built.

Now Germany was at war, the German admiralty was puzzled as to what to do with the High Seas Fleet. The answer of the Kaiser, who looked on his fleet not as a weapon but as a symbol of prestige, and of the timorous and unworthy Fleet Commanders-in-Chief of 1914-16, von Ingenohl and von Pohl, was to keep it in harbour or in the Baltic, except for gunnery exercises and swift raids by detachments. This was a tragedy for Germany, for owing to the high rate of British breakdowns, there was a time in 1915 when the two battle fleets were almost equal in numbers.

Yet although for two years the main fleets on which so much money and effort had been spent never came to grips with each other, the maritime war sharpened in bitterness and ruthlessness. German trade began to find its way through the neutral ports and ships of Holland and the Scandinavian countries. Although it was contrary to international declarations either ratified by Great Britain or to which she had stated she would adhere, the British began to carry out a system of restricting the sea-borne imports of neutrals to the levels of peacetime. There was search of neutral vessels and seizure of contraband. It caused violent protests, not least from the United States. The Germans replied on February 4, 1915, by declaring unrestricted submarine warfare in the seas surrounding the British Isles. The *Lusitania* was an early victim. Now it was the German government's turn to receive Washington's protests; and on September 1, 1915, it agreed to abandon unrestricted submarine warfare. However, British relations with the United States over British breaches of the rights of neutrals were still tense in the spring of 1916. Not in 1812, 1861-65, or in 1916 was it the American view that Britannia ruled any wave on which floated a vessel flying the Stars and Stripes.

So in 1916 sea warfare remained oddly tentative and preliminary in all its aspects. As the armies floundered in their monstrous killing matches, the unscathed navies watched in frustration. Jellicoe bore the tedium better than Sir David Beatty, commanding the battle cruiser fleet, who, a fox-hunting Irishman and a man of fashion, was of a restless, impetuous energy.

The unhappy departure of Callaghan was long past now; by his courtesy, his unfailing self-control, his complete mastery of his job, Jellicoe had won the confidence of his officers and men. As one officer put it: "Jellicoe *is* the Grand Fleet." He was fifty-seven now, tough and fit. His staff found him off duty a lively, approachable man, a generous host, but always careful and abstemious himself over food and drink. The captain of the flagship recounted: "I have in mind now how every night in harbour at dinner he would ask me: 'Will you split an apple, Dreyer?' and then cut it in halves and offer the plate to me with a charming smile." [26] In harbour he worked a fifteen-hour day, wearing his gold-rimmed half-spectacles for reading. When the fleet was cruising, however, he

[26] Dreyer, 96.

was unable to relax his personal grip on it at all: "I never left my sea cabin, which was under the bridge, to go to the after part of the ship while the Fleet was at sea." [27]

For confidence and experience had not cured him of his obsession with detail and often the detail of his subordinates' jobs. It was a fundamental element in his character; yet, as with Wellington, his subordinates varied from highly trained, highly reliable officers to men basically rather stupid, unfit for independent responsibility and, unlike the fleet's ships, unmodernised. How much could he afford to leave to their unaided capacities? Only experience of battle could tell him, as only this could confirm whether his carefully-worked-out tactics were correct; but in May 1916, after two years of war and with the Grand Fleet growing stronger all the time, battle seemed remote enough.

In fact, it had been coming nearer and nearer since January 1916, when von Pohl had been replaced as Commander-in-Chief High Seas Fleet by Reinhard Scheer, only a vice-admiral, but a brilliant officer with the keen, aggressive and bearded face of a Francis Drake.

[27] *ibid*, 42.

6

On February 1, three weeks before Falkenhayn's guns began the bombardment before the battle of Verdun and signalled Pétain's arrival as a French national hero, Scheer attended a naval conference in Berlin in which he persuaded the Kaiser that the High Seas Fleet must be used aggressively and that the power of deciding whether and when to put to sea on such a cruise must rest with the Commander-in-Chief, not as hitherto with the Kaiser himself. It was also decided to start unrestricted submarine warfare again on March 1. The High Seas Fleet, strengthened by ships from the Baltic, would begin a policy of harrying the British by advanced mine laying, airship attacks, raids on British shipping by destroyer and cruiser forces, and shelling of British coastal towns. This last activity had in 1914 caused a stupendous uproar in Britain, as if an attempt had been made to violate Britannia in her own drawing room. The German battle fleet itself would cruise in the North Sea in the hope of catching and annihilating an inferior British force. There was still no question of a decisive battle, since the Germans were now inferior in capital ships by four to seven. "The then prevailing conditions of strength," wrote Scheer, "kept us from seeking a decisive battle with the enemy. Our conduct of the war was rather aimed at preventing a decisive battle being forced upon us by the enemy." [1]

The new policy was not only rooted in Scheer's own character, which scorned inactivity, but also in the need for the navy to provide some heartening news for a nation now beginning to feel the weight of a long

[1] Scheer, 97.

and boring war; on the eastern front another gigantic Russian offensive was expected, although the Germans (under Hindenburg and Ludendorff) and Austrians had won splendid victories over the Russians in 1915. In May 1916 Scheer planned his great sortie with the High Seas Fleet. By now the German attacks on Verdun had flagged before Pétain's steady defence, and in fact on May 1 Pétain had left Verdun to assume command of Army Group Centre.

For the High Seas Fleet to gain any kind of success and then escape without destruction, careful planning, brilliant fleet handling and a great deal of luck was necessary. At Scapa and Cromarty lay Jellicoe with 26 battleships,[2] 3 battle cruisers, 10 cruisers, 11 light cruisers, 5 destroyer leaders, 53 destroyers, a mine layer and a seaplane carrier. At Rosyth there was Beatty with 5 battleships, 7 battle cruisers, 15 light cruisers, 38 destroyers, 2 submarines and 2 seaplane carriers. These two great forces made up the Grand Fleet and Battle Cruiser Fleet. At Harwich was the Harwich Force of a cruiser, 35 destroyers and some submarines under Admiral Tyrwhitt; at Dover Admiral Bacon's Dover Patrol of 1 light cruiser, 1 destroyer leader, 25 destroyers and submarines. In the Thames was a squadron of 1 modern (post-*Dreadnought*) and 7 pre-*Dreadnought* battleships and three cruisers. Covering the entire eastern coastline was the Coastal Patrol of 35 destroyers. Against this force Scheer could muster only 18 battleships, 5 battle cruisers and 7 obsolete pre-*Dreadnought* battleships, 14 light cruisers, 66 destroyers, 31 submarines, and 10 zeppelins. This was the High Seas Fleet; there was also Admiral Schröder in Flanders with 3 destroyers and 14 submarines. The British superiority was even greater than these figures suggest, for British ships nearing completion outnumbered German by 3 to 1. Not only this, but the battleships of Britain's allies outnumbered those of Germany's allies by 12 to 4.

At first Scheer considered bombarding Sunderland with cruisers in order to draw a portion of the Grand Fleet down on to the guns of the entire High Seas Fleet. On May 30, 1916, he changed his mind in favour of a cruise towards the Norwegian coast. Scouting Groups 1 (battle cruisers) and 2 (cruisers), with the cruiser *Regensburg,* and Destroyer Flotillas 2, 7 and 9, under the command of Vice-Admiral Hipper, were

---

[2] These figures are of the full paper strengths of the two fleets. As will be seen from later figures, fewer ships actually sailed to Jutland.

to sail at daylight on May 31, steer northward out of sight of the Danish coast and show themselves off Norway that day before dusk. Hipper was the bait. Scheer himself as the trap, with Battle Squadrons 1 and 3, Scouting Group 4, the cruisers *Rostock* and *Hamburg,* and Destroyer Flotillas 1, 3, 5 and 8, would follow, well back, reaching a point forty-five miles south of Lindesnes by 5 A.M. on June 1, ready to support Hipper. Battle Squadron 2, comprised of obsolete, slow battleships with thin armour and only four 11-inch guns each would guard the approaches to his bases. When British forces sailed to catch Hipper, they would be attacked by German submarines, which would also act as a reconnaissance screen. Submarines from Flanders would similarly watch Dover, the Thames and Harwich. The zeppelins would carry out air search over the North Sea.

At 9:48 A.M. on May 30 the radio room in *Friedrich der Grosse,* the fleet flagship, began tapping out the signal that led to the last general action ever fought by a British fleet. By 7 P.M. the High Seas Fleet was to be concentrated in the outer roads of the river Jade. Mine sweepers were ordered to clear a northwesterly channel west of Heligoland and the Amrum bank. This signal by radio was a serious mistake when laneline telephones and telegraphs could easily have been used; it was intercepted by the excellent Admiralty radio interception service. In 1914 Admiralty intelligence had broken the German naval code. Scheer's orders were therefore no mystery. By noon Jellicoe knew that the High Seas Fleet might be at sea next morning.

At 3:40 P.M. Scheer signalled his fleet again by radio "31 Gg 2490": it was the operation order for the fleet to sail for the Skagerrak next day. At 5:15 P.M. the Admiralty, on the basis of this signal, also intercepted, ordered Jellicoe and Beatty to raise steam. To Jellicoe the Admiralty added at 5:30 P.M.: "You should concentrate to eastward of the Long Forties ready for eventualities."

In the bleak anchorages of Scapa, Cromarty and Rosyth, surrounded by empty hills and temporary base facilities, the signals ordering the fleet to prepare to leave port fluttered up the halyards of fleet and squadron flagships.

At 5:41 P.M. Scheer signalled important changes of plan. Because he doubted whether air search would be practicable, he decided to follow Hipper more closely with his main body, sailing only an hour and

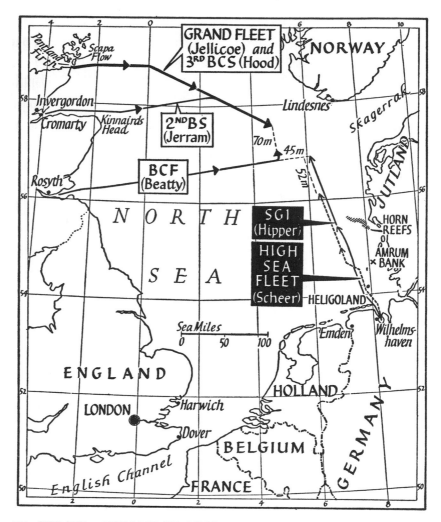

17. JUTLAND—APPROACH TO BATTLE

a half after him. He also decided to take his obsolete Battle Squadron 2 with him; it was a decision that did more credit to him as a man than as an admiral, for it resulted from the urgent pleas of the squadron's flag officer, Rear-Admiral Mauve, not to be left out and from Scheer's own wish not to depress the fine spirit of the squadron which he himself had commanded.

« 124 »

Belatedly the German command began now to use the radio to confuse the British instead of to give them precise bulletins on its intention. A coastal guardship took over *Friedrich der Grosse's* call sign; from now on the fleet would preserve radio silence until the British were sighted; Scheer would receive, but not answer, radio messages via the guard ship.

Already the British were suffering from their lack of a single fleet base, for the Grand Fleet was split between Scapa, Cromarty (2nd Battle Squadron: Vice-Admiral Sir Martyn Jerram) and Rosyth, and had to be united at sea. At 7:30 P.M. Jellicoe therefore ordered Jerram to join the Grand Fleet at 2 P.M. on May 31 in latitude 57°—45′, longitude 4°—15′ east. Seven minutes later Jellicoe signalled Beatty by landline:

> Available vessels, Battle Cruiser Fleet, Fifth Battle Squadron and torpedo boat destroyers, including Harwich t.b.d's, proceed to approximate position Lat. 56°—40′ N, Long. 5°—00′ E. Deside to economise t.b.d's fuel. Presume you will be there about 2 P.M. thirty-first. I shall be in about Lat. 57°—45′ N, Long. 4°—15′ E by 2 P.M. unless delayed by fog. Third Battle Cruiser Squadron, *Chester* and *Canterbury,* will leave with me. I will send them on to your rendezvous. If no news by 2 P.M. stand towards me to get into visual touch. I will steer for Horn Reefs from position in Lat. 57°—45′ N, Longitude 4°—15′ E. Repeat back rendezvous.[3]

At 9:30 P.M. that evening, when Scheer was still in harbour, Jellicoe's ships began weighing anchor and slipping out to sea, thick black smoke reeking back out of the tall funnels, White Ensigns streaming from the gaffs above dark, blue-grey hulls. At 17 knots, course 61°,[4] they passed the Pentland Skerries; by 10:30 P.M. the Scapa force was at sea. Beatty's battle cruisers began steaming away from Rosyth at 10 P.M., followed forty minutes later by the 5th Battle Squadron (Vice-Admiral Evan-Thomas). Jerram's 2nd Battle Squadron left Cromarty at 19 knots, course 90°, at 10:15 P.M.

The entire Grand Fleet was now at sea, ready for battle, while the High Seas Fleet lay still in the Jade roads. It demonstrated Jellicoe's skill as an organiser and the excellence of Admiralty intelligence. Jellicoe had

---

[3] Frost, 125. The following narrative of the battle of Jutland is based on Jellicoe, Bellairs, Bacon, Dreyer, Corbett, III, The Admiralty Narrative, Harper, and Frost, as a painstaking analysis by a foreigner untouched by the prejudices of most British writers on the battle. Unless otherwise stated, all timings and signals are from Frost, as are hits scored, courses and positions.

[4] All subsequent references in parentheses to exact courses and bearings are *true.*

by his speed redressed some of the disadvantages of having his fleet split between three bases, all situated so far to the northwards. Disadvantages remained, however, for the differences in temperament and style of leadership between himself and Beatty had been heightened by physical separation. The battle-cruiser fleet was an integral part of the Grand Fleet, but it had for so long been trained, exercised and stationed away from the main body as to have achieved an individual identity. At this moment two separate bases upset the homogeneity of the fleet in a particular way: because there was not enough protected water at Rosyth for gunnery practice, Beatty's 3rd Battle Cruiser Squadron (Rear-Admiral Sir Horace Hood) was with Jellicoe for gunnery practice, while in temporary replacement Beatty had been given the 5th Battle Squadron (Vice-Admiral Evan-Thomas). Its battleships were the fastest and most powerful in the Grand Fleet, but it and its admiral were strangers to Beatty and his fleet's methods.

Each impelled by 25,000 horsepower, each great mass of steel displacing up to 26,000 tons of water, the battleships steamed without lights through the darkness, stems splitting the black sea continuously into two hissing, curling lines of foam, lookouts straining without much hope for the sight of a periscope's wake, crews tense with purpose and anticipation. Already the destroyer *Trident* had confirmed Jellicoe's expectations of the danger from torpedoes by reporting attack by submarine off Rosyth; Beatty altered course to steer north of May Island to avoid it. Harmless contacts of this kind and misleading radio reports were all that Scheer got out of an ambush of thirteen submarines across Jellicoe's path. A few minutes after midnight the Pentland Skerries fell behind *Iron Duke*. Sixty miles to the southward Jerram's battleships were passing the sleeping small coastal towns of Morayshire and Aberdeenshire, with the Grampians rising behind them in the darkness. At 1 A.M. on May 31 the light on Kinnairds Head blazed out across the sea for the first time since 1914. For forty minutes it showed on Jerram's starboard beam; then the 2nd Battle Squadron in two columns steamed on into the dark waters of the North Sea.

At 1:30 A.M. Jellicoe ordered a change of course to 73°, with his battleships disposed in four parallel columns at 1,600-yard intervals, covered ten miles ahead by the 2nd Cruiser Squadron.

Meanwhile the High Seas Fleet had been raising steam and concentrating in the Jade, a great, almost landlocked bay, bordered by flat, featureless country. Flanking the exit to the outer Jade roads and the sea with two main basins, eight huge docks, building yards and floating docks was the naval town of Wilhelmshaven, the comfortable, well-equipped, long-prepared North Sea base of the German navy. When the short summer night had fallen, the dimmed lights of wartime showed on ships and shore, their reflections changing shape as the quiet waters of the Jade rippled. One by one the ships steamed slowly to the rendezvous in the Jade roads along the channel dredged between the sandbanks of Voslapp Watt and Solthomer Watt.

At 1 A.M. the great ships of Hipper's Scouting Group 1, painted in the pale grey of the Imperial navy with distinguishing coloured bands of white, red, yellow and blue on their funnels according to their position in the squadron, steamed away out of the Jade and stood northwards past Heligoland at sixteen knots. An hour and a half later *Friedrich der Grosse,* wearing Scheer's vice-admiral's white flag with a black iron cross and a black ball in the top left-hand corner, followed with the main body at sixteen knots. At 7:50 A.M. Hipper passed the end of the swept channel through the mine fields into the open sea. The morning was misty, and far away to the north in the Grand Fleet there was much signalling of questions and answers about ships' stations, bearings and distances. There was a little wind, and as the sun rose, it became a fine summer's morning.

Neither admiral was aware that his opponent's main fleet was for certain at sea. Scheer had received radio reports from U-boats of the 2nd Battle Squadron steering *northerly* (it was actually on the leg of a zigzag) and the 2nd Battle Cruiser Squadron steering south. The radio station at Neumünster told him that "two large warships or groups with destroyers had left Scapa Flow." He had also heard that because of the morning mists there could be no reconnaissance by airships. With the Jade guard ship using the *Friedrich der Grosse*'s call sign, neither Jellicoe nor the Admiralty had reason to believe that Scheer had left harbour. In fact, at 10:30 A.M. the Admiralty told Jellicoe that Scheer was still in harbour. All that morning the two fleets, the dark grey and the light grey, steamed on towards their meeting place through a calm, sunglittering sea. At 11:22 A.M. Jerram from Cromarty brought the 2nd

Battle Squadron into station to port of the 4th Battle Squadron, as Jellicoe watched from the *Iron Duke.* "Manoeuvre well executed," he signalled.

At 12 noon the fleet guide, *Iron Duke,* fixed her position as lat. 58°—07′, long. 3°—01.5′ E. *Invincible* (3rd Battle Cruiser Squadron) bore almost 90° from the fleet flagship at a distance of twenty-seven miles. Beatty, in *Lion,* bore 164°, distant 85 miles.

Jellicoe had it perfectly clear in his mind how he would fight if he met Scheer. The fundamental caution of 1914 remained unaltered.

> Neither in October 1914, nor in May 1916, did our margin of superiority justify me in disregarding the enemy's torpedo fire or meeting it otherwise than by definite movements deduced after the most careful analysis of the problem . . .
>
> The severely restricted forces behind the Grand Fleet were taken into account.[5]

For although in 1916 he enjoyed a handsome numerical superiority, there was still the question of quality. And the operational experience there had been since 1914 would not have increased any man's confidence in the quality of the Royal Navy. There had been the misunderstandings that had allowed the escape of the *Göben* to Turkey. At the battle of the Falkland Isles in 1914, two modern British battle cruisers, each with eight 12-inch guns, had taken no less than three and a quarter hours of constant shooting to sink two German heavy cruisers with only eight 8.2-inch guns. Although completely outranged the Germans had by contrast shot magnificently. "Never have I seen," wrote Captain Allen, of the cruiser *Kent,* "heavy guns fired with such rapidity and yet with such control." [6]

In the Dogger Bank battle of January 1915 (between Hipper and three battle cruisers, and the slow heavy cruiser *Blücher*—8.2-inch guns—and Beatty's battle cruisers) *Lion* had been hit twelve times, *Tiger* also heavily, while *Seydlitz* had been hit only three times. The *Blücher* had been the single British trophy; being slowed by hits, Hipper outnumbered, had had to abandon her. However, *Lion* had to leave the line, badly hurt, and with radio and searchlights out of action. Beatty

[5] Jellicoe, 304.
[6] Pitt, 112.

had signalled his remaining ships to chase Hipper, but owing to a muddle over signals in *Lion* and to the usual British blind obedience to orders, however obviously wrong, Beatty's other ships had thought they were being instructed to attack the stopped and burning *Blücher,* which they had done while Hipper escaped.

Beatty, however, had all the confidence in his ships and men that would be expected of so dashing a sailor. "Here I have the finest striking force in the world," he wrote.[7]

Zigzagging at a fleet speed of fourteen knots, Jellicoe stood towards his rendezvous with Beatty; in the circle of placid sea round the flagship could be seen from time to time neutral ships or their far-off funnel smoke, and the fleet had slowed to allow cruisers and destroyers to check the strangers. At 2 P.M. there was no sign of Beatty; the day was still fine, with little wind.

At 2:18 P.M. Jellicoe, standing on the manoeuvring platform (forebridge) of *Iron Duke,* was handed a radio message from *Galatea* (Commodore Alexander-Sinclair), part of Beatty's cruiser screen: "Urgent. Two cruisers, probably hostile, in sight bearing ESE. (100°), course unknown. My position Lat. 56°—48′, Long. 5—21."

Jellicoe was now about three hours' steaming away from *Galatea.* At 3 P.M. Jellicoe ordered the fleet to change course to SE by S (134°) and increase speed to eighteen knots. It was action stations.

At 3:16 P.M. Jellicoe ordered his divisions to keep a station 2,000 yards apart; this would give an interval of 500 yards between the ships after deployment into line of battle, allowing broadsides to bear. The fleet speed went up to nineteen knots. Perhaps no sight more impressive has been seen at sea—not even Nelson's two divisions standing in to destroy Villeneuve—than Jellicoe's twenty-four blue-grey battleships in six columns abeam, the left-centre column led by *Iron Duke* wearing Jellicoe's flag—a red St. George's cross on a white ground—their bow waves curling higher and higher, and the thick, soft smoke streaming away from their funnels into the still and sunlit afternoon. The characteristic British silhouette of a battleship was a low straight hull, from which sprang the verticals of narrow, closely placed unraked funnels and tripod masts and fighting tops. *Neptune* and the two *Colossus* class ships were

[7] Beatty, letter to his wife; quoted Chalmers, 176.

conspicuous for their ugliness, having what looked like a double-span railway bridge on the centre line over the midships turrets.

At 3:21 P.M. Jellicoe read an intercepted radio message from Beatty to his squadron commanders giving his position, course and speed. It was clear that Beatty was becoming involved with a German force; but what force? In what strength? Jellicoe ordered his destroyers to raise steam for full speed. At 3:27 P.M. there were more scraps of information—an intercepted report from *Galatea* that she had seen, to east-southeast, the smoke of ships steering west-northwest; and another from *Nottingham* (also in Beatty's cruiser screen) of five columns of smoke bearing east-northeast. Two minutes later Commodore Alexander-Sinclair (*Galatea*) signalled that he was leading the Germans to the northwest.

This scanty and ambiguous information Jellicoe considered in his quiet, methodical manner. It seemed that the battle fleet, Hood's 2nd Battle Cruiser Squadron and Beatty were all converging on the German force, in which no report had so far indicated any capital ship. Jellicoe ordered his divisional flag officers to inform their commands of the general situation. At 3:35 P.M. he sent a signal to the commodore of flotillas, in *Castor,* that sums up his appreciation at that time: "Enemy cruisers and destroyers are being chased to northward by our battle cruiser force and should be in touch with our cruisers at about 4:00 P.M."

So far, therefore, Jellicoe did not realise that Hipper's battle cruisers were present, or that Scheer's battleships were at sea. More light came at 3:40 P.M., when Beatty reported to him that there were five enemy battle cruisers and many destroyers bearing NE (32°). It omitted the crucial matter of the German speed and course, but the omission was repaired in a few moments in signals from *Galatea* and *Falmouth*. At 3:45 P.M. Beatty signalled that the enemy's course was S 55° E (112°). Ten minutes later one phase of intolerable suspense ended with Beatty's signal that he was in action. Immediately Jellicoe ordered the fleet speed to be pushed up to twenty knots—only one or two knots slower than the maximum speed of his older ships. He was now just over fifty miles from the scene of the battle-cruiser action, steaming straight for it and completely ready for battle at a second's notice. It was a tribute to his cool head, to his methodical mind and profound professional knowledge.

On the *Iron Duke*'s forebridge not much was said, but the tension was wound tauter and tauter in the face of imminent battle. Visibility was gradually worsening as mist began to veil the distances again. Somewhere out of sight ahead Beatty's ships were trading heavy armour-piercing shells with Hipper's. Would Beatty win? What situation would Jellicoe find when at last the scene of battle climbed over the horizon?

A 4:04 P.M. Jellicoe felt sufficiently anxious to take the risk of breaking radio silence for the first time to order Hood "to proceed immediately to support the Battle Cruiser Fleet." He was still worried; at 4:15 P.M. he asked Evan-Thomas (5th Battle Squadron) if he was in contact with the enemy. After a quarter of an hour came good news from Evan-Thomas: "Yes. I am engaging the enemy."

At 4:38 P.M. came the news that Jellicoe and all his fleet had longed for during the dreary, tedious months of Scapa and the training cruises—Commodore Goodenough and Captain Farie (*Champion*) reported that they had seen the German battle fleet. It was a proof of how much the critical decisions depended on other men's fallible judgements that Goodenough and Farie, although close together, differed in their estimates of the German position by twenty-five miles. Jellicoe believed Goodenough, a first-class officer, and also his estimate of the German course—N (347°). Jellicoe signalled his fleet: "Enemy's battle fleet is coming North."

It was news to pass along in a buzz of excitement, with mouths drying with anticipatory tension, through the gun turrets, magazines, engine rooms, sick bays.

At 4:45 P.M. came a curious and scanty radio message from Beatty: "26-30 battleships, probably hostile, bearing SSE steering *southeast*." (Author's italics.)

At 4:46 P.M. Goodenough sent another, model report: "Course of enemy's Battle Fleet, North, single line ahead. Composition of van *Kaiser* class. Bearing of centre East. Destroyers on both wings and ahead. Enemy's battle cruisers joining Battle Fleet from the northward. My position Lat. 56°—29' N. Long. 6°—14' E."

Goodenough had in fact miscalculated his own position; as given, it corresponded with that of Scheer's Battle Squadron 1. When Jellicoe therefore stepped down the ladder from the forebridge to study the chart in the charthouse, the German main body was plotted about seven miles east of its true position. Goodenough had also mistaken a temporary turn by Scheer for his true course, which Jellicoe therefore took to be north, instead of northwest.

The battle fleets of this epoch were in fact, like the armies, dinosaurs—heavy, powerful, thickly armoured, but with rudimentary controlling and sensory nervous systems. Although his flagship weighed ten times that of Nelson, could achieve three times the speed, and throw a projectile ten times as far, Jellicoe, through his own lookouts and his cruiser screen, could see no further and with no more certitude than Nelson.

Yet the fleets need not have been so blind; each had rudimentary air components well able to conduct air searches over a hundred miles from the fleet. Jellicoe had the seaplane carrier *Campania* (ten aircraft); Beatty the *Engadine;* Scheer had the High Seas Fleet Zeppelin Detachment. By an error *Campania* did not receive her sailing orders; when Jellicoe learned she was following well astern of the main body, he ordered her back to port, although she was gaining by three knots and her aircraft could have still operated with the fleet because of their range and speed. In any event, she would have caught up before the fleet action. *Engadine* flew an air search for Beatty, but the aircraft was sent north-northeast instead of east and found light cruisers instead of Hipper's heavy ships. The position of these cruisers was not passed to *Lion.* Beatty flew no more aircraft in the battle. Of Scheer's ten airships, only five were on air search during May 31. Because of the day's haziness they were ordered home at 4:30 P.M., just when their intervention could have decisively helped the High Seas Fleet. In fact, neither the British aircraft nor the Zeppelins could see much further than six to eight miles, under a cloud ceiling of 600-1000 feet. Jellicoe therefore depended only on the eyes and ears of scouts only tens of feet above the surface of the North Sea, and at sea it was only too easy for even experienced sailors to make errors in their own or the enemy's course and position. So far only Goodenough had given him clear and full reports; from Beatty had come little or nothing, either about the enemy or about his own battle. Yet the primary task of the battle cruisers was reconnaissance. In Jellicoe's own words: "Battle cruisers were designed and built in order that they might keep in touch with the enemy and report his movements when he had been found; hence the heavy guns they carried. They were intended to find the enemy for the Battle Fleet and to ascertain the enemy's strength in order to report to the Battle Fleet." [8]

Jellicoe and Scheer were now closing one another at a speed of fifty-six miles an hour; they were like blind men driving cars according to the instructions of others, but blind men who at any moment would regain direct sight and then have to decide the best way to deploy twenty or more battleships and issue clear orders accordingly, all at the speed with which a car driver avoids a dog.

At 5:40 P.M. another report from Goodenough confirmed Jellicoe's wrong impression that Scheer was ten miles east (further away) of where he actually was. Ten minutes earlier *Falmouth,* of Beatty's cruisers, made visual touch with *Black Prince,* in Jellicoe's own cruiser screen. At 5:33 P.M. Napier signalled *Black Prince*: "Battle cruisers engaged to SSW of me." Since Napier left out the word "our," *Black Prince* informed Jellicoe that *German* battle cruisers lay five miles to the south of her—that is, twenty-two miles from Scheer's guessed position. The two battle fleets were now only just concealed by the horizon, but Jellicoe was still virtually blind. Deployment of twenty-four battleships was a complex operation, especially since both Beatty and Hood had to effect a junction with the battle fleet and take their proper stations ahead of it. The choice of the type of deployment manoeuvre depended on a firm knowledge of the relative positions, speeds and courses of the British and German fleets. Where was Beatty? How had his battle gone? Most of all, where was the German battle fleet—exactly?

At 5:45 P.M., Rear-Admiral Sir Robert Arbuthnot, in *Black Prince* (Grand Fleet cruiser screen), sent another of that useless type of report that obscures rather than clarifies: "Battleships in action to the SSW."

At 5:50 P.M. came a clutch of three signals, including another model one from Goodenough whose contents correctly told Jellicoe that Scheer had turned north, that the battle-cruiser fleet was steering northeast. Commodore le Mesurier (*Calliope*) reported unidentified gun flashes to the south-southwest. Vice-Admiral Burney in *Marlborough,* leading ship in Jellicoe's own starboard wing column of battleships, reported "gun flashes and heavy firing on the starboard bow." Even for this vague information Jellicoe had to rely on his own battleships—an indication of the bad scouting of Beatty's battle cruisers, of the 1st and 3rd Cruiser

[8] Jellicoe, 306.

Squadrons with him, and even Jellicoe's own cruisers, but always excepting Goodenough.

The battle fleet was now running on through thickening mist; Jellicoe and his staff could hear the dull thundering of distant gunfire, but the mist muffled the direction. The decisive encounter was now only minutes away, but still Beatty remained silent. For a moment even Jellicoe's calm and self-control cracked: "I wish someone would tell me," he suddenly said to his staff, "who is firing and what they're firing at." [9]

In fact it was Beatty firing at both Hipper and Scheer. For Beatty had now been decisively beaten by Hipper alone and then had had to steam for his life away from Scheer as well. Perhaps that was why he had not carried out his basic task of sending back a constant flow of exact situation reports to *Iron Duke*.

Sir John Jellicoe, with his deep professional seriousness and interest in modern naval technology, was not at all typical of those who dominated the Royal Navy of 1916. Sir David Beatty was. Himself of the Anglo-Irish gentry, he had married the divorced daughter of Marshall Field, the American retail-store millionaire. She had bought him a steam yacht, a house in the Leicestershire hunting country and a Scottish grouse moor. Her money enabled Beatty to adopt an attitude of fine independence over questions of appointment and respect for seniors in the Service not open to a career officer without large private means like Jellicoe. However, there were disadvantages, as Beatty discovered after his marriage, for his wife was an unstable neurotic who caused him extreme mental tortures. It was all rather like the characters and plot of a play by Wilde or Pinero.

Beatty himself was an able and intelligent officer, but his origins, his social and sporting obligations and his own brave but highly strung temperament prevented him from becoming a coldly calculating professional like Jellicoe—or Hipper. It was characteristic that during the months of inactivity in 1914 and 1915 he should have expressed the private wish to fight as a soldier on the western front—but not as an artilleryman, rather as a cavalryman in a brisk charge. It was equally characteristic that on this afternoon of May 31, 1916, his flag lieutenant, on whose skill and cool head so much depended, was Ralph Seymour, a well-liked friend of

[9] Bacon, 265.

the most distinguished lineage, but not a qualified signal specialist, and indeed the man responsible for the confusion of signals at the battle of the Dogger Bank.

To a certain kind of uncritical admirer, Beatty, with his square thrusting jaw, the cap·worn at a slant, the dark hair worn long and thick, the thumbs rakishly stuck in the pockets of a monkey jacket with six buttons instead of the regulation eight, made a more Nelsonian figure than the small, inscrutable Jellicoe. They did not observe the private unhappiness and uncertainty in that hollow pose, how more like those of an actor-manager than a sailor were his good looks.

Jellicoe and Beatty were destined each to fight their own separate battle at Jutland; and it was Beatty who fought first.

At 2:15 P.M., finding that Jellicoe had not arrived at their rendezvous, Beatty steered to meet him. Hipper lay about forty miles to the east of Beatty, and Scheer about fifty miles south of Hipper. Between Hipper and Beatty lay a Danish freighter, *N. J. Fjord*. This innocent passer-by was the immediate cause of the battle of Jutland. At about 2 P.M., the German light cruiser *Elbing*, part of the west flank screen of Hipper's scouting group, spotted *N. J. Fjord* and sent two destroyers to stop her and investigate. A quarter of an hour later the *Galatea* (Commodore Alexander-Sinclair, 1st Light Cruiser Squadron, Battle Cruiser Fleet) saw to the eastwards the vertical column of smoke blown off by a halted ship. He steamed towards her and then saw the German vessels. At 2:18 P.M. he made a general flag signal: "Enemy in sight," and a radio report, received by both Beatty and Jellicoe. The presence of the enemy was a surprise to *Galatea*. "I was aft on the quarter-deck," recounted one of her officers, "quietly basking in the sun, and on hearing the bugle was in little hurry as I had heard that we were going to action stations for drill purposes some time during the afternoon. So I strolled forward to my station—a little homemade wireless office on the fo'c'sle. . . . But just as I went up the ladder . . . I was deafened by the report of the fo'c'sle 6-inch gun firing." [10]

Five minutes after receiving this signal, Beatty decided to steer for the Horn Reef to cut off the enemy. However, he made no general signal about his intentions to Rear-Admiral Evan-Thomas, commanding the 5th Battle Squadron; instead he made a specific signal to his fleet for a

[10] Fawcett and Hooper, 25-6.

change of course, which Seymour sent only by flag and not by search-light, although the *Lion*'s signal halyards were notoriously difficult to read because of the ship's design. Evan-Thomas could not read the flags and held to his existing course, while Beatty's battle cruisers steered away from him to starboard. By 2:40 P.M., when Evan-Thomas did in fact steer south-southeast, there was a ten-mile gap between his flagship *Barham* and *Lion*. Already faults in the customary British system of command had caused a dangerous division of strength. Both Beatty and Evan-Thomas were in error—Beatty for trying to give another flag officer specific detailed instructions rather than a general directive; Evan-Thomas for not using his initiative and common sense in following Beatty round without orders.

On the German side the system was very different. As soon as Hipper received *Elbing*'s radio report of *Galatea* and *Phaeton*'s presence at 2:27 P.M., he instantly swung the battle cruisers of Scouting Group 1 west-southwest and increased speed to eighteen knots; his cruisers and des-troyers followed the turn without orders.

Meanwhile Alexander-Sinclair with *Galatea* and *Phaeton* (each with three 6-inch guns) fought a sharp action with *Elbing* (four 5.9-inch guns) and German destroyers. In the thick of it Alexander-Sinclair radioed that he had seen smoke as from a fleet to the east-northeast. He did not try to get closer for more detailed information; *Elbing* hit *Galatea* under the bridge, and Alexander-Sinclair departed to the north-west, hotly pursued by *Elbing*.

At 2:31 P.M., just as tea was being served in the British ships, Beatty ordered "action stations." It was not until 3:15 P.M. that any of Beatty's battle cruisers got definite news of Hipper's presence; with the exception of Goodenough (2nd Light Cruiser Squadron), the rest of Beatty's cruisers (1st and 3rd Light Cruiser Squadrons) had been driven by German cruisers northwards, when they should have remained to the east. At 3:15 P.M. *New Zealand* sighted five enemy ships on the star-board bow. In the few minutes on either side of 3:25 P.M. both Hipper and Beatty sighted each other's ships at a distance of seventeen miles. Hipper could not see Evan-Thomas, still some 15,000 yards astern of the *Lion*, only Beatty's six battle cruisers. Although outnumbered five to six, he decided to engage without waiting for Scheer. One minute after Beatty had ordered action stations, Hipper called in his light cruisers

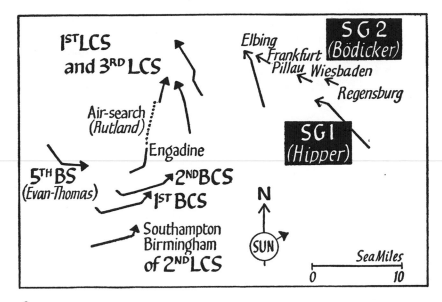

18. THE BATTLE CRUISERS MAKE CONTACT

(Scouting Group 2), sent a full radio report to Scheer and ordered fire distribution from the right. Beatty had made no signal as to his general intentions to Evan-Thomas, althought his plan was in fact to get between Hipper and his base. In the British way, only details of course and speed were signalled. Hipper was now steering northwest by west, Beatty northeast. At 3:30 P.M. Beatty changed to east; Evan-Thomas again did not follow him, and the battle cruisers and the fifth Battle Squadron again began to diverge. The blame may be apportioned as on the earlier occasion.

When Hipper in *Lützow* saw Beatty's ships swing on to their new course, he turned his own squadron almost about to southeast. Now, in these last few minutes before the guns fired, there was tremendous belated activity in Beatty's flagship. The 2nd Battle Cruiser Squadron (Rear-Admiral Pakenham) was ordered at this late stage to take station astern of the 1st. The fleet's speed was increased to twenty-four knots. Evan-Thomas was ordered, as if he were a private on a parade ground, to steer east at twenty-five knots but was still not told of the plan of battle. When Pakenham had reached his station, Beatty ordered the battle cruisers to change course in succession to ESE (100°) and at the same time a line of bearing NW (302°). It is noteworthy that in the dense traffic of signals the fleet's speed was given as twenty-four knots by flag, twenty-five by radio. Equally the position of the enemy as radioed to Jellicoe (and never corrected) differed from that given by the *Lion's* flags.

Seven minutes after Hipper had ordered a fresh fire distribution from the left, Beatty ordered the *Lion* and *Princess Royal* to concentrate on the leading German ship, his other ships to take one German each.

No dense traffic of last-minute arrangements emanated from *Lützow;* Hipper merely had to put the final polish on his dispositions. He knew his 11-inch and 12-inch guns were outranged by the 12-inch and 13.5-inch guns of the British ships and that therefore it was important for him to close as fast as possible. He therefore ordered a manoeuvre unknown to the British fleet orders—*gefechtswendung*—a rapid turn in succession, last ship first, to a designated course—in this case SSE. At 3:48 P.M. Hipper's squadron was steering at only eighteen knots, perfectly stationed in quarter line, every gun bearing, and with hulls at an oblique angle to British fire. At a speed therefore that made for perfect station-keeping and good gunnery, the pale-grey German ships, with their squat, piled superstructures, closed towards the distant British. It only remained for Hipper to signal the full situation to Scheer and open fire. The flags streamed from *Lützow's* halyards, and the five German ships fired simultaneously—a single rippling flicker of flame, a roaring concussion and a billow of smoke.

The British had been caught in the middle of a complex manoeuvre at twenty-five knots; they fired later and not together. The range was now 16,500 yards and decreasing rapidly.

"The visibility was good," wrote Beatty, "the sun behind us and the wind SE. Being between the enemy and his base [this was not in fact so], our situation was both strategically and tactically good." [11]

Yet owing to the errors and omissions of both Beatty and Evan-Thomas, really attributable to the rigid conceptions of obedience and hierarchy in the British service, Beatty's most powerful ships, the four modern 15-inch gun battleships of the 5th Battle Squadron, were mere distant spectators of a sea fight between six British and five German

[11] Chalmers, 229.

battle cruisers. Beatty had apparently committed the elementary mistake of failing to concentrate all his forces at the place and time of the decision. Should he instead have fallen back on the battleships, drawing

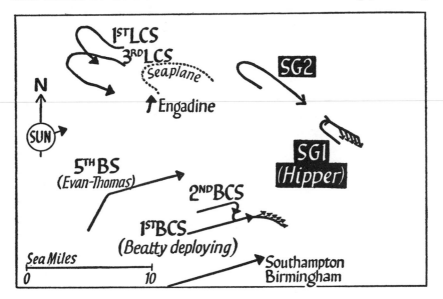

19. OPENING OF BATTLE CRUISER ACTION

Hipper after him? Beatty's admirers have thought that his decision to engage Hipper without Evan-Thomas was splendidly characteristic of a great sailor. Winston Churchill wrote:

> But Beatty's six battle cruisers were in themselves superior in numbers, speed and gun power to the whole of the German battle cruisers. . . . Why should he wait to become stronger when by every test of paper and every memory of battle he was already strong enough? . . . the fact, when at 2:32 Beatty decided that the enemy was present in sufficient strength to justify turning the heavy ships about, made it his clear duty to steam at once and at the utmost speed in their direction.[12]

Beatty's biographer, Rear-Admiral Chalmers, considered that "there was nothing rash in this decision. . . . He had yet to learn of the superiority of German materials and ship construction." [13]

[12] Churchill, 1025-6.
[13] Chalmers, 227.

Beatty himself remarked to his chief of staff in March 1916: "If I meet Hipper and his battle cruisers, I can deal with them."

It is thus agreed that Beatty's decision rested on the assumption that his ships were at least as good as the German. By contrast, all Jellicoe's plans and decisions rested on an opposite assumption. That Beatty and indeed Churchill were so ignorant of even the published facts is sufficient comment on their professional depth.

According to information public for two years before Jutland, the *Lion, Princess Royal, Queen Mary,* and *Tiger* had a 9-inch belt of armour amidships, 4-inch bow and stern, 9-inch on the main battery turrets. Their normal displacement was about 27,000 tons, and each was equipped with a main armament of eight 13.5 guns. *Derfflinger* and *Lützow* were protected by a 13-inch main midships belt, 4-inch bow and stern, both of these belts extending further along the ships' sides than in British vessels. The side armour reached up amidships to deck level, which was not so in the British ships. They displaced 28,000 tons and carried eight 12-inch guns. In addition there was four inches of deck armour. *Seydlitz,* although not as strong as *Derfflinger* and *Lützow,* was stronger in armour than the most modern British ships and carried ten 11-inch guns. Of the older ships in each fleet, *Indefatigable* and *New Zealand* displaced 18,750 tons, had main batteries of eight 12-inch guns and maximum side armour 8 inches thick; *Moltke* displaced 23,000 tons, had 11-inch side armour, main batteries of ten 11-inch guns; *von der Tann* (dating from 1909, the oldest vessel present) displaced 19,400 tons, carried eight 11-inch guns, and was in general more heavily armoured than the British ships completed in 1913.[14]

It is therefore difficult to resist the conclusion that Beatty turned to fight Hipper as he might have put his horse at a high fence in the hunting field. He paid terribly for his rashness.

At 3:48 P.M. Hipper had ordered his ships to fire; at 3:51 P.M. *Lion* was hit twice by *Lützow,* and a minute later *Tiger* was hit in the fo'c'sle by *Moltke.* All round the British ships the German salvoes were falling with an incredibly small spread, throwing up columns of spray and water a hundred feet into the hazy sky, water that came falling back across the British ships, drenching the bridges as if in a gale and upsetting gun laying, spotting and range taking. British shooting was ragged and

14 *Jane's Fighting Ships,* 1914.

wild; British shells were falling near the light cruiser *Regensburg* 2,000 yards beyond Hipper. In fact, the *von der Tann* was not fired at for some

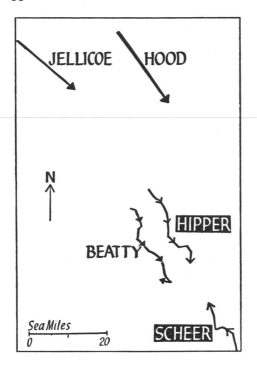

20. THE BATTLE CRUISER ACTION

time at all. This was partly owing to confusion as to the distribution of fire, as the signal for this was flying amid some of the other signals that had crowded *Lion*'s halyards and was not easy to see or read. It also seemed that the British did not appreciate how fast the range was closing. Beatty turned away 5 points to S by E (157°). Hipper, by his prompt and devastating bombardment, held the moral advantage.

Evan-Thomas, following Beatty, opened fire on the light cruisers of Scouting Group 2 (Rear-Admiral Bödicker) following Hipper, but the Germans turned away behind a smoke screen (a novelty to the British). Meanwhile Commodore Alexander-Sinclair in *Galatea*, away from whom the Germans and indeed the British had been steaming for some time, signalled: "Am I right in trying to lead the enemy?" In contrast to

« 141 »

this unenterprising officer, and Napier of 3rd Light Cruiser Squadron, Goodenough alone of Beatty's three cruiser squadron commanders carried out his proper task of scouting ahead of *Lion.*

At 3:45 P.M., with the range down to 13,000 yards, the 5.9-inch guns in the German secondary armaments opened fire. Shooting with cool accuracy and deliberation, the German ships scored hit after hit. *Moltke* landed two 11-inch shells on *Tiger,* hitting two main battery turrets and halving her rate of fire. *Lützow* hit *Lion* with a 12-inch shell, but luckily for Beatty it was high explosive, not armour-piercing. So far on the German side *Seydlitz* alone had been hit, probably by a 13.5-inch shell from the *Queen Mary,* but it only damaged an electrical switchboard. Beatty was beginning to feel the weight and accuracy of Hipper's fire; he signalled by flag and radio to his own ships for faster shooting and at the same time ordered his destroyers to get into the fight "at utmost speed." At 3:56 P.M. another salvo from *Moltke* crashed round *Tiger* and this time her shells cut deep into the British ship's hull, exploding with terrible effect, mangling and tearing structural steel, severing several steam lines and almost cutting the main one. In the hiss of escaping steam that followed the bursting of *Moltke*'s shells, as the ship reeked of fumes, the British engine-room staff worked with frenzied courage to keep *Tiger* steaming without loss of speed. Now *Derfflinger* landed two 12-inch shells on *Princess Royal*—one on "A" turret, the other putting the main control out of action for twenty minutes. Beatty turned another point away from the enemy.

At last, after eight minutes of shooting, the British scored their second hit; a 13.5-inch shell, probably from *Queen Mary,* smashed through eight inches of Krupp steel on *Seydlitz*'s "C" midships turret and down into the barbette. With a flash and a roar the powder charges blazed up, killing the turret's crew, and threatening the ship with total destruction should the flames reach the magazine. However, according to a carefully considered German emergency system, the magazine was instantly flooded. Meanwhile *Derfflinger* hit *Princess Royal* on "B" turret, forward and through the foremast and funnel. *Moltke* landed five shells on *Tiger* in seven minutes. At 4 P.M. *Lützow* hit *Lion* for the fourth time, her shell boring through "Q" turret amidships and bursting with horrifying effect inside. Like *Seydlitz* a few minutes earlier, *Lion* faced destruction by ignition of the magazine, but Major Harvey, of the Royal Marine Light

13. Admiral Sir John Jellicoe

14. Vice-Admiral Reinhard Scheer

15. Vice-Admiral Sir David Beatty

16. Vice-Admiral Franz Hipper

17. Jutland: the battle cruiser *Lion* being hit on a turret

18. The battle cruiser action: *Queen Mary* blows up

19. The German battle cruiser *Seydlitz* on fire

20. Commodore Goodenough   21. Vice-Admiral Sir Charles Madden

22. Kaiser Wilhelm II, in Grand Admiral's uniform,
talking to a dockyard worker

Infantry, although dying and mutilated, ordered the magazine to be flooded and saved the ship. *Lützow* and *Derfflinger* were also hit, but without great damage. Owing to Beatty's turns away, the range had now opened to 16,000 yards and the German 5.9-inch guns stopped firing. Although *Tiger* and *New Zealand* were both firing at *Moltke,* neither had scored a single hit in reply to five or six by the German ships.

At 4 P.M. Hipper turned away a point, and as the range opened quickly the British fire became wild again; the German shells still fell on and among the British ships in those uncannily tight salvoes. Three minutes later, with the range 17,000 yards, Beatty turned another three points away to southwest by south. A flag signal told the *Princess Royal* that the flagship's main radio had been wrecked.

The least successful German ship so far had been the old, small *von der Tann,* which had fired eleven four-gun 11-inch salvoes without making a single hit; but now, with the range widening, it was her opportunity, for her guns could be elevated to 20°, giving them a maximum range of about 22,400 yards. Flame rippled on the grey smudge in the haze that was *von der Tann* 17,000 yards away from *Indefatigable;* there was an interval of twenty-four to thirty seconds, and then three out of the four shells in the salvo smashed down on *Indefatigable.* A few minutes later, while *von der Tann* was carrying out a fleet order from Hipper to turn two points towards the British and form column on a course southeast by east, she hit *Indefatigable* abreast of the forward turret, three 11-inch shells piercing the turret and barbette armour. To the smoke reeking back from the quarter-deck from the previous hit now were added enormous rolling clouds of smoke from the fo'c'sle. Desperately wounded, *Indefatigable* sheered to port. Once more the cordite of a ship had been set ablaze; but here was no efficient emergency system, nor a dying hero; the flames flashed into the magazine and a colossal explosion threw smoke and débris higher than her masthead. *Indefatigable* rolled heavily to port and at 4:05 P.M. capsized; then the placid waters of the North Sea closed over her. Now it was five British against five German ships.

In all, Beatty had turned away nine points since fire was opened; although he now turned two points back towards Hipper, Beatty's course in the action so far constituted in fact a notable retirement. It had two effects: firstly, with the range now 22,000 yards, Scouting Group 1 ceased fire and gave Beatty's battered ships a moment's breathing space; secondly, it enabled Evan-Thomas to bring his battleships into action more quickly. The great 15-inch guns of *Barham* opened fire almost as Hipper ceased it. The *von der Tann,* last in the German line, was the target. It became an unequal fight between the battleships *Malaya, Warspite, Barham* and *Valiant,* and the two battle cruisers *von der Tann* and *Moltke.* It was a significant reward for Jellicoe's thorough care over gunnery in the battle fleet—under his direct command—that Evan-Thomas's ships shot accurately, although at extreme range and in thickening haze. *Von der Tann* took a 15-inch shell aft that did massive internal damage.

Seeing Evan-Thomas's great battleships coming into the battle, Beatty himself turned three points back towards Hipper, who had increased speed to draw away from Evan-Thomas. For Evan-Thomas, with the great range of his guns, it was an affair of target practice. Yet Hipper, knowing that Scheer was coming up from the south, fought it out with splendid coolness and courage—five battle cruisers against five battle cruisers and four of the most powerful and modern battleships afloat. At about 4:15 P.M. *Lion* and *Lützow* exchanged hits; whereas the British shells caused superficial damage, *Lützow's* exploded in *Lion's* mess decks, causing heavy casualties among the crew and setting the ship on fire. In *Lion,* as in all ships hit during the battle, a ghastly memento of Jutland for weeks afterwards was to be the smell of burned human flesh throughout the vessel. Smoke drifted thickly up into the haze, a heartening sight to the distant German ships.

Von der Tann was now fighting the *New Zealand, Warspite* and *Malaya;* after a 15-inch hit on her forward turret, she was reduced to two 11-inch guns. Nevertheless she hit *Barham* and then, shifting to *New Zealand,* hit her as well, although without causing much damage. In a duel between *Moltke* and *Tiger, Tiger* landed two 13.5-inch shells in reply to superficial hits. The British battle cruisers were shooting better now; the Germans continued to shoot with the same remorseless accuracy and closely bunched salvoes.

At 4:20 P.M. *Queen Mary* was hit in the "Q" turret amidships by a shell from either *Seydlitz* or *Derfflinger,* which were both firing at her. *Queen Mary* replied by hitting *Derfflinger* twice. However, four minutes later three 12-inch shells struck the British ship on or round "Q" turret—

it was another of those closely grouped salvoes. Within two minutes the *Queen Mary* had been struck by two more shells at about the same point. Smashed open deep into her hull by six heavy armour-piercing shells striking home in six minutes on a single part of the ship, the *Queen Mary* blew up with staggering violence, turned horrifyingly slowly over to port; then as she sank, her stern rose high in the air. An officer in *New Zealand* saw her go:

> At about 4:35 the stern of a ship projecting about seventy feet out of the water, with the propellers revolving slowly, drifted into the field of my glasses; clouds of white paper were blowing out of her after hatch, and on her stern I read *"Queen Mary."* She passed us about a hundred yards on our port beam, and a moment later there was a blinding flash, a dull heavy roar, which ceased as suddenly as it began, followed by a few seconds' silence, and then the patter of falling debris. All that was left of the *Queen Mary* was a great mushroom-shaped cloud of smoke about 600 to 800 feet high.[15]

About this time it was the opinion of a midshipman in *Princess Royal* that instead of Hipper's outnumbered and outgunned battle cruisers "we are fighting the whole High Seas Fleet." [16] About this time also Beatty received a false report that the *Princess Royal* too had been sunk. He turned to his flag captain and said: "Chatfield, there seems to be something wrong with our bloody ships today. Turn two points to port" (i.e. nearer Hipper).[17]

This remark has been widely taken to redound to Beatty's credit; but was not his realisation about his ships' weakness needlessly belated? Was it so splendid to turn two points towards Hipper, when he still enjoyed a superiority of eight capital ships to five, and when he had in fact so far turned a total of four points away from Hipper?

It was time for Hipper to break off the unequal battle; at 4:27 P.M. he ordered Scouting Group 1 to turn away together to SE (122°); as the German battle cruisers swung, three more shells hit *Princess Royal*. On *Lion* flames and smoke leaped and billowed amidships. A confused *mêlée* between cruisers and destroyers took place between the battle lines as the ships receded from each other.

[15] Fawcett and Hooper, 36.
[16] *ibid,* 33.
[17] Churchill, 1029.

At 4:33 P.M. the invaluable Goodenough's searchlight blinked out to *Lion* stirring news: "Battleships SE."

Beatty with his usual courage steered towards the reported battleships to see for himself; having seen, he countermarched. As his remaining battle cruisers turned, Hipper fired. *Lützow* hit *Lion* twice, causing more raging fires; *Seydlitz* hit *Tiger,* but without hurting her.

At 4:45 P.M. Beatty turned north; it was well timed, for at about the same moment Scheer brought his battleships into action at 21,000 yards. Their fire hit nothing. Goodenough, surely the true hero of the day, stayed amid a deluge of heavy shells from Battle Squadron 1 to radio a full contact report to Jellicoe.

Beatty, now outnumbered by twenty-one capital ships to eight, correctly intended to stay out of Scheer's grip and lead him north into Jellicoe's battle fleet. Once again, however, he did not confide his intentions to Evan-Thomas and leave that admiral to take suitable action; he issued a specific order to him to countermarch to starboard. This meant that Evan-Thomas's ships would have to turn 180° one by one round a fixed point, towards which Scheer was steaming at twenty-one knots, and then follow astern of Beatty during the run north. In fact Evan-Thomas was still steering south when, to his astonishment, he was passed by Beatty steering north. Evan-Thomas did not even know Scheer was coming up. During and after his turn Evan-Thomas was heavily shelled by the leading German battleships *Kronprinz, Kaiserin, Grosser Kurfürst* and *König. Barham,* for example, was hit several times by 12-inch shells, with heavy loss of life and the destruction of her main and auxiliary radios.

The battle had now become a running chase to the north, with Hipper's Scouting Group trying to catch Beatty, and Scheer and the High Seas Fleet trying to catch Evan-Thomas, who, owing to Beatty's orders, was unpleasantly close to the German battleships. It was now that the British received another and unwelcome surprise. The *Queen Elizabeth* class battleships were supposed to be four knots faster than the *Königs;* now Evan-Thomas found that going at his utmost speed he was hardly gaining on Scheer.

Meanwhile eight British cruisers of the 1st and 3rd Light Cruiser Squadrons retired before four German light cruisers of Scouting Group 2.

All through the long chase Evan-Thomas's ships shot splendidly; his squadron redeemed a sad afternoon for the British by taking on not only

Hipper but Scheer's leading battleships. From 5 P.M. to 5:10 P.M. *Seydlitz* was hit again and again; *Warspite* hit *Grosser Kurfürst* and *Malaya* the *Markgraf*. At this stage only the *Barham* was hit among the British ships. At 5:05 Scheer signalled a general directive for the chase north and left his divisional commanders to choose their speeds and courses, a method of command unheard of in the Royal Navy.

Between 5:10 P.M. and 5:40 P.M. a vicious running battle took place between Hipper's exhausted battle cruisers and Evan-Thomas's battle ships, with Scheer still too far astern to intervene decisively. Hipper's ships were terribly punished by accurately directed 15-inch shells—no less than twelve of them. *Von der Tann* was still in the line, although her guns were silent now; but the exhausted and dazed crews of her fellow ships maintained the extraordinary accuracy that came from fifteen years (not, as with the British, three) of long-range gunnery training—and Evan-Thomas's ships took thirteen German 11-inch shells, which inflicted severe damage, especially on *Warspite* and *Malaya* (4° list to starboard). The action between Evan-Thomas's ships and Hipper's illustrated the defects of British equipment perhaps more than the battle cruisers' encounter. Whereas the British battle cruisers had been *sunk* by 11-inch and 12-inch shells, the German battle cruisers had survived 15-inch hits and, except in the case of *von der Tann,* survived in good fighting order. All Jellicoe's forebodings had been proved by the trial of battle—and before his main fleet had become engaged.

Where was Beatty during Evan-Thomas's superb rear-guard action? He was heading for the Grand Fleet at his utmost speed, his guns silent from 5:10 P.M. to 5:40 P.M., a third of his force sunk, a decisively beaten admiral.

At 5:55 P.M. Jellicoe, still running on into the thick haze of the afternoon to the sound of continual and as yet unexplained heavy gunfire, signalled the *Marlborough,* leading ship in his starboard wing division: "What can you see?"

For five minutes Jellicoe waited for the reply. Then came *Marlborough*'s answer: "Our battle cruisers bearing SSW (189°) steering east (77°). *Lion* leading ship."

Jellicoe, his small figure now clad in a belted burberry with a scarf knotted at the neck, peered at the hazy line of sea and sky to the south-

southwest; in a few moments he and his staff saw *Lion* for themselves at a distance of five miles—not, however, as expected from previous reports dead ahead, but on the starboard bow. This was because both Beatty and Jellicoe had miscalculated their positions. She was not a cheering sight; smoke was clearly visible pouring from the port side of her fo'c'sle, and she and her fellow ships were steaming through German shell splashes that resembled a forest of momentary grey poplars. Jellicoe instantly signalled Beatty: "Where is the enemy's battle fleet?"

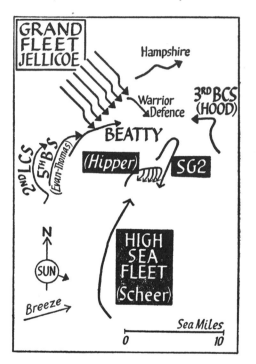

21. BATTLE FLEET ACTION—EVE OF DEPLOYMENT

Even now Jellicoe had not been given the information he needed for the critical and instantaneous decision of how best to deploy. The two battle fleets must almost be in sight; the last seconds were passing; and still no word from Beatty. While he waited, Jellicoe turned his battleship divisions together to the south and slowed to eighteen knots; when the moment came to deploy, he would be absolutely ready. Jellicoe was superb at foresight over detail—not only the detail of his own role as fleet commander, but characteristically of others' tasks. As long ago as 3 P.M. he had mentioned a minor fire precaution to his flag captain: "Dreyer, I expect you intend to put water in the cover of the sailing pinnace." [18]

At 5:40 P.M. he had asked Dreyer to take ranges in various directions and report to him the best direction, from the point of view of gunnery, to engage a fleet coming north.

"I reported to him that the most favourable direction was to the southward and would draw westward as the sun sank." [19]

As Beatty raced across the front of the battle fleet, dense smoke pouring from the twelve funnels of his four surviving ships, no flags or searchlight showed on *Lion* to answer Jellicoe's question "Where is the enemy battle fleet?"

Instead at 6:05 P.M. *Lion* sent the useless information that the enemy battle cruisers bore southeast. At 6:06 P.M., hearing heavy gunfire from that direction, Jellicoe turned his battleships from south to southeast. Two minutes later he ordered his destroyers to form a screen to port, the first indication that this might be the direction of fleet deployment. However, he made no general signal of his tactical intentions to his divisional commanders, who had to wait for specific orders before learning the plan of battle. On *Iron Duke*'s forebridge, among his staff, Jellicoe kept his counsel. As the margin of time narrowed and vanished, like the distance between the invisible fleets, as two great national rivalries, expressed by sixteen years of preparation, converged to collision point, Jellicoe himself reached the end of the line along which he had been steadily moving since that day in 1876 when he first put on the blue coat of the Royal Navy. He stood staring impassively ahead, showing no sign of the extreme test of nerve he was undergoing. For he was determined not to make a premature and possibly wrong deployment on the basis of vague information; he was going to hold on at eighteen knots until he knew exactly the bearing of the enemy.

At 6:10 P.M. Evan-Thomas in *Barham* signalled Jellicoe by flag and radio: "Enemy battle fleet south-southeast (145°)."

This signal from a battle squadron in the rear of the battle-cruiser

[18] Dreyer, 124.
[19] *ibid*, 145.

fleet was another proof of the failure of Beatty and his scouting forces (always excepting Goodenough) to comprehend and carry out their proper role.

Ahead of the battle fleet funnel smoke from dozens of vessels at full speed rose into the thick atmosphere and spread in a pall, as the Grand Fleet cruisers and destroyers raced for their battle stations. There was much confusion among the light forces. Still no word came from Beatty.

At last, thirteen minutes after Jellicoe had sent him the desperately urgent question as to Scheer's bearing, a searchlight blinked in *Lion,* and Jellicoe listened to the signalman on *Iron Duke*'s forebridge repeat the signal word by word: "Have sighted enemy Battle Fleet. Bearing SSW."

The steel tips on Jellicoe's heels clicked on the deck as he walked with his quick step to the standard compass. He stared for a half minute in silence at the magnetic compass card, while his staff watched him and his twenty-four battleships steamed on into the haze.

> I watched his keen, brown, weather-beaten face with tremedous interest, wondering what he would do [wrote his flag captain]. I realised as I watched him that he was as cool and unmoved as ever. Then he looked up and broke the silence with the order in his crisp, clear-cut voice to Commander A. R. W. Woods, the Fleet Signal Officer:
>
> "Hoist equal-speed pendant southeast."

The order astonished the others on the forebridge; this method of deployment was very unusual and had never been practised by the fleet. It was to be the subject of controversy for many years, a sign of Jellicoe's tactical mastery to his adherents, a proof of his excessive decision-losing caution to his critics.

Jellicoe's problem was to alter the disposition of his battleships from the order of cruising in six divisions abeam of four ships each (thus presenting the smallest possible target to submarines) into a line of battle (allowing the broadsides of all his twenty-four battleships to bear on the enemy at the same time). It was Scheer's sortie that had led to the present encounter; therefore it was for Jellicoe, not for Scheer, to fear a submarine trap. Scheer was already in action against Beatty and Evan-Thomas. These were the two reasons for Scheer being already disposed in line ahead. Jutland and the sea battles of the Second World War were in fact to show that Jellicoe's fear of a general torpedo attack by submarines before the fleets met did not materialise; this, however, does not prove that his fears *before the event* were unjustified. Thus Jellicoe's cruising order was very different from an order of fighting, and Jellicoe was correct to keep to it until the moment of contact.

As an order of fighting, Jellicoe had a general choice between the single line ahead and a decentralisation of his fleet into divisions—operating independently but in mutual support. Almost all the great battles of the age of sail had been fought between fleets passing in parallel single lines; and the weaker fleet, providing it had the weather gauge, almost always escaped because it had not been gripped. At the battles of St. Vincent (by an inspiration of the moment) and Trafalgar (by design) the British fought in two divisions which broke through the enemy line and annihilated the portion thus cut off. It was the innovation of a brilliant sailor (Nelson), made possible by superlative seamanship and gunnery. It depended on the superiority of British leadership and initiative over the enemy. Nelson had this confidence in his fleet. Jellicoe, on the other hand, wished to keep his fleet tightly under his own control, with its strength in no way divided. Deployment into line ahead was the result of the naval traditions of strict and rigid obedience in which Jellicoe had spent his life, of the quality of his ships and officers, and of his own character.

In view of the performance of Beatty's and his own cruiser squadrons —except for Goodenough—limp, bewildered and ineffective—and of Evan-Thomas's and Beatty's misunderstandings over simple and obvious manoeuvres, it is difficult to believe that Jellicoe was wrong to centralise his battle fleet and its tactics. The truth was that the Grand Fleet was only capable of rigid textbook manoeuvres, and Jellicoe was coolheaded enough to realise it.

He was going to deploy into single line ahead; but in which direction? He had the enemy's bearing, but not his course and speed. It was a matter of swift guesswork. In half a minute he had to decide what the relative positions and courses of the two fleets would be when they sighted each other. If Jellicoe crossed Scheer's "T," the broadsides of twenty-four battleships would bear on sixteen German ships able to reply only with guns firing forward. If Jellicoe misjudged the point and direction of the fleets' contact, Scheer instead would have the decisive advantage of crossing Jellicoe's "T." If Jellicoe deployed on his starboard wing column, or even on his centre, he ran the risk of leading his fleet into Scheer's broadside, if the German admiral were in fact already further to the north than unreliable and uncertain reports indicated. At least he ran the risk of being caught in the middle of deployment.

That was one consideration; the other was the question of visibility for gunnery, which, as Jellicoe had already found out, favoured firing to the south and then to the west. Lastly, as he had told the Admiralty in his letter of October 1914, there was an advantage in side-stepping to a flank to avoid a submarine trap.

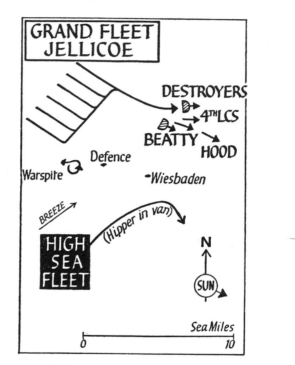

22. THE GRAND FLEET'S DEPLOYMENT

Thus, if he deployed on his port wing column, he would be certain of getting across in front of Scheer, of avoiding submarines, and also of enjoying the best possible visibility for range finding. By making this deployment an equal-speed manoeuvre he also ensured the maximum cohesion of the fleet, especially in terms of gunnery. The manoeuvre was as follows: the port wing division continued to steam in the general direction south-southeast, while in succession the other divisions turned first into line north-northeast and then again south-southeast following the port wing division.

Of the critics of Jellicoe's deployment at Jutland the most famous and most widely read was Winston Churchill in his book *The World Crisis*. The entire passage displays a fascinating struggle between Churchill's intelligence in recognising that Jellicoe was right and his belligerent emotions characteristically refusing to accept cold truths. He asserts: "Our present knowledge leads us to the conclusion that he could have deployed on the starboard wing column without misadventure," but adds: "The Commander-in-Chief chose the safer course. No one can say that on the facts as known to him at the moment it was a wrong decision." If in fact a deployment to starboard had led to heavy losses from torpedoes or gunfire, "there would have been no lack of criticism upon the imprudence of the Admiral's decision. And criticism would have been the least of the consequences." [20]

Churchill's own solution embodied that theorising from the map or chart, remote from the realities of modern battle, that was to be his worst fault as a war leader. He suggested that the fleet should have deployed behind Jellicoe's own left-centre column. The glibness of Churchill's own words and the complication of the evolutions he so lightly describes constitute an adequate comment on his suggestions: "It involved every ship in the two port divisions either reducing speed or making a complete left-handed circle to avoid losing speed, while the starboard divisions were

[20] Churchill, 1046.

taking their places behind the Commander-in-Chief. But the Fleet was not under fire [it might have come under fire at any moment—*Author's Note*] and the manoeuvre was practical." [21]

A letter from Jellicoe to his wife written soon after the battle gives a clue to the real problems facing him: "It was very misty indeed so there was a good chance of my missing him altogether [Evan-Thomas? Beatty?], but the sound of firing helped me, and at 5:40 we had got into touch, but it was so thick that I could not make out the situation for a long time. I saw firing going on from right ahead, where our Cruisers were engaging enemy Cruisers, to the quarter where our 5th Battle Squadron were fighting, and apparently Beatty was on the beam. I had to chance it so formed line of battle, and as luck would have it I got it between Beatty and Evan-Thomas." [22]

When Woods, the fleet signal officer, heard Jellicoe's order to deploy, he suggested: "Would you make it a point to port, sir, so that they will know it is on the port-wing column?"

"Very well," answered Jellicoe. "Hoist equal-speed pendant SE by E."

The signal ran up *Iron Duke*'s halyard, was tapped out in her radio room. While ships were still acknowledging, Jellicoe gave the order: "Dreyer, commence the deployment."

Two short blasts sounded on *Iron Dukes* siren, two small plumes of steam, and then her helm went over. In each of the other six columns, two blasts sounded from the sirens of the leading ships, and then they as well began to swing, leaving a wide curving swathe of wake in the paths of the ships behind them. It was 6:15 P.M. Jellicoe himself had not seen an enemy battleship. Scheer, however, steaming at twenty-one knots into the grey mist that hid Jellicoe so near to the northward, did not even expect to meet the main body of the Grand Fleet until the morrow.

---

21 *loc. cit.*
22 Jellicoe, Private Papers. Copy letter of June 7, 1916; the sketch above is from this letter.

7

The campaign of the Marne had taken a month to reach its decision: Joffre had had time to make and repair at least two major strategic miscalculations. The speed of advance in the trench battles of 1915 and 1916 had been measured in yards per week rather than in miles per hour. Beatty, on the other hand, had suffered heavy losses and had been well beaten in the course of an hour and a half. It was, as Churchill pointed out, possible for Jellicoe to lose the war during the afternoon and evening of May 31, 1916. Strategic and tactical decisions carrying the weight of future history would thus have to be made in the battle almost instantaneously, amid the heaving fountains of the enemy's shell splashes and the roar and shudder of *Iron Duke*'s own broadsides, not matured in a quiet château as a battle at walking pace smouldered away like a slow fuse. And mistakes would be irreparable, for repair needs time, and with fleets manoeuvring at a combined speed of up to forty knots, there would be no time.

The war pivoted now on this sea fight. The destruction of the High Seas Fleet would have enormous and immediate moral effects in Germany, already depressed by the barren results of her great eastern land victories of 1915 and the bloody failure of the assault on Verdun. The immediacy of a defeat at sea, the fearsome precision of its list of losses—as America was to discover at Pearl Harbor—provide a quality of sudden catastrophe absent from the swiftest and most complete of twentieth-century land defeats. For a sea defeat is a matter of the newspaper headlines of a single day. To the allies, for whom the war had brought so far few great successes, occupation and massacre in the field, a decisive British victory would bring a corresponding elation.

Beyond these immediate moral results lay the strategic consequences of German defeat. The North Sea right up to the German coast would fall to the unchallenged control of the Royal Navy. The narrow and limited exits used by German submarines could be densely patrolled and mined; the submarine campaign against allied shipping in 1917 that so nearly won the war for Germany would have been crippled. The hunt for those submarines that still reached the Atlantic would have been eased because a large proportion of the hundred destroyers guarding the battleships of the Grand Fleet could have become convoy escorts. The British Isles would be henceforth completely safe from raids or invasion, allowing concentration of all fit military manpower on the battle front.

The heavy demands of the fleet for guns and ammunition, which the army in France still lacked, would have fallen away. Above all, there was Russia, Scandinavia and the Baltic. With the main power of the High Seas Fleet destroyed, the Royal Navy could enter the Baltic through the Skagerrak and Kattegat, cutting the supplies of Swedish iron ore and other metals that were essential to German war industry. It would be possible to sail convoys to Russian Baltic ports—convoys carrying the guns, rifles and ammunition that could transform the Tzarist armies from gallant but half-armed mobs into Germany's greatest and most formidable enemy. For the Russians were beginning to fail now, despite the victories they had won and the victory of summer 1916 they were about to win—their morale corroded steadily by want of even such rudimentary equipment as rifles and bullets for assault troops. Plentiful sea-borne supplies from Britain and America might have prevented the collapse and dissolution in Russia a year later that gave the Communists their opportunity.

All these possibilities—probabilities—would be scotched and in some cases reversed if Scheer could succeed in fighting a detached portion of Jellicoe's fleet and destroying it. Germany's North Sea and Baltic Sea routes to Scandinavia would be safe. Russia would be permanently cut off from her allies. Allied and neutral public opinion would be stunned by a defeat at sea of the legendary Royal Navy. A submarine campaign could be backed by German battle squadrons free to make long sea cruises. The long British coast line would be so vulnerable to German landings that more British troops would have to be devoted to home defence. And the need for the British to build and crew fresh ships to replace those lost in a defeat would throw enormous weight on Britain's already overstrained munitions industry.

Too much thus hung on the irrevocable decisions of a moment for either the British or German admiral to take risks except when in desperate danger.

Of their total battle fleets, both admirals had at Jutland a similar proportion. In modern (*Dreadnought*) battleships Jellicoe had a huge numerical superiority—twenty-eight [1] to sixteen. Scheer's six obsolete battleships, because of their slowness, want of gunpower and their vulnerability, were a liability and should never have been brought to sea. In battle cruisers British superiority at the beginning of the Fleet action was seven to five, although *von der Tann* had no turret guns ready for action. In armoured (heavy) cruisers the British had eight, the Germans none. In destroyers Jellicoe had with him seventy-three, Scheer sixty-one. Despite the importance of the submarine in naval thinking before Jutland, neither fleet had a single submarine in company—both Scheer and Jellicoe had steamed to Jutland too fast for them to keep up.

Nevertheless the British had failed to concentrate all possible forces in the sea area off Jutland. It was another unhappy example of the Admiralty's operational feebleness. At Harwich lay Tyrwhitt with thirty-five destroyers, fretting with frustrated belligerence, waiting for orders. At 5:10 P.M. he signalled the Admiralty: "I am proceeding to sea."

The Admiralty replied: "Return at once and await order." Since the orders never came, Jellicoe was denied the help of Tyrwhitt's ships where his own superiority was at its narrowest—in destroyers. Tyrwhitt was kept in port in case a stray German cruiser should break a few tiles and windows in the towns along the east coast.

As Tyrwhitt fretted, Jellicoe was deploying. German heavy shells were beginning to pitch round *Iron Duke* and the ships in the columns to starboard of her as they made the first turn into line on a course northnortheasterly—a proof that in fact Scheer was too close for Jellicoe to have deployed safely on the starboard wing column. At 5:20 P.M. *Iron Duke* had made the second turn to southeast by east. Within five minutes

[1] Once Evan-Thomas had joined him.

of Jellicoe's order to deploy, with the deployment half completed, the twenty-four British battleships were in a single line, partly parallel to Scheer's own course and partly steering across his front.

The junction of Jellicoe, Beatty, Evan-Thomas and Hood in the presence of the enemy and in a joint deployment caused confusions probably unavoidable, but fine ship handling prevented any disasters. Hood's 3rd Battle Cruiser Squadron, having hit and stopped the German cruiser *Wiesbaden* and driven off the cruisers of Bödicker's Scouting Group 4, took station ahead of Beatty. Evan-Thomas did not attempt to follow Beatty right across the Grand Fleet but took his alternative station astern of Jellicoe's battle line with his four battleships. The major shortcoming in the final deployment lay in the situation of Jellicoe's cruiser squadrons and destroyers, who, owing to the lateness of their orders, could not reach their stations ahead of the fleet, although rolling great clouds of smoke into the battleships' vision in their attempts to get there. Indeed the greater part of the British destroyer forces was to port of the battleships and could neither protect Jellicoe's line nor attack Scheer's.

The sea was calm, oily, lazy; the sun (N 54° W) shone through shifting mists that could suddenly open into long avenues of clear vision and as suddenly close again.

The opening of the main action at Jutland was very different from that of the battle-cruiser action. Neither admiral ordered a distribution of fire; neither ordered fire to be opened; and there was no instant general cannonade. Smoke, mist and confusion prevented such a neat collision. Hipper's running fight with Beatty to the north gradually became a fight with Hood as well; and as Beatty's course changed in a slow arc from north to southeast by east, Hipper to the south of him conformed. Astern of Hipper, Scheer, who only knew that Hipper and Bödicker were heavily involved in the grey mists with enemy ships of undisclosed type and number, apparently to the northeast, steered in Hipper's wake. Scheer's fight with Evan-Thomas now became more general as his leading ships began to fire at Jellicoe's rear divisions still steering north-northeast to the turning point. *Warspite,* heavily hit and with rudder jammed, was circling at twenty-five knots, the elusive target of *Friedrich der Grosse, König, Helgoland, Ostfriesland, Thüringen* and *Kaiserin.*

A curious tragedy now took place between the main fleets before they became engaged. Rear-Admiral Sir Robert Arbuthnot, Bart., a famous rider to hounds, in the light cruiser *Defence,* steamed out from the British line towards Scheer's battleships, intent on sinking the blazing and stationary *Wiesbaden,* although his proper role was reconnaissance. Arbuthnot did not appear to see the German battleships; he did not even see *Lion,* which had to sheer violently to starboard to miss him. Before the eyes of both fleets *Defence* was blown out of the water at 6:20 P.M., a spectacle more encouraging to Scheer's fleet than to Jellicoe's.

Not until after 6:20 P.M. had funnel smoke sufficiently cleared to allow Jellicoe's seven-mile line of ships to see the sun clearly shining through the mist on to Scheer's leading vessels. "I could not of course make out anything for certain at the time," [2] wrote Jellicoe to his wife a week later. However, he drew a little diagram to illustrate the position of the fleets as he believed it to be. In the meantime *Iron Duke* and other British battleships fired at *Wiesbaden* as they passed. When Dreyer, Jellicoe's flag captain, saw three *Königs* 12,000 yards off the starboard beam on a converging course with the British, he asked Jellicoe for permission to fire. He was told to wait until Jellicoe was sure they were German ships. Jellicoe ordered him to fire at 6:30 P.M. Both the requesting of permission and the delay in its granting are interesting. The German course was now only converging with the British, not crossing it at right angles, because Battle Squadron 1 had followed Hipper round from north to east; at the moment of actual contact Scheer's "T" was not crossed. Nevertheless Jellicoe's deployment had placed Scheer in a corral —there were British ships on his flank and ahead of him. Suddenly Scheer realised he was inside a trap:

> The German van [in the words of the German official history] was faced by the belching guns of an interminable line of heavy ships extending from northwest to northeast, while salvo followed salvo, almost without intermission, an impression which gained in power from the almost complete inability of the German ships to reply to this fire, as not one of the British battleships could be distinguished through the smoke and mist.[3]

This crushing British advantage in terms of deployment and visibility was perhaps Jellicoe's greatest achievement. Now, too, his long care over gunnery was also rewarded; from 6:30 P.M. to 6:40 P.M. his battle-

[2] Jellicoe Private Papers. Copy letter of June 6, 1916. The sketch on p. 153 is from this letter.
[3] *Der Krieg zur See* 1914-18: *Nord See,* Band 5.

ships and battle cruisers fired forty salvoes, inflicting twelve hits on the *Markgraf, König, Lützow* and *Derfflinger. Lützow* had now absorbed twenty heavy shells without sinking or leaving the line. *König* was listing 4½°. Along the grey blur where sea, mist and smoke merged to the north of the German ships the British gun flashes sparkled; hardly a shot was fired by the blind and helpless High Seas Fleet.

Then at 6:31 P.M. the mists shifted and 9,500 yards away from Hipper's battle cruisers down a long avenue of clarity lay *Invincible.* It was three hours now that Hipper's ships had been in constant heavy battle, but at this fleeting and lucky opportunity of a target, *Lützow* and *Derfflinger* began another demonstration of astonishing gunnery. *Derfflinger* straddled with her first salvo, *Lützow* with her second. Two minutes later both ships fired together, and two closely grouped salvoes smashed into *Invincible* amidships. A shell burst inside "Q" turret, blew its roof off, fired the cordite charges, exploded the magazine. *Invincible* broke in half and sank immediately, carrying with her Vice-Admiral Sir Horace Hood. Yet her bow and stern remained above the surface, a macabre monument to British marine technology. As the Grand Fleet passed her, each ship could read *Invincible* on the stern part of the wreck. *Lützow* herself was heavily hit forward and, badly down by the bows, had to leave the line at 6:37 P.M. She had now been struck by twenty-two heavy shells and she was still afloat.

The ten minutes from 6:30 P.M. to 6:40 P.M. were for Scheer a battle crisis and a personal crisis. He had led his fleet of sixteen modern battleships into a close-range general action with twenty-eight British, a situation which it was the fundamental intention of German strategy to avoid. The principal cause of this was the absence of advanced information such as had been furnished to Jellicoe by the Admiralty by means of intercepted and deciphered signals. The Germans had not broken the British naval code, nor had Jellicoe made his early orders in port by radio. Because of the conditions of visibility, his ships could not reply at all to the British fire; and the British fleet had an advantage in pursuit of at least four knots, because of the presence of German pre-*Dreadnoughts;* Scheer and his fleet were in desperate danger.

At 6:36 P.M. the signal mast of *Friedrich der Grosse* flew a signal ordering a manoeuvre unknown to the British fleet: "*Gefechtskehrtwendung nach steuerbord* [Battle-turn to starboard]."

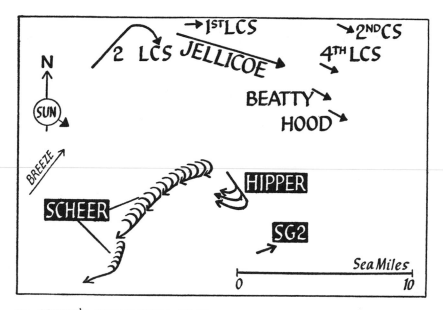

23. SCHEER'S BATTLE-TURN AWAY

Each German battleship turned 180° in succession from the rear, so that within a few minutes the High Seas Fleet was steering west away from Jellicoe at sixteen knots. *König,* the leading ship, vanished like a ghost into the mists. The British fire died away. No British manoeuvre could make a fleet disappear with such hallucinatory swiftness, and Jellicoe was baffled: "I could not see him turn away from where I was on top of the charthouse, nor could anyone else with me." [4]

"I imagined this disappearance of the enemy to be due merely to the thickening of the mist, but after a few minutes had elapsed it became clear that there must be some other reason and at 6:44 I hauled up one point to southeast and at 6:55 four more points to south, signalling at the same time to Sir Cecil Burney [*Marlborough,* 6th Division] to ask if he could see any of the enemy's battleships, and received a reply in the negative." [5]

In a private letter to Lady Jellicoe on June 7 describing the battle, Jellicoe drew a diagram to show the situation at this moment as it ap-

[4] Dreyer, 166.
[5] *ibid,* 133-4.

peared to him. "As they turned away," he wrote, "our ships in the rear shelled them badly, and the situation was as far as I could make out about this time:"

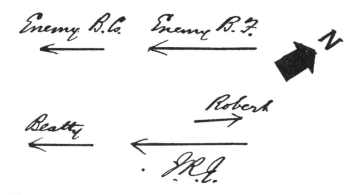

In imagining at this time that the fleets were on anything like parallel courses, Jellicoe was wildly wrong, an indication of the confusion that is an inseparable part of such a battle.

Yet battleships astern of Jellicoe had actually seen the German ships turn, but they neither turned themselves nor informed Jellicoe. Jellicoe's light cruisers equally told him nothing, possibly because they were not near enough to Scheer to know anything. Whatever the Fleet Battle Orders might say about divisional initiative, the fact was that now and throughout the rest of the battle the British fleet operated as a single cumbersome unit seven miles long, responding with passive obedience only to the specific orders of the Commander-in-Chief. Not even Beatty, commanding the scouting group (to use the German term), acted independently. He headed the battle line but did no scouting. This was not entirely his fault, for Jelicoe gave him no general directives in the course of the battle. Jellicoe has been reproached for not plunging his whole fleet into the mist after Scheer; but it was the task of the fast, big-gunned battle cruisers to find and report on the enemy fleet. Nor did either the battle-cruiser or the battleship divisions think it worth while to pass on all they saw to the flagship; it was too often assumed that what they could see, Jellicoe must be able to see as well.

However, there was no question but that Scheer's swift turn had saved his fleet, and that if Jellicoe wished to bring his sixteen battleships and six pre-*Dreadnoughts* under the guns of his twenty-eight battleships again, as during that gratifying ten minutes from 6:30 P.M. to 6:40 P.M., he would have to hunt Scheer down through the mists. For the British this was the second great battle decision. The past and the future breathed down Jellicoe's neck as he made it:

> The light was extremely baffling. These conditions were ideal for an attack by enemy destroyers and it was also quite possible that mines might be dropped by the enemy's light cruisers in rear of the retiring fleet. . . . Lastly the direction in which the enemy had retired was not known. For these reasons it was advisable to move further to the southeastward before attempting a larger closing movement.[6]

Jellicoe's refusal to be drawn was in no way a failure of nerve; it was nearly two years now since he had told the Admiralty that he would not pursue directly a retiring fleet because of the risk of mines and torpedoes. And while he was gazing at the baffling mists that had so suddenly covered Scheer, there came reports that seemed to prove the soundness of his thinking. Beatty radioed at 6:45 P.M. that there was a submarine in sight. At 6:57 P.M. *Marlborough* reported she had been hit by a mine or a torpedo and a minute later confirmed it was a torpedo—probably, although *Marlborough* did not know this, from the devoted *Wiesbaden* which still fired vigorously at anybody incautious enough to steer in range. At 7 P.M. the *Duke of Edinburgh* made a flag signal of a submarine on her port bow.

In terms of Jellicoe's knowledge at the time, a chase into the mists might reasonably have found him firstly losing ships to torpedoes and then coming suddenly on Scheer's battle line, drawn across his course—he might have been in the same kind of trap as Scheer had been at 6:30 P.M. Neither Jellicoe, with his orderly, methodical mind, nor his subordinate admirals, nor his seven-mile line of battle, nor British training, doctrine and command methods were suited to a loose, fast, fluid scramble. Once again Jellicoe was realistic enough to face the truth.

Now Scheer was eleven miles away to the west. Jellicoe still held the great strategic advantage of being across Scheer's escape routes home—Jellicoe's southeasterly and then southerly course had shepherded Scheer away into the North Sea. The German admiral had now to decide how

[6] Dreyer, 134.

to get back to the Jade without being sunk, although the Grand Fleet lay somewhere east of him on his route. He reversed his course by another *gefechtswendung* and steered east again. Scheer afterwards wrote that he intended both to rescue the *Wiesbaden* and strike a surprise blow at a portion of the British line; it may be that he intended only to steer for home, taking a passing punch at Jellicoe's rear ships as he went.

At 6:55 P.M. the High Seas Fleet swung 180° in succession again. Scouting Group 1 steamed independently of the battleships but close enough for mutual support, temporarily commanded by Captain Hartog in *Seydlitz*, as Hipper was still in the crippled *Lützow*. Within five minutes Goodenough had reported to Jellicoe that Scheer was steering east again. If the other British commodores of light-cruiser squadrons had scouted and reported with the intelligence and resource of Goodenough, the battle of Jutland would not have been fought by an admiral three-quarters blinded by ignorance of the enemy. Beatty also reported that Scheer was in sight to the west.

Jellicoe's heavy ships steamed on through the calm sea as they waited for Scheer to come out of the west. From the top of *Iron Duke*'s chart-house Jellicoe could see his line dwindling with distance from the dark bulk of *Thunderer* next ahead of him to low smudges on the horizon and tall palls of funnel smoke against the mist like a series of distant volcanoes. At 7:03 P.M. *Iron Duke* passed the bow and stern of a wreck; a destroyer was standing by.

"Is wreck one of our ships?" Jellicoe signalled.

"Yes," came the discouraging reply. *"Invincible."*

Next minute his rear divisions saw Scouting Group 1 come out of the mist; *St. Vincent, Neptune, Revenge* and *Agincourt* opened fire, hitting *Derfflinger* immediately. Once again that murky circle of calm sea, ships and funnel smoke rang with the thunder of heavy gunfire. Scheer had given Jellicoe a second chance. Instantly Jellicoe turned his battleships simultaneously three points towards the enemy to SW by S (201°), but a torpedo attack by German destroyers made him change quickly back to south.

At 7:12 P.M. Scheer followed Scouting Group 1 out of the mists and smoke and found himself in the same ghastly predicament as three-quarters of an hour before—his "T" crossed by the endless British line; not a visible line of targets for German gunnery, but merely a ring of

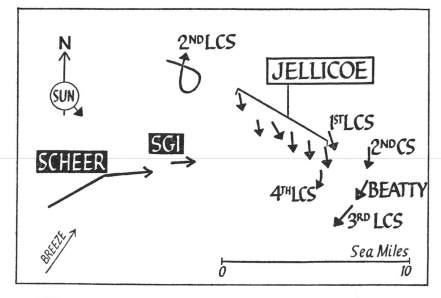

24. THE SECOND BATTLE FLEET ENCOUNTER

flickering gun flashes in the murk. No German gunnery control could take a range. As the British battleships poured heavy shells into them, the ships of the High Seas Fleet wallowed in confusion. Battle Squadron 1 slowed, and some ships stopped and went astern to allow Scouting Group 1 to take station ahead. *König* swung out of line in order to bring her broadside to bear. Scheer himself in *Friedrich der Grosse* (Battle Squadron 3, the centre division) could not see and was not told what was happening to his van; he could only sense that he faced annihilation. At 7:13 P.M. he ordered Scouting Group 1 and his destroyers to cover the fleet's escape by an attack on the British line: *"Gefechtswendung! Rein in dem Feind! Ran* [Battle-turn! Straight into the enemy! Charge]!"

Now came the most splendid and least intelligent moment in the short history of the Imperial Navy. The four remaining battle cruisers— *Moltke, Seydlitz* and *von der Tann,* led by *Derfflinger*—steamed out towards thirty-three British capital ships. They had sunk three British battle cruisers that day, fought Beatty, Evan-Thomas, then Hood and Jellicoe. They had been terribly punished by heavy shells. *Von der Tann* had no guns left in action. Their crews had been in almost continuous ac-

« 165 »

tion since 3:48 P.M. As the sea boiled and erupted round them, the pale grey ships steered eastwards to pit the best that German science, technology, metallurgy, and the German analytical mind could produce against the physical embodiment of a tradition of victory stretching back through Trafalgar and the great sea fights of the eighteenth and seventeenth centuries to the Armada. The black, white and red ensign of the Imperial Navy whipped against the grey of sea, mist and smoke; Scouting Group 1 had begun a marine Balaclava.

Ahead of it the destroyers pressed on through the British fire into torpedo range. At 7:15 P.M. Hartog, commanding Scouting Group 1 in the absence of Hipper, received a modifying order from Scheer—he was to attack the British van. Hartog ordered twenty-three knots, course south. The original order and the speed with which it was modified suggests that the German admiral in his terrible danger for a moment lost his head, an event unlikely ever to occur to Jellicoe. As Hartog's ships turned in succession they were pounded and pounded by Jellicoe's 5th and 6th Divisions at a range of only 7,500 yards. *Derfflinger* took a 15-inch shell in "D" turret, but she did not blow up. *Lützow,* which had been creeping away on her own after the first fleet action, found herself in the middle again, which put her score of hits sustained by heavy shells up to twenty-four. She still floated. By 7:22 P.M. *Derfflinger* had been hit three more times, including one under the bridge; flames roared and leaped from her. *Seydlitz* was hit; *von der Tann,* too, on the after conning tower. Still they came on. At 7:23 P.M. *Derfflinger* took two more 15-inch shells, one of which drilled through the port quarter of the barbette of "C" tunnel and burst under the guns. The powder charges flashed, but the magazine doors saved the ship. *Derfflinger* was an awful spectacle, with vast flames spurting and jumping from her after turrets and dense clouds of foul yellow smoke rolling upwards. A single telephone now constituted her fire control equipment. One turret remained in action.

Gradually Captain Hartog turned Scouting Group 1 away. Before they reached the shelter of a smoke screen laid by the destroyers, *Derfflinger* and *Seydlitz* had both been hit again. No British battleships went in to destroy these obviously badly wounded battle cruisers. Behind Scouting Group 1, Scheer's battleships made another *gefechtswendung;* but there was no attempt at parade-ground accuracy in the desperate situation— squadron commanders and individual captains turned on their initiative, in one case to port instead of starboard. Although Scouting Group 1 succeeded in drawing much of the British fire, the battleships were heavily hit. *Grosser Kurfürst* had water forward up to the main deck and a list of 4 degrees. *König*, too, was down by the head. At 7:27 P.M. Scheer was steaming southwest at seventeen knots out of danger. *Not one* of Jellicoe's divisional commanders had attempted to manoeuvre their squadrons independently to follow the German retreat. Once again it was a question of a tame "follow my leader." Meanwhile the German destroyers covered Scheer's retirement by a determined attack with torpedoes. "Jellicoe foiled them," wrote his flag captain, "by turning away first to 22½° and then increasing this to 45°. Of the twenty-one torpedoes which, towards the end of their run, passed at slow speed through our line, one was seen to pass ahead of *Iron Duke;* the other twenty were dodged by captains making drastic alterations of course." [7]

Iron Duke's 6-inch and 13.5-inch guns shelled these destroyers but at 7:31 P.M. ceased fire. She never again fired a shot in battle.

In neither main encounter did British destroyers launch a co-ordinated large-scale attack. The grouping and command organisation of the British destroyers did not make either for initiative or flexibility. The British had been given two opportunities of engaging the High Seas Fleet with every advantage of numbers, disposition and visibility. Both opportunities were the product of Jellicoe's deployment and his course thereafter and of his prudence in not following Scheer into the mist; equally they were a product of Scheer's mistakes.

Despite Scheer's courage, the event so far proved Jellicoe's superior skill as a tactician; the Grand Fleet battleships had hardly received a hit. Yet although the High Seas Fleet had been so terribly punished, not a German ship had so far been lost. Because British shells did not sink German ships, Jellicoe therefore had nothing to show for his success in blasting the High Seas Fleet for a total of forty minutes and emerging himself unscathed.

At 7:40 P.M., when all German torpedoes had been dodged, Jellicoe ordered his fleet to steer SW (212°), but Scheer was now far distant; even Scouting Group 1 was twelve miles away. Another hour and three-quarters of visibility adequate for battle remained (Beatty made a flag signal at 9:30 P.M., showing that it was still light as late as this). Now

[7] Dreyer, 151.

began a dragging anti-climax as henceforth British hesitancy, passivity, bewilderment and want of co-ordination enabled Scheer to survive those 105 minutes of remaining daylight unscathed. Jellicoe's leadership in this phase was lacking in urgency, as if he felt the battle had already been fought and had turned out well enough. He himself afterwards noted omissions on his part. With his fleet well concentrated, he still lay in Scheer's path to home and safety; for the second time his battle line had forced Scheer away into the west. Scheer, his fleet damaged and confused, ordered a course south at 7:45 P.M.

It was now the British task to hunt Scheer down and destroy him. Beatty made no attempt to chase him in a fighting reconnaissance; he continued to steam as an integral part of Jellicoe's array, about six miles ahead and to starboard of Jerram's 1st Battleship Division, although he could see German heavy ships steering southwest until 7:45 P.M. and reported this to Jellicoe. As Beatty's biographer explained: "He wished to close the enemy van, but in the low visibility he felt, quite rightly, that it would be unwise to press into close range of the enemy battle fleet without battleship support." [8]

A major purpose of battle cruisers was to undertake dangerous and risky forward reconnaissance, even to engage the enemy battle fleet long enough for the main body to come up. The considerations which made it right for Jellicoe not to risk his entire fleet in a chase into the mist did not at all apply to Beatty. Captain Hartog in *Seydlitz* had shown within the last half an hour how to take battle cruisers into close range of an enemy line. Beatty's limpness contrasts with the earlier eagerness with which he had closed with Hipper without waiting for Evan-Thomas; but that springtime of the battle was now four hours and three sunk battle cruisers away. At 7:47 P.M. Beatty sent Jellicoe a now famous signal: "Submit van of battleships follow battle cruisers. We can then cut off whole of enemy's battle fleet."

This was curious; while it was true the battleships had turned sharply away earlier to avoid torpedoes, their course was now the same as Beatty's—SW (212°). The battleships were already following the battle cruisers. If Beatty could see an opportunity invisible to Jellicoe in his station far astern down the British line, which now extended for sixteen miles, why did he not steer for it anyway? Yet his only change of

[8] Chalmers, 255.

course was a brief one or two points towards the enemy. Beatty's signal took twenty-three minutes to travel all the way to Jellicoe and all the way back again to Jerram (1st Battleship Division), only six miles astern of the battle cruisers, by which time all opportunity had been lost.

Not until 8 P.M. did either Jellicoe or Beatty order their light cruisers to hunt for Scheer; indeed, at 7:32 P.M. Jellicoe signalled to Le Mesurier in *Calliope* not to go too near the enemy. Jellicoe acknowledged afterwards that he had failed to make swift and determined use of his cruisers after Scheer's second disappearance: "I should have ordered the 4th Light Cruiser Squadron to search for the enemy when I turned to SW at 7:42 P.M." [9]

Astonishing luck made up for the slackness of the British in not hanging on to Scheer. Whereas he might well have steered east astern of Jellicoe, Scheer in fact was steering south in the belief that the British lay behind him to the northeast. The two fleets were converging again— Scheer badly hurt and in confused formation, led now by the obsolete battleships of Battle Squadron 2, with the punch-drunk battle cruisers to the southeast. Each fleet's cruisers spotted and reported on the other's heavy ships, and at 8:18 P.M. the British were given their third opportunity of a fleet action, yet again in a situation of immense advantage. The four German badly damaged battle cruisers and the high, short silhouettes of the old battleships were sharp against the bright afterglow of the setting sun; the British were veiled in the eastern dusk. Battle Squadron 2 mounted a total of six low-velocity 11-inch guns—its six ships were feebler than two of Beatty's battle cruisers. Once again the battle cruisers grappled; *Seydlitz* was hit, and now at last, with "A" turret temporarily out of action, all *Derfflinger*'s guns were silent. Both Hartog and Beatty altered course away from each other; then Hartog turned sharply to the northwest. Beatty's ships began the easy task of fighting Battle Squadron 2 and hit *Schleswig-Holstein*, *Schlesien* and *Pommern*. The old German ships fired back at their almost invisible opponents and landed 11-inch shells on *Lion*, *Princess Royal* and *Indomitable*. Rear-Admiral Mauve turned his ships sharply away together; Beatty did not follow, and the firing died.

Meanwhile Le Mesurier and the 4th Light Cruiser Squadron, heavily involved with German light forces, sighted the German main battle fleet

[9] Dreyer, 167.

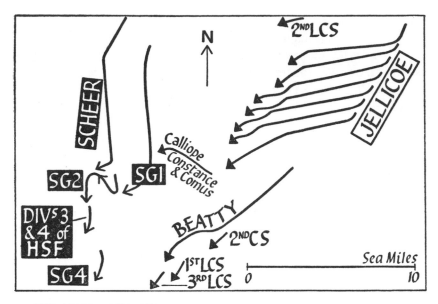

25. THE THIRD ENCOUNTER

at a distance of only 8,000 yards. Jellicoe could hear Beatty's firing in the van as well as Le Mesurier's. At 8:38 P.M. he asked *Comus*, of Le Mesurier's light-cruiser squadron, what she was firing at. The answer came: "Enemy's Battle Fleet, bearing west."

Between then and 9 P.M. Jellicoe received four other reports that indicated Scheer's presence somewhere not very distant to the west, but he did not alter course from southwest. Afterwards he wrote: "It would have been nice if I had closed the enemy Battle Fleet when *Comus* reported she was firing at it at 8:38 P.M. Had I done so I might have been able to fire a few rounds at them before they turned away." [10]

From 9 P.M. to 9:11 P.M. Jerram had the German battleships in sight, but he kept his course without investigating them. Then the fleets diverged and were lost in the mist and dusk.

During the long twilight the light forces fought a scattered marauding battle, in which the German cruiser *Frauenlob* was sunk and the British cruiser *Dublin* hit thirteen times. Each admiral could feel the presence of the other's fleet, but neither knew its true position and course.

[10] *loc. cit.*

Night closed over the calm sea, the dead fish floating belly up, the wreckage, the corpses of brave men; and still Jellicoe lay between Scheer and Germany. Jellicoe was pleased with the day. "I went back to the bridge from the conning tower," wrote his flag captain, "at about 8:30 P.M. and spoke to Jellicoe and Madden, both of whom expressed satisfaction at the good firing of the *Iron Duke*. I found that they agreed that everything that had happened had been according to expectation." [11]

The men of both fleets were utterly exhausted by the strain, noise and exertion of battle. The British relaxed a little. The thin, hollow, raucous noise of acoustic ragtime records played on portable gramophones sounded through decks stinking of cordite and flooded with water. Corned beef and biscuits were wolfed by hungry men, and at 9:30 P.M. scalding cocoa. Yet all remained at action stations still. For the Germans the danger was too great for any to succumb to that overwhelming wish for sleep, for relaxation. Scheer had got to guide his fleet home before another long summer day dawned. His solution to the problem of escape was characteristic; his fleet would steer straight for the Horn Reefs entrance to the swept channel in his home mine fields: if he met the Grand Fleet in the night he would hold his course whatever happened and smash his way through. It was only after 10 P.M. that he had sorted out his battered squadrons; from then on the High Seas Fleet and its crews were keyed for action—desperate action.

Jellicoe's problem was to cover the possible entrances that might be used by Scheer: Ems past Borkum, or Horn Reefs. He ordered the mine layer *Abdiel* to lay mines off the Horn Reefs, but the Grand Fleet course for the night was south, as if to cover the Ems. This was a curious decision, because the Horn Reefs was the nearest and most likely sanctuary for Scheer. The decision did not in fact stem from an appreciation of Scheer's likely course but from a determination not to become involved in a night action. A night exercise before the war off Vigo had convinced Jellicoe that night fighting was "a lottery." The Grand Fleet had no star shell; its searchlights were inferior to the German, and it had had no training in night fighting. Jellicoe's despatch makes the reason for his southerly course during the night of May 31-June 1, 1916, quite plain: "I rejected at once the idea of a night action between the heavy ships as leading to possible disaster. . . . I therefore decided to steer to the

[11] Dreyer, 151.

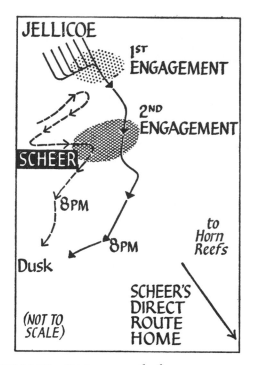

26. FLEET MOVEMENTS—MAY 31, 1916; 6 P.M. TILL DUSK

southward where I should be in a position to renew the engagement at daylight. . . ." [12]

Beatty was of the same mind: "I did not consider it proper or desirable to close the enemy battle fleet during the dark hours." [13]

Jellicoe therefore disposed his fleet in a night cruising order of three columns of eight battleships a mile apart with Beatty fourteen miles to westward. All the flotillas were stationed five miles astern of the battle fleet. This also was curious, for the Germans lay to westward and apparently Jellicoe expected them to make southward for the Ems or Heligoland; why then did he not post his flotillas ahead and to the west of his fleet? He himself says he posted the flotillas astern of the fleet because they could block a German attempt to steer for the Horn Reefs. If this were then a possibility in his mind, why were no heavy ships posted in

[12] Dreyer, 138.
[13] *loc. cit.*

the rear? Because it was Jellicoe's intention to avoid night fighting between heavy ships. As Jellicoe summed it up in a letter to his wife on June 7, 1916, "At 9 P.M. it was too dark to fight any more with heavy ships, so I turned southwards toward enemy bases, and sent my T.B.D.'s [destroyers] to attack his big ships during the night."

Thus Jellicoe's course for the night was chosen in order to *avoid* action, Scheer's to get home even if through the middle of the Grand Fleet. Once again British action was enfeebled by weaknesses in training and equipment.

At 10:41 P.M. Jellicoe received this report from the Admiralty based on a decipher: "German Battle Fleet ordered home at 9:14 P.M. battle cruisers in rear, course SE ¾E. speed 16 knots."

At 10:50 P.M. this was confirmed by reports of an action between British and German light forces that showed plainly that the Germans were not steering south. However, the Grand Fleet held on to the south. While the course of the dark hours proved that Jellicoe was absolutely correct in his decision not to fight Scheer at night, his strategic decision not to head for the Horn Reefs to intercept Scheer at daylight seems unaccountable.

From 11:30 P.M. on May 31 onwards the High Seas Fleet fought a savage running battle in the dark with the hapless British light forces astern of the Grand Fleet. The Germans illuminated the British with star shell, which gave no indication of the firer's whereabouts, and blasted them with 5.9-inch and 3.5-inch shells. The German searchlights and guns were trained to work together in a single operation: first a tiny pencil beam located a British ship, then an iris shutter snapped aside and let out the full beam on to the target, and finally the guns fired almost instantly. The British light forces fought with tremendous gallantry, but sixteen battleships as well as the German light forces proved too much. After three hours of a deadly *mêlée* in the dark Scheer was through, at the cost of two light cruisers damaged and the old battleship *Pommern* torpedoed and sunk; the British cruiser *Black Prince* and five destroyers had been destroyed. Only one British ship attempted to radio a contact report to Jellicoe; *every* German ship reported each single contact straight to Scheer.

The tremendous flashes and noise of this savage battle, with its blazing ships and brilliant star shell, were clearly seen by the battleships in the rear

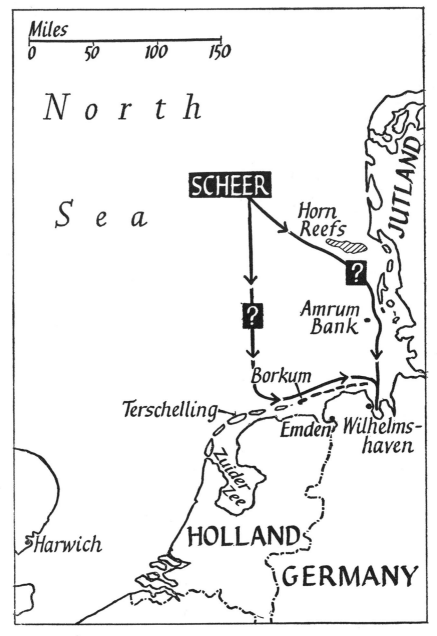

27. SCHEER'S ALTERNATIVE ESCAPE ROUTES

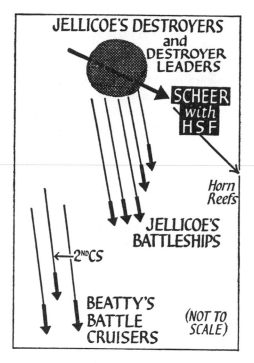

28. JUTLAND—THE NIGHT ACTION

of the Grand Fleet. *Malaya,* indeed, saw a German battleship and identified her as of the *Westfalen* class. No one thought it worth while passing the information to Jellicoe, let alone worth while turning back into the battle to help the flotillas. The passivity of the British heavy ships was absolute. The badly damaged battle cruiser *Moltke,* steering for home on her own, saw in front of her the four battleships of 2nd Battle Squadron. She was recognised as an enemy, but no British ship fired; by the strict training of a lifetime, the decision to open fire belonged alone to a flag officer. By contrast, when the searchlights of the German battleship *Thüringen* picked up *Black Prince,* her guns blew the British ship out of the water in a few moments.

During this inglorious night dozens of German fleet signals were intercepted and decoded by the Admiralty, giving Scheer's course and speed; none was passed to Jellicoe as received, and some were not passed at all. The last of them gave Scheer's position at 1:25 A.M. on June 1916.

Jellicoe wrote later of these signals, unjustly in view of the clear indications to him of Scheer's intentions as early as 11 P.M. the night before:

> These errors were absolutely fatal, as the information if passed to me would have clearly shown me that Scheer was making for the Horn Reefs. The information which was so conclusive would have led me to alter the course during the night for the Horn Reefs, instead of waiting till daylight to close the Horn Reefs if no information respecting enemy movements towards one of the other channels to his base had reached me by daylight, as was my intention.[14]

This last British lapse of all, within the Admiralty itself, robbed the British of their fifth opportunity of fighting Scheer. When at 2:40 A.M. in a miserable dawn of mist and drizzle the Grand Fleet was concentrated again for battle, the sea was empty; Scheer was home, except for *Seydlitz* (stuck on the Horn Reefs) and *Lützow* (sunk at last by the Germans themselves). *Ostfriesland* had been damaged by a British mine.

The Grand Fleet steered for its bases. It was not quite like the day after Trafalgar.

The High Seas Fleet had sunk 111,980 tons of British warships and inflicted casualties of 6,945. The Grand Fleet had sunk 62,233 tons of German ships (including *Lützow*) and inflicted casualties of 2,921.

Linking these figures with the fact of their fleet's numerical inferiority, the Germans claimed a victory. Since the British had forced the Germans back into port, they too claimed a victory. It was the British claim that rang hollowly on the world's ears—including British ears. For the legend of British maritime supremacy demanded a crushing victory without ambiguity—a victory proved by a long list of ships sunk. British propaganda did its best for Jutland, but it was a curious "victory" in that for forty years a controversy was to rage as to who was principally to blame for it. Admirers of Jellicoe blamed Beatty's rashness; admirers of Beatty blamed Jellicoe's caution. The sailors blamed the politicians' meanness over money for the weakness of British equipment; the politicians blamed the sailors, particularly Jellicoe, because he was Commander-in-Chief. Astonishing manipulations of fact were made in order to prove that, except for bad luck, the British of the Jutland era were as

[14] Dreyer, 167-8.

brilliant at building and fighting ships as in Nelson's time. The apologias and the searches for scapegoats served as a substitute for critical analysis.

Although there was no clear tactical decision, the effects of Jutland can, however, be dispassionately traced.

In the first place there were the moral results. Germany and her allies were elated, the British and theirs disappointed. In a bad year for Germany Scheer had done fine work. More than this, so far as long-term world opinion was concerned, the spell of Trafalgar had been broken; Nelson's professional descendants had been worsted in terms of losses by the new and smaller navy of a continental power. This disillusionment was true for Britain as well; the navy, as a shield of Empire, was never again accorded quite the same religious faith, and the smouldering controversy over Jutland did nothing to restore the gods.

Strategically the decisive results of Jutland lay in the battle's indecision. It proved to Jellicoe—and to Beatty when he succeeded Jellicoe as Commander-in-Chief—that the relative qualities of the two fleets were such as to make great caution necessary. The Grand Fleet made fewer sweeps in the North Sea and those not so far to the south. The passage through the Baltic to Russia was barred forever; the Heligoland Bight was safe for the entrances and exits of ocean-going U-boats. To Scheer the battle, with its lucky escape, proved that the chances of catching a detached British force, destroying it and thus achieving a naval balance (with the chance of a decisive battle later for command of the sea) were hopelessly remote. He therefore reported to the Kaiser that Germany's future naval hopes must lie in unrestricted submarine warfare. Only this could starve the British war economy before the Royal Navy performed a similar service for Germany. It was not until February 1917 that the German Government gave its consent to unrestricted U-boat warfare, but Jutland was the deciding strategic factor. U-boat sinkings brought America into the war in 1917; want of equipment and munitions took Russia out.

These are weighty consequences in terms of twentieth-century history. In fact, Jutland was also responsible for the U-boat offensive of the Second World War, because in 1939 Germany had only built a few pocket battleships like the *Graf Spee* and fast battleships like *Scharnhorst* and *Gneisenau* for commerce raiding; her main naval strength was in submarines.

In the larger sense the indecision of Jutland constituted the maritime equivalent of the land stalemate; it would be a matter of months and years before the damage done by blockade or U-boats began to have a decisive effect on the industrial capacity to make war of Britain or Germany. Jutland had closed the one open flank; at sea as well as in the trenches strategy withered into attrition; and the last military chance of avoiding a long war and utter mutual exhaustion had gone.

For the British themselves, however, Jutland has a much deeper significance, for it was in fact a defeat for British technology. More than that, as with the French at Crécy and Sedan, a social system had been exposed by battle as decadent and uncreative. Jutland proves that already in 1914, when Britain and her empire had never seemed richer, more powerful, more technologically able, dry rot was crumbling the inner structure of the vast mansion. Jutland proves that the spectacular collapse of British power and British industrial vigour after 1945 was not a sudden disaster due, as comforting legend has it, to the sale of overseas investments in 1914-18 and 1939-45, but the final acute phase of seventy years of decline. For the principal armed service of a country—in its professional attitudes, its equipment, its officer corps—is an extension, a reflection, of that country's whole society, and especially of its dominating groups.

The flag officers of Jutland were all middle-aged men when Fisher began modernising the navy in 1904. Junior commanders at Jutland (ships' captains, for instance) had also spent their young and formative years in the Victorian navy. The ten years of the Fisher era were enough to build modern ships, but it was too short a time to have more than surface effects on men whose habits of mind had already been fixed for a lifetime before the reforms began.

Fundamentally it was the Victorian navy that fought at Jutland. The Victorian navy had forgotten that it was a fighting service, an instrument of policy—just as late Victorian Britain tended to forget that her prosperity and her moral and civic excellence depended on crude competitive power. The nineteenth-century Royal Navy had no general staff, no staff college, no higher war studies. It made no war plans. It was an end in itself, justified by its size, its reputation and its elegance. Its officers were too often recruited by nepotism or influence—a form of co-optation. Co-optation is itself a form of inbreeding, and in 1900 the officer corps of the Royal Navy displayed the characteristics of professional inbreeding to the extent of Goyaesque fantasy. Arrogance, punctilious ritual, ignorance of technical progress, and remoteness from the functional reality of a modern fleet were added to the unchanged organisation of the eighteenth-century navy to produce a decadence hardly matched in any force of modern times, except perhaps by the French Imperial Army of 1870.

Efficiency meant instant, unquestioning obedience; it meant ships like a life guard's uniform. "Gunnery was merely a necessary evil," wrote Admiral of the Fleet Sir Reginald Tyrwhitt of the Mediterranean Fleet only thirty years before Jutland. "Target practice *had* to be carried out once in each quarter of the year . . . no one except the Gunnery Lieutenant took much interest in the results. Polo and pony-racing and amusements were more important than gun drill" [15]

Although the British thought of their navy in terms of "the Nelson touch"—that is, of adventurous initiative—it was in fact ruled by a discipline more rigid and pointless than that of the Prussian army. This discipline was based on the principle of absolute, unquestioning obedience of, and subordination to, one's superiors. Any discussion of service problems, however innocently remote from real insubordination, was treated as subversion. Actual disagreement with the opinion of a superior, however politely expressed and however reasonable, was crushed. A ship's captain could not even give permission for his crew to hang up their washing to dry without obtaining the approval of the senior officer present. Tiny details of individual ships' administration would be ordered from the flagship. The British sea officer was an automaton who only came to life at the impulse of a superior. That this attitude of mind survived the ten years of modernisation is shown by the radio signal of one captain in the Atlantic to the Admiralty during the war, asking for permission to issue an extra ration of lime juice

When one of these automata at last received his flag, some mysterious gift of grace then enabled him, without preparation or training, to do all the thinking and make all the decisions for the force now under his command. This was why Fisher, and Jellicoe himself, as First Sea Lord, were suspicious of all staff appointments that appeared to give junior officers an admiral's prerogative of thinking. This was why at Jutland neither the British heavy nor their light squadrons displayed tactical re-

[15] Tyrwhitt MS; quoted Marder, *From the Dreadnought,* I, 8.

source, initiative or flexibility—why, once deployed, the entire fleet of 154 ships manoeuvred stiffly only on *Iron Duke*'s signals. This was why none of the interesting manoeuvres suggested by Winston Churchill and others to grip and surround the German fleet was practicable or attempted. This is why criticism of Jellicoe's personal rigidity and caution is unfair; the failure was not on the afternoon of May 31, 1916, but in the preceding fifty years, and the responsibility was that of the British people and its politicians as well as the sailors.

Given the Grand Fleet as it was, it is difficult to fault Jellicoe's general handling of it. His prudent tactical sense enabled it to fight the High Seas Fleet twice at a great advantage and where its weaknesses of organisation and officer quality would not tell. Contrasting his low-keyed realism with Beatty's initial dash and its results, it is difficult not to conclude that more risky and aggressive tactics might have resulted in a disaster. Jellicoe himself was a product of the Victorian navy; despite his intelligence and technical knowledge he could not shake free of its rigidity and hierarchy, but he was thus well-suited to his fleet. He was not a creative genius—he never pretended he was—but an able officer who would be as effective as the prevailing system allowed. No organisation can depend on a supply of geniuses; it must always aim to allow the ordinarily able man to function at his best. In a navy with a free intellectual life, driving corporate ambition and professional curiosity, and with able and resourceful subordinates like Goodenough, Jellicoe would have been a different commander.

Two things caused the decadence of British maritime power: the long peaceful supremacy after Trafalgar and the capture of the navy by that hierarchy of birth and class that controlled so many of Britain's national institutions. Drawing most of its officers from 1 per cent of the nation, the Royal Navy never tapped that great reservoir of urban middle-class talent that made Scheer's fleet so well-educated and so intelligent. Fisher estimated that the cost of naval training excluded any son whose parents had less than £700 a year. Since there were not more than 300,000 such families in the country, the naval officer came from a well-to-do background. Although the navy was not "fashionable" in the sense of certain regiments or branches of the army, its background was still that of gentlefolk rather than of the new business middle classes, rural rather than urban. In such a world the grandee, and the grandee with money, exercised undue influence and advantage. The navy reflected social rather than functional values, preoccupation with tradition rather than technology. Fisher pointed out with some exaggeration as early as 1906 how little was the share that the nation as a whole had in its navy:

> Reckoning five people to the family, it follows that (on the basis of 300,000 families with incomes of £700 a year or more) there are not more than 1,500,000 people in all from whom officers for the navy can be taken —and of these, half, or more than half, are women and children. The remainder of the population is 41,500,000, and of these no single one can ever hope to become an officer in the navy! Surely we are drawing our Nelsons from too narrow a class.[16]

Yet the navy was only an extreme example of the grip which the privileged classes had on British national institutions—Parliament, the army, diplomacy, social and artistic life were also dominated by the alliance of money and lineage. It was a tragedy for Britain that the aristocracy and gentry had never been cut off from the national life, as had largely happened in France. It was also a tragedy that the British aristocracy was flexible and intelligent enough to preserve itself by recruiting from commerce and industry; the grandson of a thrusting iron founder would be as aristocratic in his values as any fifteenth duke.

Two things followed from this aristocratic ascendancy in modern Britain, fatal to her greatness. In the first place, the social and intellectual values of industrial society never ousted those of the aristocracy. The richer Victorian England became, the more ashamed in a deep sense did she become of the technological origin of those riches. The engineer and the businessman have never been as "respectable" in Britain as in Germany or America. In the second place, in the period after 1870, when Britain faced the technical challenges of the more complex phase of the industrial revolution and the commercial challenge of foreign competition, the leadership of the country was in the hands of the social group least likely (because of its wealth and privilege) to be aware of the challenges and to respond to them. From 1870 to 1914 Britain was decadent because a decadent ruling social group and decadent (nonfunctional) values had captured or corrupted the forces of technological and social change.

[16] Memorandum of March, 1906, quoted Marder, *From the Dreadnought*, I, 31.

The Royal Navy's officers and her organisation for war (or her lack of it) thus epitomise the domination of Britain by a small group. In the same way her ships and guns reflect the decline in the creativeness and quality of British technology.

In the first place, there were the gross and obvious defects in modern British ship design, starting with the *Dreadnought* in which the forward funnel, with all its smoke, was placed before the tripod control top. Because British battleship design was not the result of profound technical and strategical analysis, but of the personal opinions of Sir John Fisher and his committee and of later interested parties such as Churchill, fighting weaknesses were built in from the beginning. Fisher wanted fast, heavily gunned ships; therefore they could not be equally heavily armoured. The defensive weakness of British ships thus followed, most accentuated in the battle cruisers. The *Queen Mary* had 3,900 tons of armour; the *Seydlitz,* one of the comparable class, 5,200. Yet *Queen Mary* displaced 27,000 tons against the 24,610 of *Seydlitz.* The British weakness was not a matter of chance, or limited docking facilities, but choice.

It has been argued that subdivision in German ships was more elaborate than in British because British ships were designed for world cruises and therefore were given greater space for the crew's living quarters. No documentary evidence, however, has ever been produced to prove that, class for class, the crew's quarters were more spacious and comfortable in British ships. In fact, each battle fleet was designed specifically to fight the other in the North Sea; comparable classes of ships had, for example, similar fuel capacities and steaming ranges.

The German ships were also much stronger in terms of armour and internal subdivision because German engines took less space and weight (small tube boilers) and German guns were much lighter than British for an equivalent performance. The 12-inch guns in *Helgoland* weighed only forty-eight tons, yet their battle performance equalled British 13.5-inch guns weighing seventy-six tons. This enormous discrepancy displays the general obsolescence and want of modern research facilities in the British steel and armaments industries. British methods, factories and designers were committed to the "wire-wound" gun. Because the "wire-wound" system could not stand increased length and muzzle velocity, British guns had to be made heavier and bigger to get better performances. German guns, made on the "built-up" system, were much stronger in construction and thus could be lighter and smaller.[17] The steel for German guns and shells was made in special electric furnaces, giving a very high-quality steel; in Britain steel was only made by the Siemens-Martin open-hearth process.

Jellicoe himself, as Controller of the Navy, summed it up in a memorandum of May 3, 1909. After pointing out that the German 11-inch gun had better ballistics and equal penetration to the British 12-inch, and that the new German 12-inch would be very much better than ours in all respects, Jellicoe recommended that the Royal Navy would have to go to a bigger bore—13.5-inch—because the British 12-inch gun could not take extra length and extra charges to improve its performance. Jellicoe went on: "It may be asked why we cannot do what Germany has successfully accomplished with a 12-inch gun. The answer is . . . that their steel was and possibly is superior owing to the crucible method of manufacture that is used." [18]

That the British armaments industry before 1914 had chosen an inferior process of manufacture is illustrated by the adoption of the German "built-up" principle for turret guns in the new British battleships of the King George V class in the Second World War.

German technical superiority extended to the firing charges, the shells and their explosive. The last quarter of German firing charges was fed to the gun turrets in brass cartridges, the British in silk bags. British charges were thus far more likely to ignite if the turret was hit. Because of the higher muzzle velocity of the German guns and the standardised propelling charge, the flight of German shells was much more even; here was the origin of the tightly bunched salvoes that did such execution at Jutland. Also, the performance of British guns fell off after about seventy shots.

In quality of shell the general German technical superiority was overwhelming. After Jutland there were exhaustive British tests by a Projectile Committee, which reported almost exactly what Jellicoe had found in 1910 as Controller—that British shells broke up on impact with armour plate at an oblique angle. The Projectile Committee's report

[17] See *Brassey's Naval Annual* for 1914, 349-51, for a discussion of gun design and performance. The *Annual* was open to any interested member of the public or navy, including Beatty.
[18] Jellicoe Papers, II.

added that the British burster, lyddite, was too unstable and exploded on impact instead of after penetration, and that the British fuses were too sensitive and contributed to premature explosion. Indeed, a proportion of ammunition on board the heavy ships at Jutland consisted of 12-inch armour-piercing shells that had been accepted at a lower price and which had failed at proof. Such shells were fired from a gun described by the Director of Naval Ordnance in 1911 as of "uncertain" accuracy.

One reason for the general inadequacy of British shells lay in the absence of a basic study of modern war by a general staff. For the Royal Navy was up to 1913 thinking in terms of close-range bombardment, for which this shell was more suited.

It was thus mainly the Admiralty's research and development organisation and the British steel, chemical and armaments industries that robbed Jellicoe of sunk German ships during his total of forty minutes' bombardment at Jutland and therefore of the only trophies that world opinion recognised as proving victory. There was no mystery therefore about *Lützow*, only a battle cruiser, surviving after twenty-four hits by heavy shell. Much of this, of course, was known to Jellicoe before Jutland. To Beatty the report of the Projectile Committee came as a nerve-breaking surprise. In January 1918, as Commander-in-Chief of the Grand Fleet, he reminded the Admiralty that the new type of shell had not yet been supplied to the fleet; he wondered whether it would be wise to try to force a fleet action. He decided it would not.[19] Thus Beatty as Commander-in-Chief was far less adventurous than Jellicoe, steering at twenty knots for the Jutland battle, closer to German bases than his own.

The excuse is sometimes made for the loss of the three British battle cruisers (because of a flash from a powder fire into the magazine) that the German battle cruiser *Seydlitz* had almost been lost in this way at the battle of the Dogger Bank and that the Germans had profited by the experience to perfect their magazine protection. However, the British, it is said, had no experience to show them the need. Yet the cruisers *Kent* and *Conquest* had both reported cordite charges flash-ignited by exploding shells in earlier fights. The effects of a similar chain reaction taking place in the confinement of a capital ship's turret, down inside the barbette into the magazine, might well have been deduced—the more so be-

19 Chalmers, 304-5.

cause the battle cruiser *Lion* had a severe cordite fire in a turret at the same battle of the Dogger Bank, which endangered the ship. However, there existed in the Royal Navy no organisation for systematic research into questions of operational technology. The deductions were not made. It was otherwise in the German navy. In any event, even before Dogger Bank, the combination of more stable explosives and better design and construction made German vessels more flash-tight than British. After all, *Seydlitz* did not blow up; the British battle cruisers at Jutland did.

Only in one major respect at Jutland was British technology ahead of German. All British heavy ships had been equipped with centralised range finding and gun laying by a director-control system. Yet even this advantage was nullified by the quality and design of German range finders and the excellent individual German gunnery, which had been better and longer practised and was more evenly high in standard than the British.

The weaknesses of British naval technology at Jutland were in part owing to the close personal relations of private firms and Admiralty officers (who often joined the boards of such firms on retirement) and the relatively small number of firms who could undertake the work. Thus, really ruthless, independent testing and rejection of poor designs or poor quality were humanly very difficult.

A revealing glimpse into this closed world, and a clue as to why the British fleet built since 1905 was so poor in quality in so many ways, is provided by this letter from Admiral Dreyer to Jellicoe:

> I am greatly disturbed at the extent of the intrigue generated by the Armament firms against my Assistant. Your late host and his son-in-law [an incompetent manager at * * * * *] are no friends of mine and my inspectors.
>
> The Ministry has failed to get me to accept Carbon Steel for guns, Crude Trotyl, 80/20 Amatol, inferior fuses or Nitratious Cordite. . . .[20]

Yet the German navy also rested on a few shipyards and virtually on one armourer—Krupp. In fact, therefore, the shortcomings of British equipment do reflect the general obsolescence of British technology before 1914, itself reflected in her sliding performance in the world's export markets. Already the British industrial firm was too small a unit, too traditional in methods, too fond of clinging to products and techniques

[20] Dreyer, letter to Jellicoe 25.1.18; Jellicoe Private Papers.

successful in the past. It cherished the craftsman and the "practical" businessman, just as it cherished the "practical" sailor. It neglected mass, standardised production; it neglected research and despised the "theoretical" technologist. British industry no more believed in a general staff than did the Royal Navy. The connection between the general state of British technology and the equipment it designed for war is revealed in the following passage from *The History of the Ministry of Munitions:* "A Committee of Malleable Iron Founders was instituted in April, 1917. . . . But the meetings of the committee revealed, amongst many of the ironmasters, a great lack of knowledge of the results to be arrived at by research or even of the fundamental scientific principles underlying their foundry practice." [21]

The great heavy industries of Britain's early Victorian supremacy were slower to grow and slower to change their methods than those of Germany or America; yet they had an unhealthily large share of British trade. As two historians of the British iron and steel industry put it: "Britain did not retain the initiative after the fundamental inventions. The industry was slowly penetrated by science and failed to appreciate that it was entering a new highly technical phase." [22] They diagnose British industrial failure as stemming from similar causes to those of the decadence of the Royal Navy:

> The ultimate control of the British iron and steel industry has been in the past largely a family matter, which . . . accounts for men without any special training attempting to manage large industrial concerns. . . . The sense of security from inherited wealth explains an inherent conservatism, and a marked tendency to retain aged directors led to a love of compromise, a hesistant development of policy and opposition to change except when driven.[23]

British weakness in new developments such as the electrical and chemical industries or automobiles was especially noticeable. According to Professor Clapham:[24]

> Beyond question, the creation of this industry [electrical goods and equipment] was the greatest single industrial achievement of modern Ger-

[21] Vol. III, 147.
[22] Burnham and Hoskins, 246.
[23] *ibid*, 248.
[24] Clapham, 308.

many. The world had before it a new group of scientific and economic problems. In the handling of those problems Germany . . . took the lead. . . . Her success was rewarded by a foreign trade in electrical goods which no other nation could approach.

The general figures tell a story of feeble British responses to new challenges.

Percentage of World Trade[25]

	Britain	Germany
1880	23	9
1913	17	12

Steel Output in Metric Tons[26]

	Britain	Germany
1880	3,730,000	1,548,000
1910	7,613,000	14,794,000

The basis of explosives manufacture and of the twentieth-century development of plastics was synthetic dyestuffs. In 1913 Germany produced 150 thousand short tons, Britain only 5.6 thousand.[27]

In 1914 Britain had already an adverse trade balance in goods of £150 millions a year—covered by interest on British loans. By 1914 the British were no longer primarily creators, producers—dynamic, aggressive and competitive; they were usurers, possessors—comfortable, complacent and passive.

The British general decadence had the same roots as the defeat at Jutland—the propagation of social and emotional values unrelated to the hard facts of power and survival. The superiority of the gentleman over the industrialist was accepted, as was that of the arts over science, of status, right and tradition over function. Nowhere is the British collapse of the twentieth century more clearly adumbrated than in her educational system in the years before 1914, when the new Germany was pounding into the world market like one of Hipper's battle cruisers. For the future of any power lies in the intelligence and training of its people. The British, alone of the great powers, had two educational systems—

25 Clough and Cole, 605.
26 Clapham, 285.
27 Clough and Cole, 558.

one for that dominating aristocratic and middle-class group; one on the cheap for the rest, where the bulk of the nation was made artificially stupid and subordinate. Despite the excellence of British "pure" scientific research, the general educational system placed little emphasis on science, "pure" or "applied." The public schools and Oxford and Cambridge taught nothing about power, nothing about technology and business. They produced diplomats, soldiers, politicians and sailors who knew nothing about these things and indeed despised them. The children of the middle classes, who in Germany emerged as the new type of industrial leader, in Britain went off to rule the Indians. No one has yet computed the drain made by the Empire on talent so desperately needed at home.

Once again the figures tell the story. In 1908 Germany, for a population of approximately 60,000,000, had twenty-one universities, with 46,471 students, and ten technical high schools ranking with universities and issuing degrees, with 14,143 students.[28] England and Wales, for a population of 34,500,000, had ten universities and three university colleges (not issuing their own degrees), with a total of 12,000 students; no technical high schools of university rank, but instead thirty-one recognised technical institutions with a total of only 2,768 students.[29]

In a paragraph that tells the story of British decline in the twentieth century in casual accents of doom, the Report of HM Inspectors of Education for 1908-9 says: "The slow growth of these technical institutions is, however, in the main to be ascribed to the small demand in this country for the services of young men well-trained in the theoretical side of industrial operations and in the service underlying them." [30]

There was thus nothing accidental, nothing of bad luck, nothing of blame on individual officers in what happened at Jutland, nor in what happened in the forty-odd years after Jutland. It was part of a vast process of dissolution that began about 1870, when the British forgot that life is a continued response, with daily new beginnings; that nothing is permanent but what is dead. British decay began when the British forgot the sources of their power and even denigrated them. It is an astonishing indictment of British parliamentary government in its supposed golden age that, in the critical years from 1870 to 1914, the dominating politi-

[28] *Encyclopaedia Britannica,* 1914.
[29] Report of the University Grants Committee, 1908-9; Report of HM Inspectors of Education, 1908-9, 247.
[30] Report of HM Inspectors of Education, 90.

cal topic was not the modernisation and mobilisation of British resources for a desperate struggle for survival—but the future of Ireland,
than which no matter could be of lesser relevance and importance.

In distant retrospect, Jutland was one of the critical battles of history;
it marked the opening of that final phase of British world power and
maritime supremacy that was to end in 1945, with the British battle
fleet no more than "Task Force 77" in the United States Pacific Fleet, and
Britain herself reduced to financial dependency. Yet it was partly owing to Jellicoe's personal skill as an admiral that the final collapse of
British sea power was delayed until 1945 and after. However, the
British nation had no longer the energy or ambition to profit from the
respite. What Jellicoe saved at Jutland the British gave away to the
Americans by the Washington Treaty in 1922 and the London Treaty of
1930; what Scheer began in 1916 was completed by the Japanese in
1941-2.

Eighteen days after Jutland, Moltke, the forgotten man of the "quick
victory" days of 1914, died. On July 1, 1916, the battle of the Somme
began. On August 29, Pétain's victory at Verdun at last toppled Falkenhayn, but in his place in Germany's central war leadership came the formidable victors against Russia, Hindenburg and Ludendorff. On December 27, Jellicoe was made First Sea Lord, and against his specific
recommendation, Beatty, a credulous public's hero, was made
Commander-in-Chief of the Grand Fleet. At the end of 1916, when
Joffre and Haig had failed on the Somme with casualties of 614,000 and
Falkenhayn had failed before Verdun, a wave of hopelessness, reflected
by currents of pacifism and even tentative peace moves, swept over the
nations.

At last it was clear that victory was far off beyond a morass of death,
boredom and suffering; no decision on land, no decision at sea. The allied
blockade was effective enough, as German war industry and the German
household could witness; but it would be months—years—before it destroyed Germany's capacity to make war. However, the indecision of Jutland gradually produced its decisive effects on the strategy of the war.
The inter-allied conference at Chantilly in November 1916 could
only decide for 1917 on further battles of attrition on the Somme and in
Flanders; the idea of early victory and peace was abandoned. Joffre, his

credit gone, was almost immediately afterwards dismissed in favour of a man who promised what all most desperately wanted—a break-through, a sweeping exploitation, a triumph, a peace in 1917. For Nivelle—Pétain's successor as commander of the 2nd Army at Verdun, when the latter was appointed to Army Group Centre—believed he had found the "method" to break the spell of attrition. It had succeeded in a local victory at Verdun; he convinced the politicians that it could win the war. The British army would help; but the victory would be largely achieved by the French, driving straight through the German positions with "brutality" and "violence" as if they did not exist. In despair men turn to quacks who promise them their dreams. Nivelle's fatal chance was born of Jutland and the Somme. On April 16, 1917, the French attacked.

III

General Henri Philippe Benoni
Omer Pétain

A vaincre sans péril, on triomphe sans gloire.

CORNEILLE. *Le Cid.*

8

Beyond the high windows of the room—neo-classical, splendid, once the *salon* of Marie Antoinette—the park was brightly dusted with the young greens of spring. A clock like a monument standing on the chimney piece before a great looking glass measured out the seconds of a war now already two and a half years old. As its pendulum swung quietly in the tapestry-hung room in the Palace of Compiègne (itself an image of France's greatness under the monarchy and two empires) Frenchmen were dying still along the Aisne, collapsed bundles of bone and offal, dying in loneliness, terror and squalor. For although its back had been broken by the Germans a month ago—within two days of its D-Day on April 16, 1917—the grand offensive that had been guaranteed by the Commander-in-Chief, General Nivelle, to bring peace and victory was still twitching.

Behind the wide desk with its metal-shaded lamp, in an Empire armchair, sat Nivelle, bitter with the failure of the last Napoleonic offensive in French history. Distrusted even before the battle by the politicians who earlier had credulously swallowed his promises, and by many of his subordinate commanders, only victory could have saved him. Now he waited in the long, beautiful afternoon for his successor, one of those who had scorned his chances of victory—one indeed who had always scorned the chances of a general offensive against the fire of modern weapons.

It was a sad, awkward and brief meeting. The year before Nivelle had done so well as Pétain's subordinate (in command of the 2nd Army) and successor at Verdun; now his active military career was over. He was a symbol of and a scapegoat for the credulity and optimism of politicians. For a while Marie Antoinette's room held them both: Nivelle, dignified, courteous, his handsome face drawn, and Pétain, big and straight—horizon-blue uniform without decorations, horizon-blue eyes in a massive head.

That evening Pétain was Nivelle's guest at dinner. It was a frigid, silent occasion, for no words could span the gulf between the men. In the words of Pétain's *chef du cabinet:* "The meal was exquisite, but deadly." [1] Behind Nivelle lay defeat, military and personal. Before Pétain was the possibility of national catastrophe through the disintegration or mutiny of the French army. Next day Nivelle was gone and Pétain had become Commander-in-Chief. It was May 17, 1917.

Pétain knew well enough the weight of the responsibility he had shouldered. As commander of Army Group Centre, he had participated in the disaster of Nivelle's offensive and had seen its effects on the soldiers' morale; and as Chief of the General Staff in Paris for the last fifteen days he had measured the inadequacy of the French general direction of the war and its political instruments and had surveyed the balance of the war as a whole.

It was a desperate situation. Britain seemed to be losing the battle against the U-boats. The tonnage of ships sunk had risen from 470,000 in February 1917 to 837,000 in April. Sir John Jellicoe, now First Sea Lord, prophesied swift defeat at sea if the current rate of sinkings continued. In some ways the German submarines found the British Admiralty and navy even more wanting than had the High Seas Fleet. Anti-submarine warfare rested firstly on the accurate analysis of information on the time, place and characteristics of sinkings and on the general pattern of trade. The Admiralty had few trained staff officers and no modern organisational apparatus for processing such information. Its "statistics" included the incredible howler of making total weekly sailings from British ports comprise cross-Channel and coastal shipping as well as ocean-going traffic. The Admiralty for a time therefore believed that it had to protect 5,000 arrivals and departures a week instead of 200. Once again a prisoner of his own cautious temperament, the in-

[1] Serrigny, 140.

tense conservatism of the navy and the primitiveness of Admiralty organisation, Jellicoe was reluctant to introduce the convoy system. To him and his fellow admirals it seemed a risky and unproven gamble. Yet if it was wrong to gamble at Jutland, it was right to gamble against the submarines, because sure and tried methods were conducting Britain to defeat in a matter of months.

Apart from this losing battle against the U-boats, Russia had been paralysed by revolution since March. America, it was true, had entered the war on April 3, but she was quite unready and had only a small professional army. As with Britain, her military and industrial mobilisation would show few results for at least a year.

As the war thus at last changed its shape, some factors seemed permanent—Germany on the one hand, France and Britain on the other. If the new shape was to prove that of victory, it depended on French endurance, for France was still at least an equal, if no longer the senior, military partner in the democratic alliance. Could France hold on? Nivelle's offensive had been born of the post-Moltke, post-Jellicoe stalemate; it had always been founded more on faith and desperate wish than on dispassionate examination of the chances. The Russian Revolution had been the outcome of similar sacrifices without result. It had been the product of despair. Now despair had come to the French army too—with Russia as an example and an encouragement.

For Pétain there was no novelty in taking over an army in a state of crisis. An integral part of his make-up now was Verdun. He had arrived there to find the battle apparently already lost, the defence system already submerged beneath the German offensive, the French troops already apparently in a state of helpless rout and disintegration. His calmness and patience had triumphed over the appearance of accomplished defeat; the defences of Verdun had been rebuilt, and swift disaster had been replaced by half a year's murderous attrition.

On the morning of May 17, 1917, the new Commander-in-Chief held his first meeting with the staff of *Grand Quartier Général.* Some were no strangers. There was the sad-faced Debeney, Chief of the General Staff, who like Pétain had been a pre-war instructor at the Ecole de Guerre. Like Pétain, he was also an infantryman who had always believed in the dominance of modern fire power over all other factors on the battlefield. The Chief of the Third Bureau, de Barescut, had been at

Verdun—in charge of the complex rearward organisation of routes, transport and supplies that had saved the fortress as much as had the endurance of the fighting troops.

As was the custom in the French army, Pétain had brought with him his personal staff or *cabinet.* The *chef du cabinet,* General de Serrigny, had been Pétain's colleague ever since the latter had become a corps commander in 1914. It was one of those "military marriages" between a commander (who shouldered the responsibility) and a personal staff officer (who supplied original ideas, draft plans, and a wide-ranging intellectual curiosity). Such relationships had become an important feature of modern armies, with their complex problems of command. Serrigny made an excellent complement to Pétain, who was a farmer's son and perhaps too narrowly a professional soldier. Serrigny was sophisticated in both intellect and experience; literature, history, economics, politics and science were among the subjects of his wide reading. In the two and a half years of their association Serrigny had passed on some of this general culture to his chief. As Serrigny put it:

"In the evening I remained alone with General Pétain round the fire [during the battle of Verdun]. . . . When the sector was calm the talk turned generally towards strategy, foreign affairs or the organisation of the army. . . . The day that the general took over the supreme command he possessed a veritable *corpus* of political and military doctrine." [2]

Serrigny and the other members of the *cabinet*—Lieutenant-Colonel Duchêne and Captain Picard—were to work in the superb music room, next to Pétain's office.

The staff of the G.Q.G. eyed Pétain warily. Under Joffre and Nivelle the Third Bureau (operations) had enjoyed enormous prestige and influence both within the headquarters and with the armies as emissaries of the Commander-in-Chief—the *"missi dominici,"* as they were nicknamed. In the forces of each belligerent there was a chasm of suspicion and incomprehension between the fighting troops and the staff officers planning and theorising at G.H.Q.; this chasm was deepest in the French army, where G.Q.G. operations staff were members of an exclusive élite, the *"brevetés"* of the Ecole de Guerre. Unlike the German staff and to some extent the British, they displayed an arrogant reluctance to allow the realities reported from the front to interfere with their military phi-

[2] Serrigny, 71.

losophising. In Pétain's dour realism the staff had always seen a want of "guts," of the French offensive spirit. His rudeness in the past to G.Q.G. officers made him no more congenial to them. So G.Q.G. was now, to its distaste, ruled by one of those they had always in a sense contemned —a fighting soldier, one who had seen the realities of modern war as a brigade, divisional, corps, army and army group commander.

In G.Q.G., on the other hand, Pétain found an organisation that foreshadowed the ludicrous snobberies of cartelised industry fifty years later. Between rank and rank, bureau and bureau, *breveté* and *non-breveté*, lay impassable *glacis* of professional and social distinction; and in an atmosphere of grim institutionalism and rivalry any sense of urgent collective endeavour had long since died. For G.Q.G., war was no more than something to be planned and administered like a routine, and boredom was consequently the inevitable furniture in every room in the rambling palace. Pétain at first watched and listened; patience was a great and characteristically peasant quality. But the impact of the new Commander-in-Chief, by personality alone, was instantaneous. There was his physical presence. "I had the impression," wrote Lieutenant de Pierrefeu, "of a marble statue; a Roman senator in a museum. Big, vigorous, an impressive figure, face impassive, of a pallor of a really marble hue." [3]

Colonel Repington, military correspondent of *The Times,* had been impressed by Pétain's personality a year before, in March 1916, when he had visited him at his headquarters at Souilly while the fight for Verdun had been in its crisis: "A fair Pas-de-Calais man of medium height, with a firm and reserved aspect and a masterful regard; a soldier before all, and one with strong will and decided opinions." [4]

Only three weeks before Pétain became Commander-in-Chief, Repington had watched him (as Army Group Commander, Army Group Centre) and Serrigny going through the morning reports: "I was struck by the quick and businesslike methods of both, and by the acute, pungent and penetrating remarks of the general." [5]

In conference Pétain's aloofness and majesty dominated not only his staff and colleagues but also the politicians who had treated Nivelle so

[3] Pierrefeu, II, 9.
[4] Repington, I, 157.
[5] *ibid,* 546.

insultingly. Paul Painlevé, the Minister for War, like Repington, never forgot the Pétain of Verdun crisis—that "impassive face, his haze that nothing troubled in the gravest of circumstances; his organiser's brain that only left the inevitable to chance . . ."[6]

Pierrefeu, a journalist who had edited the daily official communiqué under Joffre and Nivelle and who was thus a connoisseur of commanding generals, summed up the effects of Pétain's personality: "Pétain did not appear to me only as a soldier; his greatness does not only derive from his skill at directing a battle, but emanates from his entire personality. No one evokes better than he what the Romans called 'great men.'"[7]

Overwhelming physical presence Pétain had always had. Serrigny remembered his first sight of him at the turn of the century: "Cold, glacial even, this good-looking blond fellow, already going bald, attracted women and men alike by the intensity of the gaze of his blue eyes."[8]

Yet here too was the clue to Pétain's other side—the warm springs of emotion that ran beneath the ice. For he had always been a master of the bedroom as well as of the battlefield. In 1916 he had in fact been run to earth with a girl in the Hotel Terminus at the Gare du Nord in Paris by Serrigny in order to be given Joffre's order to take command at Verdun. Pétain was never without a mistress, would compulsively flirt with any pretty woman, even a princess on an official visit. His adventures were fine subjects for his famous sardonic wit; when he was at the Ecole de Guerre he could be seen at his favourite restaurant "amusing himself by telling gamey anecdotes to his friend Commandant Fayolle which the latter pretended not to understand."[9]

Pétain brought with him to G.Q.G. a definite and revolutionary strategy:

> The decision of war not being attainable [he had written on May 10 in a rare paper in his own hand] without having first annihilated or at least reduced the enemy's reserves, we must devote all our forces to the work of weakening these. For this there is no need whatsoever to mount major attacks in depth with distant objectives. These attacks take long to prepare, are costly in effectives because in general the attacker loses more than the

[6] Painlevé, 284.
[7] Pierrefeu, II, 9.
[8] Serrigny, Preface, viii.
[9] Serrigny, Preface, viii.

defender, and do not give the benefit of surprise. . . . The method of wearing out the enemy while suffering the minimum casualties oneself consists in multiplying limited attacks, mounted with great artillery support, so as to strike the vault of the German edifice without pause until it collapses. When they can no longer rebuild the edifice, but only when, we will be able to go over to the pursuit.[10]

As a sign and symbol of the change of régime the detailed 1:5000 battle maps that Nivelle had used were replaced in Marie Antoinette's *salon* with a single strategical map of the western front on a scale of 1:200,000. An innovation of Serrigny's was a map showing relative strengths (divisions fresh, worn-out, or in the line) on both sides at any time. Later a graph, brought up to date every day, was added. This was a long way from Marengo.

Next day (May 18) Pétain and Serrigny journeyed to see Field-Marshal Sir Douglas Haig, Commander-in-Chief of the British army in France. They had already met in Paris during Pétain's fifteen days as Chief of the General Staff. Haig was impressed: "As regards Pétain personally, I found him businesslike, knowledgeable, and brief of speech. The latter is, I find, a rare quality in Frenchmen!" [11]

It was agreed that a French army of six divisions, deployed between the Belgians and the British, would come under Haig's orders for the forthcoming British offensive in Flanders. Pétain rejected Haig's request to relieve British troops south of Havrincourt, but promised him general French support by means of three limited offensive battles—one on the crest of the Chemin des Dames ridge on a total front of fifteen kilometres; one to disengage Reims once the German reserves had drained away; and one on the left bank of the Meuse.

However, Pétain and Serrigny came away struck by the mistrust of their allies over the French offensive plans. Certainly the British had valid grounds for doubt, for Nivelle had handed over a confused, continuing battle and a shaken army.

Along the front of the collapsed "victory" offensive—Malmaison-Chemin des Dames-Brimont—the 5th, 6th and 10th Armies were still struggling to hold their small gains and to carry out that old familiar western-front operation of "wearing" the enemy by attrition. These

[10] *ibid*, 136.
[11] Blake, 232.

Lens

Douai

Mons

BELGIUM

Arras

Maubeuge

BRITISH

Cambrai

le Cateau

Bapaume

GERMAN LINE · APRIL 1917 AFTER WITHDRAWAL TO SIEGFRIED LINE

Somme

1916

Peronne

St Quentin

Oise

DEC.

Roye

Ham la Fère

Oise

Craonne

FRENCH

Laon

Aisne

Compiègne

DEC. 1916

Aisne

Soissons

FRENCH

Oise

Projected breakthrough

Reims

Projected pursuit

Miles

0   30

29. NIVELLE'S PLANS

armies were exhausted by a month of savage fighting in unseasonable wet and bitter cold; their morale sagging under the weight of 96,125 casualties (French official figures—highly optimistic) between April 16 and 25 alone, of the decisive nature of their repulse, and of the lamentable failures in organisation and control by the French command itself.

« 200 »

Nivelle had believed that the methods that had recaptured Fort Douaumont at Verdun—massive artillery preparation, then a rapid assault by infantry behind a creeping barrage—could be applied to a general offensive and would lead to a break-through and open warfare. By "violence" and "brutality" the infantry would flood over the three successive German positions in one bound, as if a man could walk through a brick wall, were he to will himself strongly enough. None of Nivelle's orders revealed objective study of German defensive measures. It was true Nivelle expected the enemy defences to have been destroyed by the preliminary French bombardment; but here too he built not on reality but on his own wishful dreams. French industry had not yet supplied the necessary types of artillery in either quantity or quality. The French army still suffered from the neglect of heavy artillery and howitzers before the war. The principal weapon for smashing the German defences, strongly built into tough chalk hills, was the 155 mm. short Schneider howitzer. Nine hundred were needed; in fact there were only 428. The French had therefore to rely on their 75's and on long-barrelled heavy guns, all with flat trajectories that would not demolish deep fortifications and which increased the risk of French fire falling on French infantry. Ammunition was in some places very short and nowhere adequate for the long pursuit that was expected to follow the break-through. In any event, the allotment of guns and shells was grossly inadequate to the width and depth of front to be demolished.

In terms of infantry tactics, Nivelle's offensive ignored all the expensive lessons of 1914-16 on the futility of successive close waves of assault, ignored the German tactics of infiltration that had come so near to breaking up the defence of Verdun in the first forty-eight hours. Liaison between the different arms, detailed staff work and artillery control, organisation of the rear (especially medical services) displayed again that French unwillingness to organise minutely, to be thorough and painstaking, that had, since the August battles of 1914, cost them so many unnecessary casualties and the highest sickness rates of the three western-front belligerents.

Because Nivelle's plan had been openly discussed in Paris, and because a copy of it had been captured by the Germans, there had been no surprise. Instead the Germans had thinned their exposed forward positions and reinforced their reserves. Forty-eight French divisions therefore had

« 201 »

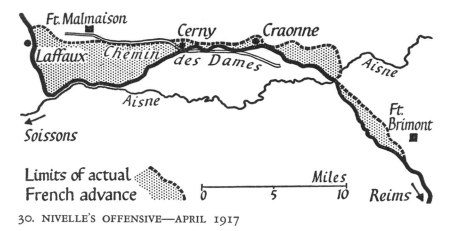

30. NIVELLE'S OFFENSIVE—APRIL 1917

tried to drive forty-two German divisions out of dense and largely unde-
stroyed defences. Despite the frantic heroism of men who had screwed
themselves up to one last effort, the French had been bloodily defeated.

By the end of 1915 the French army had already suffered 1,961,687
casualties, of which 1,001,271 were killed or missing—more than the
total French army deployed in August 1914. In 1916 the French had
lost 362,000 at Verdun alone. Except for the Marne the French army
had won no success. Now there were signs—justifying British misgivings
—that after two and a half years of war the French army had passed
the limits of endurance. G.Q.G. postal censorship reports indicated how
deeply and widely the physical miseries and moral disappointment of
Nivelle's offensive had affected the troops involved. On May 3 there had
even been a mutiny in the 2nd Colonial Infantry Division when it had
been ordered to prepare for another assault on the Chemin des Dames.
Agitators had encouraged the troops not to move and handed out leaflets
with such stirring headlines as:"Down with the war! Death to those
responsible for it!"

Other agitators had suggested that "they didn't want to fight while
their friends in war factories were making ten to fifteen francs a day." [12]

Nevertheless, on the day after seeing Haig, Pétain issued his basic
strategic instruction—Directive No. 1: personal and secret—to army
group and army commanders: "The balance of opposing forces on the

[12] Mermeix, 107.

northern and northeastern fronts does not for the moment permit of thinking of a break-through followed by strategic exploitation. Therefore we must seek to wear out the enemy with the minimum of losses to us." [13]

The instrument of the wearing process would be "attacks with limited objectives, unleashed suddenly on a front wide enough to make full use of the numbers and various types of existing artillery." [14]

These attacks would not be pressed further and further over the same killing ground as on the Somme; they would be switched from point to point and "follow one another as quickly as possible in time, in order to grip the enemy and take away his freedom of action." [15]

This meant surprise, and this in turn meant a new mobility of deployment based, in Pétain's (or Serrigny's) words, on "an appropriate organisation of the front"—a network of roads, railways, supply dumps and cantonments by which huge numbers of men, horses and cumbersome pieces of equipment could be moved, fed and watered at relatively short notice.

Above all, Pétain's offensives would be shallow in depth, so that no salients would be created ripe for concentric counterattack.

When Pétain was laying down this strategy of patience in May 1917, 3,200,000 allied troops faced 2,800,000 German on the western front—109 French divisions, 62 British, 6 Belgian and some Portuguese. Against the narrow allied superiority of numbers had to be set the extra cohesion enjoyed by the Germans with an army all of the same race, equipment and training and under a single command. There was also the inherent power of the defensive. Even without reckoning on the results of the Russian disintegration, which might eventually free fifty German divisions, Pétain's strategy was prudent. It would equally have been prudent in 1915 and 1916, although politically difficult or perhaps impossible. The belated mood of disillusion following Nivelle's failure made Pétain's cold realism acceptable in 1917.

As a justification for the great allied offensives on the western front in 1915 and 1916, attrition was retrospective. The original hope and intention had always been a break-through into open country and then

[13] Laure, 14.
[14] *loc. cit.*
[15] *ibid,* 15.

the wide manoeuvres in whose tradition all generals had been brought up, which had always been a norm of war, and one so unnaturally supplanted by siege operations. To acknowledge even to themselves that decisive success was beyond their power would not have been easy for men the *raison d'être* of whose professional life and present command was to achieve victory. The inexperience of Joffre and Haig and their armies in siege warfare in the field, and their own wish and hope for success, led them into a false optimism which a cold and rigorous analysis of the balance of forces would have demolished. More than this, there was a too literal acceptance of Napoleon's and Clausewitz's ideas on the supreme power of will and the necessity of striking the enemy's centre of gravity. "Will" came to mean obstinacy, or "pluck"; the enemy's centre of gravity to mean his most powerful defences. Only an exceptional man could have stepped outside the military training and tradition of a lifetime, could have remained free from the influence of the desperate hope pressing upon him from politicians, public opinion and his own subordinates. Pétain was such a man.

The fact was that the German front in the west was impenetrable, given the opposing forces and equipment, and had been since 1914. Pétain had recognised this as long ago as October 1914. Serrigny's diary for October 29 recorded: "They keep on telling us to attack, but Pétain begins to realise the uselessness of such operations" [16]

On the German side, defensive technique and equipment had evolved always in advance of the allied offensive methods. In the words of the *British Official History:* "With their usual thoroughness, having decided to stand upon the defensive, they gradually evolved a system which amounted to something more even than defensive strategy and tactics and may be described as a philosophy of the defensive." [17]

In 1915 and 1916 the French had had a mass array of trained troops but lacked the heavy artillery and shells for an assault on such defences; the British in 1916 had had the artillery (although with poor and unreliable shells, fruits of a scrambled expansion of war industry), but about half the British troops had been raw levies, superficially trained. Therefore in 1916 there had been the contrast between the subtle infiltration tactics after a brief hurricane bombardment of the first German assault

[16] Serrigny, 4.
[17] *British Official History*, XI, Preface.

on Verdun and the rigid linear tactics of the British attack on the Somme, after a laborious fortnight's shelling. It was the contrast between an army whose backbone was an abundant supply of first-rate, peace-time-trained officers and N.C.O.'s and one suddenly expanded from a tiny force and whose leaders from platoon to division were therefore without experience and thorough training. Here was the reason for the ghastly massacres on the Somme, too subtle and too prosaic a reason for those who sought scapegoats.

Faced with the basic fact of German defensive power, generals and politicians spun in circles in their efforts to find a way round it, or over it, for no one wished to draw the only realistic conclusion from it— that victory without fresh allies was impossible. There were the eastern-ers who thought that sweeping victories of manoeuvre might be won against Turkey or in the Balkans. As at Gallipoli in 1915, surprise might have won an intitial success, but sooner or later the German reserves would have arrived and the allies would have faced a similar situation as in the west. As the Second World War proved, Europe has no "soft underbelly." "Easternism" was escapism. But so was "Westernism"; for by April 1917 the pursuit of victory in the west had reduced the French army to a state of collapse.

The fact thus remained, too blank and awful for most to admit, that Germany was unbeatable by the military means available to her enemies in 1914-17.

The consequence of ignoring this fact, or being unaware of it, was the series of massacres for which the generals have been so bitterly blamed. Yet who forced them to attempt the impossible? Fundamentally it was the very people whom the casualty lists horrified and who were to blame the generals after the war: the public and the politicians. To beat an enemy as powerful as Germany necessarily involved massacres. Because the western allies suffered relatively lightly in the Second World War, it does not mean that the massacres were avoided by brilliant leadership. It is simply that the Sommes and Passchendaeles took place at Lenin-grad, Stalingrad and Moscow. The Normandy invasion was not launched until the Red Army had inflicted and sustained casualties on a similar scale to the western-front battles of the First World War.

The logical consequence of stalemate was a compromise peace. Until after the agony of the Somme was over in November 1916, the implacable, illogical hatred of the home fronts, especially in Britain, made peace without triumph unthinkable. The troops in France knew the reality of war and how far it was from the slogans and attitudes of propaganda. For them the war rapidly became not only terrifying and horrible, but tedious, a job of work, a condition of life. At home the public lived in an atmosphere of noisy emotion, Victorian in style; it saw the war in the simple shapes and crude colours of nineteenth-century religious or temperance tracts. The home public simply did not know what it was talking or feeling about; its conception of the war was no nearer reality than the plot of a penny novelette was to real love and marriage. And the soldiers could not tell them the truth.

So far as the British army was concerned, there was in the first place the national taciturnity, reinforced in the case of officers by a public school training in silence and stoicism. For the soldier on leave in Britain the gulf between the front and his home circle was unbridgeable. How could one tell the people one loved, living still so comfortably and safely, talking such naïve nonsense about the war, the reality of one's own experience—the daily boredom and squalor, the terrors, the familiar and no longer awful sights of mutilation, the rats and the lice? How could one convey one's curious sense of kinship with the Germans suffering in the opposite trench to these clean, bright civilians who thought of the war in terms of honour, glory, victory, "our gallant lads" and "the wicked Hun"? The front and Blighty remained worlds separated by a mental portcullis that dropped perhaps on the ship or at the delousing station. There were no radio reports, as in the Second World War, to bring the truth straight from the battlefield to the home; the popular newspapers instead purveyed illusion to feed illusion.

It was an aspect of the tragic folly of the war that it was the soldier's own family, in their lust for victory, that kept the soldier in the trenches; that it was the mental attitude of the very people who watched so fearfully for a war-office telegram that made it likely that they would indeed so receive news of the death of a loved one.

For the desire for total victory was not rational. The fruits of the victory, or the fate it would prevent, could never be proportionate to the sacrifices. The Kaiser was not Hitler; Imperial Germany, for all its crude manners and brash and bullying methods, was not Nazi Germany. "Civilisation" belonged to neither side exclusively. If Britain and France

23. General Philippe Pétain

24. General Robert Nivelle

25. Paul Painlevé

LIVING QUARTERS:
26. The Château de Beaurepaire, occupied by the British C-in-C
from March 1916 to April 1919

27. A dugout near Miraumont, occupied by the Royal Artillery,
March 1917

28. French troops deserting during the mutinies of 1917

29. The Passchendaele campaign, 1917: a canal and bridge
destroyed in the fighting

30. Albert Thomas, Haig, Joffre and Lloyd George

31. General Sir Henry Wilson

32. Field-Marshal von Hindenburg

represented liberal nineteenth-century individualism and democracy, Germany represented the technology and collectivism of the future. If France in the post-Impressionists had the most creative painters, Germany was leading in modern architecture and industrial design. A roll call of the great creative artists, scientists, writers and dramatists of the early twentieth century in no way supports the view that the future of civilisation lay with any one nation or alliance or with their existing ruling groups.

Nor were there decisive differences in the extent of the greed manifested by each side's war aims. In the last months of 1916 and the first of 1917, while America was still neutral, the central powers and the allies each stated the outline terms upon which they were prepared to discuss peace. As Lord Hankey points out, those put forward by the allies were essentially those which after two more years of slaughter were imposed by the Treaty of Versailles. The terms make a fascinating comparison.

Germany wanted the Belgian Congo; in 1919 Britain took all Germany's African colonies, partly in the guise of a League of Nations "mandate." Germany wanted the Briey-Longwy coal and steel basin in France; France took the Saar as a protectorate. Germany wanted either the fortress of Liége or the passing of Belgium under her influence; the allies occupied for ten years the whole of the Rhineland. Germany and Austria wanted Italian territory on the Austrian frontier; Italy took Austrian territory both there and down the Dalmatian coast. Germany and Austria wanted Rumanian territory on the Austrian frontier and Serbian territory on the frontiers of Austria and Bulgaria; the allies destroyed Austria entirely except for the rump round Vienna and the Alps.

It would thus be difficult for the historian to draw up a balance sheet of the vices and virtues of each side that would justify the character of a crusade against evil given to the war by the combatants. Nor, punitive though the eventual peace terms were, can the penalties of defeat, or of a compromise peace, be reasonably related to the scale of sacrifices endured to avoid defeat or achieve victory.

At the heart of the war, therefore, lay a monstrous irrationality that coloured all policies and all events, that made it the colossal tragedy it was and gives it a special historical fascination. It was a war of religion without religion, of ideological fanaticism without ideologies; it was a war whose fuel was fear and crowd-madness, a reservoir of emotion only drained by the deaths of up to one in thirty-seven of the population.

In 1914 universal education and the popular press had created a mass public opinion, but it was an opinion still based on ignorance of the world—especially the world outside one's own country. Another country was another planet, inhabited by mysterious, inferior but probably hostile beings. The social novelists of the time portray a lower middle class of simple, ignorant people in whose lives there is an intolerable discipline at work, iron taboos in private life, and a near-poverty that allows little outlet for creative recreation. The true picture of the life of the mass of those who went to the war in 1914 is not the Arcadian legend of tea on the lawn under the cedars but of a grey dreariness that permitted little self-expression and little joy. Emotional colour and fulfilment, a sense of power and achievement, these the people had to seek outside their own lives; they found them vicariously in Kaiser and Fatherland, King and Empire, in parading troops and battleships in review. And when some spark like Mafeking set them off, all their repressions exploded in public riot.

The radio and the television speak to men or to families individually. In 1914 you had to go out into the street—to the palace, parliament or even the local post office—to hear the latest news and official announcements. This meant crowds; and crowds in 1914 meant Mafeking again. Only by the end of 1916 was the consequent emotional debauch beginning to end in a sober dawn wherein the havoc could be measured.

Once the war had begun it moved according to its own inner dynamics, unrelated to policy or intent. Those dynamics were similar to those of revolution. In the first phase there were moderate men enlisting "mob" support in achieving moderate objects. The "mob," its fear of the enemy once aroused, outran moderation; "war to the end" became the goal. The moderate leaders either gave expression to this frenzy or were thrust aside. Now the sacrifices already made demanded extra recompense; each country's price for peace rose; peace became less and less possible; the war was feeding on itself. As in revolutions, mass emotion at last began to cool, as casualties and shortage of food and goods made life more and more unpleasant. It was the moment for the Cromwells, Dantons and Napoleons to keep the machine rolling when more and more people wanted to stop it. In Britain Lloyd George replaced Asquith; in Germany Ludendorff and Hindenburg established a military dictatorship in place of Bethmann-Hollweg; in France it was Clemenceau, although not until November 1917.

Yet the romantic spell of war had lain less powerfully on France than on Britain and Germany; the spell worked best on rootless urban populations, and France was still predominantly a country of small towns and peasant proprietors. There was of course Paris—Paris which had produced all the changes of régime since 1789, Paris that contradicted more than expressed France—but 1870-1 had cured the Parisians of facile enthusiasm for war. Between 1914 and 1917 the French had fought dourly for a completely realistic objective: to clear the Germans off their territory.

Now in the spring of 1917 France, who of the western belligerents had suffered most, was the first to give way to an infinite weariness of spirit, a lassitude of despair and disillusion. Before Pétain could begin to apply his Directive No. 1, at a moment when France found her effective great-power allies reduced from two to a single one, at the beginning of the long wait for the Americans, the new French Commander-in-Chief received reports that told him he faced the imminent disintegration of his army. Ahead of Pétain lay a test of generalship more difficult than a great battle. Success would bring no lists of prisoners and captured guns, no triumphant entries into liberated towns, no sweeping arrows of advance on the maps in the newspapers. Yet if the French army were still in the field when the Americans arrived in force in the summer of 1918, it would prove that Pétain was indeed *un grand chef*. The consequences of his failure, on the other hand, would almost certainly be German victory.

In the first place, if the French army collapsed, Haig would have to face a hazardous retreat to the Channel ports under attack by overwhelming odds—a retreat that would involve the loss or destruction of the vast network of communications, camps, supply depots and ammunition dumps so expensively constructed since 1914 as a base for the British army in France. Secondly, the British Empire, after a disaster of this magnitude, would face the central powers with only the dubious help of Italy and the far-off chance of rescue by America. The British Empire would do so, not as in 1940 at the beginning of the real fighting when spirits were fresh, but after terrible losses in the field and at a time of weariness and discouragement. In these circumstances, would Britain have fought on alone against Imperial Germany as she was to do against Nazi Germany?

Whether this question would have to be faced and answered depended on Pétain. On May 19, 1917, three days after he took up his command, the discontent that had been simmering in the French army since the beginning of the month boiled over into widespread open mutiny.

9

The mutiny that marked the beginning of a general slide of the army out of the grip of habitual discipline and the control of its officers took place on May 19 in a divisional depot of the 32nd Corps. In almost every respect its course was characteristic of what followed in half the divisions of the French army.

The firing charge was supplied by news that certain troops in the depot were being posted as reinforcements to the 162nd Regiment of Infantry; that is, they were destined for the German mincing machine, details of whose efficiency had been widely disseminated by experience and rumour. Even a grim and tedious depot cantonment seemed preferable. A shapeless crowd gathered on the bleak roads of the camp, discontent, fear and *vin ordinaire* leading to bleats of protest. Agitators gave direction to the demonstration, and the song that had taken Russia out of the war sounded through the depot—the *Internationale*.[1]

Now the crowd felt the electric tremor of the desire for violence. It swarmed to the house of the officer commanding the depot, and the leading spirits at the front of the mob got in. By luck or good sense, the officer commanding was elsewhere. To smash his furniture had therefore to be the unsatisfying substitute for manhandling his person. Nothing more could be done in the way of riot, so the mutineers drew off to organise themselves on true Russian lines. Until now the officers, N.C.O.'s and depot staff might all have been on leave so far as the maintenance of discipline was concerned. This was a fact quite as alarming as the mutiny

[1] The general account of the mutinies is drawn from Mermeix, Laure, Palat and Carré.

itself. When the officer commanding returned to his depot, he was visited by three "soldiers' delegates" who presented him with a list of grievances the troops wished to see remedied. Next day neither bugle nor the bellowing of N.C.O.'s could get the troops on parade: the personnel in the depot had become like a single, sullen, growling, immovable beast, and so they remained.

In some ways the mutiny in the 128th Infantry Regiment (which began on May 20) was even more truly expressive of the immediate causes and course of the men's despair.

On the opening day of Nivelle's offensive the morale of the regiment had been good, if perhaps brittle, as it went up to join the 2nd Corps of the 10th Army (designated for the strategic exploitation of the breakthrough). For thirteen days during the repulse of the offensive and the consequent muddles and indecision the regiment was ordered to and fro in meaningless, exhausting and tedious marches, in rain, sleet, high winds and biting cold; it slept in the open. On April 29 it had been ordered to take a certain hill (Mont Spin); it attacked on May 8 with great courage and dash, either despite its unpleasant fortnight's manoeuvring or, as is more likely, because the prospect of action restored the regiment's spirits. Nevertheless the German defences were too strong; 128th Regiment found that only one of sixteen gaps marked on their battle maps as opened by gunfire was in fact so; the regiment's gains were small.

It held on in a precarious situation for eleven more days of danger and cold and was then relieved. Hardly had it reached its rest area when the regiment learned that its successors had lost its gains to a German counterattack. Thus far the regiment had been treated to almost a month of extreme and quite pointless physical hardship, culminating in danger and heavy casualties without result. Now the regiment was "resting" again. As with most French rest areas, the only discernible difference from the line was the absence of enemy shells and bullets. Only two out of the three battalions in 128th Regiment had a roof over their heads. Food was scanty and dire, welfare and recreational facilities of a Crimean standard, sanitation and washing facilities medieval. Troops shivering and worn out with cold and danger wanted warmth, cleanliness and food. All they got were floods of cheap wine—upon which so many of the mutinies were to be fuelled.

On May 20 the 128th Regiment was ordered back into line. This meant on the one hand danger of death in the muddled operations and on the other the end of any chance of leave. There were plenty of politically interested parties ready to point this out, and round such nuclei of rebellion clustered the miserable soldiers. These indignation groups matured into an open-air strike meeting, and two companies refused to march. However, the "strike" was mastered by the officers; the regiment marched.

The shock of fear at orders for the line also began the mutiny of a battalion of the 18th Infantry on May 26. After three weeks in a "rest" area, it was ordered to be ready to move at midnight by motor transport. By 10 P.M. the troublemakers were at work. Mutiny here had a different sound—that of drunken riot and sporadic rifle shots—as groups of men lurched through the camp. When the trucks finally clattered away into the darkness, the battalion was 144 men short. These men now became a group elated with the sense of liberation given by successful disobedience, so they set off at daybreak for the nearest railway station, Fère-en-Tardenois, with the intention of taking the first train to Paris. To stop them the *gendarmerie nationale* had to turn out in great force. Surrounded, the mutineers were marched back to camp.

Next day (May 27) orders for the line exploded a mutiny in the 158th Infantry Division. Four battalions herded angrily round the divisional headquarters with raucous shouts and ugly gestures of violence. The G.O.C. and his officers went out to meet the crowd, braided kepis and neat uniforms against shabby serge, the choler of outraged authority against the rage of ill-used servants. The soldiers' shouts called for leave, to which they reckoned they enjoyed a right. Had not their "delegates" already given the G.O.C. details of their demands? The G.O.C. could not get them to disperse; they stayed together in the warm and safe anonymity of the crowd until the moment had come when they should have begun to march up towards the German guns. Officers and loyal troops did succeed in herding the mutineers off along the road to the front, but they could not restore discipline; they could not or dared not single out the leaders of the mutiny for arrest. The march was a shambles; the battalions shed deserters continually.

From May 19 onwards Pétain received reports of seven or eight fresh, serious outbreaks every day. For a commander-in-chief it was a terrifying experience—worse than a defeat in the field—for as the bonds of discipline and obedience dissolved, authority had no means with which to hold the army together except the increasingly doubtful one of loyal troops. The feebleness and apathy of most commanders on the spot sharpened the sensation of helplessness in the face of general dissolution.

In a single day two more separate incidents manifested the twin themes of Communism of a march on Paris—both highly dangerous developments from what had begun as a military "strike." All three regiments of the 9th Division, once again after being notified of an early return to the trenches, formed a protest march in which the singing of the *Internationale* was alternated with shouts of: "Leave!" and "We won't go up the line!"

And in the 5th Division similar protests took place in two regiments, but, significantly, they had both been out of the line for some time and personnel had enjoyed regular leave. Equally significantly the shouted grievances here were not military: "Our wives are dying of hunger—they're killing them in Paris—that's where we want to go. The Government must be told; they are the ones that turned down the German peace offer. We're going to the Chamber of Deputies." [2]

Elsewhere a battalion took to the road to strident shouts of *"à Paris!"* —one of those roads up which so many masses of their burdened comrades had marched to slaughter, sometimes past saluting *grand chefs* in the cruel splendour of spurred boots and tight uniform. Behind the mutineers came in pursuit a regiment of cuirassiers; a use had at last been found for cavalry in the war. Like bullocks, the dejected troops were herded back to camp by the horsemen.

Yet another regiment left its cantonment shouting *"à Paris."* Like children running away from home, the soldiers hid in a wood for three days. As it camped peacefully, loyal troops surrounded the woodland. The officer commanding the sector was a man of good sense; he used no force but sent amongst the mutineers middle-aged family men from a territorial regiment who succeeded in persuading the younger fellows to return to their duty.

Not even units with the finest war records were immune from the profound discontent. In one such army corps there was a large number of mutineers, who shut themselves in their huts or threatened to open fire on anyone who came near them. In the end their resolution, too, crum-

[2] Mermeix, 173.

bled into surrender. However, as with all other mutinies, the affair had taken place in a back area, not in the battle zone. This was a cardinal point of comfort to Pétain as, between May 20 and the middle of June, reports came into Compiègne of disorders big and small, in no less than sixteen army corps (fifty-five divisions), most of which had taken part in the disastrous attacks of April 4 and 16—and all of which lay nearer to Paris (which, politically, was France, and therefore key to a revolution) than did the rest of the army.

Half of Pétain's army therefore was mutinous. If the Germans—who had known most of the French secrets—knew this and attacked, would the mutineers fight for their native soil or, as with the Russian army, would they make for the interior to spread revolution? Might they not do this even without a German offensive? The troops in the line so far had proved reliable; but how long would they remain so if a general "strike" in the rear prevented their regular relief?

"It is useless therefore," in Pétain's own words at the time, "to minimise the gravity of such acts of indiscipline and their disturbing action on neighbouring units. . . . The evil exists, it is an undeniable fact. It could have the most disastrous consequences for the army and for the country. It is important to define its causes, then to seek remedies." [3]

Defining the causes displayed the G.Q.G.'s mode of thinking about military events in all its happy illusion and absence of self-criticism. The Third Bureau (Operations and Training), supported by the Postal Control, furiously blamed the mutinies on political agitation, the French Trades Union Congress, and the syndicalists, and on the government for not preventing defeatist agitators from demoralising the army from the rear—indeed on anything but the operations and training of the French army through four bloody campaigns.

Inaugurating a command by coping with a desperate crisis did not come more easily with habit, rather the reverse. Behind the mask of cold authority and resolution, Pétain was shaken. "He was extremely pessimistic," wrote Serrigny. "Debeney, who had stomach trouble, also saw things blackly; every evening General Franchet d'Esperey came to see us and subjected us without relief to a régime of sauna baths;[4] with his natural impulsiveness he saw the situation sometimes good, some-

---

[3] Report to the Minister of War 29.5.17; quoted Carré, 81.
[4] *douches écossaises.*

times ugly. On the days when his impression was bad, the morale of the General-in-Chief was not brilliant." [5]

On May 29 Pétain made his first report to Painlevé, Minister of War, on the mutinies. It was Wellingtonian in its brutally cold and candid good sense. After summarising the mutinous incidents that had occurred so far, he turned to their causes:

> . . . It is difficult to determine how far one particular cause is significant rather than another. It is therefore necessary to place them in two different categories: those which emanate from life itself at the front, those that are due to outside influences.
>
> Against the first, the General-in-Chief is armed up to a certain point. He is unarmed in the case of the others, and only the government can act effectively here.
>
> Concerning life at the front, one finds, at the base of the troops' indiscipline, general weariness, the question of leave, drunkenness and, it is necessary to acknowledge it, the faults of the command during the recent offensive.
>
> As an accessory to this, one can point out a weakening in the repression of crimes and military offences. [6]

In the contrast between promise and result in Nivelle's offensive Pétain saw the key to the military causes of the mutiny.

> The orders for the great offensive . . . had obviously aroused exaggerated hopes. It was repeated that our troops would reach Laon on the first day.

Nivelle in his speeches on tour to inspire the troops had said that the German withdrawal to the Siegfried Line, the preliminary attack by the British and Army Group North to draw the German reserves, and the artillery bombardment which would lay the German defences flat would all lead to victory "certain, swift and small in cost." And Pétain went on:

> These promises were broadcast as far as the soldier in the ranks. . . . In fact, we have progressed little despite very severe losses, the destruction counted on has been totally insufficient, the struggle has been very hard, and, having begun on April 16, is not finished today.

[5] Serrigny, 146-7.
[6] Carré, 82.

Nivelle's indecision after the great failure of April 16 had added to the demoralisation:

> All that period of orders and counter-orders which followed till the end of the month has been disastrous. The troops put in the line on April 19 received successively information that they would attack on the 23rd, then the 25th, then the 29th, at last May 3 and 5. Successive counter-orders of this kind are depressing in the extreme for those carrying them out. To prepare to attack is to face the probability of death. One deliberately accepts this idea once. But when they see the awful moment postponed again and again the bravest and the steadiest become demoralised. In the end, physical resistance and nervous tension alike have their limits. The troops who attacked on May 5 were at the end of their tether, having been in the front line for seventeen days under intense and continuous fire.

In this paragraph lies perhaps the essence of Pétain's quality as a soldier; his profound understanding of what war meant to those who have to fight it, his compassion, his knowledge of the possible, and his ability to express these things so lucidly.

This paragraph in a confidential official report recalls one of the most moving passages in military literature, in which, after the war, Pétain recalled his anguish at the sight of his soldiers passing his headquarters outside Verdun to and from the battle:

> My heart lurched as I saw our young men of twenty going into the furnace of Verdun, and reflected that they would pass too quickly, with the lightness of their age, from enthusiasm in their first engagement to the weariness caused by suffering . . . how saddening it was when they came back, either on their own as wounded or stragglers, or in the ranks of companies decimated by loss! Their stares seemed to be fixed in a vision of unbelievable terror . . . they drooped beneath the weight of their horrifying memories. When I spoke to them, they could scarcely answer.

Now in 1917, as he wrote his report to Painlevé on the mutinies, he drew on his unrivalled experience to suggest how the troops should have been rested after Nivelle's attacks:

> . . . one must lay down as an absolute rule that a man coming back from hard fighting (Somme, Verdun, Aisne) will not rest properly if he is exposed to shelling and even the sound of gunfire. It is utopian to believe that troops can recover physically and morally from their emotions and from

exhaustion in an area under bombardment, or if they know that they are likely to be sent suddenly back into the line.

It follows that . . . it is necessary to send troops relieved from the front to complete rest in the rear.[7]

This did not mean softness or indulgence:

On the other hand, one must oppose the very distinct tendency, shown in certain units and even among their commanders, to *demand as a right* prolonged rest after any period of fighting.[8]

Pétain's report had now dealt with those causes of the mutinies that had originated in purely military shortcomings. In turning to outside causes, he wrote a coldly accurate, beautifully organised and absolutely devastating indictment of French politics and French society in the third spring of the war.

He began with an analysis of the evil done by an irresponsible press, linking this analysis with particular social questions.

Never [wrote Pétain] has the press been worse directed than since March. *It might really have wanted, systematically and deliberately, to ruin the discipline and the morale of the army* as well as that of the nation . . .

Ever since the opening of our offensives, the papers . . . have openly criticised the ideas and methods of the High Command. In their columns, reprinted *in extenso,* are found the numerous parliamentary questions put by M.P.'s on the conduct of operations, the recruitment of black troops, the functioning of the medical services, etc. . . .

The articles display little enthusiasm over anything concerning our own success. On the other hand . . . the press never runs dry of wildly inflated praise for the exploits of our British allies. . . .

On matters not directly relating to the army and its operations, the papers are not less depressing to the morale of our soldiers.

There were, for example, wild reports on the situation inside Russia.

[The press] makes no attempt to conceal our grave anxieties henceforth about the military worth of this powerful ally. It describes . . . the measures taken by the revolutionary government in regard to the army; setting-up of soldiers' committees in each regiment, abolition of salutes for officers . . .

[7] Carré, 84-5.
[8] *ibid,* 85.

There was, Pétain considered, another press topic equally as dangerous as the Russian Revolution:

> . . . the idea of *Peace* and the word itself appear in terms of longing in the weekly journals. They gave the widest and loudest publicity to the agitation worked up by the Socialist party for the Stockholm conference, where socialists of allied, neutral and enemy countries were to meet to discuss peace.

Yet Pétain was fair to the press over this question of peace:

> The papers, it is true, are almost unanimous in only contemplating peace with honour. . . . But the big word is let fall: *Peace,* approaching peace and, as many do not hesitate to describe it, *imminent.*

The question of peace was linked to the deplorable state of the national economy:

> The press does nothing to hide the worries of the government over this subject; it criticises the measures it takes, which are declared to be vexatious, badly thought out (which is only too true) and in any case useless.

Then there was the publicity given to strikes in industry, especially when the soldier knew that his fellow citizens called up for war work were getting fifteen to twenty francs a day.

Pétain now summed up the combined effects of press publicity in sentences that fall like salvoes:

> To dangle prematurely before the eyes of men who daily face death, men subject to the horrors of the battlefield, men worn out by the misery of life in the trenches, the lovely mirage of peace is to wish deliberately to weaken all the moral resources and high ideals that have so far been the glory of the French army in this long war.

> To present the soldier with all the seriousness of the economic crisis without giving him at the same time reassurance that the government will devote all its powers to deal with it, is unforgivable frivolity.

> Nothing is more depressing to the fighting man than henceforward to think about the prospects . . . before their wives and children left at home of lack of fuel and want of food next winter.

So far as future direction of the press was concerned, Pétain laid responsibility firmly in the lap of the government. Then, pausing to denounce all propaganda in favour of revolution as treason and demand that revolutionaries should be hunted down and punished, the Commander-in-Chief swung his attack on Members of Parliament who visited the front on parliamentary missions:

> Since the beginning of 1917 the number of such representatives has continued to multiply, particularly in the zone of operations. Not content with seeking information and asking questions on the precise subject of their mission, many of them ask general officers for all kinds of information, they invite criticisms and recriminations against the High Command, they even gain knowledge of secret documents. . . . They then go down the scale to corps commanders to junior officers, as far as the other ranks, from whom they receive in a muddled way all that is current in the way of complaints.
>
> Sometimes even—a graver matter—they promise to look after the soldiers' interests in high places . . . they encourage discontent by promising everyone the granting of leave as an absolute and inalienable right.
>
> In every respect, even the presence of these people at the front creates a state of mind in no way helpful to discipline . . . the government ought to remind members of both Houses of Parliament visiting the armies that it is their duty to limit themselves strictly to the terms of the particular and restricted mission entrusted to them.

Here Pétain had touched on the fundamental issue of parliamentary control of the army—not merely of control over grand strategy, but direct and detailed, in the style of the deputies on mission of the Revolution.

Pétain finally saw special significance in the way the factors causing the mutinies had been combined:

> The crisis has been aggravated in a singular manner by the fact that all the causes have exerted their influence during a relatively short lapse of time. We started active operations in March. Almost at the same time the Russian revolution broke out. A bitter end of the winter sharpened economic difficulties. To cap it all supervened the vast deception and deep discouragement produced by the failure of our April offensives and the losses that they caused.

So much for diagnosis; what of cure?

> The first measures that I have in mind—to regulate the granting of leave, to suppress drunkenness and to establish a rotation of units between rest, training, the line and battle—should have a curative effect.
>
> But it is on the other hand essential that the High Command impresses on all ranks that it is resolved to make everyone observe the strictest discipline

and obedience, from top to bottom of the military structure. It must ruthlessly make examples where necessary and bring them to the knowledge of the army.

Lastly it is the government's responsibility to act immediately to bring about a change in the line taken by the press and to take legal action against any revolutionary agitation. It is part of its duty to make use of all its influence to control the action of Members of Parliament in the way indicated above.

In reminding the government of its duty to stop revolutionary and pacifist agitation behind the front, and in particular demanding that leave trains and Paris railway stations should be cleared of agitators, Pétain only repeated the terms of a long letter written by Nivelle as long ago as February. It was the job of M. Malvy, the Minister of the Interior since the beginning of the war. But Malvy was a Radical Socialist; there were, so the phrase went, no enemies on the left, and therefore no action had ever been taken. Thus Merrheim, head of the metalworkers' union (whose membership was to rise from 7,500 in 1912 to 204,000 in 1918) and a friend of Malvy, was free to organise and conduct a vigorous peace campaign. Malvy had less sincere, less respectable friends in such curious political go-betweens as Bolo Pasha (in German pay) and Almereyda, the editor of the pacifist and revolutionary paper *Le Bonnet Rouge*. It was a fantastic situation, for *Le Bonnet Rouge* still received a French government subsidy while it was carrying German propaganda. Painlevé, the Minister of War, an able mathematician but renowned for his inability to make a decision, refused to take action against Malvy; he refused even to believe the charges Pétain made against him. Pétain therefore took measures on his own authority to clean up the trains and railway stations.

Alarmed by the feebleness of commanders in the face of mutiny, Pétain sent them a strongly worded signal:

> To excuse their not having done their duty, certain officers and N.C.O.'s hide behind the fact that since the incidents are collective in character, it is difficult to single out the leaders. Such a reason is not valid. It is always in fact possible to turn a collective act into an individual one. It is enough to give some man an order to carry out (beginning with the bad-hats). If they refuse, they are immediately arrested and sent for trial.[9]

[9] Serrigny, 147.

He specifically covered with his own authority those who acted firmly and promised retribution to weaklings.

Yet the mutinies were still spreading with a horrible spontaneity. Revolution and an end to the war had now become themes that began to dominate purely military grievances. The mutiny still had no centre; indeed, its alarming quality lay in the sudden spontaneous burst into flame, first in this unit and then in that, all along the front of Nivelle's offensive. A brigadier was howled down, manhandled, and lost the stars from his uniform and the flag from his car; a town hall that housed an H.Q. had its windows stoned; in most places the *Internationale* was sung or red flags brandished. Elsewhere the mutineers freed the prisoners from a detention camp; in a chasseur regiment the officers were stoned and the C.O.'s house shot at, the incident culminating in a gun battle with loyal troops. Two thousand demonstrators paraded to shouts of: "Long live the Revolution! Down with the war!" "Long live peace!" "Down with tyrants!" In all these incidents there was the same ugly, jagged violence of bitterness and anger. Leaflets and posters tried, often successfully, to harness the discontent:

> French soldiers! [said one poster] the hour for peace has struck! Your last offensive has pitifully failed! It has caused you frightful losses, and you have no further strength to carry on the useless struggle! Where are you heading for? In your towns and countryside the spectre of hunger already joins the spectre of death! If you do not know how to get rid of that gang of degenerates and careerists who are leading the country to ruin, if you do not know how to get out of England's grip and obtain immediate peace, France as a whole will go down the road to unavoidable death. French comrades! Down with the war! Long live early peace! [10]

Between May 28 and June 10, 1917, the danger of complete French collapse sharpened, as the mutiny flared and smouldered throughout the army, even touching territorial units along the quiet front of Alsace-Lorraine. In Painlevé's words: "There did not remain more than two divisions that could be absolutely relied upon, if the Germans had launched a large-scale attack." [11]

On the other hand, no units had so far abandoned the front line in the

[10] Carré, 100.
[11] *ibid,* 102.

Russian manner; it was a grim comfort to the authorities that the mutineers appeared still to put the *defence* of their country first.

However, the danger of national collapse was heightened by parallel unrest among the working classes of the great cities. There was strong agitation for peace, with or without social revolution; there were strikes and industrial protests. As with the army, Russia was the great precedent and inspiration. On June 4 soldiers' wives who were also war workers were fired on by Indo-Chinese soldiers while demonstrating in the boulevard Berthier. In a country under censorship a rumour therefore spread from Paris to the front with the speed of a fuse to the effect that bloody civil war had broken out in the capital. Members of the government were only too aware of the horrifying sensation of sitting on a mine that showed every sign of being about to explode. The President of the Republic, M. Raymond Poincaré, wrote in his *Memoirs* of a riot on June 2, 1917:

> From the Elysée Palace I heard the shouting that rose from beside the *Grand Palais* and which lasted two hours. When information was received, it turned out to be a matter of 2,000 to 3,000 women strikers who had passed along the Avenue Alexander III and the Champs-Elysées and were heading for the Ministry of Armaments, where they had sent delegates. They carried banners and screamed out in tumult.[12]

As the history of five countries during the war was to illustrate, there was a breaking point for nations as well as for individuals. How soon it was reached depended on the scale and speed of human wastage and the social and political cohesion of the state. The "agitators," "pacifists" and "revolutionaries" that were so often looked upon at the time as the causes of national collapse were in fact merely among its symptoms. For whereas war began by cementing the social structures of the belligerent countries, it ended by loosening them; all the peacetime centrifugal forces came back into play with vastly greater power.

Of the western belligerents, France had made the most intense human effort and had suffered the heaviest losses. In 1914 she had been in terms of human and industrial resources no longer a great power. Her friends and her enemies continued to regard her as one. Most Frenchmen— soldiers and statesmen—equally did so; given her place in Europe, per-

12 Carré, 103.

haps they had no choice. But the role of a great power imposed terrible strains. In the war of 1870-1, which she had lost, France opposed a population of 36,000,000 to Prussia and her allies' 40,000,000; in 1914 she opposed 39,000,000 to Germany's 67,000,000. Yet in 1914 France managed to place an army in the field little inferior in number to the German army in the west. She had originally mobilised over one in twenty of her adult male population, against Germany's one in thirty. In terms of purely human mobilisation—"the nation in arms"—this achievement was prodigious and made more so by a scarcity of young men in an ageing population. However, the French effort from 1870 to 1914 to maintain her traditional greatness vis-à-vis Germany was too narrowly military. French industry and technology, like those of Great Britain, had not responded to the challenges and opportunities of the second, post-1860, industrial revolution. France, too, was stagnant. In 1914 the French steel industry had produced only 5,000,000 tons against the German 17,320,000 tons (to give the basic index of industrial capability). In the "new" industries of chemicals and electrics, the French were particularly weak: French capital investment in the latter was in 1913 only a third of Germany's. Now in 1917, with an army still of 2,877,000 men in the field, and her reserves of military manpower reduced to 380,000, mostly of the 1919 class, and her northern industries in German hands, war production threw a breaking strain on a peasant agriculture, on an old-fashioned, small-scale industrial system, and on a society little fond of or accustomed to collective discipline.

Since France had, by 1914, already become a second-class power in all but strictly military terms, her shortage of young men in a population of only 39,000,000 meant that, without strict prudence and economy of lives, she would fairly soon become second-class in military terms as well. However, her soldiers and politicians had conducted the war as if the French Empire of 1914 enjoyed a relative strength in the world similar to the First Empire—as if the Third Republic occupied the same position in Europe as the First. It is true that the initiative exercised by Germany from 1914 onwards, by reason of her presence on French soil, would have induced all but the strongest-minded Frenchmen to attack. Nevertheless (as Plan 17 showed) French soldiers and politicians had always made fundamentally false and oversanguine assumptions about French national power, and their strategy for the years 1914-17 had been still based on these assumptions. By their unrealism they had imposed strains on France too great to be borne; they had hastened the present crisis, in which there were in fact no new elements but the precedent of Russia.

For anti-army propaganda had been a feature of militant socialism and radicalism ever since the Dreyfus affair at the turn of the century had shaken the nation's confidence in her military hierarchy. Indeed, anti-militarism had become a fashionable, intellectual movement, especially among schoolteachers; between 1909 and 1910 there had been violent propaganda calling on soldiers to desert or to carry out military strikes (as was now happening in 1917). As war grew nearer, anti-militarism had faded before a new patriotic solidarity that culminated in the *union sacré* of 1914-16. Now, with the *union sacré* destroyed on fruitless battlefields and in the muddles and injustices of French home-front organisation for total war, anti-militarism's moment had come again; in the trench and the home alike it was difficult for miserable people to see what personal benefit victory could bring, with all its cost, that would not equally be bought by immediate compromise peace. For in France there was no gulf between the front and home. No inhibitions of mind or upbringing stopped the French from pouring out their hearts to their loved ones far away. The troops on leave came out of the home railway stations still filthy from the battlefield; the hospital trains crowded with newly wounded passed throughout the country.

The mutinies were therefore not merely the result of Nivelle's failure, but part of a general national sense of defeat. They marked the public bankruptcy at last of those ideals of the Revolution, in fact long outmoded, that had governed French life since 1789. Those ideals were rooted in the thinking of the eighteenth century; their emphasis was on individual liberty rather than mass collective action, on politics rather than economics or technology, on government as a debating society or a constitution rather than as a political general headquarters. Energy that might since 1870 have gone to exposing and remedying the senescence of French industrial power and social institutions was directed at curiously eighteenth-century quarrels such as church-versus-lay education, republicans-versus-conservatives (over Dreyfus), and of course also directed at the endlessly revolving intrigues of Parliament and party. Since 1914 the ideals of the Revolution had failed to inspire successful solutions of the enormous problems of mass organisation posed by the war. The home front and the zone of the armies alike were a morass of shortsighted improvisations, a chaos of waste and confusion. Pétain's superbly organised defence of Verdun in 1916 had gained glory by its very rareness.

Now in Pétain France had at last a great organiser, a "technocrat"; a man who had never concealed his contempt for Republican ideals and parliamentary government; a man of France rather than a man of Paris. Yet in his own military sphere, too, Pétain faced the consequences not only of Nivelle's failure but also of the forty years since Sedan and in particular of the Dreyfus affair.

Whereas in Germany the army had stood apart from politics, secure in its prestige and able, in the words of a French historian, "to pride itself on being the first in the world, and be so,"[13] the French army had been affected by waves of public sentiment even before Dreyfus. After 1870 it became the banner round which a defeated nation rallied, the focus of the desire for *revanche* and the return of Alsace-Lorraine. And in a lay bourgeois republic that barred most official careers to Catholic aristocrats it gradually became the province of the old nobility and gentry and of religious sentiment. As the living belief in *revanche* faded, however, a new wave of sentiment after 1887 ridiculed the army, the tedium and narrowness of life in provincial garrisons, the stupidity and brutality of officers and N.C.O.'s—and this was now an army drawn apart from the nation in a professional, religious and class isolation.

The antagonisms between the lay and bourgeois values of the Third Republic and the religious and aristocratic ones of the army were exploded by the Dreyfus affair, in which a Jewish officer was wrongly convicted of espionage for Germany, and when evidence later suggested that this conviction was wrong and that an aristocratic officer was guilty, the army chiefs tried to save the face of a Catholic and aristocratic institution by blocking further processes. They were devastatingly defeated, but only after a protracted struggle. From 1900 to 1904 the Minister for War had been General André, a freemason, a republican and an anti-churchman who attacked the Catholic-aristocratic dominance of the army so violently that it became a purge. Higher promotions were taken from the Commander-in-Chief and vested in the Minister for War; officers down

13 Contamine, 21.

to the regiment were "vetted" for anti-religious sentiment by André's masonic spies.

The French army therefore had endured a profound crisis ten years before the war, and one whose reasons had absolutely nothing to do with its functional efficiency for war, but which indeed greatly damaged this. The number of enrolments at St. Cyr fell; the quality of new officers deteriorated; every mess was divided into religious and political factions. In the words of Raoul Girardet: "In most units, all feelings of solidarity, all moral cohesion seemed on the point of vanishing." [14]

The patriotic revival after 1910, and the consequent rise in the army's prestige, was too late to repair all the damage. In 1914 the French regular officer and N.C.O. were inferior to the German not merely in military education but in leadership, in management of their men. Instead of the close sense of teamwork that united the officers and men of a German company, the flexible discipline of the German army, there was too often deep personal and professional gulfs between officers, N.C.O.'s and privates in the French army; there was a brutally stiff discipline that had survived from the Second Empire.

In retrospect, therefore, the survival of the French army until 1917 was a prodigy brought about by the courage and stoicism of the ill-led and misused *poilu*. It now fell to Pétain in the middle of a great war to repair the mistakes and the negligence of forty years—if he were granted time enough.

First, however, there remained the mutinies. In themselves they were a delicate enough problem for the Commander-in-Chief. Too stern and wholesale a repression might drive the entire army into angry rebellion. On the other hand, indulgence might encourage it to melt further into disintegration. With so many armed units in mutiny, authority had to be restored not so much by force as by moral authority—by the impulsion of the Commander-in-Chief's will. Everyone believed that Pétain possessed force of will. Moral authority—especially with the soldiers— he enjoyed more than any other French commander of his seniority. He had not been a château general but a fighting commander who had risen step by step from command of a brigade; he had no disasters or avoidable massacres behind him. Instead there was Verdun, a victory for organisa-

[14] Girardet, 264.

tion, in which thrift in lives had been Pétain's dominant theme. Pétain, the troops believed, was the general who was aware of them as individuals rather than as figures in military accountancy. He had never made speeches or orders of the day about "guts" or "the offensive spirit" or "glory"; above all, he was the man who kept his word.

His own reputation was therefore Pétain's strongest weapon in the crisis of 1917; this lends special interest to his post-war comments on leadership:

> The true chief is one who knows how to ally firmness with wisdom, professional knowledge with resolution in action, the art of the organiser with that of the executor. It is thus that he wins confidence.
>
> In this conquest of confidence, there is also an element of personal prestige: clear-sightedness justified by events, ability to avoid the false move, coolness in difficult circumstances, calm in adversity and modesty in success.
>
> In reality, confidence is not to be ordered, it is to be merited.[15]

Pétain tackled the immediate crisis by swift and severe punishment of ringleaders in order to break the nerve of the wavering mass. Here both he and his officers throughout the army were hampered by the slowness of the system of military justice. In 1916, as part of the parliamentary war on the army's autonomy, the *"cours martiales,"* with their swift and summary proceedings, had been abolished, leaving only the *conseils de guerre,* a more elaborate system that allowed for much delaying on the part of the defence; splendid as a principle, functionally unsound in a crisis. Military justice had been further enfeebled on April 20 by the abolition of the Commander-in-Chief's right to confirm a death sentence, which now rested with the President of the Republic.

Therefore Pétain wrote to his army commanders on June 1 ordering them to bring mutineers before the *conseils de guerre* without the usual French preliminary judicial investigation. A week later he wrote to the Minister of War, Painlevé, in his own name and those of his army commanders, to request the instant restoration of the summary *cours martiales.* On June 9 Poincaré, by presidential decree, gave the Commander-in-Chief the right to confirm death sentences. Just before this, the case of two particular mutineers illustrated how feeble was republican government and how closely and tightly connected were the mutinies with shaken national solidarity.

15 Pétain, *le Devoir des Élites,* 29.

The appeal of the two mutineers against the death sentence had been specifically not endorsed by every echelon in the army, from their captain to Commander-in-Chief. Yet Painlevé had recommended the President to grant them mercy. Painlevé was asked by the Senatorial Army Commission why these men had been spared and others, whose crimes were less serious, executed. Painlevé replied:

> I was obliged against the advice of all their officers to pardon these men because their execution would have provoked a general strike in the big town of Ste. Etienne, against which the government would have been defenceless. . . . One of the condemned is in fact a member of the Teachers' Syndicate of the Loire Department and the other is one of the leading members of the Ste. Etienne labour exchange.[16]

While the military courts were briskly dealing with leading mutineers and, backed by the Commander-in-Chief's written support, officers and N.C.O.'s were renewing their authority, Pétain had already begun to remedy the troops' grievances. On June 2 he inaugurated a new leave system:

> The Command's efforts [ran his instruction] should be aimed at making sure that everyone has seven days' leave every four months . . . at all times when the situation permits [the percentage of men on leave] can be raised to 25 per cent and even 50 per cent in large formations withdrawn for refitting.[17]

For the first time there would be a proper leave organisation to make sure that the soldier reached home as quickly as possible, personally clean and in a clean uniform. Trucks from camp to station, information and welfare centres and canteens in major stations, barbers' shops, even a traveller's guide—all things that the British and German soldier took for granted in the way of welfare were introduced to the French army by a note of Pétain's dated June 8, 1917.

Pétain also requested the Ministry of War to supply 400,000 bunks; he himself organised workshops to make 5,000 a day.

He was particularly concerned about food—his own mess had an excellent table—because the cookery of the French army combined primitive organisation with poor-quality rations. By an instruction of June 2

[16] Mermeix, 177.
[17] Carré, 170.

Pétain laid down that mobile cookers should be placed as far forward as possible in order to supply the man in the line with hot food.

> Supervision of food [he reminded his officers] is as important for the soldier's health as for his morale. It is by concerning themselves with these details, apparently trivial, that company commanders will gain a deep and lasting influence over their men which will amply repay their trouble in time of battle.[18]

On June 9 Pétain reported a lack of green vegetables to the Under-Secretary of State for War and demanded a hundred truckloads a day—priority for the army.

He also ended the boom for the private traders who had battened on the troops by encouraging military co-operatives and founding a central store to supply them.

Wine was, of course, the fuel of the mutiny—the easy barrier against the horror and boredom of the war. Pétain ordered canteens to be closed on the eve of a unit's departure for the line and lectured his officers:

> In many units, the example comes from the junior officers' mess . . . where it is easy to get into the habit of drinking too much. The N.C.O.'s naturally follow in the same error. The result is that among the troops the need becomes so pressing that a man does not hesitate to go long distances on foot to refill his water bottle with *pinard* . . .
>
> It is sad to see men who have been the admiration of the world for three years degrade their military virtue in a few hours. The struggle against drunkenness will be pursued with vigour.[19]

When the situation allowed, Pétain spent days away from Compiègne touring among the units of his shaken army, inquiring into grievances, suggesting or ordering remedies. There were few parts of the front where his white-flagged car was not seen, and his own bulky figure in horizon blue with a plain kepi, for in the months after June 15 he visited ninety divisions. He made a point of talking to everyone—officers, N.C.O.'s and men—and he encouraged them to speak freely to him. There was nothing of "public relations" about these tours: "no bonhomie, no affectation of fatherliness, no display of feelings, because the soldier is only duped for a moment by this kind of play-acting."[20]

[18] Carré, 133.
[19] *ibid*, 134.
[20] Pierrefeu, II, 35.

Pétain would gather a small informal group round him, discuss such lowly but vital matters as the quality of bread or food.

"He spoke as man to man without trying to lower himself, dominating everyone with his spell. . . . He remained calm and impressive, truly the general-in-chief and with a regal presence." [21]

When his car drove away from a unit, Pétain left behind a memory of integrity and humanity—above all, of trust. What he had promised over leave, food, better camps, would be done. Officers and N.C.O.'s had received a valuable lesson in man management, in simple care for their men, which the French army desperately needed. It was a lesson that sometimes came accompanied by a freezing blue glance and phrases that rasped.

Thus it was that the commander-in-chief of the sociologically most backward army on the western front demonstrated the techniques whereby the leadership of a mass organisation could be made a living reality to the individuals in its ranks.

From June 10 onwards the mutiny faded rapidly. Between May 25 and June 10 there had been eighty grave cases of collective mutiny, from June 10 to July 10 only twenty. On June 20, five weeks after he had become Commander-in-Chief, Pétain therefore reported to the government:

> Although examples of indiscipline are today more scattered, one cannot be sure that calm has been definitely restored. The relaxation has resulted from: 1. fear caused by the heavy punishments suffered by those most guilty; 2. action taken on the subject of leave; 3. the feeling experienced by the agitators that the general movement of revolt has failed because of a want of co-ordination. The reasons put forward by them for the mutiny, such as the stopping of leave, or lack of rest, have been only pretexts to mask the revolutionary and pacifist character of the disorders . . . the morale of the army tomorrow depends on the future activities of agitators and on the strength of the means that the government leaves at their disposal.[22]

This was another salvo at Malvy.

On June 18 he sent a letter to his army commanders to inform them of the general situation in regard to the mutiny:

[21] *loc. cit.*
[22] Carré, 126.

The first intention [he recalled] was immediate repression in order to stop the trouble spreading.

With the achievement of this object it was necessary to cut short the disorders by changing conditions wherein dangerous germs could multiply, whence my Instruction about leave. . . .

I set about suppressing serious cases of indiscipline with the utmost urgency. I will maintain this repression firmly, but without forgetting that it applies to soldiers who have been in the trenches with us for three years and who are *our soldiers*.[23]

Nevertheless verdicts of guilty were passed on 23,385 men—the equivalent of two divisions, or one in every hundred men of the field army on the western front. Although 432 were sentenced to death, only fifty-five were shot; the remainder were sent to penal settlements in the colonies.

By the middle of July the mutinies had entirely ceased; they died away with a surprising speed that leaves a mystery as to which of Pétain's actions had most effect in reconciling the army to endless continuation of a dreary and dangerous war. In its immediate causes the mutiny had been a strike against more offensives. Pétain too was convinced of the futility and impossibility of such events before the arrival of the Americans and had told his subordinate commanders so. Army and Commander-in-Chief had thus reached separately the same conclusion. Perhaps it was indeed the realisation that Pétain thought the same as they did, and that there would be no more massacres, which reconciled the soldiers again to the trenches and stopped the mutiny blazing into a national revolution.

No more grand offensives then—but what was Pétain going to do with the largest of the armies of the allies during the twelve months of waiting for the Americans' arrival *en masse?*

[23] Carré, 128.

10

Germany dominated her alliance; accordingly, that alliance had fought the campaigns of 1915 and 1916 to a single fundamental strategy and often under German command. Failures were generally the result of unsound calculation rather than of lack of co-ordination. With the allies there was in this war no dominant partner, as there was after 1941 in the Second World War, and therefore no machinery for grand strategy and the common allocation of resources. Periodic conferences had, however, attempted to fix a common policy based on the simultaneous use of the military power of France, Russia and Great Britain—and Italy. In 1916 the superiority of the allies (major powers: France, Britain and Russia) over the central powers (major powers: Germany and Austria) was in population 266,553,130 to 115,215,000. However, steel production was nearly at parity (France, Britain and Russia, 15,329,792 tons; Germany and Austria, 17,078,139 tons).[1]

With the Russian Revolution of March 1917 the power-relationship of the war was transformed. If Russia made a separate peace with the central powers, France and Britain would then be outnumbered in total population by Germany and Austria by 115,553,130 to 84,370,000. In steel production they would be inferior by 12,036,000 tons to 17,078,139 tons. This was a heavy inferiority.[2] America's belligerence brought another 93,400,000 people and the overwhelming steel production of

[1] *Statesman's Year Book* for 1920, p. xxviii.
[2] *ibid.*

45,060,607 tons to the aid of Britain and France, but it would be a long time before this potential new strength was realised.[3]

In May and June of 1917, when Pétain was formulating his strategy for the French army, it was not yet clear how completely Russia had foundered as an ally, although French and British strategical calculations were dependent on the number of German and Austrian divisions likely to be held on the eastern front. Estimations of Russia's future illustrated the hazards of prophecy and the dire influence on calculation of the calculator's own hopes. Ludendorff's opinion (retrospectively) was: "The outbreak of the Revolution threw a strong side light on conditions in Russia. The army and nation were rotten to the core, or it would never have taken place. . . . I felt as though a weight had been removed from my chest." [4] He added: "The Revolution was a serious blow to the *Entente,* as it inevitably entailed a diminution of Russia's fighting capacity and brought considerable relief to us. . . . For G.H.Q. this consisted first of all in the saving of troops and munitions in the east; and the exchange of worn-out divisions from the west for fresh troops from the east was undertaken on a large scale." [5]

At the beginning of June, Paleologue (who had just ceased to be French Ambassador at St. Petersburg) and Gaston Doumergue (who had just returned from a mission to Russia as Ambassador Extraordinary) expressed their conviction that nothing more was to be expected from Russia but early collapse. Buchanan, the British Ambassador to Russia, sent back reports that spring and summer full of gloomy detail about Russia's civil and military dilapidation, but with true British optimism, he did not draw Paleologue's and Doumergue's grim conclusion, but like a fond relative at a deathbed, saw gleams of hope of recovery in the most transitory and trifling pieces of good news.

Haig shared Buchanan's robust optimism. In a memorandum for the War Cabinet of June 12, 1917, on "The Present Situation and Future Plans," written to justify his launching a grand offensive in Flanders, he stated:

> In my opinion the only serious doubt as to possibilities in France lies in the action to be expected of Russia, but even that doubt is an argument in

[3] *ibid.*
[4] Ludendorff, II, 43.
[5] *ibid,* 414.

favour of doing our utmost in France with as little delay as possible.

Russia is still holding large German forces and every week gained makes it more impossible for the enemy to transfer divisions to the west in time, if we act promptly.

There is still room for hope of increased Russian assistance, and successes in the west will surely increase the prospects of it.[6]

An intelligence appreciation made at G.H.Q., France, on June 11 had hazarded this resounding guess, which influenced Haig's memorandum of the following day:

> Even if the position in Russia should change for the worse in the immediate future, there appears no reason to anticipate that Russia will make a separate peace. . . .[7]

These documents were prepared, it is true, before Brusilov's last Russian offensive began on July 1, 1917, a brief and useless event as had been foretold by despatches from Buchanan and British military observers with the Russian army. Nevertheless, as far back as May 9 the Chief of the Imperial General Staff had submitted in a memorandum to the War Cabinet that the probable secession of Russia would increase the German gun and rifle strengths on the western front to slightly more than that of the allies.

> It is obvious [the memorandum added] that offensive operations on our part would offer no chance of success; and our best course would be to remain on the defensive, strengthen our positions, economise our reserves in manpower and material, and hope that the balance will be eventually redressed by American assistance.[8]

After a German counterstroke on July 19 had flung the Russians back in utter and final deliquescence, Haig still did not think, as did Pétain, of an inevitable movement sooner or later of the mass of the German army in Russia to the west, and its use in an offensive in such vast superiority of numbers as to dwarf his own and the French past efforts in 1915-17, and the effort he was even now preparing.

On July 25, six days before his offensive was to be launched, he wrote to the War Cabinet: ". . . even if my attacks do not gain ground, as I

---

[6] *British Official History,* 1917, II, 431, App. XII.
[7] *British Official History,* vol. *cit,* 427.
[8] *British Official History,* vol. *cit,* 98.

hope and expect, we ought still to persevere in attacking the Germans in France. Only by this means can we win. . . ." [9]

The furthest Haig went at this period over the Russian collapse was to consider the effect on his *own* offensive of piecemeal transfers from the east. Not until the early winter did he comprehend that Russia's failure exposed his own army and the French to the most dangerous attack launched by anybody since 1914; not until then did he accept that it was the allies who were the weaker side, whereas his calculations in the spring and summer were based on the opposite assumption.

In short, Haig decided to attack the most powerful army in the war with only an army group supported by one ally in disintegration and the other paralysed by moral failure. It was not at all that he was being urged by the Prime Minister to venture on an offensive, as were such British Commanders-in-Chief as Wavell and Auchinleck in the Second World War; on the contrary, Lloyd George now distrusted the whole conception of the Flanders operation. Nor should Haig have been in ignorance of Pétain's opinion. According to Brigadier-General Charteris, Haig's Director of Military Intelligence, the French Commander-in-Chief recommended "that the British as well as the French armies should confine their fighting to small operations with limited objectives." [10] On May 19, Pétain told General Wilson, the British liaison officer between G.Q.G. and G.H.Q., that: "In his opinion, Haig's attack towards Ostend was certain to fail, and that his effort to disengage Ostend and Zeebrugge was a hopeless one." [11]

Next day Wilson passed on Pétain's intentions and opinions to Haig in a long letter, of which the following are critical paragraphs:

> 2. He [Pétain] was opposed to any operations with such distant objectives as those which the Admiralty and the Cabinet were asking you to carry out—but he added that this was no business of his. . . .
> 5. His attacks . . . would be for strictly limited objectives, and when objectives were gained the whole movement would automatically cease.
> 6. He did not believe in another Somme. [12]

[9] *British Official History*, vol. *cit*, 106.
[10] Charteris, 289.
[11] Lloyd George, 1266.
[12] Terraine, *Haig*, 352.

It is thus difficult to follow the reasoning of Haig's latest and most able biographer, Mr. John Terraine, that Haig's decision to carry out the Flanders offensive was based on a sound and realistic belief in whole-hearted and general French support, the more so in view of the suspicion of French intentions that Haig and his staff manifested to Pétain and Serrigny at their first meeting. Indeed, when Haig finally recommended to the Cabinet in his June 12 memorandum that the offensive should take place, he had already been told on June 2, by Debeney, that the French army was in a bad state of discipline and that the French attack promised for June 10 would be delayed four weeks. It is even more difficult to follow Mr. Terraine when he suggests that Haig's continued belief in sub-stantial French help was owing to dissimulation or false promises on the part of the French. On the information that reached Haig about the French and their new commander-in-chief (or from them), both before and after the French mutinies began, a shrewd general would have real-ised that little could be expected of the French army that summer. In fact, Haig's apparent assumption of French support was as ill-founded as his assumption of continued Russian help, which Mr. Terraine himself cannot swallow. The third justification for undertaking the Flanders operation was the Admiralty's intense desire to see the Belgian U-boat ports captured. Once again it is curious that Haig should take this so seriously when privately he had characterised Jellicoe, the First Sea Lord, as "an old woman." Mr. Terraine agrees, however, that the Ad-miralty's wish fitted in well with Haig's own conception.

If Haig really did believe in powerful French support and even Rus-sian co-operation as late as June 12, and in the light of the information available to him, it argues powerfully that his military judgement here lacked shrewdness and perspicacity. Mr. Terraine's analysis of the evolu-tion of the Passchendaele campaign is perhaps the least convincing pas-sage in an otherwise excellent biography.

Events, too, proved Haig wrong; his offensives failed either to take the ground expected or to ruin the German army; and in 1918 he was to be saved by the closest margin from defeat in the open field. In 1917 Haig, as a commander in a coalition, committed the fundamental error of making an isolated offensive instead of waiting for a concentration of all allied forces in space and time. It must be remembered that there was

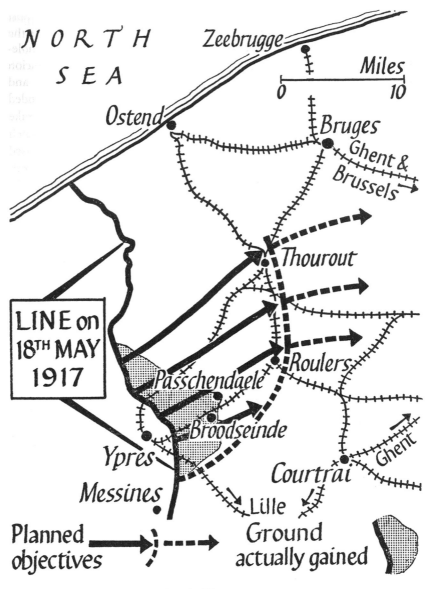

NORTH SEA

Zeebrugge

Miles
0   10

Ostend

Bruges

Ghent &
Brussels

Thourout

LINE on
18TH MAY
1917

Passchendaele

Roulers

Broodseinde

Ypres

Ghent

Messines

Courtrai

Planned
objectives

Lille

Ground
actually gained

31. THE PASSCHENDAELE CAMPAIGN, 1917

not a single U.S. division yet in the line. He also misjudged his own capabilities and possibilities and those of his enemy. It is difficult not to think that this error really sprang from a profound streak of stubborn pride in himself, his army and his country, from a conviction that the British could win this war before the Americans arrived, and that therefore he made the facts of the situation fit his ambition. Indeed, he wrote in his diary on May 26, 1917:

> There seems little doubt, however, that victory on the Western Front means victory everywhere and a lasting peace. And I have further no doubt that the British Army in France is capable of doing it, given adequate *drafts and* guns. . . .
>
> For the last two years most of us soldiers have realised that Great Britain must take the necessary steps to win the war by herself.[18]

There is also that element of playing-field "spirit" and "pluck," of backbone rather than intellect, that was so much a central feature of a public-school education of Haig's epoch. Haig's official papers as well as his private diary entries express all these moral qualities and limitations.

It is not merely historical hindsight to show how and why Haig's calculations were unsound; for there was, after all, another Commander-in-Chief who at the time read the situation correctly and who adopted a correct policy—Pétain. He had arrived in Compiègne after spending fifteen days in Paris as Chief of the General Staff and principal military adviser to the French government, fifteen days in which he and Serrigny were able to add to their unique knowledge of battle an understanding of national war policy and grand strategy, its machinery and its personalities. Pétain's policy was expressed in the sentence, "We must wait for the Americans." Foch, who had succeeded him as Chief of the General Staff in Paris, and who was as temperamentally different as it was possible to be, agreed with him.

"Foch, apropos the collapse of the Russian front, denounced to me," wrote Painlevé, "the chimera of a grand general offensive following in a few months after that of April 16, given the state of our assault divisions."

The date of the American's expected deployment in force thus became the determining factor in French military and industrial policy: 2,500 Renault light tanks were ordered for July 1918 when expansion programmes for aircraft, artillery and other equipment were to be com-

[18] Blake, 233-4.

pleted, as well as those for road and rail communications and elaborate base installations. If Haig wished to launch and persist in his own general offensive in Flanders in 1917, Pétain would hardly dissuade him. Pétain was primarily interested in the French army and in France; the British would help them either by keeping the German army occupied in another attrition battle or in taking over a large section of the French front. On the whole, Pétain would have preferred the British to have extended their line, but since they proposed to attack, he would co-operate to the extent of a single army and limited operations.

Thus in the third year of the war, the French army under Pétain abandoned general offensives aimed at victory and settled down in and behind its trenches for a twelve-month period of re-equipment, retraining and reorganisation. It was a remarkable phenomenon—a kind of unilateral armistice—that owed something to disillusion, something to that unhurried patience of Pétain's that set him apart from all the politicians of the war and most of the generals.

And indeed the French army's operational weaknesses were such that twelve months was by no means too long a time for reform, for in those months had to be remedied the results of more than fifty years' military history. Just as the mutinies exposed the social and political old-fashionedness and inadequacy of the Third Republic and of the army as one of its institutions, so in this "unilateral armistice" of 1917 Pétain picked up the bill for the purely military inadequacies of the French army and its recent traditions—inadequacies proven by the heavier losses incurred by the French than the Germans in every campaign since August 1914, whether offensive or defensive. There were the petty inferiorities, such as that of the quality of leadership of French to that of German junior officers and N.C.O.'s, the standard of tactics from platoon to army corps or the standard of staff work, organisation and inter-arm liaison. There were large inferiorities, such as in trench and heavy artillery (now partly remedied), in aircraft, in gas, in techniques of fortification, and in generalship and staff work in handling mass operations. There was above all the confusion in the French army's ideas of battle—the absence of sound common principles of action from company to army groups; the persistence of romantic Second Empire notions of glory, dash and personal bravery in the face of a war that was really a matter of organising death on mass-production techniques. The origins of the mess that faced Pétain lie certainly as far back as Sedan, probably as far back as Isly and possibly even as far back as Marengo.

Although it included about 30 per cent conscripts, the French army of 1870 in its mental climate and institutions had differed little from that of the Restoration—a professional long-service force of toughs, brutalised by barrack life, by a rigid discipline, blind obedience and the active discouragement of thought or study. This force lived physically and mentally divorced from the life of the nation and the ideas of the century, demoralised by life without a purpose in a long peace, dreaming crudely of glory if war should come. It was beaten with cruel completeness by a Prussian army that made use of the latest ideas and techniques of the nineteenth-century industrial and social revolution, led by "intellectual" commanders, whose soldiers were drawn by conscription from the entire nation.

When, after 1870, the French set out to create the effective instrument of *La Revanche,* they therefore imitated the Germans. The new French army would rest on conscription, would have in its *territorials* the equivalent of the German *Landwehr.* Yet the backbone of a conscript army is its regular N.C.O.'s—of which the French always had only a third of the number of the German Army. As in Germany, regiments would be permanently stationed in provincial towns but for political reasons would not similarly recruit from the surrounding region. Unfortunately imitation did not extend to the German *Kriegsakademie* (founded in 1818 with Clausewitz as the first administrative head) or to the formation of a general staff. Like the Royal Navy, the French army had no brain, no higher education. A supreme war council was created in 1872 but did not really begin to function until 1887.

Nevertheless the army of the republic in the 1870's and 1880's had reacted strongly against the cultivated stupidity and conformism of the Imperial Army. The *règlement d'infanterie* of 1875, written while memories of the bloody encounters outside Metz were still fresh, emphasised the domination of the battlefield by modern fire power. The new Ecole de Guerre was set up in 1878, sixty years after its Prussian prototype. These years of rejuvenation in the French army were also the years of its greatest prestige within the nation as the instrument of the revenge that, as Déroulède never ceased to remind his countrymen, might and should be imminent.

However, in the 1880's the memory of the reality of modern war and the national worship of the army faded together. It was Colonel Cardot, as chief of the Ecole de Guerre in 1885, who, by reviving a belief in the possibility of troops in close formation succeeding in a resolute attack under fire, began the intellectual civil war in the French army that was to cost so dear in 1914-18. How did Cardot believe such attacks to be possible? In his view it was the attackers' will power, their morale, which won the action by achieving the impossible and thus paralysing the defenders' capabilities. Cardot was among the first French military thinkers of this era to fall into the typical French error of dealing in ideals, where the Germans correctly thought in terms of technique or principles derived from technique. It was ironical that at the moment when Cardot was arguing the possibility of a brave battalion walking up to and over long-range field guns, machine guns and rifles, technical improvements made fire power even more deadly. Smokeless powder allowed smaller bores and cartridges, and invisible marksmen; repeating mechanisms doubled a rifle's rate of fire; better explosives permitted higher muzzle velocities and deeper penetration to artillery, so that Séré de Rivière's belt of frontier forts in masonry was obsolescent at the moment of completion. Nevertheless the *règlement* of 1887 reduced the front of a division from 2,800 to 1,600 metres and stated: "Brave and energetically commanded infantry can march under the most violent fire even against well-defended trenches, and take them." [14]

The German view, however, was that steady infantry should not be attacked in front but must be outflanked if possible.

While Cardot's ideas were gaining ground, the French army itself was slumping back into the inertia, conformism and dreary routine that had characterised it between 1815 and 1870. The movement towards reform, towards a spirit of free criticism and contact with the most modern manifestations of the age had never really stirred the great mass of the regular army, stuck in its dull provincial garrisons. Only the memories of 1870 and the idea of an early war of revenge had kept the army in a mood of tension and expectancy. Now both the memory and the idea had faded. The intellectual quality of the army deteriorated, along with its sense of reality.

"When firing," wrote one officer, "it was not a question above all of

[14] Contamine, 61.

placing shots in the bull, but of exactly taking the regulation posture, although this posture was uncomfortable for the rifleman." [15]

"Little change since the Second Empire," noted another officer in 1887. [16]

And another: "At the end of the nineteenth century it was not lawful for an officer, and above all for a captain on the staff, to think and express himself freely. . . ." [17]

Meanwhile France, smaller, less industrialised than Germany, was falling further and further behind in quality and quantity of equipment, except in field guns. From 1900 onwards began that German development of mobile heavy artillery and howitzers (150 mm.), long-barrelled artillery (105 and 150 mm.) and heavy mortars (210 mm.) that was to dominate the western front from 1914 to 1917. In 1901 the Germans introduced the Mauser rifle with which they were to fight the war; the French were to keep their Lebel of 1893 until 1915. Whereas the French merely improved their frontier fortifications, the Germans carried out a complete reconstruction of the fortified region of Metz on the most modern principles of concealment and construction.

Between 1900 and 1914, as the quality of the French army stagnated in training, equipment, personnel and professional thought, the intellectual civil war over tactics and strategy sharpened. Foch, as professor at the Ecole de Guerre, followed Cardot in believing in the superiority of the attack; others considered that gunfire could reduce all armies to helpless immobility. Captain Mayer, indeed, a brilliant military writer and critic, vehemently attacked Foch's ideas and prophesied a siege warfare of years on a front from the frontiers to the sea. He had little influence and less promotion. While the Germans became more and more convinced of the need for thin extended fronts, authoritative French voices called for battles almost as dense and narrow as those of 1870. After 1905 there were the lessons of the Russo-Japanese War to be considered. In 1909 Colone de Maud'huy, then at the Ecole de Guerre, wrote:

> To march under fire, impossible before steady troops, will become easy in front of a nervous adversary. The perfection of armament has increased the power of local defense, for which smaller means will suffice to stop

[15] Simon; quoted Girardet, 271.
[16] Quoted Girardet, 273.
[17] loc. cit.

superior numbers for a limited time . . . entrenching tools will quickly make a fortified position out of any place where one halts, and that will be true of both sides, whence siege warfare will result.[18]

This followed closely the thinking of Grandmaison, head of the Third Bureau (Operations) of the General Staff for five years under three Commanders-in-Chief; he was one of Foch's star pupils, and his name has been associated with the idea of attack in modern war as a charge of the old guard at Waterloo, but a successful one. Yet in his book, *Infantry Training for Offensive Battle,* published in 1906, Grandmaison struck a note of prudence:

> In open ground, a frontal attack by infantry under fire is impossible. In attack it is the task of the guns to constitute that fixed element of superiority of fire necessary to preserve a barrier against the enemy so long as the laborious approach of the infantryman lasts . . . it [the artillery] will precede every step of its infantry by its fire. . . .[19]

Pétain's own lectures at the Ecole de Guerre in 1911 made no blazing contrast with the views of Grandmaison and Maud'huy: the Russo-Japanese and the Boer Wars were emphasised as proving that shock action by massed infantry in the style of Cardot, which had formed the basis of the *règlements* after 1875, was impossible. The novelty in Pétain's lectures lay in his presentation, which credited himself with innovation and succeeded in making him the leader and symbol of a "school" for the rest of his life.

But it was in February of the same year that Grandmaison, too, became leader of a "school"—that of the offensive. He closed the second of two general staff conferences with these assertions:

> It is always necessary in battle to do something which would be *impossible* for men in cold blood. For example: march under fire. Such things only become possible for men in a high pitch of excitement against men in low morale. The experience of every age shows that in the offensive, safety is gained by first creating this depression in the enemy that renders him incapable of action. There exists no other means but attack, immediate and total. . . . Our conclusion will be that we must prepare ourselves and others by encouraging with enthusiasm, with exaggeration and in all the infinite details of training everything that bears—however little—the mark

[18] Contamine, 169.
[19] Grandmaison; quoted Contamine, *loc. cit.*

of the offensive spirit. Let us go as far as excess and this will not perhaps be far enough.[20]

As a summary of techniques of moral preparation that would enable the soldier to walk or run for a mile up to the muzzle of a machine gun, Grandmaison's words are unexceptionable. However, ringing aphorisms like these are ripe for wide publicity—and for oversimplification and misapplication. Between the lectures of distinguished minds at the Ecole de Guerre, or at conferences of the General Staff, and the unsophisticated intellects of colonels and captains in dreary regimental barracks in the provinces, there was a barrier of time and distance through which ideas penetrated only slowly and then simplified into caricature. In military as in feminine fashion, the provinces and the mass tend to adopt a style at the moment it has become *démodé* in the capital.

The muddle over tactical conceptions was reflected and made worse by strategical controversies. Should operations be based on first waiting for the Germans to commit themselves and then launching a massive counterattack from deep inside France? Or should the French themselves launch an immediate offensive? Should the divisions of the French army be disposed in an extended line, like the Germans, or massed in depth for manoeuvre like Napoleon's lozenge formation? Plan 15, conceived by General Bonnal in 1905, favoured a preliminary defensive followed by an offensive by a deep phalanx of armies. Plan 17, by Joffre, preferred an immediate offensive by forces not as densely disposed as Bonnal's, not as extended as Schlieffen's. On the other hand, Captain Grouard, like Mayer another officially ignored outsider, predicted in his book, *Guerre Eventuelle* (1913), that the Germans would swing through Belgium and that the French should not themselves take the offensive but wait for the moment for a counterstroke. His views did not prevail. Nor had General Colin, whose studies of the disastrous war of 1870 proved that French doctrine had then been offensive, not defensive, any decisive influence.

A French historian sums up the state of the French army's military ideas in 1914: "In reality, it is with justification that an expert on the training methods of 1914, Ory, the controller general, was able to say to me that rather than a doctrine there existed French military opinions, so involved and diverse was the forest of our specialist literature." [21]

20 Contamine, 167.
21 Contamine, 188.

From such involved diversity perhaps two generalisations may be drawn. Usually it is the victor of the last war who, complacent with success, fails to progress in weapons and methods; the vanquished who is spurred by defeat into reform. However, it was the victor of 1870, not the vanquished, who had made the better preparations in doctrine, training and equipment for 1914. Secondly, the relative French failure stemmed primarily from an old-fashioned—almost a pre-industrial—way of thinking; that is, thinking in terms of ideals, of general concepts, rather than of problems of technique. Indeed, not only the Cardots but even more their popularisers invested purely tactical questions with emotional and moral values. But the military French in their professional habits, as in their social history, only reflected the general obsolescence of the ideals and institutions of the Third Republic.

Retribution for the failure to train the army and its commanders in a coherent and realistic system of war came in Lorraine and in the Ardennes in August 1914: in the first six weeks of war (four of heavy fighting) the French had lost 110,000 dead and 275,000 wounded. This loss worsened the situation, for the ranks of the scarce junior regular officers and N.C.O.'s had been decimated.

Neither the Germans nor the French (apart from individuals) had foreseen stalemate in the trenches; both armies were trained and equipped for rapid, open manoeuvre. Yet the Germans were far better placed to adapt themselves. They still had their backbone of regular officers and N.C.O.'s. They had plenty of medium and heavy artillery, especially howitzers. They had always been trained and equipped to dig. Above all, they had the habits of organisation—they were accustomed to painstaking thoroughness. In 1914-17 these gifts, carefully fostered for so long, were displayed in the German war zone by the deep, comfortable dugout of the front line as well as by the whole organisation and equipment of the front. By contrast the French soldier would not dig, would not take pains to make his defences strong, comfortable and clean; the French officer could not or would not master the intricate problem of mass organisation posed by the new type of war. It was not, as Pétain and others wished to prove, that Nivelle's general idea of a swift breakthrough was inherently absurd—Ludendorff succeeded in a similar conception on March 21, 1918—but that from army group to company there were innumerable lapses in organisation, cumulative examples of slipshod performance, a basic lack of tactical doctrine and training.

This, then, was the military system that Pétain had to remake from the foundations, while he continued to face a German army with a record of continuous and single-minded progress dating from Gneisenau's and Scharnhorst's reforms after Jena in 1806. The difference between Pétain and his shrewder contemporaries such as Mayer, Grouard or Colin before the war lay not so much in their views, but in that Pétain alone of them became Commander-in-Chief at a time when disillusionment made the French temporarily willing to accept reality rather than blood-warming ideals, and he could thus order his reforms to be adopted. Thus in a fundamental sense Pétain's command in 1917 meant the temporary eclipse of a whole French military tradition and even of a certain national habit of mind. Pétain personified the dour, enduring realism of peasant France; in a moment of reality it had triumphed over the intellectual brilliance of Paris. It was interesting that in 1940, when Pétain once more took over in the middle of disaster—this time not merely to the army but to the country—the slogan of his *Etat Français* incorporated the basic realities of *travail, famille, patrie,* instead of the republican abstractions of *liberté, égalité, fraternité.*

He had laid down his fundamental policy in his Directive No. 1, to army and army group commanders, dated May 19, 1917, and issued before the mutinies had exploded into crisis. Not until June 20 was he able to follow it up with Directive No. 2, on tactical doctrine and training. By rotation large units were to be pulled out of the line into training camps where, as in peacetime, they could be progressively trained up to large-scale combined exercises based on Petain's conception of the limited, minutely organised offensive. Together all arms could analyse the problems of organisation and liaison, so that no essentials were left to hazard. They would be guided by two principles: thrift with the infantryman and prodigality with guns. Training camps and schools for these purposes were to be built.

Pétain was particularly worried about the poor quality of liaison between the arms and of collective organisation by commanders from brigadiers upwards. Therefore Directive No. 2 ordered army group commanders themselves to direct study centres where their senior officers could analyse the lessons of the recent battles in regard to close co-operation between infantry, guns and aircraft and the use of new weapons, and from them evolve sound methods of attack and defence.

Yet such a programme depended for its success on the general deployment of the army and on the quantity and type of new weapons now in production. On July 4, 1917, Directive No. 3 shared out resources between the army groups—Army Group North (Franchet d'Esperey) H.Q., Vic-sur-Aisne; Army Group Centre (Fayolle) H.Q., Châlons-sur-Marne; Army Group East (Castelnau) H.Q., Mirecourt. It also gave guidance on deployment and discussed programmes of re-equipment.

The defence zone was to be echelonned in depth to absorb sudden attacks, and this would require more major units in the zone. Nevertheless these units could be easily rotated between the line, rest, construction work in the rear, and training. From troops not in the defence zone, Pétain began forming a very large general reserve, a novelty on the western front. Divisions in this reserve were to be intensively retrained, and march and railway tables (as well as the roads and railways themselves) were to be minutely organised so that the command could quickly switch these reserves to any part of the front. For Pétain, mobility consisted not in dashing improvisation but in elaborate organisation. This was something of a novelty for the French, in whom the administrative traditions of the army of the first Empire and of colonial wars had always been strong.

In the future, as Directive No. 3 made clear, metal would replace *cran* as the basis of success. The section on artillery breathes Pétain's and Serrigny's memories of that long duel of massed heavy artillery at Verdun on which the battle had turned. Each army corps would have as corps artillery a light regiment of 75's and a heavy regiment made up of two groups of 105 mm. and two groups of 155 mm. long Schneiders (an increase of one). Each division would be equipped with one regiment of 75's and two groups of 155 mm. short Schneiders (both extra). There would be a general artillery reserve—a battering train—composed of a large number of 75's either horse-drawn or on trucks, six groups of heavy artillery pulled by tractors, and lastly the A.L.G.P. (*artillerie lourde à grande puissance*). Yet in following the German model of 1916, Pétain and his artillery advisers were already out of date. In General Gascouin's words:

It is curious enough to note that it was at the moment of the war when the German artillery was reverting quite visibly to medium and medium-heavy guns, that we adopted bigger and bigger calibres, an A.L.G.P. more and more powerful. . . . Admirers and imitators of the German large calibres, we carried out a true *tour de force* to create for ourselves an imposing large-calibre artillery in two years. And yet, at the moment when heavy artillery reached its height on the French side, it was already to a certain extent old-fashioned in the eyes of the German G.H.Q.

This latter seems to have realised early enough that it is the destruction of human material above all that it is important to achieve and that for this kind of effect the very heavy guns do not give the best performance.[22]

More original in Directive No. 3 were the paragraphs on air power. They expressed Pétain's belief that this would prove a decisive weapon. Each corps or unit of heavy artillery would be equipped with a reconnaissance squadron and a balloon unit. Apart from tactical squadrons with army groups, G.Q.G. would control a central strategic striking force for use in a great battle.

On the question of tanks, Pétain was hampered by France's narrow industrial base; only 150 Schneiders and St. Chamonds had so far been produced by spring 1917; he allotted a group of each type to each army group. He set up, however, a G.Q.G. tank park to receive the new Renaults as they left the factory and to organise them into units.

These three directives, together with the various notes and instructions on the food, welfare, rest and leadership of the front-line soldier, were on the foundation of nearly twelve months of reform and re-equipment in the French army. At the same time Pétain tried, without long-term success, to eradicate the blind obedience, the excessive sense of hierarchy that had never ceased to characterise it; he attempted to create a more free and open mental climate, a closer sense of comradeship between the ranks. A note of May 19 had already stated that blind obedience was no longer adequate and had added: *"The person to receive an officer's professional confidences is his superior . . .* it is up to the latter to justify the trust, which rests on mutual esteem and on the same devotion to the country."[23]

A note of June 14 pressed home the point. There should be frequent

22 Gascouin, 177-8.
23 Carré, 148.

meetings to discuss problems: these meetings "should allow subordinates *to give their opinions freely* and to bring points of detail to their superiors' attention that might otherwise escape them." [24]

Army, corps and divisional commanders were ordered to hold regular weekly meetings with the commanders of their artillery and other special services. Pétain added a characteristic reminder: "It is particularly important . . . that general officers and staff officers show themselves frequently in the trenches. By talking to front-line officers and N.C.O.'s they will keep themselves informed of the moral and material state [of the troops]." [25]

Pétain could not erase the effects of the truly catastrophic losses of 1914-17; reserves of manpower would remain desperately thin; as 1940 was to show, the army's morale would never entirely recover. Yet from a nineteenth-century army, reduced to the point of total collapse in May 1917, Pétain created a twentieth-century force nearly equal to its British allies and German enemy in organisation and equipment.

Throughout the summer and autumn of 1917, while Russia lay in a prolonged agony of dissolution and the British drove their lone offensive forward yard by yard in Flanders, the novel processes of intense staff study and general reorganisation went on in the French army. In order that the Third Bureau (Operations) and the Second (Intelligence) should work united—that operational studies might be based on the realities perceived by good intelligence rather than on wishful abstraction—Pétain placed both sections under de Barescut. To take charge of air affairs Pétain appointed Colonel Duval, at one time Chief of Staff to Fayolle at Sixth Army; Duval was not only convinced like Pétain that air power would prove a decisive weapon, he had that restless intellectual temperament that was not afraid of novelty and experiment. Thus G.Q.G. was stirred out of its routine, lethargy and boredom into hard thinking; its old separation was overcome by frequent inter-bureau conferences and by Pétain's own daily meeting with bureau heads.

Yet it was a measure of French backwardness that the basis of many staff duties in 1917 was examination of existing German techniques. There was for example the counterattack in depth (*Gegenstoss aus der Tiefe*) that had proved so shattering a surprise during Nivelle's opera-

[24] *ibid*, 151.
[25] *ibid*, 152.

tions. Whereas in the great battles of 1915 and 1916 the defender had been content, apart from local and piecemeal counterattacks, to defend his ground, in April and May 1917 the Germans had launched massive counterattacks at the moment when the attackers paused in greatest weakness and exhaustion. Instead of a narrow belt of strongly held trenches, the Germans now preferred a loose, deep web of strong points, the forward zone thinly held to avoid casualties from artillery. For the Germans, riflemen were no longer the backbone of defence; they became escorts to the machine guns, protectors of the guns. When specially selected, however, the infantry formed the essential component of the attack—the *Stosstruppen* or shock troops. These German innovations were the result of General Ludendorff's intense personal interest in techniques of attack and defence. The replacement of Falkenhayn by Hindenburg and Ludendorff had been followed by great changes in German methods and organisation.

From June 1917 the Second Bureau sent out information and analytical studies on these new German methods. The Infantry Bulletin dated June 10, 1917, contained an appendix about "German ideas on positional warfare." On June 30 G.Q.G. issued a complete translation of "Instructions on the counterattack in depth," issued by the German command on January 31, 1917. In particular the Second Bureau studied German operations along the Chemin des Dames. It published on August 28 an analysis of the German attack at Cerny on July 31. In the first place it noted a revolutionary feature—the extreme brevity of the preliminary bombardment, properly called, which lasted only five minutes. The attackers arrived in the enemy's position when the defenders were scarcely leaving their dugouts. In both battalion and company the assault organisation was flexible and varied according to need. In particular the *Stosstruppen* were not permanent formations but created for each operation by thinning out men from the ordinary units. In the words of the Second Bureau study, the *Stosstruppen* formed "an advanced guard which leads and reconnoitres." [26]

On September 15 the Second Bureau followed this study with a translation of the German instruction on "The Construction of Defensive Positions," which prescribed a wide zone of bunkers and fortified shell holes, switch lines, concealment, camouflage, subtle defences to canalise

[26] Pierrefeu, II, 43.

and ensnare attackers. French and British defensive techniques at this time still generally rested on the continuous trench system, although one of Pétain's earliest instructions as Commander-in-Chief had laid down that the second position was to be at "such a distance from the first that it cannot be subjected to preliminary bombardment at the same time as the first." [27]

He, like Joffre and Haig, had also condemned the existing allied practise of packing the front line: "It is useless to have plenty of men in the first line; [it] would only increase losses without increasing the solidity of the defence. It is much more by an increase of the means of fire power . . . that one will increase the strength of the defence." [28]

The original of this instruction bore this addition in the Commander-in-Chief's own hand: "Modern tactics are no longer Napoleonic tactics. They are dominated and conditioned by the progress of armaments, by the extraordinary growth in fire power. 'Formation in line' is replaced by 'Formation in depth' whose organisation and cohesion rests primarily on the 'combination of arms.' " [29]

Right at the end of the year (on December 20) Pétain signed an "Instruction on the Defensive Action of Large Formations in Battle." This Instruction embodied all his own ideas and experience and also the lessons learned from the enemy; and it was issued at a time when it had become certain that the campaign of 1918 would open with a German general offensive in the west. Subordinate commanders did not universally welcome its emphasis on yielding ground forward, on elasticity. For the very soldiers who believed with a moral fervour in attack (like Foch) also believed with a similar fervour in never yielding a yard of ground. Once again they confused emotion—gallantry, pride in themselves and their country—with technique.

How then could the Commander-in-Chief ensure that his instruction was understood, accepted and obeyed throughout a mass army? It was a problem that equally faced Haig and Ludendorff—a problem in mass communication that none of the three effectively solved. In each case the course of battle demonstrated how far the prejudices and want of understanding of subordinates—the inertia of the huge military machine—

[27] Laure, 43.
[28] *ibid*, 44-5.
[29] *ibid*, 44.

had overcome the will and purpose of the distant Commander-in-Chief and the means of supervision and enforcement at his disposal.

Because of his fundamental strategy of waiting for the Americans and in the meantime making the most thorough possible preparations to meet a violent German offensive, Pétain's programme of reform and tactical study was heavily weighted towards defence. His conception of the offensive during 1917 did not really move beyond that of a limited operation in which a massive artillery conquered ground by methodical preparation over several days and then the smallest possible number of infantry occupied the ground behind a creeping barrage. The six divisions of Anthoine's 1st Army (co-operating in Haig's Flanders efforts) were allotted 300 heavy and medium guns and howitzers, 240 75's and 200 aircraft—a very much heavier weight of armament in proportion to strength than in previous battles, and nearly double that of Nivelle's offensive. At the end of the Flanders campaign Anthoine had suffered only 8,525 casualties.[30]

Apart from Anthoine's operations, Pétain launched two more of his limited offensives in 1917. Both were designed to recapture specified valuable ground and to inflict disproportionate losses on the enemy. Equally, both were designed to test the recovery of the army from the moral failure of the summer, to prove Pétain's military system and to provide clear-cut victories to hearten the army and the nation.

To the 2nd Army (General Guillaumat) Pétain gave the task of pushing the Germans away from those commanding positions north of Verdun where Falkenhayn's terrible and tragic battle had finally stalled in 1916. Guillaumat was expected to advance no further than limits strictly drawn at 3,000-4,000 yards. His front extended astride the Meuse for eleven miles and his weight of artillery for troops engaged was absolutely unparalleled in the French army. Sixty per cent of his force were gunners, only 40 per cent infantry. In one army corps gunners outnumbered riflemen by two to one. For eight clear and blazing days of August this huge artillery concentration smashed and battered the German defences, ploughing and reploughing the ground. On August 26 the minutely organised attack followed the minutely planned bombardment; the heights of Mort Homme and Hill 304 fell, and 10,000 German prisoners were taken. The success was complete: the battle as perfect a

[30] *French Official History*, V (ii), 719, 1281.

piece of organisation as a chronometer; the casualties small. On October 23 the same process was repeated at Malmaison west of the Chemin des Dames ridge.

The attack was carried out by the 6th Army (Maistre) and its limits, too, were set at 3,000-4,000 yards. Once again an enormous artillery concentration (986 heavy guns and 624 field guns) systematically destroyed the German defences over a front of slightly more than seven miles. For six days and nights the guns worked carefully over the ground before the attacking troops went in. Once more the colossal weight of the bombard-

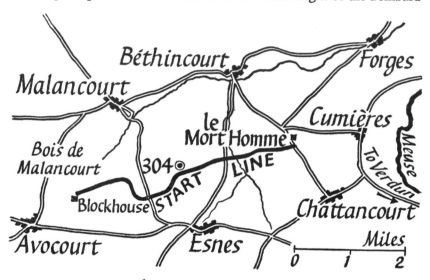

32. VERDUN, AUGUST 26, 1917

ment and the painstaking exactitude of the planning gave the French a complete and cheap success. In four days the Germans had been driven back behind the River Ailette and its marshes along the whole front of attack with the loss of 10,000 prisoners. As Pétain had intended, the French advance had turned the German defences on the Chemin des Dames; on November 2 the Germans evacuated the positions and the entire length of the road along its crest was in French hands. Pétain altered the G.Q.G. communiqué with his own hand to read: "We have made a big advance." [31] Malmaison had been another clear-cut small

[31] Pierrefeu, II, 58.

victory: neat and compact and satisfying as a gift package; indeed a gift to cheer a tired and discouraged country.

Yet Malmaison and the Verdun attack owed part of their success to the draining of the German front to face the British; and as perfectly mounted limited operations they had their rivals in such victories as won by Sir Herbert Plumer at Messines and Broodseinde, using even greater concentrations of artillery. The British, too, in the search for better methods, were copying the Germans: the attack organisation of British battalions and companies in late 1917 owed much to the *Stosstruppen.* Neither Plumer nor Pétain was likely to win the war by these economical and methodical small battles. However, they represented the final perfection of allied military thought in the war—or, rather of that period of the war before the German 1918 offensive had changed the entire character of battle. Haig came to the small perfection of Broodseinde by way of great ambition shattered, Pétain to Malmaison because he had never seen any other kind of possibility.

It was left to the Germans under Ludendorff to find the missing key to break-through and deep exploitation. Two German offensives in the autumn achieved these magical results (as they seemed in 1917) and at the same time gave a clear demonstration to Pétain and Haig of their own future fate.

On September 1, 1917, after hurricane bombardment of only five hours and without registration a force of eight German infantry and two cavalry divisions under General von Hutier (8th Army) attacked the Russian bridgehead over the Drina at Riga. It was one of several operations aimed at finally liquidating the eastern front by enforcing an armistice. The Russian defences, paralysed by the sudden saturation bombardment, collapsed as Hutier's divisions flooded through in small infiltrating parties. French G.Q.G. published a study of this "laboratory" battle as an appendix to its intelligence bulletin of December 17, 1917.

The second German offensive was of a general character and led to a victory that made all previous offensives since 1914 seem laborious and limited. At 2 A.M. on October 24, 1917, the German-Austrian army in Italy opened a six-hour hurricane bombardment by gas and explosive shell on the Italian positions round Caporetto. At 8 A.M. the assault, on the pattern of Riga, went in—working ceaselessly forward through the Italian defences in small parties, always seeking the flank and rear. The

Italian army, which had launched eleven offensives of its own without other result than the usual mutual attrition, collapsed; a war of blazing pursuit followed, in which the Germans and Austrians took 275,000 prisoners. Only on the Piave did the Italians succeed in stopping the on-rush.

At both Riga and Caporetto the Germans therefore proved that they had solved the problem that had defeated the allied generals—that of the break-through and its wide exploitation. Only with the wasted and un-exploited British tank success at Cambrai in November—unconnected with Haig's main effort towards Passchendaele, which indeed made no use of surprise, speed or shock—did the allies find their own belated so-

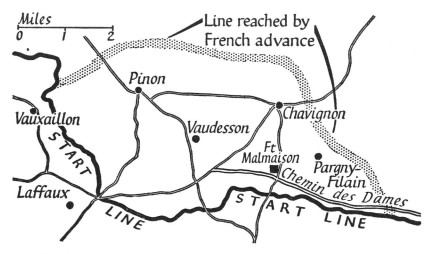

33. MALMAISON, OCTOBER 23, 1917

lution. And this was swiftly followed by a successful German counter-stroke, using the techniques of Riga and Caporetto.

As a principle Pétain believed that the allies must eventually launch their own general offensive—after the Americans had deployed. It was a principle that helped to soothe impatient politicians. Yet it was not clear how and when the principle would become fact. Pétain's eventual general offensive was rather like the Communist promise of the withering-away of the state: an event scheduled for a tomorrow that never came. For Pétain's judgement and will were clouded by his emotional make-up quite as much as were those of Nivelle, Foch, and Joffre and the "young turks." There was in him a passiveness—Serrigny did not hesitate to call it "weakness"—that chimed perfectly with the defensive in war. Although the war so far did not justify the ebullient optimism of Haig and Foch, Pétain himself, after Verdun and the mutinies, went further than impartial realism in his cold and sombre assessments—into fatalistic pessimism. He saw events more coldly stark than they were, while his peers saw them rosy and gold with future glory and success. There is nothing like the society of optimists for turning a realist into a pessimist, and Pétain even as a young officer had had a reputation for sardonic and deflationary wit.

His emotional qualities were generally low in key then. Yet this was not so in regard to all things; Pétain had that capacity for love and compassion, for being moved by suffering, which revealed emotions almost feminine in their warmth and strength. There were his mistresses and flirtations; he was terrified of loneliness. He was unhappy whenever his military "family" was broken by postings. All this expressed thwarted affection seeking reciprocation. In his early youth there had been no such reciprocation in his childhood home on the farm on the bleak downlands near St. Omer: "My father had married again; my stepmother turned out to be stony-hearted; the paternal house was practically closed to me." [32]

Thus it was that where Pétain's cold, controlled exterior concealed very powerful emotions, they were of a nature to increase, not diminish, his passivity and pessimism. The memory of his soldiers' faces at Verdun never ceased to haunt him. He could never pass an ambulance without a tightening of the throat. The suffering of a battle struck him with a horrifying immediacy—an immediacy that underlined his preoccupation as Commander-in-Chief with France's exhausted reserves of young men. A general offensive meant the Somme, Flanders or Verdun once more—could he bring himself to commit the French army to such an enterprise ever again?

It is likely that his passive tenaciousness was in fact more in tune with the French character in the twentieth century than was the school of the offensive. Studies of French child art and of French upbringing indicate an intense sense of defensive possession over property drawn with tight

[32] Serrigny, 322.

enclosing limits, and a powerful discouragement of outward aggression and expansion. The keynote is conservation.[33] And it is this kind of battle that the French preferred to remember and celebrate—Verdun and the Marne, not the victories of 1918.

Yet as the crisis of Nivelle's failure and the mutinies faded, Pétain's policy and character seemed to some politicians and soldiers less and less to fit the possibilities of the war situation.

Colonel Herbillon, liaison officer between the Prime Minister and G.Q.G., described Pétain's view of the future on September 21, 1917:

> General Pétain took me for a walk in the park of Compiègne. I told him that the government had sent a note to the Russian government to encourage it to display some energy. He showed himself pretty sceptical over the results of these various notes, which to him seemed like a cautery on a wooden leg. For him, there is nothing much more to be expected from the Russians . . . he did not hide that his constant preoccupation is the crisis of effectives he foresaw in several months. . . . The English operation used up plenty of men so we were obliged to think in terms of economy.

Pétain told Herbillon:

> We must always foresee definite abandonment by Russia, and that day we will have against us considerable forces. . . . I am reproached as being a pessimist because I explain the situation without oratorical flourishes, but they would do well to listen to my reasons.[34]

On the same day, absorbed by the success (to his mind) of his Flanders offensive, Sir Douglas Haig gave orders for a further attack towards Passchendaele; he still hoped for a break-through and ordered a pursuit force including five cavalry divisions to be made ready for a deep exploitation.

Friction between Pétain and the politicians had begun while he was still carrying out his great reforms of the army. At the very outset of his command-in-chief there had been the problem of getting Malvy, the Minister of the Interior, to stop the vast amount of pacifist and anti-army

[33] For an analysis of French upbringing, see *Childhood in Contemporary Cultures,* edited Margaret Mead and Martha Wolfenstein, Part II, essay no. 7; Part V, essay no. 18; Part VII, essay no. 18.
[34] Herbillon, 141-2.

propaganda in the country and in particular that part of it directed at troops on leave. Under Clemenceau's lashing attacks, Malvy became at last a liability that brought the Ribot government down; in September 1917 Painlevé became France's fifth wartime Prime Minister. Malvy at his own ill-judged request was placed on trial and Almereyda and Bolo arrested.

For Pétain, however, Painlevé's accession to the premiership brought other troubles. There was the old issue (on which Joffre had given battle) of parliamentary interference in the army, revived by Painlevé's wish to appoint under-secretaries of state to each army group. In Pétain's absence in Belfort on a visit, Serrigny telephoned the President of the Republic and told him that the Commander-in-Chief would resign if such under-secretaries were appointed. The highhanded bluff was successful. But it was another example of how the politicians of the Third Republic were dogged by analogies from the First.

Painlevé lasted until November 13. There was nobody left but Clemenceau, terrifying, ruthless, indeed a dictator. As in 1940 and in 1958, parliamentary government *à la française* was a dispensable frivolity when the country was in ultimate danger, when there was real work to be done.

On December 6, Pétain met the new government for the first time at a meeting of the War Committee. He gave them his appreciation of the strategic balance:

> Thanks to her transport movements from east to west Germany will soon have 200 divisions and 1,600 heavy batteries on the Anglo-French-Belgian front. She will be able to hold her line with 100 divisions and 600 heavy batteries. She will thus have 100 divisions and 1,000 heavy batteries available to prepare for use in a great offensive in the spring. We are on a tight-rope.[35]

Now that Caporetto had proved that sweeping victories were after all possible, politicians and public opinion began to find Pétain's ideas lacking in glamour. At the next meeting of the War Committee on December 13 he was criticised by the presidents of both Houses of Parliament for being excessively defensive. Pétain answered them himself with frigid dignity and simplicity:

[35] Laure, 37.

"I am eager to say that if another method is believed superior to mine, I am ready to stand down and return in silence into the ranks."

"There can be no question of that," intervened Clemenceau. "I alone am responsible here. I am not in favour of the offensive, because we have not the means. We must hold on. We must endure. . . ."

After the two presidents of the Houses had left, however, Foch, Chief of the General Staff, had his say: "We must not on the other hand exaggerate the dangers. The defensive is easily maintained in the present war. We can hope to hold on easily." [36]

This, like so many of Foch's reverberating pronouncements, was a gross miscalculation. But Foch was dangerous; Foch was in Paris, close to the government, and Foch, with his passionate offensive ardour, his powerful personality, his rages and gesticulations, was more likely to chime in the long run with Clemenceau's violently aggressive temperament than was Pétain, although personally they disliked each other. There was a clash here of military policies, of temperaments; but over all loomed the question of an allied supreme commander and an interallied reserve. Caporetto and the necessity to send swift help to the Italians exploded the question.

On October 28 there was a meeting of the War Committee in Pétain's office at Compiègne—the Prime Minister (still Painlevé), Foch, Debeney, Barescut and Serrigny. It had been agreed to send six French and three British divisions to rescue the Italians; it was now agreed to send as well a French general to consult with the *Commando Supremo*. Pétain argued strongly that he should go; it would enable him to prepare the ground for taking the Italian army under his supreme command. Caporetto and the present discussions were in truth a proof that there was but a single front in the west in terms of strategy.

On hearing Pétain's suggestions, Foch, the Chief of the General Staff in Paris, flew into a rage. The two men were fire and ice—Foch wiry, bow-legged, eyes like coals in deep sockets, long moustache spreading at the tips like cedar branches, big curved nose; Pétain massive, still, cold-eyed. Foch, pre-war propagandist of the offensive at the Ecole de Guerre, removed from command of Army Group North after the bloody results of his real offensives in 1915 and in 1916 on the Somme, was once again rising in influence by sheer force of personal magnetism.

[36] Painlevé; quoted Laure, 38.

"Foch declared," wrote Serrigny, "that the Commander-in-Chief wanted to poach on his preserves and he noisily went out of the room. I followed him to calm him down. We walked together on the terrace of the palace; at my request, he decided to go back. A few moments later General Pétain, as ever weak, had given way and next morning Foch left for Italy!" [37]

On November 5, in the last days of the Painlevé ministry, the inter-allied conference of Rapallo was persuaded by Lloyd George to set up a Supreme War Council to draw up a single strategy for 1918 and to co-ordinate the available forces. It was part of his devious manoeuvres against Haig, whom he wished to dismiss, but because of his own insecure parliamentary support (so different from that of Churchill in the Second World War) and of the King's friendship with Haig, could not. The military representatives on the council were Henry Wilson and Foch—men alike in that they possessed personalities of magnetic power allied to military judgements often of wild unsoundness. Neither Haig nor Pétain was in favour of the new council or their own national military representatives. They were united in preventing Foch and Wilson acquiring real powers and, above all, troops from their commands.

In December, however, Pétain's prestige with Clemenceau began to slip. That ruthless killer began to find him too cautious, too defensive—altogether too low-keyed. He began to interfere in Pétain's command: on December 19 he suggested to Poincaré, President of the Republic, that Debeney, C.G.S. at G.Q.G., was too akin to Pétain in temperament and outlook (which was true). Pétain accepted Debeney's replacement by Anthoine, a big, bluff sort of fellow, a gunner, the late 1st Army commander. At the same time Clemenceau stopped publication of the "Bulletin of the Armies," which he felt gave Pétain a direct hold on French opinion. They clashed, too, over Clemenceau's wish to bring back older men from the army to industry—at a time when the French army was wasting at a rate of 40,000 men a month, had no reserves and had had to break up two divisions in November and December. Nor could Clemenceau see the justice of Pétain's request for a labour force of 500,000 for elaborate construction work in preparation for the German torrent in 1918. A further snub for the Commander-in-Chief was Clemenceau's circular that divisional generals at sixty, brigadiers at fifty-eight

[37] Serrigny, 171.

and colonels at fifty-six should be taken out of active commands.

The year of 1917 closed in gloom and uncertainty for the allies. On December 22 the Treaty of Brest-Litovsk finally brought Russia out of the war; five days later by the Armistice of Tocsani, Rumania was out as well. The uncertainty for Pétain lay also in the equivocal nature of the relationships between himself, Clemenceau and Foch, and in the still open question of an allied Supreme Commander commanding his own inter-allied reserve.

However, the convoy system had beaten the U-boats. The rate of sinkings of British merchant ships had fallen from 169 in April to 85 in December. The Americans, instead of being cut off from Europe, were landing in France in larger and larger numbers. On the other hand, the High Seas Fleet, virtually retired from the war in favour of U-boats, had twice been near mutiny because of discontent and idleness. Jutland was still throwing its long shadow.

On December 22, Pétain issued to his senior commanders a Directive for the future (No. 4) that by its cold good sense, abundantly borne out by events, further diminished his credit and further stirred up opposition to his "system." Referring to Russia's final demise as an ally, he drew the conclusions: "The *Entente* will not recover superiority in combat effectives until the moment the American army is capable of putting a certain number of large formations into the line; until then, under the pressure of unavoidable wastage, we ought to adopt a waiting strategy with the idea . . . of going over to the offensive again as soon as we can, which alone will give us final victory." [38]

He told his commanders that battle would always be offered on the second line, never the front line, and his "Instruction for the Application of Directive No. 4" made his tactics clear. Each army was to lay out its defences so that the attacking German infantry would have left the cover of their guns by the time they reached the main position. Reserves were to be held back near roads and railways and their possible moves planned in advance. Above all, the troops were to be trained once more in manoeuvre in the open field.

Static warfare and open warfare [wrote Pétain] must no longer be placed in opposition. One fights in positions and between positions, these positions being more or less organised, more or less demolished, more or less quickly

[38] Laure, 45.

taken by attacks and counterattacks and, eventually, one fights outside the fortified zone, on ground free of all defended localities. At all times and on all kinds of ground in this battle, movement is one of the essential characteristics of offensive manoeuvre as of defensive manoeuvre.[39]

In November and December the number of German divisions in the west crept up from 149 to 161. The significance of the Russian collapse now became clear to Haig—perhaps because his own offensive had now ended and therefore no longer blocked his mind. On December 3 he told his army commanders:

> The general situation on the Russian and Italian fronts, combined with the paucity of reinforcements which we are likely to receive, will in all probability necessitate our adopting a defensive attitude for the next few months. We must be prepared to meet a strong and sustained hostile offensive.[40]

It was thus generally accepted that, after three years of appalling sacrifices on the western front, whose only result had been a statistician's disputable claim that the German losses had been marginally higher, the war had revolved full circle. The campaign of 1918, like that of 1914, would open with a German offensive of tremendous power. Pétain could see that the thinned and shaken allied troops and their flimsy defences were unlikely always to stop the Germans, as Joffre and Haig had been stopped, in a narrow battle zone. Yet this clear-sightedness, embodied in his general and training instructions, aroused bitter opposition—led of course by the fiery Foch.

On New Year's Day Foch wrote to Weygand that the allies must impose their will on the enemy by attacks or counterstrokes. On January 6 Pétain held a conference of army group commanders at Compiègne. He told them that by March 1 the Germans would have eighty divisions and 1,000 heavy batteries in reserve. He thought the allies would be attacked on a very wide front of fifty to eighty kilometres—possibly round St. Quentin because von Hutier, the victor of Riga, was now in command between the Oise and the Cambrai-Péronne road. The allies had only fifty-five divisions in reserve, and therefore the line must be drastically thinned to supply more reserves.

[39] Laure, 48.
[40] Edmonds, 276-7.

Meanwhile Foch had been passing on his own ideas about forestalling the Germans by attacking them to Clemenceau, who found Pétain more and more negative in his approach. Pétain wrote to the Prime Minister on January 8 to contrast Foch's ardent ideas with the hard facts of the military situation. But politicians, instead of accepting nasty truths, prefer to reject those who utter them. Clemenceau carried out a campaign against Pétain's ideas of mobility and the yielding of ground, a campaign that found sympathy in every subordinate French commander whose mind had become fixed in the habits of trench warfare and who could not accept that the Germans might succeed where they had failed —in making deep penetrations. On January 24 Clemenceau passed on to Pétain the views of his "Inspector General of Defence Construction," General Roques, to the effect that the Commander-in-Chief did not attach enough importance to barbed wire and fortifications—that too many troops were in training, not enough digging.

All this movement against Pétain showed that after the bad fright of spring and summer 1917 the "moral" school of war (always attack, never yield ground, fight in the front line) was reviving. It made more difficult the Commander-in-Chief's task of preparing his army according to common principles of training and doctrine. It meant that in one more crucial campaign the chances of success would be reduced by this fatal French idealism—by this "moral" school that was no more based in the winter of 1917-18 on analysis of technical realities than in 1887, 1914 or the spring of 1917.

While the long trains trundled across Europe from Russia to France with their loads of victorious troops and massed equipment and the weight of German strength crept up and up opposite the allied line like a dark tide secretly climbing an embankment, the squabble over a supreme commander went on among the allies. It was not, as it should have been, purely a matter of functional organisation. While this was certainly much in Lloyd George's mind, he was also looking upon a supreme commander as a means of clipping Haig's power.

At the beginning of February the Supreme War Council created an executive committee under Foch that would form an inter-allied reserve. For Haig this meant Wilson (British representative on the committee) as an ambiguous kind of rival or superior; for Pétain it meant Foch. Both national commanders-in-chief found that they had no reserves available to contribute to the central reserve. Instead they co-ordinated their own mutual help. On January 25 Humbert (3rd Army) was instructed by Pétain to prepare detailed plans for going to the aid of the British right wing.

On March 3 Pétain told his monthly meeting of army group commanders that there were now two hundred German divisions in the west, of which at least half were in reserve, preparing for a grand offensive at an early date. Pétain now appreciated that the blow would fall on the British between the Oise and the Scarpe, with a diversion in Champagne.[41] In fact, there was only eighteen days' grace left.

He had done his best to make the French army ready for its last battle. He had repaired most of the effects of Nivelle's and Joffre's offensives; he had retrained the army and re-equipped it. He could not make dead men rise to fill the ranks of reduced or broken-up divisions, and he had only partly succeeded in making his own ideas prevail over those of which Foch was the most distinguished adherent; but at least the army that had been about to disintegrate when he assumed command now had a fair chance of surviving the German fury.

For it was early spring, 1918, and the French army was still in the field, and never more realistically trained and equipped. This was Pétain's achievement. However, Pétain had yet to command this army in a great general battle. Was the army in fact strong enough to support the shock? Indeed, had Pétain himself the necessary reserves of will power and fighting spirit, after living through two such appalling experiences as Verdun and the mutinies? The answering of these questions depended now on the German army and its commander, General Ludendorff.

[41] *French Official History,* VI (i), p. 218.

IV

General Erich Ludendorff

"All this is madness," cries a sober sage:
But who, my friend, has reason in his rage?
"The Ruling Passion, be it what it will,
The Ruling Passion conquers Reason still."
Less mad the wildest whimsey we can frame,
Than e'en that Passion, if it has no Aim;
For though such motives Folly you may call,
The Folly's greater to have none at all.
                    ALEXANDER POPE, *Moral Essays.*

11

The *de facto* Commander-in-Chief of the Field Army of the German Empire was a man very different from Pétain, with his cold dignity and sagacity, from Haig, that inarticulate upper-class Briton, from Jellicoe with his cool prudence, or from Foch, with his Gascon fire and gesticulation. General Erich Ludendorff, First Quartermaster-General, personified the restless energy and surging power of the German Empire; he also personified its ugliness, its crudity and its fatal unwisdom. Under his *pickelhaube,* bright, keen protuberant eyes stared out of a suety, pudgy face ornamented by a straight nose, a bristling moustache, a pursed mouth, and sometimes an eyeglass. His head was round, hair cut short and bristly, his brow high and broad; a beefy neck bulged into the uniform collar with the gold and carmine general officer's collar badges. Ludendorff was tall and straight, but his sword belt sagged slightly round and beneath a heavy stomach. His manner, his entire personality expressed restless ambition and impatience, an enormous appetite for action. "Your husband," a painter told Frau Ludendorff, "gives me cold shivers down my back." And Frau Ludendorff comments: "Even in his family we knew that grim countenance. They used to say: 'Be careful! Look out! Today Father looks like a glacier.' "[1]

Yet he had not always been so forbidding: "There was a time when Ludendorff could be cheerful and free from anxiety. His features did not

[1] Frau Ludendorff, 26.

always wear that look of unbending obstinacy, the expression of a man whose feelings had been turned to ice." [2]

Like Lloyd George, Ludendorff was the result of 1916, the watershed year of the war; he too was appointed as a cure for failure. Up till then German political policy had been defensive, ready to take any opportunity of opening negotiations for a peace of reconciliation; this was the policy of Bethmann-Hollweg, a Chancellor submerged by the magnitude and savagery of events. German military policy after the fall of Moltke had also been defensive; local offensives at Verdun and against Russia in 1915-16 had been limited deliberately in scope; this was Falkenhayn. Bethmann-Hollweg's attitude was admirable, but, as the British and French were quick to discover, only hate and fear of the enemy and lust for victory really enlist the support of the masses. Falkenhayn's conception of limited war prevented the Germans smashing Russia in vast offensive operations in 1915-16 as they were to do in 1916-17; because of Falkenhayn German concentration in the west was a year late. Verdun was apparently a bloody failure, although in fact the French army and Pétain himself had been shaken by it.

No decision in the east; defeat in the west; stalemate at Jutland; a nation staggering under the strain of a war for which it had still not been spiritually mobilised; and so on August 20, 1916, Falkenhayn had been replaced by those victors of the resounding limited battles against Russia —Field Marshal von Beneckendorff and von Hindenburg, the Commander-in-Chief, East, and Lieutenant-General Erich Ludendorff, his Chief of Staff.

The Kaiser being titular Commander-in-Chief of the Field Army, Hindenburg became Chief of the General Staff. Ludendorff was offered the title *"Second* Chief of the General Staff"; he refused it. He, like his country, thought himself second to none. He took the title "First Quartermaster-General." Hindenburg was the symbol of command, the object of national reverence. Like Joffre between 1914 and 1916, he was showered with a fan mail of outstanding volume and neuroticism; like Joffre, he was the recipient of rich and unsolicited personal gifts and of appeals for personal help that indicated that in the mind of the appellant the Commander-in-Chief had the power to remedy minor civil and personal wrongs and also possessed supernatural powers. The fan mail

[2] *ibid*, 19.

33. General Erich Ludendorff

34. General Otto von Bülow

35. General von der Marwitz

COMMANDERS IN THE MARCH OFFENSIVE, 1918:

36. General Oskar von Hutier

37. General Sir Hubert Gough

38. German troops attacking

39. German field artillery advancing

40. British heavy artillery retreating

41. A German 5.9 inch howitzer

42. Field-Marshal Sir Douglas Haig   43. Marshal Ferdinand Foch

44. Crown Prince Rupprecht of Bavaria

45. General Sir Julian Byng

46. Foch shakes hands with the United States C-in-C,
    General John J. Pershing

of the national commanders-in-chief gave a glimpse into the terrifying abysses of war psychology.

Hindenburg was born in 1848, the year that the liberals failed to unify Germany. His outlook remained that of a mid-nineteenth-century Prussian officer and Junker: an unquestioning and naïve patriotism, a feudal sense of duty to the monarch, an austere simplicity of character and mode of life. Politically his ideas were schoolboyish. Yet, with his massive dignity and calm, he represented the best of Junker qualities as well as the limitations. He was unspoilt by public adulation.

As a soldier his reposeful strength constituted a counterpoise to Ludendorff's restless oscillations of temperament. In this military marriage Ludendorff was the prime mover; his were the plans, the orders, the driving will. Yet Hindenburg was no mere splendid figurehead ornamenting the bows of the ship, but ultimately the captain who always appeared on the bridge in a storm when Ludendorff began to panic. For example, after Haig's attack at Arras on April 9, 1917, which broke deep into the German positions, Ludendorff was white and restless with anxiety, and O.H.L. began to catch this mood. But Hindenburg calmed the staff by his display of serenity; he put his hand on Ludendorff's shoulder and said: "We have lived through more critical times than this together." [3]

In contrast to Hindenburg, an aged military aristocrat already in retirement at the outbreak of war, Erich Ludendorff was a commoner and a violently aggressive careerist. He was the son of a businessman and was born in 1865, in a white single-storeyed house in an orchard at Kruszczewnia in Posen. In 1904 the younger Moltke had appointed him Chief of the Operations Section of the Great General Staff, where he pressed so vigorously for an increase in the rate of conscription and in the mobilisable strength of the army as to make his posting to a regimental command in 1913 appear a mark of unpopularity. By temperament, influence and training, Ludendorff was a complete believer in Count Schlieffen's military ideas. For him, as for Schlieffen, a victory must be crushingly decisive to be worth a campaign. In the east he had raged with frustration as Falkenhayn held him back from the mammoth successes he saw possible.

Unlike Schlieffen, Ludendorff was above all a man of action; inactivity and waiting made him psychologically ready to explode. On July 31, 1914, he had written in a letter to his wife: "I am thirsting for a man's

[8] Wheeler-Bennett, 98.

work to do, and it will be given me in full measure. Pray for me, beloved, that my efforts may be crowned with success." [4]

His experience of war was even more immediate than Pétain's; for he began the conflict by the superb piece of personal leadership on the battlefield that won him the *Pour le Mérite* and his country the citadel and town of Liége. Because of this feat he had been sent by Moltke with Hindenburg to take over the shaken 8th Army in East Prussia from Prittwitz. Ludendorff impressed that headquarters: on September 4, 1914, a staff officer wrote in his diary: "Ludendorff is a first-class fellow to work with. He is the right man for this business—ruthless and hard." [5]

However, the same officer was later to note how Ludendorff tended to give way to panic, or to lose his temper, at times of crisis and great anxiety.

Hindenburg himself in his *Memoirs* admired "the intellectual powers, the almost superhuman capacity for work and untiring resolution of my Chief of Staff." [6]

This capacity for work was allied to rigid exactitude and punctuality. His wife recalled: "Time was not reckoned in our house by hours, but by minutes. He would say for instance, 'Today I shall be back at four o'clock for some food.' He would come back on the stroke . . . and walk straight into the dining room. If the soup was not already on the table, he would say teasingly, 'Well, there's a nice thing, there's nothing to eat in your well-managed house today.' " [7]

The arrival of Hindenburg and Ludendorff at supreme military control in Germany on August 20, 1916, had signified early conflict between O.H.L. and the Chancellor, Bethmann-Hollweg. Ludendorff stood for complete and ruthless mobilisation of all German resources in order to win a decisive victory in the war and dictate a German peace. Bethmann still hoped that out of the indecision of the war at that time a compromise peace might prove possible. The conflict centred round the question of unrestricted submarine warfare. The British blockade, arbitrary as it was in its methods of control of neutral trade, had wrecked the German export trade, was beginning to deny German war industry essential raw

[4] Frau Ludendorff, 70-1.
[5] Hoffmann, I, 41.
[6] Hindenburg, 84.
[7] Frau Ludendorff, 31.

materials, and, above all, was beginning to rot German morale by the simple expedient of making women and children go hungry and thus raising the figures for German infant mortality and sickness.

Only unrestricted submarine warfare could answer this. Indeed, with the stalemate in the west and the east and in the North Sea after Jutland, the submarines provided the only apparent means of achieving decisive victory or averting defeat by slow starvation. The Admiralty staff believed they could starve Britain in six months; Ludendorff and Hindenburg put their weight behind the Admiralty. Bethmann-Hollweg, appalled by the effects on neutrals and above all on America of such ruthlessness, opposed the measure as destroying the last hope of peace. Rather he demanded that Germany should send out peace proposals. On December 6, 1916, the year's campaign ended with the fall of Bucharest to German forces and the collapse of the Rumanian army. This provided the victory that would prevent the peace overtures appearing as a proof of weakness. On December 12 the proposals were communicated to the allies and to America.[8]

They were unfortunately timed, for five days beforehand the moderate Asquith had been replaced as British Prime Minister by Lloyd George, with a policy of ruthless warmaking until final and total victory. A national war machine is, as both Lloyd George and Winston Churchill found, the most exhilarating of all vehicles to drive. It was unlikely that such a lover of power as Lloyd George would step tamely down from the driving seat into the peace-conference chair within days of his closing his fists over the controls amid general popular acclaim. Bethmann's proposals were rejected by the allied governments, and on January 10, 1917, the allies' conditions were communicated to President Wilson. These were so stiff that only a defeated Germany could have considered them.[9] They were exactly what Ludendorff expected and hoped for; they destroyed Bethmann by proving that Germany had no alternative but to fight to a finish, employing any means she could, whatever the consequences. This meant unrestricted submarine warfare and possible American entry into the war as an enemy. The naval and economic experts were convinced that the war would be won before America could become sufficiently armed and mobilised to constitute a danger. Bethmann

[8] See above, p. 206-207.
[9] See above, p. 206-207.

stuck to his guns; the Kaiser had to choose between his civilian head of government, a second-rater of fine sincerity and good will but of crumbled prestige, and Hindenburg and Ludendorff, powerful, mob-worshipped and crowned with past victories. The Kaiser accepted Beth-mann's resignation, and the war became a fight to the last breath. From now on until the eve of national collapse the office of Imperial Chancellor was to be filled with dim personages manipulated by the military dictatorship of O.H.L.

Yet in planning Germany's grand strategy Ludendorff was subject to the same insoluble dilemmas as Schlieffen, Moltke, Falkenhayn and, three decades later, Hitler—dilemmas posed by Germany's fundamental geographical disadvantages. The dilemmas of wartime grand strategy were in fact no more than those facing German world policy in peace-time. Except for her narrow North Sea coast Germany was cut off from direct access to the world; she, with all her powers of technological creation and production, was imprisoned in middle Europe by her great neighbours of France and Russia and by British sea power. Beyond Europe the world's markets and the world's various and vast resources lay in allied ownership or allied control.

In military terms Germany had already achieved astonishing victories; her armies everywhere lay deep on enemy soil. These successes had not solved her fundamental problem; only the submarines could do this. On February 1, 1917, they began to sink on sight; on April 2, 1917, the U.S.A. declared war on Germany. This and the Russian Revolution were the cardinal events of the First World War and probably the twentieth century. United States belligerence was caused not by German miscalculation (for the Germans were not to know that in March revolution would begin to take Russia out of the war) or brutality, but by the pure accident of German geography. Whereas the British blockade, because of British sea power and the situation of the British Isles, could be carried out without acts of violence to neutrals, the German blockade could not. Whereas the British and the French could carry on a lucrative trade with the U.S., Germany could not. This was how German geography determined the side on which America would fight. Pro-allied sentiment alone would not have brought her in.

By June 1917 the dissolution of Russian military power under the effects of the revolution had made it clear to Germany that the war on two fronts was nearly over; that for the first time since 1914 Germany could concentrate forces on the western front that would outnumber the British and the French sufficiently to make a general offensive possible. In 1939-40 Hitler created a similarly advantageous situation by the pact of alliance with Soviet Russia, and destroyed it, and himself, by choosing to invade Russia in 1941 with the British Empire, supported by American industry, still unbeaten at his back. In 1917 it was an irreparable tragedy for Germany that she should have commenced unrestricted submarine warfare only a few months before the stalemate it was designed to break dissolved without it. On December 16, 1917, a Russo-German armistice at Brest-Litovsk closed down active operations on the eastern front. Germany, having held off Britain and France through three campaigns and fought France to a standstill, had smashed one of the three great powers originally against her. But America was in, mobilising, training and producing fast; and the submarine campaign, despite vast successes, had not proved decisive. In military and industrial power Germany was a match for France and the British Empire together; in America, however, she now had an opponent with all her own energy and technological organisation, but on a scale that dwarfed her.

At the end of 1917 Germany faced therefore a fresh embodiment of her eternal problem—a war on two fronts. It was 1914 all over again, except that instead of two enemies separated in space (as with France and Russia) Germany now had to deal with two enemies separated in time. At the moment France and Britain were alone; from the summer of 1918 onwards America would have an army of over a million fresh, well-fed men on the western front.

On November 11, 1917, a conference was therefore held to discuss Germany's national grand strategy for 1918. It was not held in Berlin under the chairmanship of the Kaiser, the Imperial Chancellor, or even of Hindenburg, none of whom was present. It was held at the army group headquarters in Mons of Crown Prince Rupprecht of Bavaria, under the chairmanship of Ludendorff; and the others present were the Chiefs of Staff of Army Group Crown Prince Rupprecht and Army Group Imperial Crown Prince, General von Kuhl and Colonel von der Schulenburg, and Lieutenant-Colonel Wetzell, head of the Operations Section of the General Staff. This demonstrated the inadequacy of the political machinery and talents of the German Empire in the face of so basic a political task as the planning and directing of a national struggle for survival. Clausewitz had written:

> In one word, the art of war in its highest point of view is policy . . . it is an irrational proceeding to consult professional soldiers on the plan of a war, that they may give a *purely military opinion* upon what the Cabinet ought to do; but still more absurd is the demand of theorists that a statement of the available means of war should be laid before the general, that he may draw out a purely military plan for the war. . . .[10]

Yet in Germany since the fall of Bethmann the situation that Clausewitz had denounced as absurd had in fact arrived. The war was run from O.H.L., by Ludendorff and Hindenburg, themselves immersed twelve hours a day in the purely military business of fighting battles. Neither of these distinguished generals had by talent, experience or knowledge adequate grasp of politics or policy, whether home or foreign. Hindenburg acknowledged this ignorance:

> It was against my inclination to take any interest in current politics. Perhaps my liking for political criticism is too weak, and possibly my soldierly interests are too strong. When holding my high posts of command in the east, and even after I was appointed Chief of the General Staff of the Field Army, I had never felt either necessity or inclination to mix myself up in current political questions more than was absolutely necessary.[11]

Colonel Bauer, who worked closely with the First Quartermaster-General at O.H.L., wrote of Ludendorff:

> His strategic plans had, of course, to take the political and economic situation into account. But his views and his economic and political plans found no support in the government. . . . In matters of economics he lacked the basic education in many respects, as is only natural. . . . Home affairs and the press were not so much his cup of tea. . . . Only too willingly, he left this field to the Reich Chancellor who was of course responsible for it, even though to Ludendorff all political questions were military questions.[12]

In fact Ludendorff was constantly badgering the Imperial Government —over the necessity for a propaganda bureau, over direction of labour,

[10] Clausewitz, III, 126.
[11] Hindenburg, 220.
[12] Bauer, 109-11.

over all the vast field of the material and spiritual mobilisation of the nation for war. His memoirs are full of bitter complaints about the weakness, indecision and sloth of the Imperial Government. As he summed it up:

> Lloyd George and Clemenceau had control of their Parliaments. . . . At the same time they stood at the heads of the entire administrative and executive authorities; I, on the other hand, had no constitutional power to influence the German government in order to enforce my views as to the steps necessary for the conduct of the war, and I was frequently confronted with the lack of understanding and energy of the departments concerned.[13]

Why then did Ludendorff (or Hindenburg) not become Chancellor and thus political as well as military dictator? Ludendorff explains:

> Many had already approached me with the suggestion that I should become Chancellor. This, though well-meant, was a mistaken idea. The work I had to encompass was enormous. In order to carry on the world war I had to control the machine. This alone required an unusual capacity for work. It was inconceivable that I should take over in addition the conduct of a Government which on account of its extremely clumsy working methods required even more than one man's whole time and strength. Lloyd George and Clemenceau might be dictators, but the details of the war did not concern them. Germany's dictator would have to be in Berlin, not at O.H.L.[14]

Ludendorff on numerous occasions in his memoirs thus laments the absence of a strong man in Berlin. Yet as his conduct towards Bethmann and his successors showed, he was the last man to have tolerated political direction of the war by a German Clemenceau. So the German government became an unwilling and slothful front organisation for O.H.L.; German policy was decided by Ludendorff partly on narrowly military grounds, partly on jejune political ideas of a proto-fascist nature. Her war aims now became and remained until the moment of defeat grossly annexationist; there was even talk of retaining the Belgian channel coast. There was an astonishing contrast between industrial and technological Germany and political Germany. The Germans designed and built a modern industrial machine excellent in every detail but its steering

[13] Ludendorff, 706-7.
[14] *ibid*, 530.

mechanism, which was defective, a machine that they had no idea how to steer, anyway. The French and British had by comparison rather old-fashioned and poorly built machines, but the steering systems were somewhat better and they used them generally with greater skill.

Ludendorff came to the Mons conference of November 11, 1917, with his mind already made up: in 1918 Germany would decide the issue of the war with an offensive victory in France before the Americans arrived in force. It was the Schlieffen Plan again: a gamble under acute pressure of time, making use of a temporary superiority of numbers that in itself was far from overwhelming.

Ludendorff saw no alternative: "The condition of our allies and of our army all called for an offensive that would bring about an early decision. This was only possible on the western front. . . . The offensive is the most effective means of making war; it alone is decisive. Military history proves it on every page. It is the symbol of superiority." [15]

There was justice in Ludendorff's assessment of the state of his allies and his own army. In regard to Austria, as he explained, "We had to take into consideration that Austria-Hungary might actually arrive at the end of her military power. It was clear that her political power could not last one hour longer." [16]

Bulgaria was no sounder: ". . . she would remain faithful to us as long as all went well with us." [17]

And Turkey "was faithful to the alliance but at the end of her strength." [18]

All then rested on the German army. Yet the defensive battles in the west, with all their imprisoning horrors and long continuance, had finally begun to break up its moral cohesion.

> The army had come victoriously through 1917; but it had become apparent that the holding of the western front could no longer be counted on, in view of the enormous quantity of material of all kinds which the *Entente* had at their disposal. . . . Against the weight of the enemy's material the troops no longer displayed their old stubbornness; they thought with horror of fresh defensive battles and longed for a war of movement.[19]

[15] Ludendorff, 543.
[16] *ibid*, 540.
[17] *ibid*, 541.
[18] *loc. cit.*
[19] *ibid*, 541-2.

This longing for escape from trench warfare in fact amounted to a powerful moral lever on Ludendorff's strategic judgement: "In the west the army pined for the offensive, and after Russia's collapse expected it with the utmost relief. . . . It amounted to a definite conviction which obsessed them utterly that nothing but an offensive could win the war. Many generals, among them the most distinguished, spoke in the same strain." [20]

Thus Haig's offensives of 1916 and 1917, like that of Falkenhayn at Verdun, had had effect on the defending army.

If there were thus powerful reasons to impel Germany to attack in the west, there were also splendid results to be obtained from a success—results in terms of her own self and allies, rather than of her enemies. Hindenburg sums them up:

> I hoped that with our first great victories the public at home would rise above their sullen brooding and pondering over the times, the apparent hopelessness of our struggle and impossibility of ending the war otherwise than by submission. . . . My hopes soared even beyond the frontiers of our own homeland. Under the mighty impression of great German victories, I saw the revival of the fighting spirit in hard-pressed Austria-Hungary, the rekindling of all the political and national hopes of Bulgaria and the strengthening of the will to hold out even in far-away Turkey.[21]

Here Hindenburg touched on a crucial matter—German national, as opposed to military, morale. In Germany, too, the neurotic war fervour of 1914-16 had disappeared. The same forces of disintegration—left-wing and pacifist agitation—that had almost brought France down in 1917 were working powerfully in Germany, exploiting similar social and personal grievances. Only warm, well-fed people can afford the luxury of abstract ideas such as patriotism, liberty or honour; families living on an almost fatless and meatless diet in cold, often unlit houses, their children pale and listless and menfolk dead or far away, begin to think only of realities—of reunited family life, of food and comfort and the modest pleasures of peacetime. The government came to seem the obstacle between them and peace. In Germany, as in France and Britain, there were the war profiteers; in Germany, because of her obsolete political system,

[20] *ibid*, 542.
[21] Hindenburg, 328.

the inequalities between rich and poor, town and country, were more glaring. Social disintegration did not respect frontiers.

As Hindenburg and Ludendorff read Germany's grand strategical situation at the end of 1917, therefore, an early decision of the war was imperative.

There was an alternative—that adopted twenty-six years later by Hitler, of *Festung Europa*. It would have involved the ruthless and centralised economic exploitation of German-controlled Europe behind the shield of the German army fighting a defensive battle lasting a year or more, until the allies agreed to a compromise peace out of exhaustion and disappointment. Already Germany had begun to organise middle Europe into a single economic region, and the maintenance of it had become an important war aim.

This alternative policy was apparently considered by Ludendorff and Hindenburg, but curiously it is discussed in Hindenburg's memoirs, not in Ludendorff's.

> The result of our great offensive in the west has given rise to the question whether we should not have been better advised virtually to adopt the defensive on the western front in the year 1918, supporting the armies previously employed there with strong reserves, while we concentrated all our military and political efforts on the business of restoring order and creating economic stability in the east and assisting our allies in the execution of their military tasks. . . . I rejected [this idea] after mature reflection.[22]

His reason was that while Germany's allies could not hold on much longer, Germany's enemies were still fit and willing to fight for years. A quick solution was therefore essential. The policy of *Festung Europa* would of course have been a repetition of Falkenhayn's, except that the *Festung's* economic hinterland would now include Rumania, Poland and large tracts of western Russia. It was Ludendorff's misfortune that, at a time when decisive victories were possible, he had been curbed by Falkenhayn, and that, when he became Quartermaster-General, circumstances in 1916-17 had similarly curbed his intellectual belief in and temperamental predilection for smashing offensive blows. Now in November 1917 he found himself for the first time free to follow his natural bent. From the start it was unlikely that a Falkenhayn policy for 1918

[22] Hindenburg, 340.

appealed to him at all, whatever the objective considerations. Yet it is possible that a limited and defensive strategy, so wrong in 1915-16, might have become right in 1918. From July 1918 until the moment of final collapse the central powers were forced to carry out this policy, the great offensive having failed and having consumed the German reserve of good troops. The character of this defence under the worst possible conditions and under heavy allied attack suggests at least that the *Festung Europa* policy for 1918 would have been no more disastrous than the offensive, and not so risky.

Ludendorff proposed nevertheless to decide the war by an offensive in the west. Yet neither his book nor Hindenburg's visualises a concrete military object or a concrete political object that could be gained by military success. The ultimate purpose of the attack was vague and cloudy:

> The crown of success would be an operation in which we could bring to bear the whole of our superiority [wrote Ludendorff]. It was our great object. . . . Everything was based on the assumption that we should do well in this respect and although, of course, I expected our own Army to be weakened, I hoped it would be less so than that of the enemy. By continuing to attack we should still retain the initiative. More I could not aim at.[23]

The nearest Ludendorff gets to a political strategy of which his battle would be the instrument is:

> Germany could only make the enemy inclined to peace by fighting. It was first of all necessary to shake the position of Lloyd George and Clemenceau by a military victory. Before that was done peace was not to be thought of.[24]

Lieutenant-Colonel Wetzell, Chief of the Operations Section of O.H.L., in a memorandum after the war, defined the political attitude of the Supreme Command as follows:

> The one point of view which had clearly emerged was that a thorough-going success on the western front was necessary in order to arrive at a conclusion of this formidable struggle favourable to Germany. Only a far-reaching military success which would make it appear to the Entente powers

[23] Ludendorff, 588.
[24] *ibid*, 594.

that, even with the help of America, the continuation of the war offered no further prospects of success, would provide the possibility, in the opinion of the Supreme Command, of rendering our embittered opponents really ready to make peace. This was the political aim of the Supreme Command in 1918.[25]

Once again here were not clear-cut objectives but cloudy aspirations; and so far as these went, they rested on complete misreading or non-reading of Clemenceau's and Lloyd George's characters and those of their countries. Insight into the minds of others, so essential a quality of greatness in a commander, Ludendorff lacked. As his wife wrote of him during his political plottings after the war: "Ludendorff never possessed any knowledge of human nature, otherwise he could never have been at the mercy of those influences which brought about his downfall." [26]

Nothing could illustrate more the mindlessness of the efficiency and power of the German Empire than this great military offensive within a political vacuum.

So it was that in Mons on November 11, 1917, four able military minds evolved basic plans for a military absurdity, an absurdity to be prepared and carried out with a technical, tactical and organisational finesse never equalled on such a scale by France and Britain.

From Verdun to the Swiss frontier the ground was unsuitable for a grand offensive. Ludendorff and his subordinates therefore had the three hundred miles from just east of Verdun to the North Sea from which to select a point, or points, of attack. Two areas of weakness were apparent: the British in Flanders, the French in the Verdun salient; Kuhl argued for the first, von der Schulenburg for the second. Haig's stubborn half-year of slogging towards Passchendaele had drawn the mass of his forces and their elaborate base and communications installations into a narrow space between Ypres and the coast. If the German army struck through the critically important railway junction of Hazebrouck towards the sea, left flank on the La Bassée canal, Haig would be taken in flank and rear without room for manoeuvre. It was in Kuhl's mind that Haig would probably attack again in the spring beyond Passchendaele and thus tee himself up even better for the German drive. Such indeed had been Haig's intention, had he received the reinforcments he demanded. Kuhl

[25] Lutz, 22.
[26] Frau Ludendorff, 232.

acknowledged that the wide and marshy valley of the Lys, protecting the British front at the point of break-through, would only be certainly freed from floods by April.

Von der Schulenburg disagreed with Kuhl: France might be broken by a military catastrophe; Britain, however, would survive a disaster in Flanders. Therefore they should aim at smashing the French by a double attack on the Verdun salient, bringing about a wide collapse in the French line.

There was the legendary town of Verdun as an immediate prize and as a subject for propaganda. Franco-American military co-operation would be dislocated. With the French paralysed by defeat, the German mass of manoeuvre could be transferred to deal with the British.

Ludendorff himself was in favour of attacking the British, fearing that they would otherwise attack him in Flanders while he was involved at Verdun. The conference came to no final conclusions, but Ludendorff's summing-up defined the ground for further staff studies:

> The situation in Russia and Italy will, as far as can be seen, make it possible to deliver a blow on the Western Front in the new year. The strength of the two sides will be approximately equal. About thirty-five divisions and one thousand heavy guns can be made available for an offensive. That will suffice for *one* offensive; a second great simultaneous offensive, say as a diversion, will not be possible.
>
> Our general situation requires that we should strike at the earliest moment, if possible at the end of February or beginning of March, before the Americans can throw strong forces into the scale.
>
> We must beat the British.
>
> The operations must be based on these conditions.[27]

His own first preference was for an attack to take the British mass in their right flank, but launched further south than the Lys or Arras:

> In particular an attack near St. Quentin appeared promising. After gaining the Somme line, Ham-Péronne, operations could be carried further in a northwesterly direction, with the left flank resting on the Somme, and lead to the rolling up of the British front.[28]

[27] *British Official History,* France and Belgium 1918, The German March Offensive, 139.
[28] *British Official History,* vol. *cit,* 140.

Following this early conference, Kuhl, von der Schulenburg and Wetzell carried out more detailed studies. A remarkable aspect of this planning was that none of the planning officers had any doubt that the German army would succeed in breaking through the opposing defence system, an achievement that had eluded France and Britain. The German planners worked in the opposite way to Haig, Joffre and Nivelle. Whereas the allied generals had drawn up plans on excellent strategic principles with splendid distant objectives, and then failed so badly in tactics as to reach no strategic objectives at all (this was surely the apotheosis of chair-borne strategy, if that phrase has any meaning), the Germans began with the tactical problem of the break-through. As Ludendorff put it:

> Tactics had to be considered before purely strategical objects which it is futile to pursue unless tactical success is possible. A strategical plan which ignores the tactical factor is foredoomed to failure.[29]

On November 20, Kuhl sent Ludendorff a paper strongly and elaborately arguing in favour of the Hazebrouck axis of advance, starting from a front Festubert-Frelinghien. The Arras area was too strongly defended. As for St. Quentin, a break-through would certainly be fairly easy, but the exploitation might prove too great a task for the available forces, involving as it did holding off the French to the south while rolling up the British northwestwards.

On December 15 Wetzell sent in a brilliant analytical staff study of German and allied strength, deployment and reserves. Its keynote was cool realism:

> Any prospect of success in the West depends upon other principles than those which hold good for the East or against Italy. We must be quite clear what these principles are before estimating what is attainable . . . otherwise we shall be led astray and select objectives which, in view of the character of our opponents, we are not likely to reach.[30]

Wetzell wanted to attack at Verdun, or, as an alternative, in Flanders through Hazebrouck. Like Kuhl he felt the St. Quentin project to be beyond German strength, unless it was regarded as a preliminary opera-

[29] *British Official History*, vol. *cit*, 141.
[30] Ludendorff, 540-1.

tion to draw British reserves away from a second, and principal, blow towards Hazebrouck.

On December 27, Ludendorff held another conference. He made no choice but ordered planning and physical preparation to go forward for the offensive towards Hazebrouck (code name *George*), with a subsidiary attack near Ypres (*George Two*), the Arras attack (*Mars*), the St. Quentin operation (*St. Michael*), and attacks either side of Verdun and in the Vosges. He gave March 10 as the completion date for this work. It was a jeweller's tray of glittering possibilities from which it was clear that Ludendorff could not bring himself to choose. Since the great battle must begin in only about ten weeks' time, it indicated a dangerous lack of clear strategic thought. Even in his memoirs Ludendorff does not conceal his psychological difficulties in deciding where to commit his country's final reserve of strength in a gamble with its future.

> As is always the case, there was a great deal to be said for and against each proposal. . . .
> Strategically the northern attack had the advantage of a great, though limited, objective. It might enable us to shorten our front if we succeeded in capturing Calais and Boulogne. The attack on Verdun might also lead to an improvement in our front. . . . The centre attack seemed to lack any definite limit. This could be remedied by directing the main effort on the area between Arras and Péronne, towards the coast. If this blow succeeded the strategic result might indeed be enormous, as we should separate the bulk of the English army from the French and crowd it up with its back to the sea.
> I favoured the centre attack, but I was influenced by the time factor and by tactical considerations. . . .[31]

In mid-January of 1918 he went on a tour of the front to hold staff conferences. At the end of it, on January 21, Ludendorff at last made his decision. *George*, across the Lys to Hazebrouck, was so dependent on the wetness of the weather that it might not be possible until May—too late. *Mars*, as Kuhl had from the first maintained, was too risky in view of the strength of British positions about Arras. Therefore *Michael*, against which both Kuhl and Wetzell had argued as being overambitious, would constitute the great offensive. In support of it, and several days later, there would be a reduced *Mars* attack south of Arras.

[31] Ludendorff, 590.

34. ALTERNATIVE OFFENSIVES

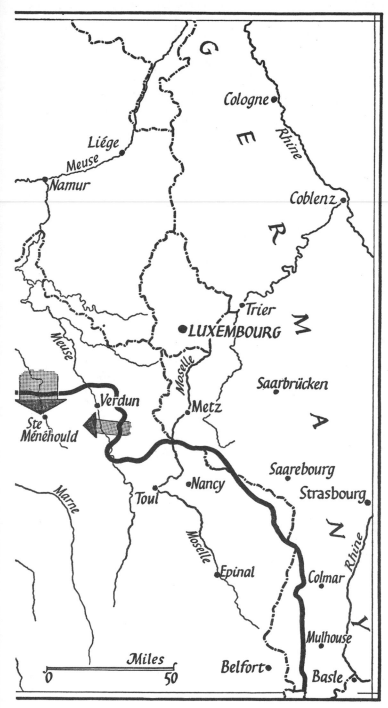

CONSIDERED BY LUDENDORFF

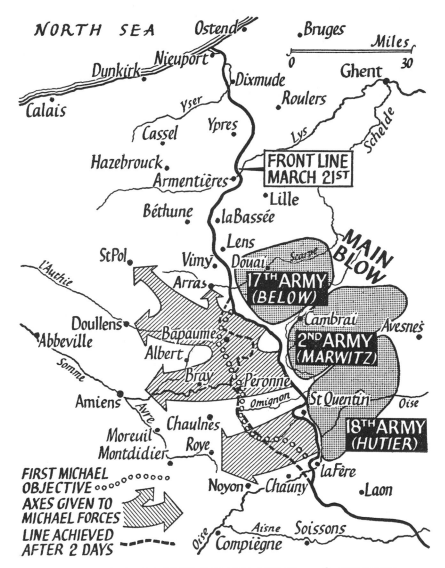

35. LUDENDORFF'S FINAL PLAN FOR THE MARCH 1918 OFFENSIVE

Preliminary orders issued three days later gave the operation's general objectives: "Attack *Michael* should break through the enemy front with the objective La Fère-(left flank) Ham-Péronne, and then, in combination with *Mars'* (left flank), push forward to Péronne-Arras and beyond." [32]

For an offensive of this war-deciding importance, the objectives appear inadequate. They do not reveal the clear shape of a strong, attainable design; rather, they seem to express the uncertainty of a mind that has seen no further than a tactical success and hopes that events will guide his thought for the second stage. The contrast is sharp with Manstein's *Sichelsnitt* plan for 1940, which in so many ways was a successful replay of *Michael*. In *Sichelsnitt* the preliminary blow fell first in the Belgian plain, to grip and distract the enemy; then the major attacking group broke through in the south to take the allied forces in Belgium in flank and rear. From Sedan onwards the objective was always the coast at Abbeville. In *Michael* no such final targets were assigned, and the subsidiary attack was launched after the main blow and achieved nothing. All these characteristics of *Michael* reflected Ludendorff, with his burning mental restlessness and physical activity, his appetite for detail. Even more revealing that Ludendorff's strategic architecture was not a great coherent design but an agglomeration of little elements was the fact that *Michael* was not necessarily alone to constitute the campaign of 1918; it might be followed by other major attacks—despite the fact that Kuhl and Wetzell thought German strength too slender even for *Michael* itself. Ludendorff told the Kaiser and the Imperial Chancellor in Hamburg on February 13: "We must not imagine that this offensive will be like those in Galicia or Italy; it will be an immense struggle that will begin at one point, continue at another, and take a long time; it is difficult, but it will be victorious. . . ." [33]

Ludendorff's organisation of the offensive forces also suggested ambiguity. At the end of January 1918 the 18th Army was transferred from Crown Prince Rupprecht of Bavaria's army group (which otherwise and hitherto contained all the *Michael* forces) to that of the Imperial Crown Prince; responsibility for *Michael* was thus split between two army group commands. In 1940 all the troops involved in the great break-through between Namur and Sedan were allotted to Rundstedt's Army Group A. Dynastic reasons may have been in Ludendorff's mind, but he had his own military explanation: "I meant to exercise a far-reaching influence

[32] *Der Weltkrieg,* Band 14, 78.
[33] Ludendorff, 588.

on the course of the battle. That was difficult if it was being conducted by one group only; every intervention was only too apt to become mere interference from above." [34]

Ludendorff's reasoning was sound enough, given his intention to direct the battle himself. Was it, however, a correct decision for Germany's over-all supreme commander to involve himself in one offensive on one of the war fronts? Allied as well as German experience certainly suggested that decisive events should not be left in the hands of subordinates. Ludendorff's method was the opposite of Moltke's in 1914.

Throughout the winter, troops from the eastern front (all those under thirty-five) had been sent by train to the west for training and re-equipment. From the western-front trench system, too, troops had been withdrawn in rotation for intensive training in offensive tactics. The general principles of these tactics and tactical organisation were to serve the German army well for another forty years—in France in 1940, in the western desert, 1941-43, and in the desperate battles against odds of 1943-45. Instead of the fixed objectives and designated limits of advance of British planning in 1917 and of the linear tactics that the British began to abandon for major operations only late in the 1917 campaign, German tactics were based on infiltration by storm groups of all arms except tanks—riflemen, light machine guns, flame throwers and mortars. These groups were not fixed units, but of any size and composition up to battalions according to the task in hand. They were not to worry about their flanks, not to preserve a continuous front line, not to stop in order to overcome points of resistance. Like a tide coming in over a rocky foreshore, they were to flow always forward and round by the paths of least resistance. The training pamphlets drove home the principle:

> The objective of the first day must be at least the enemy's artillery; the objective of the second day depends on what is achieved on the first; there must be no rigid adherence to plans made beforehand.
>
> During training in the past, objectives have too often been indicated as first line, second line, intermediate line and artillery protection line; the aim of the break-through should be the enemy's artillery, when the lines will fall of themselves.

[34] Ludendorff, 592.

The reserves must be put in where the attack is progressing, not where it is held up.[35]

Behind the storm groups came the battle groups—mixed forces again, including guns and engineers—whose task was to clean up resistance bypassed by the storm troops.

The rigid hierarchy of command under which the British and French had fought their battles of 1917 (army—corps—division—brigade—battalion) was also abolished in favour of a more flexible, more instantly responsive system. Army commanders gave a general directive under which divisional commanders fought their own battles. The battalion commander actually controlling the fighting on the battlefield had direct access to the divisional commander. Corps and brigades were often merely "holding" commands for supply and reinforcement.

All this was the shape of military things to come. It is fair to say that although the British had become in the course of 1917 infinitely more flexible and subtle than at the beginning of that campaign—and far more so than some give them credit for—they were very far from the complete revolution of tactical thought and organisation achieved by the Germans. The orders and events of the last battles of 1917 showed the British to be still essentially rigid and hierarchical, with the traditional fixed military units. The British command regarded men with rifles as the principal component of an attacking force although they were supported by machine guns as they followed the barrage. In the Second World War also the British laid excessive emphasis on rifle-armed infantry. The German infantry, on the other hand, now formed part of the mechanised fire power of a battle group of all arms, except tanks which the Germans had chosen to neglect.

The German tactics and organisation required high qualities of leadership and initiative from the section leader upwards. It was therefore remarkable that the army Haig thought to have ruined in 1917, and which indeed Ludendorff himself regarded as approximating to a militia, could be, and was, trained to carry them out with general success.

On March 10 Hindenburg issued the operation order for *Michael*:

[35] *British Official History*, vol. *cit*, 156-7.

His Majesty commands

1. The *Michael* attack will take place on March 21. Break into the first hostile position at 9:40 A.M.

2. The first great tactical object of Army Group Crown Prince Rupprecht will be to cut off the British in the Cambrai salient and gain, north of the junction of the Omignon stream with the Somme, the line Croisilles-Bapaume-Péronne-mouth of the Omignon. Should the progress of the attack of the right wing [17th Army] be very good, it will be carried further, beyond Croisilles. The subsequent task of this army group will be to push forward in the direction Arras-Albert, to hold the Somme near Péronne securely with the left wing, and with the main weight of the attack on the right wing to upset the balance of the British front on the 6th Army front as well as on the front of the attack, and thus free further German forces from position warfare for the advance. . . .

3. Army Group German Crown Prince will first gain the line of the Somme south of the Omignon stream, and the Crozat canal. The 18th Army will also be prepared to extend its right wing as far as Péronne. This army group will study the question of reinforcing the left wing of the 18th Army by divisions from the 17th, 1st and 3rd. . . .

The blow to break through the British front and envelop the mass of Haig's forces by an advance northwestwards was thus to be struck by the 17th Army (Below) on the right flank and the 2nd Army (von der Marwitz) to its south. The 18th Army's advance was subsidiary, designed to support the other armies on its right flank and hold off the French on its left. Of the forty-seven[36] *Michael* assault divisions, fourteen were allotted to the 17th and twenty-one to the 18th Armies; and out of the 6,608 guns, the 18th received 2,623 and the 17th fewer—2,234. Since the 17th Army had an assault sector of nine and a half miles and the 18th Army twenty miles, the 17th Army was given nearly double the weight of guns but in men only half the weight again. It was also anomalous that, although the 17th Army commander, Otto von Below, had a fine record of success, it was von Hutier, the 18th Army commander, and his artillery specialist, Colonel Bruchmüller, who had planned and fought the prototype break-through battle of Riga. The over-all deployment of strength and talent seemed unbalanced in view of the British deployment and defences opposite *Michael*—thirty-three

---

[36] All *Michael* figures from German Official History, *Der Weltkrieg,* Band 14, Appendix 38a.

attack divisions of the 18th and 2nd Armies mostly against the fourteen divisions of Gough's 5th Army (partly in dilapidated defences newly taken over from the French) and fourteen attack divisions of the 17th Army mostly on the front of Byng's 3rd Army of fourteen divisions. Despite the unprecedented weight, technique and power of the *Michael* forces, many of the preparations displayed the lack of a clear and dominating theme; this was Ludendorff again.

As February turned to March, the wide landscape of northern France was alive with creeping and stealthy movements; forty-seven divisions and over six thousand guns, with all the vast stacks of ammunition, food, fodder, hundreds of thousands of horses, trucks and tractors that such a force required, were being placed behind a front that already held twenty-eight "trench" divisions. There were also fixed installations to be built—aircraft hangars, light railways. Unlike the British and French preparations of 1915-16 and some of the British of 1917, which had been openly conducted, the German *Michael* preparations were intended to be secret: to lead to strategic surprise. Through the night countryside and shuttered villages the assault divisions marched towards the front; by daylight they had disappeared; only just before D-Day did they leave assembly areas well in the rear. In railway stations there were no familiar sights of hordes of troops waiting for transport: when the trains stopped, the troops instantly dispersed.

All this was a staggering exercise in staff work. In the words of the *British Official History:* "The concentration of these vast forces and their subsidiary services on the battle area constituted a gigantic problem which was solved with complete success." [37]

The problems of defensive organisation to meet such vast forces were far from adequately solved by the allied command although in fact allied intelligence penetrated the German cover plan with remarkable acuity.

Where the allied front might be smashed anywhere along the three hundred miles from Verdun to the sea, it was clear that a single general should direct the battle, that a single general should control the reserves on whom the outcome of the fight depended. On January 23, 1918, Joint Note No. 14 of the Supreme War Council called for the national Commander-in-Chief's views on the formation of a central inter-allied

[37] *British Official History*, vol. *cit*, 153.

reserve for the western and Italian fronts. Next day Haig, Pétain and Pershing met Foch and Wilson (military representatives on the Supreme War Council) in a meeting full of barely concealed acerbity, especially between Foch and Pétain. The upshot was that the American army was to be the only central reserve; neither Pétain nor Haig could spare troops out of their own reserves; in any event, Pétain and Haig had agreed to help each other with reserve divisions if either needed them in the face of a German blow.

From January 30 to February 2, 1918, the Supreme War Council again chewed over the question of a central reserve and somebody to command it. It was a drifting, shapeless debate. At the end resolutions were proposed by Lloyd George, and passed, that created an allied central reserve for the west, Italy and the Balkans, and put its deployment in the control of an executive committee under the chairmanship of Foch, who nevertheless could not give strategic directions. Later Pétain and Haig informed the committee that they could spare no troops for the reserve. The central reserve was still being endlessly and fruitlessly discussed when the Germans struck. Had Haig not had so deep a distrust (with justice) of Henry Wilson and Lloyd George, and Pétain likewise of Foch, the national Commanders-in-Chief might not have regarded the appointment of a supreme commander so much as a mine under their own authority.

As it was, Haig and Pétain each prepared for his own battle, the one based on the necessity for covering the Channel ports, the other for covering Paris and heart of France. The split in allied strategy was modified by the limited and detailed arrangements made by the two Commanders-in-Chief for mutual help on either side of the junction point of their armies. By these final schemes General Humbert (3rd French Army) with six divisions would arrive in the area either of Montdidier-Noyon or of Amiens (behind Gough's 5th Army) on the evening of the fourth day after a request for help, or rather later round St. Pol. Humbert's troops would either be used for a counterstroke or to take over part of the British line.

There was a marked contrast between the defensive measures of Haig and Pétain on their own fronts. Pétain had accepted since the summer of 1917 that Russia's fall would lead to a German offensive in 1918; he had therefore been training and preparing for nine months. France was at the end of her manpower, as Pétain had long foreseen. In a sense the French infantry had therefore become escorts and protectors of their artillery, which was the real key to Pétain's defensive methods. Pétain kept thirty-nine of his ninety-nine divisions in reserve—40 per cent against the British 30 per cent. The French defensive systems were based on an outpost zone to be held very lightly, a main position beyond the reach of the enemy's preliminary bombardment, and behind it a reserve position. Pétain, however, foresaw that the attack might burst into open country and he had instructed his troops to be trained in delaying battles of manoeuvre. Nevertheless the French army was unevenly prepared in these ideas, because throughout the winter of 1917-18 all those officers suspicious of their novelty had continued to receive support from Foch, the Chief of Staff, and from the French government.

Nineteen of the French reserve divisions were behind their right between the Argonne and the Vosges, placed either to parry a German stroke at Verdun or round the southern flank of the western-front trench system via the Swiss lowlands. Another group, eighteen strong, was behind the French centre in Champagne, covering Paris; four of them were west of Soissons in reach of Gough's 5th Army. The remaining two French reserve divisions were behind the Belgians in Flanders.

In every respect, bar a higher ratio of troops to frontage, the British were less well-placed than the French to sustain a blow of the weight and type planned by Ludendorff; and most of their troubles were to be attributed to the extreme lateness of Haig's acceptance of the fact that 1918 might open with a major German offensive, not a continuation of Passchendaele.

It was Haig's view—and is still that of his defenders—that the 1917 Flanders campaign had done far greater damage to the German army than to his own in terms of attrition of reserves. This is not certain and rests on speculative accountancy of a dubious and optimistic kind. In terms of demoralisation the question is equally open. As Ludendorff points out, the German army dreaded another defensive battle like Flanders in 1917, whose horrors had deeply shaken it. However, the British army had been also badly shaken. In the German counter-attack at Cambrai after the successful British tank attack, some British troops—survivors of Passchendaele—had collapsed in rout. Rising figures for drunkenness among officers and men, for cardiac and psychological disorders, for desertion and absence for 1917 and 1918 all illustrate increasingly shaky nerves in the British army.

Whereas the Germans made good—and vastly more so—their 1917 losses by transfers from Russia, Haig had hoped to make good his own from the still copious reserves of fit young manpower in the United Kingdom—607,403 trained "A" men on January 1, 1918.[38] Restored to its full strength, the British army in France would, he had hoped, attack again in early 1918. However, instead of the 605,000 men he demanded, he was promised only 100,000. His twelve-battalion divisions were to be reduced to nine, like the French and German. This reorganisation into nine-battalion divisions was not completed until March 8. Older British military opinion regretted the change; the best minds welcomed it for the same reasons that the Germans had adopted it—as making for greater fire power and flexibility.

In the meetings and correspondence relating to this and other problems, Haig was (as the *British Official History* put it in regard to a War Cabinet meeting of January 7 on the prospects for the next twelve months) "in the equivocal position of having to convince the War Cabinet that, although the Passchendaele operation had inflicted many losses on the Germans, they were still very powerful." [39]

Haig's army, then, was not strong enough for the offensive; but for defence?

In January 1917 the fighting troops of the British army in France had totalled 1,168,466, less about 60,000 R.E. transport personnel; in January 1918, it was 1,097,906, a diminution of only 3 per cent. At the opening of Haig's Flanders offensive in July 1917 the Germans had held the thirty-two miles of front from the Lys to the sea with thirteen divisions against an attack by forty-nine divisions, ten to twelve German divisions being in reserve. That was one line division to 2.46 miles of defence, odds during the first assault of nearly 4 to 1. In March 1918 British held 126 miles of front with fifty-five divisions in the line or in army reserves—one division to 2.2 miles, a slightly denser force. The German maximum strength on the front of attack in 1918 was 1.72

[38] *British Official History*, vol. *cit*, 52.
[39] *op. cit*, 60.

divisions to the mile,[40] favourable odds of little more than 3 to 1. If only "attack" divisions are counted, this becomes 1.4 divisions to the mile.

In other words, in terms both of odds and of density of troops within the actual defense system, the British in March 1918 were better placed than the Germans in July 1917, who had succeeded in blunting the first British assault. However, whereas the Germans in July 1917 had had ten to twelve reserve divisions for thirty-two miles of front, Haig in March 1918 had only eight in general reserve, for 126 miles. If army reserves are included, the figure for reserve divisions rises to eighteen; but correspondingly the density of troops in the defence system must be reduced.

Nevertheless the figures alone suggest that the British defence system itself should have been capable of absorbing the German blow for some days, even if paucity of reserves brought about a progressive later collapse. The difference not shown by the figures lay in the fact that the German defences in Flanders in 1917 had been long prepared according to an ingenious and carefully considered directive, and the troops within them well trained in elastic defence, whereas British preparations in 1918 were belated, uneven, and incomplete, both in terms of defences and training.

Only on December 14, 1917, did G.H.Q. issue a general instruction on defensive layout and tactics. It was the first time since 1914 that the British had studied defence. They paid the Germans the compliment of copying the methods used against themselves in 1917. Unfortunately they copied the letter, not the spirit. They adopted the basic German ideas of a dense net of machine-gun posts and fluid, mobile grouping for counterattack, but they tried to fit these things into the stiff British organisational hierarchy, the static British way of defending ground by staying put on it. Moreover, they continued to think of machine guns as supporting a defence based on the infantry, whereas the Germans treated riflemen as escorts for the machine guns, the true spine of resistance.

More particularly the British copied the wrong German manual—not that of December 1916 (Conduct of the Defensive Battle: *Die Führung der Abwehrschlacht*) which laid down general principles and tactical methods, but an August 1917 edition of a companion manual on the layout and construction of field defences themselves (*Allgemeines über*

[40] *British Official History,* II, France and Belgium, 1917, 108 fn.

Stellenbau). Had the British had plenty of time—which they had not—and plenty of labour to dig and build—which they had not—the result would still have been a caricature of German methods.

The British G.H.Q. Instruction of December 14 ordered that the existing trench system should be modified into a Forward Zone, a Battle Zone and a Rear Zone, each belt to be a network of defended localities.

In the role allotted by the Instruction to the Forward Zone there was an ambiguity; instead of being an area thinly held by machine guns merely to delay and dislocate attacks (as were French and German forward zones) it was, in the words of the *British Official History,* to be "sufficiently garrisoned and strengthened . . . to compel the enemy to employ strong forces for its capture." [41] In the 5th and 3rd Armies about a third of their total strength was therefore posted in this zone, ready to receive the German hurricane bombardment.

Some two or three miles behind the Forward Zone lay the Battle Zone, containing two-thirds of the guns and a proportion of troops that varied from army to army, but roughly a third more than in the Forward Zone. This was the line of main resistance and was some 2,000-3,000 yards deep. This also could be saturated from the German gun line. Four to eight miles behind the Battle Zone was to be a Rear Zone—a second position—but in view of the shortage of labour, it was only to be marked out at first and completed later. In the German system two-thirds of all troops within the defensive zones were kept mobile for manoeuvre and counterattack; in the British copy the proportion was reversed.

At the same time troops and command unaccustomed to defence, to whom the new tactical ideas were unfamiliar and even uncongenial, had to be retrained in the brief time available, and the shaken and decimated Passchendaele divisions rested.

By March 21 British preparations were far from complete. The Forward Zone—which on the German system mattered least—was in the best condition of the three in the 3rd and 5th Armies; the Battle Zone incomplete, without any kind of dugouts in the 5th Army, without machine-gun dugouts in the 3rd. In the 3rd Army the Rear Zone had been wired, but not dug; in the 5th there was simply a line of turned turf, known as the "Green Line."

The 5th Army's defences were specially rudimentary because only in

[41] *British Official History,* France and Belgium 1918, The German March Offensive, 42.

January had it taken over a large part of its present front from the French, who, as ever disinclined to dig and following Pétain's concepts of a deep mobile defence in open country, had done little fortification. The reason why the 5th Army had taken over this front so dangerously close to the time of the expected German blow was Haig's reluctance to extend his line at Pétain's request so long as there was a chance of re-commencing Passchendaele in the spring.

However, given long and thorough preparations on sound principles, the actual defence system ought, on German precedent, to have held out for several days. The lack of such preparations was the direct consequence of Haig's late summer and autumn battles of 1917 and of his persistence in the face of news from Russia in thinking more of his own offensives than of a German one, bigger than them all, in 1918.

Haig's deployment of forces in March 1918 is also open to question. Like von Kuhl, he was rightly impressed by the possibilities of a German advance across the Lys towards the Channel coast. The Germans had only fifty miles to go to reach the coast and much less to reach Haig's communications and base organisations. Here lay the 2nd Army with twelve divisions for a front of twenty miles across the base of the Passchendaele salient, which was not to be held strongly. This army and the Belgians formed a large salient endangered by a thrust through Haze-brouck; the line could have been much shortened and the strategic balance improved by withdrawing to a back line covering Dunkirk. As it was, a German success on Haig's left flank could not be immediately dangerous, and his allotment of troops to the Ypres sector appears excessive—especially when compared with the strength of his right flank, which linked him to the French and also covered the Channel ports. The 1st Army, holding a front of thirty-three miles from Gavrelle to Armen-tières, was given 14 divisions and 1,450 guns and howitzers. This part of the front had long been in British occupation and was tactically strong by reason of the shallow and marshy valley of the Lys and the Vimy and Lorette ridges to the rear of the existing line. From Gavrelle to a little north of Gouzeaucourt (on 1st Army's left) Byng's 3rd Army had 14 divisions and 1,120 guns and howitzers to twenty-eight miles; from Gouzeaucourt to the French left at Barisis Gough's 5th Army had 12 divisions (and 3 cavalry divisions) and 1,566 guns and howitzers for forty-two miles. Taking Byng and Gough together, this gave them 26 infantry divisions and 2,686 guns to defend seventy miles of front, behind which lay the twin objectives for the Germans of separating the British from the French and outflanking the British from the south. The allotment of reserve divisions equally was stronger in Flanders, weaker behind Byng and Gough. This deliberate weakness of Haig's right flank was accentuated by the incompleteness of its defences, above all in the 5th Army.

Haig's satisfaction with his dispositions is the more difficult to understand because the weakness of the 5th Army's defences was well known at G.H.Q., and because as early as an army commanders' conference on February 16, Haig himself had said: "We must therefore be prepared to be attacked . . . possibly from Lens to the Oise."

On March 2 the intelligence statement at the army commanders' conference considered that: "There are strong indications that the enemy intends to attack on the Third and Fifth Army fronts, with the object of cutting off the Cambrai salient and drawing in our reserves." [42]

This was confirmed by the weekly intelligence summary of March 10 and by the last such summary before the battle (March 17): ". . . there is no reason to alter the view already expressed that an offensive is intended in the Arras-St. Quentin sector, combined with a subsidiary attack in the Bois Grenier-Neuve Chapelle sector." [43] Gough himself was convinced that Hutier was intending to break through round St. Quentin and make for Amiens.

G.H.Q. instructions to Gough on February 9 on the conduct of the battle were ambiguous. He was "to secure and protect at all costs the important centre of Péronne and the river Somme to the south of that place. . . ." He was in the first place to meet a serious attack in his present position, but "it may well be desirable to fall back to the rearward defences of Péronne and the Somme, whilst linking up with the Third Army on the north, and preparing for counterattack."

In his book *Douglas Haig,* Mr. John Terraine regards this as a firm instruction to Gough to fortify the Péronne bridgehead and fight a main battle there after a withdrawal from a lightly held forward line, and considers that Haig believed this henceforward to be the basis of the 5th Army's battle plan and work of field fortification.

[42] *British Official History,* vol. *cit,* 105.
[43] *op. cit,* 107.

What was the reason for the complacency displayed by Haig over his right flank? Judging by the pace of his own offensives, he reckoned that he—or Pétain—would have time enough to switch reserves to Gough and Byng while they gave ground (there was far more room behind them than behind the 1st and 2nd Armies) before a heavy German attack. In the words of the *British Official History:*

> Both G.H.Q. and G.Q.G., judging from previous experience, anticipated that a German offensive, even if successful on a large scale, would do no more than occasion a more or less gradual withdrawal of the troops on the front attacked, which would allow time for the Allied reserves to be brought up and assembled at a safe distance behind that front, and sent into action deliberately in accordance with the pre-arranged plan.[44]

In fact, in his planning to meet *Michael* in March 1918, Haig thus made mistakes of deployment and miscalculations of timing similar to those of Gamelin in his preparations between Malmédy and the North Sea to meet *Sichelsnitt* in May 1940: a left wing too strong, and a right too weak. In 1918 Gough and the 5th Army, therefore, faced the same kind of danger as did Corap and the 9th French Army in 1940.

Rather like meteorologists plotting the approach of a hurricane, allied intelligence pierced through the elaborate German efforts at conceal- ment. By March 21, 1918, 191 German divisions and 3 brigades were in France and Belgium; 47 attack divisions were poised behind the *Michael* front. Against these 191 divisions were arranged 63 British (including 2 Portuguese) and 99 French; of 7 American divisions so far in France, only one was fully trained and ready to fight.

In artillery the Germans opposed 8,910 field guns and howitzers and 4,922 heavy and super heavy guns to the 8,814 field and 6,368 heavy guns of the allies.[45] But of the German total, overwhelming strength was allotted to *Michael,* and faced the British, less plentifully equipped with guns than the French. The three *Michael* armies had 4,010 field and 2,598 heavy guns[46] against only 1,710 field and 976 heavy guns[47] in the British 5th and 3rd Armies. In trench mortars, which the Germans had developed as a powerful and mobile close-range support artillery,

[44] *British Official History,* vol. *cit,* 117.
[45] *British Official History,* vol. *cit,* 103.
[46] German Official History, *Der Weltkrieg,* vol. *cit,* Appendix 39h.
[47] *op. cit,* 114-5.

the German superiority on the *Michael* front was crushing: 3,534 against a total of only 3,000 for the entire British army in France.[48]

The final week was a time of immense exertion and movement behind the German front. On March 15 ammunition dumps were completed. Between March 11 and 19 the guns and trench mortars came up and were slotted into their places in the vast scheme on March 20, the very eve of battle. On March 16 the forty-seven divisions of the *Michael* offensive group began marching the last stages to the front; the bands played them along as they sang *"Muss i denn, muss i denn."* [49] The army was in wonderful spirit, elated by its vast numbers, by the hugeness of the preparations, the wealth of equipment. On March 15 Lieutenant Sulzbach, of the infantry-escort artillery of the 18th Army, wrote in his diary: "One can only be amazed again and again at the careful work done by headquarters and at the preparations being made down to the last detail—that is after all the source of our greatness . . . all kinds of new equipment are in evidence, things that were lacking in 1914." [50]

Did not the shortest route to victory, peace and home lie through the British trenches? As for Nivelle's troops before the 1917 offensive, this was supposed to be the last—but this time successful—effort.

And in truth the last of Germany's strength had gone into the western preparations—into contracting a muscle that could strike one great blow and no more. Even the attacking army, whose power and equipment so impressed its members, illustrated the effects of four years of relentless blockade. "It was admittedly a serious question," wrote General von Kuhl in a report to a Reichstag commission after the war, "whether the army was still sufficiently mobile to be fit, as it was hoped, for larger operations in the open after breaking through the enemy lines." Kuhl referred to "the great lack of horses, and the fact that those available had been weakened by shortage of fodder, the lack of petrol and oil, rubber tyres, etc." [51]

There were no further reserves of manpower but eighteen-year-olds of the 1900 class and boys even younger. And behind the army the homeland was in a desperate state of misery and semi-starvation, of vio-

[48] *op. cit*, 153 fn.
[49] Sulzbach, 143.
[50] *ibid*, 142-3.
[51] Lutz, 73.

lent class conflict and political tensions. As with France in 1917, social revolution on Russian precedents was becoming a danger, as anti-war agitation spread through the factories and armed forces. Only the hope of victory in *Michael* held Germany together. Thus eventually the Royal Navy had won a great maritime victory in the war. In 1917 German infant mortality (one-five years old) was up 49.3 per cent over 1913, and mortality of children between five and fifteen up 55 per cent. At the beginning of 1918 German civilian adults had a diet of only 1,000 calories a day—enough for a child of three or four—less than half that necessary for the maintenance of health and strength. Every material aspect of German life was affected by similar penury.[52] A great European nation was living as a starving pauper, with all the moral hopelessness and collapse of will that goes with pauperism. On January 24, 1918, came a violent manifestation that German society could not survive more trials—250,000 workers came out on strike in Berlin, with proportionate numbers in Bremen, Hamburg, Essen and Leipzig, demanding peace with no annexations and no indemnities.

Michael was then a desperate and final gamble. It was an attempt by purely military means to decide on the battlefield a war involving total national economic, military, social and technical power, a war that Germany was losing.

On March 18, Ludendorff established an advanced headquarters in Avesnes, using buildings and telecommunications vacated by Hutier's headquarters. "From there we would easily reach all parts of the front by car," wrote Ludendorff. "I intended to see a great deal for myself, and to send my staff officers to the scenes of important events in order to obtain impressions at first hand. . . . Our offices there were not good, everything was cramped, but they had to do." [53]

Next day the Kaiser turned up at Avesnes in his luxurious court train.

At noon on the twentieth Ludendorff, Hindenburg and their staff met to take the decision whether or not to unleash the offensive the next day. It was a decision to daunt the will and harass the mind.

"Every delay must have increased the difficulties of troops crowded together close up to the enemy," wrote Ludendorff. "Already the tension

52 Bell, 671-2.
53 Ludendorff, 595.

was very hard to bear. The psychological pressure of the mass was urging them forward. . . . And yet our artillery relied on gas for its effect, and that was dependent on the direction and strength of the wind." [54]

The previous day and night had been violently rainy and windy; Ludendorff had had to face the agonising possibility of postponement. At 11 A.M. on the twentieth he received a fresh report from his meteorologist, Lieutenant Dr. Schmaus. "It was not strikingly favourable, but it did indicate that the attack was possible." [55]

At noon Ludendorff made his decision and issued his orders: *Michael* would begin next morning.

Now for Ludendorff began the worst period—the long work of preparation was over, the battle not begun. He had nothing to do, and throughout his life inactivity had been the most hateful and unbearable of things. There was still plenty of time for the wind to change and ruin the great bombardment, time for all sorts of things to go wrong. It was out of his hands. "Now it could no longer be stopped," he wrote. "Everything must run its course. . . ." [56] At such a moment a commander is the helpless victim of a fate he himself has determined.

During lunch that day Ludendorff made a confidence to his neighbour, Lieutenant-General von Tieschowitz, the significance of which was grotesque: "Do you know what it says for tomorrow in the *Brüdergemeine?* [57] It is the day of the Chosen People. Now can we not look upon the offensive that begins tomorrow with confidence?" [58]

The British knew the offensive was coming, knew by all the cumulative evidence of air and ground reconnaissance and interrogation of prisoners. Although there had been no warning bombardment of several days, nor even the increased fire of batteries making sure of registration, they were aware of the gigantic battering engine that had silently and stealthily made itself ready in front.

The evening and night of March 20, 1918, were quiet, too, but full of

[54] Ludendorff, 596-7.
[55] *ibid*, 598.
[56] *loc. cit.*
[57] Literally: "lay Brothers." In England, the Moravian Brothers. A community of Protestant pietists often referred to as *Herrnhuter* because their first settlement was in Herrnhut in Saxony. Founded in 1727 by Nikolaus Ludwig Graf von Zinzendorf, later with branches in England, North and South America and Czechoslovakia.
[58] Foerster, 132-3. Throughout this part the work by Foerster referred to is *Der Feldherr Ludendorff in Unglück.*

creepy signs that the attack was imminent. By 9 P.M. a mist along the 5th and 3rd Army fronts had thickened to fog, dampening sound, isolating every man, post and headquarters within the small islands of their own visibility. Apprehension prickled along the silent front.

After midnight the fog thickened further, a wall across the beam of a dimmed and shaded torch or lantern, a soft wall of silence.

At 4 A.M. (German time) the German army synchronised its watches three times for absolute accuracy. The fog wreathed and billowed quietly in the dark for another forty minutes. Then, on the stroke of 4:40 A.M., the German guns fired together all the way from Barisis to Armentières.

12

It was like the majestic outburst of orchestral power in Siegfried's Funeral March from *Götterdämmerung* after the opening growls of the brass and woodwind—themselves paralleled in *Michael* by the months of stealthy preparation. And indeed the bombardment of March 21 was as richly and elaborately orchestrated by Bruchmüller in his orders, fire tables and plans as a score by Wagner.

The bombardment began with two hours of fire by the complete orchestra of guns, from field artillery to super-heavy, on targets fixed without registration by air reconnaissance and by mathematical calculations that included allowances for the flight of shot under different weather conditions: the targets were guns, command posts, camps and telecommunication centres. Gas shells were used—blue and green cross—and reached as far as the British heavy-gun line. After twenty minutes the mine throwers stopped firing. After fifty minutes all the artillery except Schwefla (code name for long-distance fire) switched to the British infantry positions for ten minutes—explosive shell on the forward zone, gas further to the rear.[1]

The bombardment went on for five hours in all, switching from target to target, zone to zone, alternating between gas and high explosive, changing its orchestral pattern of instruments according to need, until the British communications and command organisation from army headquarters downwards was in shreds, and until the 5th Army and to some

[1] Bruchmüller, 95 ff.

extent the 3rd Army had been reduced to isolated, unco-ordinated elements of gassed and blasted troops.

"I awoke," writes a British heavy-artillery officer in the 3rd Army, "with a tremendous start conscious of noise, incessant and almost musical, so intense that it seemed as if a hundred devils were dancing in my brain. Everything seemed to be vibrating—the ground, my dugout, my bed. . . . It was still dark." [2]

All British accounts agree on the paralysing effect that this moving, changing deluge produced as the shells homed through the fog and the dark on to individual key installations with astonishing precision and regularity. Near some new deep cable trenches "the German shells fell in parallel lines, five yards apart, the craters nearly touching." [3]

Half-blinded, and with speech muffled by their gas masks, those troops not pinned to shelter by the roaring storm groped their way to their battle stations. With all communications cut, thousands of questions were asked to which there was no answer.

The sun rose at 6 A.M., but the fog still lay thick along low ground—thickest on the 5th Army's right in the valley of the Oise—blotting out the defence's observation of no man's land, blinding machine guns. The bombardment went on. Its climax was a smashing blow with explosive shell on the British forward zone and front positions. It lasted five minutes. Then, without a pause, the German fire changed to a creeping barrage, tightly behind which came the German infantry, silent, no cheering, grim and eager.

It was 9:40 A.M.

This was the moment when the spell of paralysis in the west began to be lifted—a spell laid on at the Aisne on September 13, 1914. Suddenly the pulse of the war changed its rhythm from the slow, sluggish movement of long hibernation to the quick beat of rapid events.

In the sky a flat white disc of sun; on the ground fog, treacherously varying in thickness from sector to sector, blending over the front lines with smoke from shell bursts and German smoke canisters. Hardly had the German creeping barrage swept over the British front positions than

[2] Behrend, 53.
[3] *British Official History,* vol. *cit,* 162 fn. 2.

the storm troops arrived. They loomed through the fog in small parties, sweeping over defended localities whose defences and garrisons had been already obliterated by the guns, creeping fast up the valleys that led into the heart of the British positions—valleys covered by the cross fire of blinded machine guns—ignoring the isolated garrisons that still fought. Allowing for variance between different sectors of the 3rd and 5th Armies, the Germans had achieved overwhelming tactical as well as strategic surprise. In the British armies under attack, both among the fighting troops and throughout the command, there was complete anarchy, a chaos of rumours and ignorance. In the British artillery there was a total breakdown of co-ordinated counterfire owing to the smashing of tele- and radio-communications.

At 11:07 and 11:30 A.M., Sir Douglas Haig first received formal reports from the 5th and 3rd Armies that they were being violently attacked (he had heard the news before 8 A.M. as he was dressing). By then the Forward Zone in the 5th Army, containing a third of its troops and much of its field artillery, had in the main collapsed and dissolved —in many places before its machine guns had fired a shot. "A disastrous feature," in the words of the *British Official History,* "of the success of the German attack in swamping the forward troops was not only the complete loss of a quarter or more of the battalions of the divisions attacked, but also the capture or destruction of a large proportion of their machine guns and Lewis guns, the lack of which was to prove a most serious handicap during the subsequent days of battle." [4]

The signal book of an acting brigade major of infantry[5] gives an immediate picture of the speed of the collapse. By 6:50 A.M. there was no communication by cable forwards or rearwards or to flanking brigades. By 10:30 A.M. B Company of the 11th King's had lost forty out of 150 men. At 11.15 came a report by a captain who had been called from a trench by a rumour to see a mob of his men running towards Battalion H.Q. "I was told," ran his signal, "the enemy had broken through and was upon us." He tried to organise a defence but was outflanked.

At 11:45 A.M. a signal reported that the front line "gave way at 10:15 A.M." [6]

[4] *British Official History,* vol. *cit,* 167.
[5] Captain Desmond Young, 42nd Infantry Brigade of 14th (Light) Division in the 5th Army.
[6] Young's Signal Book.

As the sun rose higher and grew hotter, the fog at last dispersed; the confused and savage battle was fought on under a blue sky in the warmth of spring. By 2 P.M. the Germans were everywhere up to the Battle Zone of the 5th Army and ready to attack it; they were already infiltrating deep into it by the valleys of the Somme, Omignon and Cologne, and the Heudicourt valley. In the 3rd Army the situation was hardly better, but not so uniformly bad. The Flesquières salient had held, but between the Bapaume-Cambrai road and Fontaine les Croisilles (ten miles) the defence was already clinging desperately to the rear fringe of the Battle Zone.

Till midday Gough believed his front could hold together for two or three days without other reinforcement than the two G.H.Q. divisions behind him. By evening he was not so optimistic; he ordered a retreat behind the Somme and the Crozat Canal, which would form a salient into his line and lengthen it by four miles.

In this sector all three zones of the defensive system had been lost. The Germans had in a single day broken clean through into open country.

During this disastrous day Haig issued no operation orders: it was too early to assess the situation, and he lacked information. He did, however, begin to reverse his strategic deployment by ordering three divisions from the 1st and 2nd Armies to the 5th and 3rd, and by releasing three G.H.Q. divisions to the armies under attack.

Pétain did not wait for an appeal from Haig for help before ordering five French divisions to be ready for a move at any time after noon on the twenty-second.

A disaster in itself, March 21 presaged an even greater disaster, as the decimated and disorganised troops in the 3rd and 5th Armies faced another day's furious assault. March 21, 1918, echoes in British history like such other swift and unexpected catastrophes as Tobruk and Singapore. There had to be scapegoats (Gough or Haig, according to taste) and an excuse. The excuse was the fog. It certainly made things very difficult for the defence, but it also created trouble for the attackers, pressing on over enemy ground in complex tactics of infiltration. According to Ludendorff, the fog was no help to the Germans: ". . . fog impeded and retarded our movements and prevented our superior training and leadership from reaping its true reward." [7]

[7] Ludendorff, 598.

The British failure, in fact, was partly owing to the fog, partly owing to Haig's strategic deployment with heavier weight on his left, but above all to the abiding and ubiquitous influence of Passchendaele which led to the lateness (and consequent errors and omissions) of British defensive preparations and to lowered morale in the defending troops. ". . . no less than 19 out of 21 divisions in the front line of the Fifth and Third Armies," says the *British Official History,* "had been engaged in the Passchendaele battles, in which they lost a large proportion of their best soldiers whose places had been filled, if filled at all, by raw drafts and transfers." [8]

Even had Haig received all the reinforcements he had demanded, these too would have been raw drafts by the exacting standards set by Hutier's, Marwitz's and Below's troops.

The German success was not solely owing to British shortcomings. Their troops had been led with dash and had skilfully executed clever tactics. The bombardment, however, had been a special triumph, for by its short duration and use of gas it had paralysed the defence without smashing up the ground. In the words of the *British Official History:* "The deadly rapidity of the enemy advance was assisted by the good and practically undamaged surface of the ground quite unlike the laboured progress of our own troops over the cratered surface and clinging chalk of the Somme, or the liquid mud of the later stages of Passchendaele." [9]

Behind the British front the pressure of the German success made itself felt as long-fixed organisations packed up in haste and began to retire down crowded roads—army and corps headquarters, the ponderous tractor-drawn heavy artillery. The night of March 21-22 was one of sleepless movement. A heavy-artillery officer recalls the time his unit abandoned their home of six months: "It was a painful moment, and when I looked back and saw the vivid flashes of the field guns firing away in the midst of our once spotless headquarters it seemed—as indeed it so nearly was—the beginning of the end of all things." [10]

The German rear was also a scene of tight-packed crowding and pressure. The German transport services displayed the ruthless mobilisation

[8] *British Official History,* vol. *cit,* 254.
[9] *op. cit,* 256.
[10] Behrend, 73.

of every kind of vehicle that an exhausted and blockaded country could put on the road—motor trucks with iron tyres, farm carts, carriages, traps, dogcarts. British prisoners noted how skeletal the horses were; even those of the cavalry were like old cab horses.

Despite the general and unprecedented success of the day, the German command that evening as it pondered all the reports was not entirely satisfied. The 17th Army (right wing of *Michael*) was stuck in front of the British Battle Zone, despite brutal fighting and higher casualties than had been expected. For March 22 it was ordered to continue attacking, weight on its left wing in co-operation with the 2nd Army. This army, charged with the principal role of break-through and rolling-up, was similarly stalled in front of the Battle Zone, except on the left, where it had participated in the sweeping successes of the 18th Army. Its orders for March 22 were to take the objectives assigned for the 21st. Above all, the expected collapse of the Cambrai salient under the armies' concentric attacks had not taken place.

Only Hutier had made the progress looked for from all armies; indeed, so swiftly had organised resistance melted opposite him that Crown Prince Rupprecht, his army group commander, thought the British 5th Army must have been in the middle of a withdrawal when the Germans struck.

Thus the pattern of tactical success so far did not correspond with the *Michael* planning. Already Ludendorff was presented with a choice between opportunism and tenacity of purpose. True to Schlieffen, Ludendorff preferred the flank to the frontal assault. He assigned six fresh divisions to Hutier (or the army group to which he belonged), none to the 17th Army, whose attack north of Cambrai in conjunction with the 2nd Army was supposed to be the pivot of *Michael*.

The second day of *Michael* was not so smashingly successful: no surprise, no Bruchmüller, but a hard-fought exploitation of those factors of the twenty-first. The Flesquières (Cambrai) salient was not pinched out, and no collapse of the British front occurred there. North of it, the 17th Army made slow progress until late in the afternoon; Crown Prince Rupprecht changed its axis of advance wider towards Bapaume. South of Flesquières the 2nd Army bundled the British 3rd and 5th Armies out of the rest of its defensive system in bitter fighting, reaching Tertry (on the Omignon) and Ytres (seven miles southeast of Bapaume). It was the British 5th Army, however, that constituted Haig's (and Pétain's) greatest cause of alarm. Under Hutier's incessant spoiling attacks it was beginning to disintegrate. The troops themselves were enfeebled by loss of men, guns, defences and coherent organisation—drunk with lack of sleep. In the 5th Army command there was a confusion of policy and intentions between Gough and his corps commanders that suggested that heads were not far from being lost. At 10:45 A.M. on the twenty-second Gough had laid down his policy: "In the event of serious hostile attack corps will fight rear-guard actions back to forward line of Rear Zone, and if necessary to rear line of Rear Zone." [11] (None of which really existed.)

Under Hutier's blows this policy was interpreted "as an executive order for retirement." [12]

At the end of the day Hutier was solidly on the Crozat Canal and the Somme. The greatest German success was thus still on the wrong wing. Yet the Germans had succeeded (where the allies had failed) in maintaining the momentum of their offensive through the second day. Lieutenant Sulzbach of the infantry-escort artillery in the 18th Army noted, however, in his diary: "The roads are so crowded that progress is slow."

Ludendorff at Avesnes was not entirely happy: "The result of the situation on the 17th Army front was that the enemy in the Cambrai salient was not cut off, nor could the opposition to the 2nd Army be indirectly reduced. The latter had been obliged to rely on its own unaided efforts and had, therefore, not got ahead so fast as was desirable from the point of view of assisting the 17th. And so again Crown Prince Rupprecht's Group could not gain ground between Croisilles and Péronne to the extent that had been originally intended." [13]

Haig's diary on March 22 describes the development of the battle with characteristic optimism, but at 8 P.M. came bad news on the telephone from Gough: "Parties of all arms of the enemy are through our Reserve Line." Haig "concurred in his falling back and defending the line of the Somme and to hold the Péronne bridgehead." [14]

He also at once asked for help in this undertaking from Pétain, whose reserves were already coming to the rescue in far greater quantity than

[11] *British Official History*, vol. *cit*, 266.
[12] *op. cit*, 266.
[13] Ludendorff, 599.
[14] Blake, 296.

Haig had originally requested on March 21. Instead of only three divisions to the area Noyon-St. Simon, he ordered Humbert (3rd French Army) to move up to defend the line of the Somme and Crozat Canal, including Tergnier, with seven divisions. Advanced elements of these troops were noted by the Germans coming up that evening via Chauny and Noyon.

On March 23 the feebleness and disintegration of the 5th Army was accentuated. Every man who could hold a rifle (even if he could not aim it) had been combed out of rearward units and the three Army G.H.Q. reserve divisions had been sent into the fight. Eight out of the 5th Army's original eleven divisions were no more than remnants. As the battle foundered into headlong retreat, up to six miles were lost in the day; a gap opened between the 5th and 3rd Armies; everywhere troops and horses and trucks and tractors struggled down the choked roads. At the moment when Hutier surged over the Somme and the British evacuated Péronne, G.H.Q. ordered: "Fifth Army will hold the line of the Somme River at all costs. There will be no withdrawal from this line. . . . The Third and Fifth Armies must keep in closest touch . . . and must mutually assist each other in maintaining Péronne as a pivot." [15]

Now Haig, too, suddenly appreciated that he faced catastrophe. On March 23 he wrote in his diary:

> General Pétain arrived about 4 P.M. . . . In reply to my request to concentrate a large French force (20 divisions) about Amiens, P. said he was most anxious to do all he can to support me, but he expected that the enemy is about to attack him in Champagne. Still, he will do his utmost to keep the two Armies in touch. If this is lost and the enemy comes in between us, then probably the British will be rounded up and driven into the sea! This must be prevented even at the cost of drawing back the Northern Flank on the sea coast.[16]

This entry suggests that the beating wings of panic were round Haig's head as well as Pétain's. On the twenty-first he had asked for three French divisions—now twenty!

Pétain agreed to take over the British front as far as Péronne. This was an admission that the 5th Army was ceasing to exist, except as desperately tired but often still resolute groups fighting a kind of fast-

[15] *British Official History*, vol. *cit*, 368.
[16] Blake, 296-7.

moving battle for which they were no better trained and practised than Corap's 9th Army on the Meuse in 1940.

The 3rd Army, too, was in danger, partly because of the 5th Army's collapse on its right, partly because it had wasted valuable troops in holding on stubbornly to the Flesquières salient rather than shorten its line and avoid risk of encirclement. The 3rd Army lay along the Green Line (which did not exist as a defensive system) except on its far left, where it was in front of the Battle Zone, and its right, which now lay in open country.

This day, March 23, was the crisis of the battle. The Germans had achieved a complete breach nearly forty miles wide in the allied line on the front of the 5th Army. Across this gap was loosely strewn the wreckage of Gough's command. It was the situation of May 15, 1940. As in 1940, it was the speed of developments that so shocked the allied command. Haig suddenly wanted twenty French divisions to fill this gap astride Amiens; a "G.H.Q. line" and a "Purple line" were ordered to be dug in frantic haste as backstop positions, extending in depth back to the old "B.C.D." positions of 1915 covering the Channel ports; in the next few weeks 5,000 miles of new trenches were to be dug, 23,500 tons of barbed wire and 15 million wire pickets erected. It was a vast achievement, surely possible long before the battle began.

Behind the British front there were festival scenes of loot at base canteens and stores. The retreat was not always festive. Near Ytres on the night of March 23-4, for example:

> Agitated staff officers galloped wildly across country, vainly searching for troops for whom they had orders but could not find. Roads and villages were packed with transport and units on the move; everywhere those who had been "pushed off" the roads made their way . . . to the accompaniment of the rattle of machine-gun and rifle fire and shell-bursts; flames from burning stores, canteens and hutments threw such a glare over the old Somme battlefields as to illumine the darkness and provide light by which all could see.[17]

However, in 1940 the continuing force and momentum of the German drive ensured that the gap should remain unclosed, the panic amongst troops and generals unquenched. Rather, the rate of disintegration was sharpened by the continued speed of deep penetration. In 1918 Luden-

[17] *History of 17th Battalion, Royal Fusiliers,* 215.

dorff had a similar opportunity: he must convert this fleeting moment of total success into permanent domination of the enemy; they must not recover their heads or their balance. The moment would not last long, for the French reserves were moving up fast now, and his own troops, after three days of marching and fighting, were tiring.

In 1940 the Germans smashed through where they had intended; their reserves, their communications and their forward planning were ready for relentless pursuit. Not so in 1918. Below's 17th Army and the right of Marwitz's 2nd Army were still slogging slowly forward against unbroken resistance. The original *Michael* plan had not so far succeeded. Under heavy pressure of time and of unfolding events, basing himself on uncertain information, Ludendorff had to take fundamental strategic decisions as to where he should throw his reserves and in what direction the offensive should be pressed.

So far he had had little to do but wait on events and fret restlessly at Avesnes. This was his first test of command in the battle. At 9:30 A.M. on March 23 he issued his new orders: they revealed an incoherence similar to that of the original *Michael* planning. Once again, instead of a clear and dominating theme, there was a grabbing after disparate objectives. After the line Bapaume-Péronne-Ham had been reached "Seventeenth Army will vigorously attack direction Arras-St. Pol, left wing on Miramont. Second Army will take Miramont-Lihons as direction of advance. Eighteenth Army, echeloned, will take Chaulnes-Noyon as direction of advance, and will send strong forces via Ham." [18]

Ludendorff elaborated these orders at an afternoon conference at Avesnes with Kuhl and Schulenburg:

> The object is now to separate the French and British by a rapid advance on both sides of the Somme. The Seventeenth and Sixth Armies and later the Fourth Army will conduct the attack against the British north of the Somme, in order to drive them into the sea.
>
> They will keep on attacking at new places in order to bring the whole British front to ruin. The Seventeenth Army will take St. Pol as the main direction and will push with its left wing via Doullens in the direction of Abbeville. South of the Somme the operations will be conducted offensively against the French by a wheel to the line Amiens-Montdidier-Noyon and then an advance southwestward. In so doing the Second Army must push

[18] *British Official History*, vol. *cit*, 376.

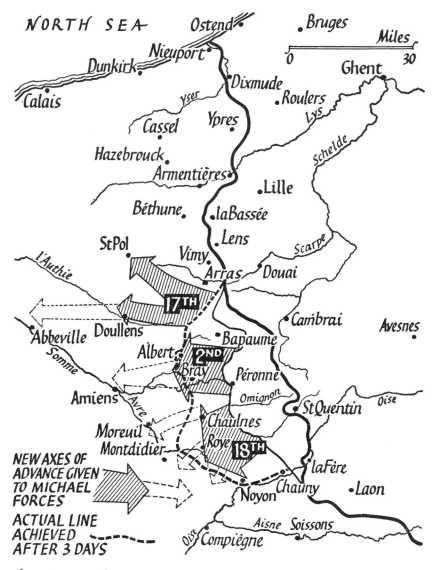

NORTH SEA

Ostend
Bruges
Miles
0   30
Nieuport
Dunkirk
Ghent
Calais
Dixmude
Yser
Roulers
Lys
Cassel
Ypres
Hazebrouck
Schelde
Armentières
Lille
Béthune
laBassée
l'Authie
StPol
Vimy
Lens
Scarpe
Arras
Douai
Cambrai
Avesnes
Abbeville
Doullens
Albert
Bapaume
Somme
Bray
Péronne
Amiens
Avre
Omignon
StQuentin
Oise
Moreuil
Chaulnes
Montdidier
Roye
laFère
Chauny
Laon
Noyon
NEW AXES OF
ADVANCE GIVEN
TO MICHAEL
FORCES
Aisne Soissons
ACTUAL LINE
ACHIEVED
AFTER 3 DAYS
Oise Compiègne

17TH **2ND** **18TH**

36. LUDENDORFF'S ORDERS OF MARCH 23

« 316 »

forward on both sides of the Somme on Amiens and keep close touch with the Eighteenth Army.[19]

Instead of choosing one axis of advance—probably through the gap opened by Hutier—Ludendorff thus chose *three,* and those divergent in purpose and direction. There was here revealed a state of mental restlessness and incoherence that might ill support defeat and danger if these came about. The predominant of the three purposes appeared to be an advance towards Amiens on either side of the Somme, to split the French and British. It should have been the sole purpose—as it was in 1940. In any event, Ludendorff's fresh orders were at least a day late. The fleeting opportunity existed on March 23, and the reserves should by then have been assembled behind Hutier and a plan of exploitation already issued. By the evening of the twenty-first the pattern of success had already been clearly adumbrated; by the afternoon of the twenty-second it was obvious that Hutier alone was achieving a great success. The decisions should have been made then. As it was, the moment when the battle quivered in the balance had passed before Ludendorff's new orders and dispositions took effect. From this day forward the real danger of catastrophe to the British faded, although the apparent course of events continued to create sharpening alarm.

It was an irony therefore that, with the cardinal moment of the battle already missed by Ludendorff, the Kaiser's entourage should give way to victorious exultation in the manner of August 1914.

> This evening [wrote Admiral Müller on March 23 in his diary] His Majesty returned from Avesnes bursting with news of our successes. To the guard on the platform he shouted as the train pulled in: "The battle is won, the English have been utterly defeated."
>
> There was champagne for dinner. The communiqué was read telling of our great victory under the personal leadership of His Majesty the Emperor. . . .

The Kaiser went even further in his extravagant anticipation of victory. He presented Hindenburg with the Iron Cross with Golden Rays, a decoration that even the great Moltke had not merited, and which had last been awarded to Blücher after Waterloo.

By their system of feeding the advance with reinforcements rather

[19] *op. cit,* 396-7.

than relieving whole units by rotation, the Germans had succeeded in keeping up their forward speed. However, it was a crushing moral and physical strain on the troops to continue to march and fight under incessant air attack and to sleep (if at all) in the open under shellfire. The fatigue of the ordinary soldier was a factor of growing importance as the attack progressed. The battle had now entered a region of eerie desolation and total destruction; the old Somme battlefield and the zone evacuated by the Germans in their retreat to the Siegfried line in 1917. The horror of it was enhanced, not diminished, by the passage of time; rust and rank growth gave it the haunted quality of a scene of ancient catastrophe. To troops themselves, plainly fed and with ill-fed families, short of all the comforts of life, the opulent plenty revealed by abandoned British canteens and camps was depressing. Lieutenant Sulzbach noted in his diary on March 23 the provisions in the enemy quarters, oats for the horses in vast quantities, preserves, cheese, bacon, wine. He took it as evidence that what had been said about the U-boats successfully blockading England was not altogether true.

Thus the German army suddenly discovered how shabby, pinched and ramshackle a force it was (except in weapons) compared with its enemies. British food and clothes were hungrily plundered. In Ludendorff's words: "That they [the German troops] did not achieve all the success that was possible was due . . . above all, to their not being always under the control of their officers. They had been checked by finding food depots, and valuable time had thus been lost." [20]

March 24 was apparently another bad day for the allies. Although Hutier's 18th Army received only two further divisions on March 23 (as well as three on the twenty-first and again on the twenty-second), it pressed on towards its day's objective of the line Chaulnes-Noyon, driving before it the débris of the 18th and 3rd Corps of the 5th Army and the ill-organised advanced elements of the French. However, Hutier was between six and ten miles short of his objective at the day's end, although the British had lost the line of the Somme except between the Omignon and the Tortille. With so little in front of him, Hutier's shortfall indicates that the German momentum was already running down because of fatigue and supply difficulties. North of the Somme the 2nd and 17th Armies gained some ground westwards in heavy fighting as the

[20] Ludendorff, 601.

British 3rd Army swung back its right to keep touch with the 5th. Bapaume was captured, but the Germans were generally about seven miles short of their objectives. The battle here remained bitter, step by step, in no way like Hutier's pursuit.

In the allied command, however, March 24 saw the beginning of an acute crisis. Suddenly a crack snaked across the smooth surface of allied solidarity, as centrifugal fears tugged the alliance apart. The threat to Amiens and his right rear greatly worried Haig. He was concentrating a reserve thinned out of his left wing. This would strike a counterblow against the northern flank of the German advance. However, in Haig's view the link between the British and French depended on Pétain placing twenty divisions astride Amiens at utmost speed, whereas their original arrangement called for only six. By sending seven, Pétain had more than honoured his word already.

At 11 P.M. Pétain arrived at Haig's château at Dury; he struck Haig as "very much upset, almost unbalanced and very anxious." [21] He handed Haig a copy of an order to all French armies, of which the nub was this:

II *Intentions of the General Commanding in Chief*
Before everything to keep the French Armies together as one solid whole; in particular, not to allow the G.A.R. [Reserve Army Group, H.Q. Montdidier, General Fayolle] to be cut off from the rest of our forces. Secondly, if it is possible, to maintain liaison with the British forces.
To conduct the battle on these lines.

Pétain made it clear that Fayolle would not concentrate twenty divisions astride Amiens, partly for the reasons expressed in his order, partly because of his fear of another German offensive in Champagne (which did take place in May and for which basic preparations were known to have been made), and partly because he and the French government intended above all things to cover Paris. Indeed, Fayolle had been ordered to fall back southwestwards on Beauvais if heavily attacked.

All this was profoundly alarming to Haig. He wrote in his diary: "I at once asked Pétain if he meant to abandon my right flank. He nodded assent and added 'it is the only thing possible, if the enemy compelled the Allies to fall back still further.' " [22]

Haig's assessment of this new situation in his diary was: ". . . to keep

21 Blake, 297.
22 *loc. cit.*

in touch with the British Army is no longer the basic principle of French strategy. In my opinion, our Army's existence in France depends on keeping the British and French Armies united." [23]

To look now into the crack opened in the alliance was to peer into a bottomless crevasse of disaster. Yet was Haig entirely just to Pétain? Had his own dispositions before March 21 rested on the basic principle of keeping in touch with the French army? It was natural that Pétain would not want to have his reserve army group involved in any catastrophe occurring to the British, because as a French Commander-in-Chief his first task was to preserve his army and defend the heart of his country. There is strong evidence that Pétain believed that Haig had already abandoned *him* and was retreating northwestward. That very day Pétain had told the French government, "urgently to press the English to decide to rally on him and not force him to extend himself indefinitely to reach them." [24]

It is clear from his orders and his conversation that Pétain believed that a situation had already arrived like that of May 18-19, 1940, with all the allied forces north of the Somme being herded away into the sea and the prospect of those south of it fighting a later battle on their own to cover the heart of France. He wanted to make sure that the mass of the French army should remain intact for this moment. It never seems to have occurred to Haig, on the other hand, that in a desperate situation like this, he might—or might have to—abandon the Channel ports and fall back southwards behind the Somme from Abbeville eastwards. Yet Pétain—as 1940 was to show—was right in refusing to extend himself northwards; right, that is, if his reading was correct that the British and French were already as good as separated and the British beaten. For in 1940 the disaster of Dunkirk occurred because the allied northern army group stood its ground after the German break-through south of it, instead of falling promptly back across the Somme before the panzers could cut its line of retreat. In 1918, too, Haig's strategy risked a Dunkirk.

The only result of the meeting at Dury was that Gough and the line south of the Somme was put under the command of Fayolle.

Haig now was really agitated, as the language and tone of his diary illustrates. That night and next morning he (or his Chief of Staff) was

[23] *loc. cit.*
[24] Herbillon, 229-30.

in urgent touch with London to get the C.I.G.S. (now Wilson) and the Secretary for War (Milner) to come out to France at once to persuade the French government to appoint Foch or another man of resolution as supreme allied commander. It is clear that Haig's sudden desire for the immediate appointment of a French supreme commander (as opposed to his long-standing approval of the idea in principle) was really based on a more solid desire for twenty French divisions astride Amiens. He would thus be able to stand his own ground and the French would come to him. As he told Wilson on the morning of March 25, according to the summary in his diary: "Everything depends on whether the French can or will support us *at once* with twenty divisions of good quality, north of the Somme. A far-reaching decision must be taken at once by the French P.M. so that the *whole* of the French divisions may be so disposed as to be able to take turns in supporting the British front as we are *now confronting the weight* of the German Army single-handed." [25]

Haig, Pétain: certainly selfishness is the child of crisis.

For the twenty-fifth, Crown Prince Rupprecht ordered both the 2nd and 17th Armies to attack energetically westward. For the 17th Army this switched the axis from St. Pol to Doullens: west instead of northwest, a significant modification of Ludendorff's directive of the twenty-third. The 18th Army was to reach Noyon-Chaulnes. But the scale of German success and its future chances were now declining steeply. The troops were desperately tired; supplies of food and ammunition were slow to come up through the devastated zone of 1916-17. In 1940 motor transport kept the advance rolling; in 1918 there were only the failing muscles of man and beast, and although Pétain would not transfer half his reserves to Amiens, he had sent help to the British 5th Army as promised—indeed, more and faster than had been promised. By the agreement between the two Commanders-in-Chief on March 7 the total of six French divisions to be sent if needed were not to arrive in either the Montdidier-Noyon or Amiens area until the evening of the fourth day. In fact, by the morning of the twenty-fifth (fourth day) Humbert's 3rd French Army was deployed in a strength of seven divisions and Debeney's 1st French Army was on the way with six divisions. However, French motor transport and railways were now at capacity and although, on the evening of the twenty-fourth, Pétain ordered his Army

[25] Blake, 297-8.

Group East to release six divisions to Fayolle, their arrival would take time. In the words of the *British Official History:* ". . . even using the maximum capacity of the railways, it would be several days before they could arrive." [26]

While his chances thus slipped away with every hour, Ludendorff at Avesnes was continuing to run his battle with the maximum of violent energy and leadership and the minimum of consistency. That morning he and von Kuhl conferred. The result was that the directive of March 23, only two days old, was greatly modified, and the battle plan further fragmented. He told Kuhl: "First of all, the British front on both sides of the Scarpe as far as the Lens basin must be shaken and smashed by the attacks *Mars North* and *Mars South* and *Valkyrie,* in combination." [27]

These attacks would then go forward either side of Arras. *As well as this,* an emasculated *George (Georgette)* would be launched between the La Bassée canal and Armentières but could be dropped if the other new attacks were successful. Directions of advance: the 6th Army on Boulogne, the 17th still on Doullens-Abbeville, the 2nd on Amiens. Instead, therefore, of feeding Hutier with all his available reserves in order to consummate the single great objective of separating the British from the French and destroying the British in isolation, Ludendorff started up fresh, smaller-scale operations. He fixed D-Day for *Mars* as the twenty-eighth, owing to the need for preparation. In any event, therefore, it could not affect the present battle for three days.

In all, this was a complete reversal of strategy. The divergent exploitation of the *Michael* break-through was abandoned after two days. Hutier's 18th Army was now hardly more than a flank guard to drive off the French, now known to be coming to Haig's rescue in force. It was the 2nd and 17th Armies (who had never broken through) and the *Mars* attack that were to constitute the major effort.

On the battlefield the balance swung further against the Germans on March 25, as French and British reserves arrived, and their own troops became more and more exhausted. The 18th Army still did well, especially to the south of its front, driving Humbert's French troops beyond Noyon and the Oise and reaching nearly to Roye. The French, who had arrived without the bulk of their artillery, upon which they now so

---

[26] *British Official History,* vol. *cit,* 455 fn. 2.
[27] *British Official History,* vol. *cit,* 494.

much relied, did not display appetite for stubborn defence. Marwitz's 2nd Army had a tough day, however, for, as its report says, "the enemy's resistance seemed to get stronger." Like the 17th Army, it had had to beat off strong British counterattacks.

Yet from the British side the flowing retreat often seemed uncontrollable. A heavy gunner in the 3rd Army describes the major event for him of March 25:

> As I was closing the door the General shouted, "Come back!"
> "How long will it take you to get to Colonel Thorp?" he asked.
> "About four minutes, sir."
> "Then get off as quickly as you can and tell him to continue to retreat *at once*. The Germans captured Albert half an hour ago. [Not true: Author's note.] Make for Doullens. . . . Hurry up. . . ."
> Within twelve minutes we were all on the move again with real dismay in our hearts. . . .[28]

At 2:10 P.M. a brigadier-general told Colonel Weston, of 17th Battalion, Royal Fusiliers: "The Corps Commander's Orders are that the Irles-Pys-Courcelette line is to be held at all costs. Officers are, if necessary, to use their revolvers to keep the men back." [29]

As a whole the 5th Army front fell back about four miles and during the night of the twenty-fifth–twenty-sixth the right flank of Byng's 3rd Army north of the Somme even further, actually exposing Gough's left along the river. But the 5th Army had now finally disintegrated. Only 18th and 19th Corps remained as formed bodies in the line; the rest of Gough's command lay in reserve or attached as remnants to French units.

Urgent though his desire for French help might be, Haig was as calm and resolute as ever in the conduct of his own battle. He issued orders that afternoon that assumed that the French would be made or induced to come to him, and that he could continue to occupy his unattacked front from Arras to the sea, covering his ports and bases. Byng's army was to swing its right slowly back to the Ancre, while reserves were concentrated for offensive action south of Arras. It cannot be doubted that Haig's strategy in the battle had been based—and still was—on retirement (when necessary) northwestwards on his ports, not southwestwards

[28] Behrend, 103.
[29] *History of 17th Battalion, Royal Fusiliers*, 223.

on to Pétain. This basic principle had begun to operate *before* Pétain took his equivalent step of ordering Fayolle to fall back on Beauvais if heavily attacked.

In the allied command, March 25 was a day of crisis conferences at Compiègne and Dury, but there was no single meeting at which all the interested parties were present. Haig was as active as ever in trying to organise a system by which Pétain's reserves should be forced to come to him. At 4 P.M. he met Weygand (Foch's Chief of Staff), Milner and Clemenceau. Ever inarticulate, he handed Clemenceau a note that stated that in order to prevent a serious disaster, it was necessary for the French to act at once and concentrate as large a force as possible north of the Somme near Amiens. It was a day of vast gloom, during which French G.Q.G. packed up in unseemly haste because of the danger of air attack and went back to Chantilly. Here at 11 P.M. Pétain was visited by Pershing, the American Commander-in-Chief. Pétain continued to see the battle situation as desperate, still believed he was going to be attacked in Champagne, and, as he told the American, he "had few reserves left." Pershing, who had fought so hard against Pétain to keep his American troops as a separate army, was so struck by the apparent danger that he offered Pétain immediate use of four U.S. divisions (equal to eight French) instead of reserving them to form the 1st U.S. Corps.

In fact, the events of the following day, March 26, followed the general tendency since March 23; Ludendorff was losing the battle. No final decision had been achieved, while German dominance and superiority of forces faded hour by hour. By a misunderstanding of Byng's orders, the right wing corps of the 3rd Army had pulled back overhastily behind the Ancre; otherwise, in the words of the *British Official History:* "On this day the crisis on the front of the Third Army may be said to have ended, and also on that of the Eighteenth and Nineteenth Corps, these formations being all that remained in the line of the Fifth except the position of the Third Corps away on the extreme right of the battle front near the Oise." [30]

Whereas the British were beginning to sort out the mess caused by the retreat, the Germans were suffering more and more from fatigue. Their advance had outrun adequate artillery and ammunition and even, for forty-eight hours, food. Despite the German mobilisation of every kind

[30] *British Official History,* vol. *cit,* 532.

of transport, communications across the devastated zone of 1916-17 had proved insufficient to nourish the attack. The iron tyres of the trucks particularly cut up the road surfaces.

In the 18th Army Lieutenant Sulzbach recorded in his diary that he had "requisitioned" some pigs and chickens as supplies had not kept up with the front line. He added that the Germans were "worried by air attacks and feel defenceless against bombs. They are unused to having no defences in which to shelter. Losses are considerable. The mood is gay, though, for the chief aim of separating the British and French seems to have been achieved."

Ludendorff summed up the situation:

> On March 25 the 17th and 2nd Armies had passed far beyond the line Bapaume-Combles, fighting hard all the way; the 18th Army had taken Nesle and met with but little resistance. The 17th Army was already exhausted. . . . The 2nd Army was fresher but was already complaining of the old shell-holes. It could get no further than Albert. . . . The 18th Army was still full of fight and confidence. . . .[31]

Only the 18th Army therefore made important progress on March 26 —about five miles towards Amiens and Montdidier—but it, too, was now faced with a continuous line of resistance. Indeed, as the *British Official History* puts it, "The battle was now becoming stabilized. . . ." [32]

However, in the confusion of the fighting and in face of continued German advances, the allied command saw the danger of catastrophe as still growing. When the crisis of battle had already passed, therefore, the crisis was now reached in the allied command. It centred round Haig's desire to induce the French to send twenty French divisions behind Amiens, so that both continuity of the allied line and British occupation of Flanders and the Pas de Calais would be preserved. The locale of the resulting conference of allied politicians and generals was the *mairie* of Doullens, a depressing grey-shuttered, red-brick little town. The conference was preceded by a meeting of British army commanders (Plumer, Horne and Byng) under Haig's chairmanship. Byng was heartening: desperate fatigue had taken most of the edge out of the German attack; both sides were staggering with exhaustion. Haig told his commanders, ". . . my object is to gain time to enable the French to come and support

[31] Ludendorff, 599.
[32] *British Official History*, vol. *cit*, 534.

us. To this end we must hold our ground, especially on the right of our 3rd Army [near Bray] on the Somme, where *we must not give up any ground.*" [33]

Horne would therefore yield three Canadian divisions which would be concentrated behind the 3rd Army. Haig was displaying admirable courage and steady nerves, as well as a clear and single-minded strategy. The apparently desperate situation revealed his qualities as a commander to better advantage than the offensives of 1916 and 1917.

Meanwhile the situation was doing the opposite for Pétain. *Michael,* on top of Verdun and the mutinies, was too much for him. In a battle as in personal relationships there was a streak of pessimism and acquiescence in him that his organising skill and understanding of the troops could not outweigh. At bottom, he was just not a fighter by temperament. At Doullens in 1918 Pétain was out of step. At Bordeaux in 1940 only the fighters were out of step. As the notabilities were assembling in informal conversation before the big conference, Pétain took Clemenceau on one side to give him his appreciation of the battle situation. Clemenceau, aghast, reported the exchange to Poincaré, President of the Republic: "Pétain sets one's teeth on edge with his pessimism. Imagine, he said something to me that I would confide in nobody else but you. It is this: 'The Germans will beat the English in the open field, after which they will beat us as well.' Should a general speak or even think like this?" [34]

At noon Poincaré took the chair. Present were Clemenceau, Loucheur (French Minister of Armaments), Foch, Pétain, Haig, Wilson, Milner and Generals Lawrence (Haig's C.G.S.) and Montgomery (for General Rawlinson, British Military Representative at Versailles).

Pétain was in a state of very great emotional tension. Haig noted that he "had a terrible look. He had the appearance of a Commander who was in a funk and had lost his nerve." [35] Certainly in the course of the meeting Pétain's pessimistic views were expressed with a startling emotional warmth.

Haig spoke first. North of the Somme he was confident of holding his ground. South of it he could do nothing. Pétain followed, defending his

[33] Blake, 298.
[34] Poincaré, X, 60.
[35] Blake, 298.

measures since March 22. "It is evident," he added, "that everything possible must be done to defend Amiens." [36]

At the mention of Amiens the restless Foch could no longer contain himself. He burst out in sharp, spitting sentences: "We must fight in front of Amiens, we must fight where we are now. As we have not been able to stop the Germans on the Somme, we must not now retire a single inch!" [37]

This was the moment; Haig took it. "If General Foch will consent to give me his advice, I will gladly follow it."

The general meeting temporarily broke up into private discussion groups, after which Clemenceau read out a draft agreement charging Foch "with the co-ordination of the action of the British and French Armies in front of Amiens."

This was not what Haig wanted. "This proposal seemed to me quite worthless," he wrote in his diary, "as Foch would be in a subordinate position to Pétain and myself. In my opinion, it was essential to success that Foch should control Pétain." [38]

He proposed therefore that Foch's co-ordinating authority should extend to the entire western front and all nationalities. This was agreed. At last after three and a half years of war the allies had a supreme commander, at least in embryo. This was the great achievement of the Doullens conference. However, the conference did not lead to the results most urgently hoped for by Haig. For Foch, despite his ostentatious energy and fire-eating, was not to concentrate twenty divisions astride Amiens as soon as possible (only eight by early April), did not—and could not—significantly speed up the movement of French reserves already ordered by Pétain. Whatever the moral importance of the new supreme command, in hard facts of divisions and dispositions it made little difference to the battle. Although Foch ordered Fayolle to defend, support and then relieve the present British 5th Army line, "defending the ground foot by foot" in order to protect Amiens at all costs, Fayolle continued to fall back southwestwards and the 5th Army westwards for so long as the Germans retained their impetus.

[36] Account of M. Loucheur, quoted *British Official History*, vol. *cit*, 541.
[37] *op. cit*, 542.
[38] Blake, 298.

Nevertheless with Foch's appointment the heaviest moral strain on the allied command passed, its passing helped by the delayed realisation that the battle was already going better.

It was on this day, March 26, that the moral strain was switched for the first time to the German command. Now it was Ludendorff under test. While the 18th Army deepened its salient by up to nine miles beyond Roye, forming a defensive flank along the Oise from Noyon to Chauny, the 17th and 2nd Armies were still unable to get forward rapidly. The 17th Army in fact had fought itself to a standstill. It was this army's disappointing performance right from the first day that had wrecked the original *Michael* plan. It stemmed from two causes. Firstly, its preliminary bombardment had only followed Bruchmüller's general principles, but had not been planned and organised with the same exact care as that of the 18th Army. Secondly, its troops and command had not fully accepted the principles of rapid infiltration by small battle groups; the 17th Army tended to employ its troops in old-fashioned density and waste time in reducing strong points in its path instead of bypassing them. This army's failure enraged Ludendorff more and more. Characteristically he tried to drive it on as he had driven on the assault group at Liége. On the telephone to Crown Prince Rupprecht he went off in one of his violent fits of temper.

"He was quite beside himself," wrote Rupprecht, "and dissatisfied with the Chief of Staff, whom he talked of removing from his post." [39]

Irritability, instability—that evening Ludendorff altered his battle plan radically yet again. His alterations were based on a wild exaggeration of his enemy's weakness. Helped by *Mars* and *Valkyrie,* the 17th Army was to go on attacking towards Doullens-St. Pol. The 2nd Army was now to place its main weight south of the Somme, capture Amiens, and face southwest on a line Moreuil-Airaines. The 18th Army was to continue southwestwards across the Avre, deployed ready for a further advance to Compiègne-Tartigny.

Yet, like a fire at last mastered by the pumps, *Michael* was dying. On March 27, the 2nd and 17th Armies were firmly and finally stuck. Only on the 18th Army's front did the flames leap and run further; and it was on a narrow front of twelve miles between the Oise and the Avre, where the French were pushed back beyond Montdidier some ten miles.

[39] Rupprecht, II, 357.

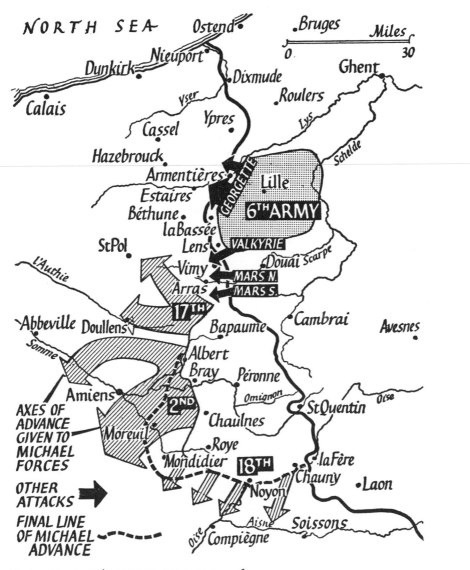

37. LUDENDORFF'S ORDERS OF MARCH 26

The threat to Amiens was no worse. On March 28 *Michael* burned lower still; the Germans made only three miles towards Amiens between the Avre and the Somme and a few small gains near Montdidier. Worst of all, *Mars,* launched at 7:30 A.M. against the Arras sector, had been stopped and defeated with serious losses by the same afternoon.

Once again Ludendorff, in his ambition and impatience, changed his mind. All the vast and divergent objectives were abandoned; at last and too late *Michael* shrank to the capture of Amiens.

"Amiens is now the objective," ran O.H.L. orders that evening; "to secure that place all the efforts of this and the following days will be directed; the attacks near Montdidier and eastward of that town are only diversions designed to delay enemy forces." [40]

To his chagrin Ludendorff had to acknowledge that *Michael* had failed; he gave orders for *Georgette,* across the Lys, to be organised as the second great blow to be struck in eight to ten days' time. While March 23 was the turning point in *Michael,* March 28 was the fundamental turning point of the campaign of 1918. The Germans had struck with their maximum fresh strength against a strategically vulnerable joint weakly protected. German writers—Hindenburg, Kuhl, Wetzell—make it clear that *Michael* was intended to be the single, war-deciding effort of 1918. This was why it was christened the *"Kaiserschlacht."* The offensives that followed were always weaker than *Michael,* temporarily and locally dangerous, but never producing, as had *Michael,* a general crisis; offensives diminishing in scope and effect.

By the end of March even Hutier had stopped. On April 4 and 5, after reorganisation and fresh bombardment, Hutier's troops tried to get moving again towards Amiens. They were stopped east of Villers Bretonneux. *Michael* was dead. As a performance and achievement on the battlefield it had no peer in the war, but battles are not, however, displays of virtuosity. They are the means to the end of strategy, and *Michael* was therefore a titanic failure. Its failure was less owing to such defensive skill displayed by Haig and Pétain as to Ludendorff's own incoherent generalship.

Georgette was launched on April 9, after another of Bruchmüller's masterpieces of ordnance (he had been seconded). The 6th Army attacked across the shallow valley of the Lys; and next day the 4th Army extended the front of the offensive northwards beyond Armentières. *Georgette* had a front of about twenty miles instead of *Michael*'s fifty,

[40] Edmonds, 295.

and only twelve[41] out of twenty-six divisions in *Georgette* were "attack" divisions, as against forty-seven in *Michael*. The offensive struck defences far better than those improvised by Gough, but *Michael* had drawn off enough British strength to make both reserves and line troops dangerously slender. The collapse of three Portuguese brigades on April 9 opened the dyke, and the Germans began to advance strongly towards Hazebrouck. Having few reserves of his own, Haig launched appeals for French reserves to Foch that for a man as stolid and self-controlled as Haig came near to the language of desperation. He found Foch, if anything, less accommodating than Pétain had been. On the eleventh the Germans got within five miles of Hazebrouck, and Haig availed himself of that classic resort of military extremity, an Order of the Day: "There is no other course open to us but to fight it out. Every position must be held to the last man. There must be no retirement. With our backs to the wall and believing in the justice of our cause each one must fight to the end. . . ."[42]

In fact, however, the Germans never reached the runaway pace of *Michael;* it was a tough, exhausting struggle against a well-conducted defence. By April 18 *Georgette,* too, had stalled. By April 30, despite the capture of Mount Kemmel from the French on the twenty-fifth, local efforts to restart the battle had failed. The performance of the German troops had not the keen edge of *Michael,* an omen of decline for Ludendorff.

> Our troops had fought well; but the fact that certain divisions had obviously failed to show any inclination to attack in the plain of the Lys gave food for thought . . . the way in which the troops stopped round captured food supplies, while individuals stayed behind to search houses and farms for food, was a serious matter. This impaired our chances of success and showed poor discipline. But it was equally serious that both our young company commanders and our senior officers did not feel strong enough to take disciplinary action, and exercise enough authority to enable them to lead their men forward without delay.[43]

Ludendorff now faced the implications of the repeated failure of his fundamental plan for 1918 of destroying the British. The policy defined

[41] German Official History, *Der Weltkrieg,* Band 14, Appendix 38g.
[42] Terraine, *Haig,* 433.
[43] Ludendorff, 611.

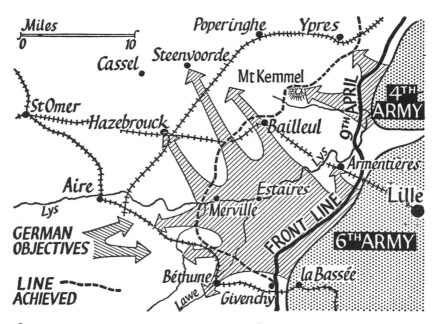

38. THE GEORGETTE OFFENSIVE, APRIL 1918

before March 21 was bankrupt. He had now to start again. In all the opportunism and incoherence of his strategy he did cleave to his orignial intention in regard to Haig's army. French reserves having at last moved in quantity to Amiens and the British front, Ludendorff considered that another direct assault there would fail. First the French reserves must be drained back behind their own front. The means to this would be a great offensive on the Chemin des Dames. Then, and finally, he would deal with the deserted British. It seemed almost that, as his resources and margin of time shrank, his planning became more grandiose. Since March 21 he had lost 348,300 men and inflicted roughly equal damage. However, in that time 179,703[44] Americans had arrived in France. Three American divisions (equal to six European) were already in Pétain's line. The Chemin des Dames offensive could not be ready until the end of May—a month later than the original Lys operation proposed by Kuhl in December 1917 and rejected by Ludendorff as being too late in the year. And the decisive blow against the British could hardly take

[44] Réquin, quoted Lutz, 63.

place earlier than late June. Ludendorff's new policy would have better suited growing rather than waning relative strength.

On May 27, after a bombardment organised by Bruchmüller that reached twelve miles behind the front, the Germans struck on the Chemin des Dames. In addition to eleven trench divisions already in the line, Ludendorff employed thirty divisions (only fifteen completely fresh). Facing the force was General Duchêne's 6th French Army with four French divisions and three exhausted British ones (sent from the Amiens front for a rest). The 6th Army occupied a strong and elaborately prepared position on the Chemin des Dames ridge. Immediately behind it was the river Aisne; Duchêne thus elected to fight in a narrow bridgehead on the German side of the river. Behind the Aisne were echeloned reserves consisting of two more British and seven more French divisions. May 27 was an instantaneous disaster—the fruits of the unresolved conflict of the Pétain and the Foch conception of defensive methods. On May 5 Foch had issued a directive to Pétain and his army group commanders: "Necessary before all," he wrote, "to dispute ground with the enemy step by step . . . there can be no question of lines of advanced posts or of observation, and of lines of resistance. . . . Any retreat, even very slight, would thus play the enemy's game." [45]

This resounding piece of unrealism was an invitation to the French army to ignore Pétain's precepts on elastic and withdrawn defence.

Duchêne and his army group commander, Franchet d'Esperey, were of Foch's mind; they packed the narrow strip north of the Aisne. Pétain made it clear that he considered this a mistake and that battle should be offered south of the river. Foch's supreme authority—so much stronger over the army of his own country than over that of Haig's—decisively weakened that of Pétain, never in any event the man to start a quarrel. Pétain acquiesced. This kind of struggle went on throughout the summer, to the detriment of the French army.

On May 27 there was again fog to cloak the assault. The Germans, as on March 21, swarmed through troops and defences stunned and shredded by Bruchmüller's guns. They surged over the Aisne, engulfing the French and British reserves, and covering ten miles in the day.

It was an instant, shattering success, its scope as unexpected as it was tempting. Hindenburg describes how the news came to Avesnes: "At the

[45] Laure, 85.

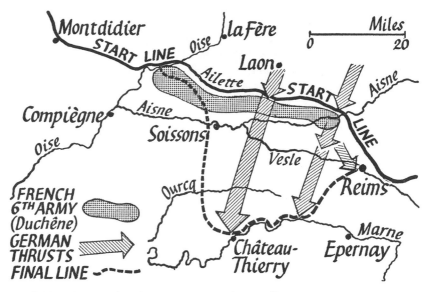

39. CHEMIN DES DAMES OFFENSIVE, MAY 1918

outset we were bound to anticipate that our attack would come to a halt on the Aisne-Vesle line and would be unable to get beyond that sector. We were therefore not a little surprised when we received a report about midday . . . that smoke from German shrapnel could already be seen on the southern bank of the Aisne and that our infantry would cross the same day." [46]

Should the offensive be stopped now that it had fulfilled its purpose of breaking through the French line in order to draw away reserves from Flanders? Or would it be a waste and a pity not to invest more German reserves in converting a huge tactical success into a sweeping and perhaps decisive strategic victory over the French?

The temptation was presented to a commander whose nerves and mind were burning with the cumulative effect of two years of responsibility and overwork, culminating in the strain of the current campaign and its lack of decisive success. Ludendorff seemed to find refuge from larger worries in yet more intensive detailed work. He lived on the telephone to his subordinate commanders, interfering over trivia, nagging, chasing, raging. Now he snatched at the chance presented by the break-

[46] Hindenburg, 361.

through on the Aisne. The racing advance went on, deeper and deeper towards Paris, eighty miles away. On the evening of May 29 the Germans were beyond Soissons and level with Fère-en-Tardenois, though, on the left flank of the advance, Reims held out.

Pétain issued orders that such reserves as he had within a few days' march were not to be thrown piecemeal into the confused and flowing battle, but systematically installed with their artillery on a line running through the eastern fringes of the forest of Villers-Cotterets, the Marne, western fringes of the Mountain of Reims to Reims itself. On this line the German offensive faltered, stalled and died. Round Château-Thierry two U.S. divisions fought alongside the French.

Ludendorff was left with a deep salient badly served by railways and its flanks menaced from Reims and from the deep cover of the forest of Villers-Cotterets. Therefore he was forced to launch yet another unpremeditated operation to widen the shoulders of the salient and improve its communications. On June 9—time was slipping away rapidly now, along with the remaining German reserves—Hutier's 18th Army attacked Humbert's 3rd French Army between Noyon and Montdidier. Humbert's dispositions were a compromise between those of Foch and Pétain. An overpacked forward zone was quickly lost, but Hutier's attack suffered badly in the course of struggling through the main position. On June 11 Ludendorff stopped the battle. Yet another linked subsidiary operation southwest of Soissons also failed.

Thresh about how he might, the situation was now closing darkly round the German field commander. Clemenceau had been quite unshaken by the German advance to the Marne. The decisive battle—in Flanders still—had yet to be fought. However, German strength was melting. In Crown Prince Rupprecht's Army Group, for example, several cavalry rifle regiments were re-formed in April and two divisions broken up in May. Even so, the average field strength of a battalion had sunk from 807 men in February to 692 in May. According to German information, about fifteen U.S. divisions had reached France in April, May and June. As Ludendorff put it: ". . . not only had our March superiority in the number of divisions been cancelled, but even the difference in gross numbers was now to our disadvantage, for an American division consists of twelve strong battalions." [47]

[47] Ludendorff, 637.

In addition there was the temporary but very heavy reduction in effective strength caused by the influenza epidemic, which reached the Germans before their enemies, and whose effects were more severe on them because of poor diet. There were also signs now of failing morale among the fighting troops, as well as at home. It was a time when forebodings of failure began to squeeze the stomach. On July 23 a colonel at O.H.L. noted in his diary: "Talk with General Ludendorff and von Plessen. Former describes how sometimes depression among commanders too. Therefore whole burden on himself. They were advising him not to continue the offensive, saying he was overdrawing the bow, but he must risk it, he thought. Particularly the H.Q.'s of the 7th [in the Marne salient] and 9th Armies seem to have warned." [48]

He must risk it. Ludendorff in his memoirs argues the case for carrying on the offensive.

"The battalion strength had been reduced, but was still high enough to allow us to strike one more blow that should make the enemy ready for peace. There was no other way.

"Again and again our thoughts returned to the idea of an offensive in Flanders. . . . But an offensive at this point still presented too difficult a problem. We had to postpone it." [49]

He decided to attack the weakened French front on either side of Reims: "Immediately following this operation we meant to concentrate artillery, trench mortars and air squadrons on the Flanders front, and possibly attack that a fortnight later [early August]." There were hopes that if the offensive at Reims succeeded, "there would be a very decisive weakening of the enemy in Flanders." Nevertheless "I gave serious thought to the question whether, in view of the spirit of the army and the condition of our reserves, it would not be advisable to adopt the defensive. But I finally decided against this policy, because, quite apart from the bad influence it would have on our allies, I was afraid that the army would find defensive battles an even greater strain than an offensive. . . ." [50]

His decision taken, Ludendorff was happier, because this meant more intensive work, absorbing detail, the familiar narcotic.

---

[48] Förster, 14.
[49] Ludendorff, 638-9.
[50] *ibid*, 639-40.

"The general, with all his characteristic energy," recalled Colonel Mertz von Quirnheim of O.H.L., "and fully confident of success, threw himself first of all against the enemy on the Marne. This energy was all the more astonishing since in so doing he had to override so many different considerations put forward by colleagues he valued. . . ." [51]

The offensive, *Marneschütze-Reims,* was very carefully prepared and the assault forces very strong—fifty-two divisions. However, the concentration had been noted by the French, and on July 5 Pétain warned General Maistre (Army Group Centre, in the place of d'Esperey, now sent to command the allied forces in Salonika) that his 4th and 5th Armies on either side of Reims would be attacked in order to encircle the city. Maistre was ordered to meet the offensive on the main position, covered by outposts held as thinly as possible. Meanwhile a major French counterstroke was being prepared for July 18 against the western flank of the Marne salient; after four months of offensive battle the initiative no longer rested in firm German hands but hovered now between the lines like a turncoat.

On July 15, and for the last time, the German hurricane bombardment beat and roared along the allied line. On the west of Reims the German 7th Army smashed through the French defences of the 5th and 6th Armies, partly because once again the bulk of the defenders had been posted too far forward, partly because two Italian divisions gave way. Six German divisions got across the Marne at Dormans and created a bridgehead four miles deep. However, east of Reims, Gouraud (4th Army) had deployed his army completely in accordance with Pétain's defensive orders. The result was a total and crushing German defeat. As usual when an army was not getting forward fast enough, Ludendorff telephoned its chief of staff to drive it on by his own restless energy. He displayed some of that wild temper, *furor teutonicus,* noted by Colonel Bauer, which became more and more ungovernable as the war situation worsened.

Ludendorff's tone was not exactly friendly [wrote General von Einem, G.O.C. 3rd Army, in a letter on July 19[52]] when he asked Klewitz [Chief of Staff 3rd Army]:

[51] Letter 16.9.41; quoted Förster, 15.
[52] Förster, 16.

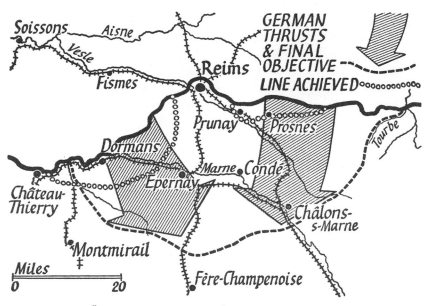

40. MARNESCHÜTZE-REIMS, JULY 1918

"Why isn't the attack getting any further? It must be pressed home at once."

Klewitz answered calmly:

"The Army Commander has ordered it to be discontinued because the prerequisites of the Chemin des Dames are not in evidence here. The French have pulled their artillery back a long way and the present French positions are laughing at the withering fire."

At this, clarity and insight at once came to Ludendorff and he replied:

"I quite agree about the discontinuation of the attack. I am the last man to order an attack that merely costs blood."

Now not merely *one* offensive, but the whole offensive of 1918 had slowed down and stalled. This was the moment of balance, of immobility, before the war began to roll against Germany with unstoppable momentum. The immobility in these few days from July 15 to 18, 1918, did not only exist on the battlefield; it existed in Ludendorff's mind and personality. On the evening of July 15 he rang up Kuhl, as Kuhl recounts in a letter of July 16.

"Ludendorff telephoned me and was very depressed about the poor outcome. I nevertheless advised Ludendorff to continue the attack today, and mentioned March 21 with the 2nd Army, when we made no progress either. . . . But he felt we could not risk the losses associated with that." [53]

The mood of depression and mental vitiation lasted through the sixteenth and seventeenth. On the sixteenth, Mertz von Quirnheim noted in his diary: "Pretty depressed mood. . . . Difficult question what is to be done next."

And on seventeenth: "I am convinced that neither Wetzell nor Ludendorff know [sic] what they must do next."

Next day Ludendorff held a conference with army commanders and chiefs of staff. He had got himself rolling again in terms of will and energy. "Ludendorff was confident," wrote General von Lossberg,[54] "and eager to attack, and to the joy of us all still held to the intention of carrying out an attack in Flanders [code name—Hagen]."

But while they were still talking news came that the French had launched a massive counterstroke under General Mangin from the cover of the forest of Villers-Cotterets, without any preliminary bombardment at all. Fire had been opened with the creeping barrage, behind which the advance of eighteen divisions (with seven in reserve) had been led by swarms of light Renault tanks. The German line had collapsed, and by midday the French had pressed four miles through the standing corn. Ludendorff's conference on Hagen went on, form without meaning. Ludendorff was now, as he recounts, "naturally in a state of the greatest nervous tension." [55]

He returned to Avesnes at 2 P.M. and was met at the station by Hindenburg. Over lunch the very great danger to the troops in the Marne salient caused by the French success was discussed. From this day forward danger and desperation never left Ludendorff. Yet the brutality and weight of the French counterstroke, coming only three days after the dismal failure of the last of so many supreme German efforts, seemed to smash the governor that controlled Ludendorff's restive energy, so that the powerful machine began now to race itself to pieces. The instability and incoherence so long implicit in his military thinking suddenly

[53] op. cit, 17.
[54] von Lossberg, 343.
[55] Ludendorff, 668.

burst out into the open before his astonished headquarters, and in the stress of this cardinal moment of defeat, he turned his rage on Field-Marshal von Hindenburg himself.

Colonel Mertz von Quirnheim noted the incident in his diary and six months later wrote a fuller account of it:

> At lunch the situation was discussed in a serious atmosphere but with no sign of strain on the minds of those present. General Ludendorff did not speak his mind. . . . Turning to me, the field-marshal said suddenly that the simplest and most complete solution of the present crisis was, in his opinion, to summon up all troops immediately, including those from Flanders, and to start an offensive across the high ground north of Soissons in a southerly direction against the left flank of the enemy's attack. Then, all of a sudden, General Ludendorff joined in the conversation. He declared that anything of that sort was utterly unfeasible and must therefore be forgotten, as he thought he had already made abundantly clear to the field-marshal. The field-marshal left the table without a word of reply, and General Ludendorff departed, clearly annoyed and scarlet in the face.

This astonishing scene was replayed with even more melodramatic performances that night after dinner:

> . . . the field-marshal waved his left hand over the maps, and in such a fashion that the outspread fingers of his hand moved over the high ground northwest of Soissons, and in a subdued voice, but pronouncing the words quite clearly, said:
>
> "This is how we must direct the counterattack, that would solve the crisis at once!"
>
> At this, General Ludendorff straightened up from the map and, with an expression of rage on his face, turned towards the door, letting out one or two words like "madness!" in profound irritation. The field-marshal followed his First Quartermaster-General and said to him just as he was brushing past me:
>
> "I should like a word with you."
>
> . . . Both of them disappeared into Ludendorff's study.[56]

This was the day when military defeat for Germany became a fact and this was how Ludendorff faced it. There were months of disappointment and disaster ahead; but Ludendorff's command of himself was not to improve.

[56] Förster, 18-19.

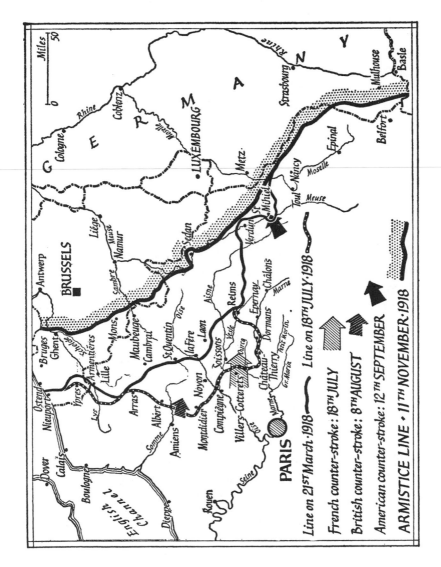

41. THE WESTERN FRONT: JULY-NOVEMBER 1918

As the war had opened, so it was about to close—with the disintegration of the personality of the *de facto* Supreme Commander of the Field Army of the German Empire.

« 341 »

13

The French success of July 18 did not lead to a swift and progressive collapse of the German forces opposite the attackers. The allied troops and command were not trained to deep, fast penetration; after the first surprise the Germans displayed their familiar aptitude for swift re-organisation and skilful defence. On July 19 Mangin only progressed two to three miles. The situation of the German forces in the Marne salient—and especially in the bridgehead south of that river—remained hazardous. At O.H.L. Ludendorff was like a beetle on its back, waving and wriggling furiously to no effect. At the head of the German army during these critical days was violent rage, indiscriminate blame, funda-mental panic, paralysis of command.

On the morning of July 19, General von Lossberg (Chief of Staff, the 4th Army, and since 1917 the acknowledged expert on defence in depth) arrived for a conference with Ludendorff and the staff of O.H.L. It was another unpleasant and embarrassing performance.

> When I reported [wrote Lossberg] I found Ludendorff in a really agi-tated and nervous state. To my regret, he made some very unjustified re-monstrances against the Chief of the Operations Section [Lieutenant-Colonel Wetzell] and others of his colleagues who, he implied, had "failed" in their assessment of the fighting forces. This scene was a really painful one. The Chief of the Operations Section, Wetzell, said nothing, like a good soldier, but he obviously found these rebukes hard to take. His eyes grew wet from inward emotion which he otherwise fought down bravely.[1]

[1] Lossberg, 344.

The key to Ludendorff's agony of indecision was *Hagen,* the offensive intended finally to destroy the British. If he stopped the movement of reserves and guns to Flanders in order to prevent a disaster in the Marne salient, *Hagen,* the consummation and justification of his four great previous offensives, would have to be postponed. And with the year more than half gone and his reserves pouring away, was postponement really other than abandonment? Abandonment of *Hagen* meant acceptance that Germany could not win the war. On the night of July 20-21 the bridgehead over the Marne south of Dormans was evacuated; elsewhere the French counteroffensive was held. This solution of the immediate tactical crisis did not terminate the strategical crisis. Ludendorff sent officers—including Lossberg—to investigate and report on the state of units in the Marne salient. When Lossberg reported back to Ludendorff, he found the First Quartermaster-General still in a state of intellectual dislocation. "When I entered his room, Ludendorff made a very discouraging impression on me. Contrary to his usual practice, he interrupted my account frequently with digressions about points of detail for which the seriousness of the situation truly left no time."

Ludendorff on the other hand can hardly have found Lossberg encouraging. Lossberg suggested that in order to permit *Hagen* to take place all the troops along the front of the Marne salient and westwards should be withdrawn to the Siegfried line. If *Hagen* failed, then the troops in Flanders, too, should retire to this position. According to Lossberg's account, he further recommended to Ludendorff that a rear position should be prepared from Antwerp to the Meuse. Even *Hagen* was now seen by Lossberg as "tactical." Ludendorff was thus told by one of his most able officers that July 18 was no nightmare to vanish with the break of the next day, but enduring reality. He was recommended to abandon all ambitions of winning the war by a victory in the field, to retreat, and then to adopt again the dour defence of 1917. Lossberg describes how Ludendorff took his advice.

> My address and my suggestions made a noticeable impression on Ludendorff. He considered for quite a while and then said—in essence—something like the following:
> "I consider your suggestions relevant, but I cannot carry them out—for political reasons."
> To my question: "What exactly are these political reasons?" Ludendorff

replied: "Consideration of the impression that would be made on the enemy, on our army, and on the people back home."

Lossberg asserts—although other officers at O.H.L. at the time strongly deny the likelihood—that Ludendorff decided at that time to offer his resignation, which was declined by Hindenburg. Nevertheless, whether or not he did so in a moment of panic, there is no doubt that Ludendorff was in a gruesome state of nerves. In a letter of March 11, 1941, Mertz von Quirnheim recalled "that following the unsuccessful thrust of July 15 and the defeat of July 18, the General suffered to the verge of emotional collapse and at times lost control of himself." [2]

Ludendorff was incapable of thinking the situation through with Lossberg's relentless logic. As with Hitler twenty-five years later, fear of the political consequences of a sound military policy of defence was blended with a reluctance to part finally and brutally with the ground won in the past and with the triumphs sought in the future. He proceeded pragmatically, as he was driven by the pressure of daily situation reports. On July 22 in the evening it was decided to retire from the Marne to the Vesle, running across the base of the salient. The first stage—retirement to the line Fère-en-Tardenois-Ville-en-Tardenois—was fixed for the night of July 26-27. There remained the question of the weakness of the flanking armies to the west of the salient: the 18th and 17th.

It had to be made good [wrote Ludendorff] by reinforcements. These could only be drawn from Army Group Crown Prince Rupprecht.

The offensive in Flanders could not bring a rapid and decisive success. According to all indications, the enemy was ready for it. If he avoided the attack, as he had done east of Reims, we should be unable to force a decision. . . . O.H.L. therefore decided to abandon this offensive. The Rupprecht Army Group was to stand on the defensive and to surrender reserves to reinforce the 18th, 9th and 7th Armies; this it was quite capable of doing. . . . I had as yet no idea how, if at all, [Ludendorff adds:] we should be able to recover the initiative after taking up the Vesle position.[3]

Hindenburg's memoirs sum up the catastrophic results of July 18:

We could have no illusion about the far-reaching effects of this battle and our retreat. . . .

[2] Förster, 25.
[3] Ludendorff, 674-5.

From the purely military point of view it was of the greatest and most fateful importance that we had lost the initiative to the enemy. . . .

The effect of our failure on the country and our allies was even greater, judging by our first impressions.

How many hopes, cherished during the last few months, had probably collapsed at one blow! How many calculations had been scattered to the winds.[4]

The decisions of July 22 were far from constituting a clear and resolute strategy; Ludendorff was far from recovering his head; this was all demonstrated that afternoon, when the First Quartermaster-General—that iron and frozen man who did not confide even in his wife—showered intimate confidences on Mertz:

> 5 P.M. Have just been with His Excellency [noted Mertz in his diary]. He informs me of the decision to withdraw from the Marne and outlines the military necessity to me. His Excellency in very grave mood. He said to me:
>
> "I am not superstitious or rather, yes, I am. You know, I had no confidence in July 15."
>
> With this he opened the right-hand drawer of his writing table and took out a rather tattered prayerbook of the *Brüdergemeine*. From this he read out to me the text given there for July 15. He interpreted it, in contrast to the texts on our other days of attack, as unfavourable. Then he read me the texts for March 21, April 9, May 27 and June 9. Afterwards, we talked long and seriously. I was really inwardly quite moved. His Excellency then said goodbye with the words:
>
> "The good Lord will, I hope, not forsake us."
>
> I answered that this certainly would not be.

Mertz's diary entry cheerfully ends:

> His excellency quite broken.[5]

Ludendorff's forebodings about July 15 (of which he gave no sign before or since, except to Mertz) are less important than the fact, corroborated by Tieschowitz, of his superstition, which recalls the omens and auguries of ancient wars and the elaborate superstitions ("gremlins" and lucky charms) of modern combatants (such as air pilots) subject to great stress and danger.

[4] Hindenburg, 386.
[5] Förster, 25-6.

By August 4 the crisis in the Marne salient was over, and the Germans were well dug in behind the Vesle and the Aisne. However, at O.H.L. the strategic paralysis continued, along with Ludendorff's personal collapse. Mertz's diary entries give a vivid—perhaps too vivid—picture of an extraordinary fortnight:

> July 23, evening: . . . Wetzell and I feel we are dying of half-measures. Ludendorff will spend himself completely without finding the strength to decide on anything dynamically effective.
>
> July 24: Serious question of His Excellency Ludendorff's nervousness and of disjointedness in the work he produced. . . . His Excellency is working himself to death, worrying too much about details. This situation is really grave.
>
> July 25: Graf Schwerin [Chief of the General Staff of the Balkan Army Group, temporarily in Avesnes] very much disturbed by the appearance and nervousness of His Excellency. It really does give the impression that His Excellency has lost all confidence. The army chiefs are suffering terribly as a result of it. Hence telephone conversations lasting one and a half hours on the day's agenda.[6]

Other officers on the staff of O.H.L. or visiting it later considered Mertz's account overcoloured, but his general picture agrees with that of Lossberg. Lossberg was the witness of a further, but more or less suppressed, quarrel over orders between Ludendorff and Hindenburg on July 26.[7] General von Oldershausen, later one of Mertz's critics on the grounds of exaggeration, himself noted at the time Ludendorff's tremendous internal stress and loss of appetite.

Equally at O.H.L. and at subordinate headquarters, officers remarked how Ludendorff married total strategic indecision with endless detailed interference over minor troop movements.

On August 2 Ludendorff, gradually recovering himself in view of the relative quiet and safety of the front, issued a strategic directive. It contained the familiar incoherence:

> The situation demands that on the one hand we should place ourselves on the defensive, on the other that we should as soon as possible go back into the attack again. . . . In our attacks . . . it will not so much be a

6 Förster, 28.
7 Lossberg, 350.

question of conquering further territory as of defeating the enemy and gaining more favourable positions.[8]

In fact, as Lossberg had pointed out, what was needed was a clear acceptance of the inevitability of the defensive, and a consequent retreat in good time to the Siegfried line, both much shorter and much better fortified than the deep, lightly defended salient towards Amiens.

On August 7 Ludendorff had to issue a secret order to the O.H.L. staff in order to repair the damage done by his own fortnight of disintegration:

> To my regret the existence of despondent outlooks and rumours has been established and their source traced to Supreme Headquarters. At home and in the army, all eyes are turned upon the O.H.L. Whether rightly or wrongly, each member of Supreme Headquarters is looked upon as being well informed and corresponding value is put upon all he says. For this reason every member of Supreme Headquarters must even outside the O.H.L., remain conscious of his responsibility. . . . The O.H.L. is free from despondency. Sustained by what has previously been achieved on the front and at home, it prepares stout-heartedly to meet the challenges that are to come. No member of O.H.L. may think and act in a manner other than this.[9]

It was not Ludendorff, but Haig, who put an end to the paralysing uncertainty at O.H.L. On July 24 Foch had held a conference at the Château de Bombon. This gave formal approval to Haig's suggestion of a Franco-British joint attack east of Amiens, a suggestion made when Haig on July 17 rejected Foch's own first idea of a British attack on the Festubert sector.

At the Bombon conference it was agreed that three lateral railways must be freed. One of them (Paris-Avricourt—south of Château-Thierry) would be cleared by the current battle in the Marne salient. A second (Paris-Avricourt—south of Verdun) demanded an American offensive against the narrow German salient of St. Mihiel. The third was the Paris-Amiens line. It would be disengaged by a combined offensive by the British 4th Army[10] and Debeney's 1st French Army. Two days

---

[8] Förster, 37.
[9] Förster, 39-40.
[10] This was the new number given to the old 5th Army which had disappeared from the order of battle. It was commanded by Lieutenant-General Rawlinson.

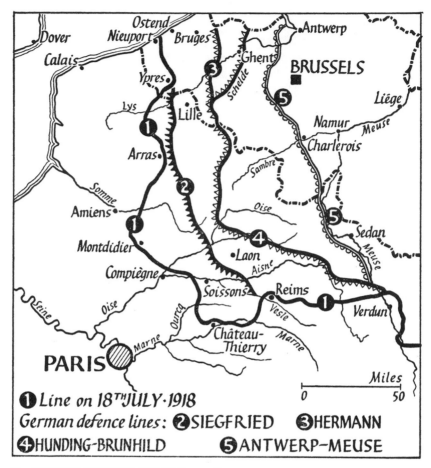

Line on 18ᵀᴴ·JULY·1918
German defence lines: ②SIEGFRIED ③HERMANN
④HUNDING-BRUNHILD ⑤ANTWERP-MEUSE

42. GERMAN DEFENCE SYSTEMS, 1918

later Foch issued his orders for the Amiens operation, placing Debeney under Haig and fixing the date as August 8.

Like the attack of July 18, August 8 marked a great change in allied tactics and planning since the great battles of 1917. To the end of the Passchendaele campaign Haig had adhered to the technique of a preliminary bombardment lasting for days, of open and deliberate preparations. This was despite suggestions put forward as early as August 1917 for achieving surprise and shock effect by attacks secretly prepared, led by tanks, and launched after an unregistered hurricane bombardment of a few hours. The German command was less conservative than the British; this technique had been the basis of Riga (September 1917) and Caporetto (October 1917) as well as of March 21, 1918. Only after the Passchendaele battle had ended did the British command try out new techniques of surprise and shock by use of tanks at Cambrai, a battle revolutionary in itself, but inadequately prepared and thought out in terms of strategy and without military result. The German successes of 1918 had finally discredited the methods of Passchendaele and Malmaison.

Indeed, the allies now surpassed the Germans, for on August 8, 1918, four hundred and thirty tanks replaced the hurricane bombardment as the method of paralysing and smashing through the enemy's defence system. Nevertheless it would be wrong to assume, because the future belonged to the tank, that in 1918 it was a more effective weapon than Bruchmüller's guns. The allies chose to develop the tank, the Germans their already excellent and abundant artillery and mustard-gas shell (which the allies did not possess in quantity until a year after the Germans). The German choice was influenced by the indecisive performance of tanks in 1916-17 and by their shortage of suitable factories and plants, a shortage that did not apply to guns and gas. On March 21, 1918, the majority of types of tanks by then with the allied forces had little more capacity for deep penetration and mobility than Bruchmüller's guns. Low speed and poor reliability would have limited their major effort, like the German guns, to the first day. Even by August, when the British armies had received large quantities of light and faster tanks ("Whippets"), no more was achieved in terms of break-through and demoralisation than had been achieved by Hutier on March 21.

Yet this was enough.

The front of the attack on August 8 lay astride the Somme between the Ancre and the Avre, with the French 1st Army holding about a third of it south of the Amiens-Roye road. The 4th Army included the Canadian Corps and the Australian Corps, which because of a more flexible system of training and discipline and of a more able and enterprising type of officer, recruited from wider social backgrounds than the British, were the most formidable troops in Haig's command. The 3rd Corps (British) would act as left-flank guard. Rawlinson was given the Cavalry Corps for exploitation. The 1st French Army included five army corps, of which three were to take part in the battle. In all, Rawlinson employed ten Dominion divisions (at full strength), four British, one American and three cavalry divisions in the initial assault or in reserve—441,588 men and 415 tanks. This powerful striking force, supplemented by Debeney's army, was faced by von der Marwitz's 2nd Army with only seven divisions in the line and four in reserve, all badly under strength, perhaps 3,000 rifles apiece. In Marwitz's opinion, reported to O.H.L. on August 3, only two of these units were fully battle-fit, another five good enough for trench warfare only. In fact, like Gough's 5th Army before March 21, Marwitz's troops were the overextended survivors of bloody offensives. Like Gough's troops, too, they had had no time and no labour to prepare adequate defensive systems. Unlike Gough, Marwitz and his staff failed to deduce from the evidence that a smashing blow was impending. In the German 2nd Army there was a listlessness, apathy and nonchalance that indicated how far morale had declined after the failure of the spring and summer offensives.

In the morning of August 8 there was fog along the 4th Army front. At 4:20 A.M. Rawlinson's and Debeney's guns fired: not a bombardment but a creeping barrage. Behind it the infantry and tanks moved straight away through the fog and smoke. It is ironical that whereas Ludendorff had considered the fog on March 21 to have hindered the attackers and the British official historian had judged it a major factor in the collapse of the British defence, the effects of the fog of August 8 were not seen by these writers as entirely similar. Sir James Edmonds writes: ". . . it assisted to cover the launching of the attack . . . but it did not clear completely until nearly 10 A.M. and embarrassed both the troops and the tanks in keeping direction and formation. . . . Under these conditions the attacking brigades became split up from the start into small groups . . ." [11]

Ludendorff refers to "the dense fog, rendered still thicker by artificial means," [12] and Hindenburg says "the thick mist made supervision and control very difficult." [13]

[11] *British Official History,* Vol. IV, 1918, 41.
[12] Ludendorff, 679.
[13] Hindenburg, 391.

As the tanks reared, loomed and lumbered through the shifting vapour, Marwitz's army collapsed in rout and confusion. All the scenes in and behind the British front on March 21 were now replayed in German uniform. However, Marwitz's army did not show moral stubbornness equal to Gough's command. The scenes of panic, dissolution and insubordination were really more reminiscent of the conduct of Nivelle's troops after the failure of the April 1917 offensive and on the eve of the mutinies. By the end of the day Rawlinson had advanced up to four miles and according to German accounts had virtually annihilated the line divisions opposite him. There were neither defences nor strong field forces to bar a fast British penetration and pursuit. "August 8," wrote Ludendorff, "was the black day of the German army in the history of this war. This was the worst experience that I had to go through, except for the events that, from September 15 onwards, took place on the Bulgarian front and sealed the fate of the Quadruple Alliance." [14]

It was not the extent of the defeat, or the strategic danger it created, that gave August 8 its blackness, for they were no greater than on July 18. Nor was August 8 a "turning point." Ludendorff, Hindenburg and the British official historian agree that it was on July 18 that the course of the campaign was reversed. The special quality of brutal calamity that belonged to August 8 came from other factors. In the first place, it blocked any small loophole of hope that the result of July 18 might not be final. Secondly, it brought home to Ludendorff a phenomenon that he had preferred to ignore—the catastrophically rapid decline in the morale and discipline of the German army. Above all, it knocked Ludendorff himself down psychologically at a moment when he had barely got to his feet after the smashing blow of July 18.

> The report of the staff officer [Mertz] I had sent to the battlefield [wrote Ludendorff] as to the condition of those divisions which had met the first shock of the attack on the 8th, perturbed me deeply. I summoned divisional commanders and officers from the line to Avesnes to discuss events with them in detail. I was told of deeds of glorious valour but also of behaviour which, I openly confess, I should not have thought possible in the German army; whole bodies of our men had surrendered to single troopers, or isolated squadrons. Retiring troops, meeting a fresh division going bravely

[14] Ludendorff, 679.

into action, had shouted out things like "Blackleg," and "You're prolonging the war". . . . The officers in many places had lost their influence and allowed themselves to be swept along with the rest.[15]

In fact, there was nothing suddenly new in all this. In the winter of 1916-17 there had been copious reports of the poor morale and discipline, of the revolutionary attitude, of troops and repatriated prisoners of war from Russia. The German army, like the French, had been infiltrated by left-wing propagandists and agitators who argued that the war was irrelevant to the real interests of the rank-and-file combatants. As in France in the summer of 1917, so in Germany from autumn 1917 onwards there was continued disorder on troop and leave trains.

"Reports of this kind became more numerous in February and March 1918," wrote Kuhl in his report to the Reichstag Committee after the war. "Shots were fired from the windows of the trains. The men got out at every opportunity and could be induced only with difficulty to get in again. Many disappeared at the stations without ceremony." [16]

By June indiscipline along lines of communication had become as bad as that in the French army twelve months before, except that it had not yet turned "collective." Officers who tried to maintain order on trains and stations were stoned to shouts of "Knock him down!" Even hand grenades were thrown out of the windows of trains. On June 17 a troop train bore the scrawled assertion: "We're not fighting for Germany's honour, but for the millionaires!"

How far a war of nation states, fuelled on a nationalistic "ingroup" psychology, had become modified by a new international class war, with "ingroup" psychology based on class solidarity, is illustrated by the extraordinary similarity between events in France in 1917 and in Germany in 1917-18. On the one hand, the attitudes, reports, recommendations and actions of the German and French high commands over their men's declining interest in glory are so exactly alike as to be interchangeable. On the other, the pattern of insubordination and agitation, the language of left-wing propaganda, are equally so.

The German problem was sharpened by the division in the army in 1918 into "shock" and "trench" divisions. There had been neither equipment nor time for training to allow the entire army to be prepared for

[15] Ludendorff, 683.
[16] Lutz, 143.

mobile operations before March 21. Therefore only the offensive mass of manoeuvre had been retrained and re-equipped. To fill its ranks the best troops had been stripped from the rest of the army, whose passive and dreary task was to continue to occupy the trenches on quiet fronts. The system worked splendidly while Ludendorff was attacking; the troops of March 21 displayed a standard of skill and initiative never equalled by the more evenly trained and equipped allies. But when the "shock" divisions had been shattered in offensive battles and the allies recovered the initiative, the brunt of the defensive fell in the first place on the poor-quality "trench" divisions.

Encapsuled in his dreams of great victory, Ludendorff had failed to appreciate or preferred to ignore the extent and speed of rot in his army, until, too late, the facts were brutally thrust into his face by Haig on August 8.

The British did not develop or exploit their success with Hutier's relentlessness. August 9 was a day of hesitation and missed opportunities; the communications network and the habits and methods of command, so long accustomed to static warfare, could not be adjusted to control a fast-moving and fluid battle. Only three miles were gained, and Marwitz found enough good troops to patch the gap. At Avesnes, however, the panic went on without slackening. It was a day of incessant telephone calls, visits and counter-visits between the command and staff at O.H.L. and the attacked front. Tschischwitz (Chief of Staff, 2nd Army) told Kuhl (Chief of Staff, Army Group Rupprecht) that the 2nd Army must retire behind the Somme. He was followed on the line by Marwitz who said the same. Kuhl then spoke to Ludendorff, who expressed the view that the 2nd Army had lost its nerve. Mertz had come back from the front to report that both Marwitz and Tschischwitz were finished. Tschischwitz was therefore being replaced by von Klewitz.

Like Hitler at Stalingrad, Ludendorff could find no better policy than to hold the existing front at all costs. Events had now made Lossberg's strategy of timely withdrawal to the Siegfried line even better sense and more urgent than on July 19. Kuhl therefore argued in anguished frustration that the policy of holding present fronts at all costs exposed them everywhere to danger, left them naked, used up all their resources. Ludendorff's mind was still closed. Kuhl wanted the 2nd Army to hold on long enough to cover the 18th Army's retreat from the Montdidier salient and then itself to retire behind the Somme. Ludendorff would not heed him. In despair, Kuhl got Major von Leeb[17] to repeat Marwitz's report to Wetzell. Ludendorff broke into the conversation to say that the position must be held. As with Hitler at Stalingrad and Churchill at Singapore, reality was to be forced to fit the dream.

> Eventually, after long arguments [wrote Kuhl], Ludendorff agreed late in the evening to a withdrawal to a line l'Echelle-Conchy-Riquenberg-Matz. This was carried out in the night of August 9 to 10.
>
> Ludendorff is continually insisting on having a say in all the particulars, talking to all the armies and their chiefs, arranging details often quite contrary to his orders to me. Then when one talks to the army commanders, one hears they are doing something entirely different from what we ordered. This makes everything terribly difficult. At the same time he is extremely restless and does not listen to a single suggestion.[18]

Next day, in Avesnes, Ludendorff explained the general situation to the Kaiser; the severe defeat, the poor state of the troops, the necessity to fight for every foot of ground. There was more to it than this. Ludendorff had already accepted national defeat.

> I had no hope of finding a strategic expedient whereby to turn the situation to our advantage. On the contrary, I became convinced that we were now without that safe foundation for the plans of O.H.L. on which I had hitherto been able to build, at least so far as this is possible in war. Leadership now assumed, as I then stated, the character of an irresponsible game of chance, a thing I have always considered fatal. The fate of the German people was for me too high a stake. The war must be ended.[19]

Major Niemann, O.H.L. liaison officer to the Kaiser, describes how Wilhelm II took this:

> The Kaiser maintained his outward calm, but anyone looking at his face could see in the taut features, the deep furrows of mental anguish and the burning eyes, the overpowering inward emotion that was straining for release:
>
> "I see we must balance the books, we are at the limit of our powers. The

---

[17] Later Field-Marshal von Leeb; at this time an officer on the staff of Army Group Rupprecht.
[18] Förster, 45.
[19] Ludendorff, 684.

war must be brought to an end. . . . I shall expect the gentlemen in Spa within the next few days, then!"

Full of trust, his eyes smiled at the field-marshal and a firm, warm handshake showed the First Quartermaster-General that he could count as well on the full confidence of his royal superior in future.[20]

As a sign of his complete personal defeat after August 8, Ludendorff had already offered his resignation to Hindenburg, who had refused it.

It was less than a month since Ludendorff in good heart and bounding ambition had told Hintze, the Secretary of State, "I hope to make the enemy ready for peace with my next stroke." [21] In four weeks Germany had accepted the decision of a four-year conflict. The rest is a chronicle of progressive national collapse taking place at an equal speed in the armed forces and at home. Yet the collapse had begun at O.H.L. with the breaking of Ludendorff by the events of July 18 and August 8.

The general conference in Spa, to which the Kaiser had made reference on August 10, took place on the fourteenth. As well as the Kaiser, Ludendorff and Hindenburg, there were present Hintze and Graf Hertling (the Chancellor). It had been preceded the day before by a private discussion in Hindenburg's room at the Hotel Britannique that excluded Wilhelm II. The result of both conferences was that in view of the military situation and the state of home morale, Hintze was to put out feelers for a negotiated peace. The Kaiser indicated the Queen of Holland as a possible intermediary.

The disasters of July 18 and August 8 had sent leaping waves of dismay throughout Germany's allies. The Emperor Charles of Austria, his Chancellor and his Commander-in-Chief, visited Spa for inconclusive talks that only proved one thing—that Austria's flag, too, was beginning to come fluttering down the mast.

Yet at this time when Ludendorff was pressing peace negotiations upon the German government, the German army still occupied more French territory than in 1917, was still an organised, coherent array of more than 2,500,000 men, had behind it the powerful defence systems of the Siegfried and Hunding-Brunhild lines. Its British and French enemies had no overwhelming superiority of numbers; the French reserves were exhausted. The allies were incapable, morally and physically, of a mas-

20 Niemann, 355.
21 Memo of Oct. 1918, quoted Förster, 11.

sive and shattering break-through like that of March 21; throughout the late summer and autumn of 1918 Foch and Haig limited themselves to a linked series of local spoiling offensives. What then was the factor that made Ludendorff opt for peace after his first defeats?

It was the Americans—not the handful of divisions in the line, but the huge and growing reserve of well-fed, unwearied and unshaken men they supplied. Whereas in August the average field strength of a German battalion had sunk to 660-665 men, and the only fresh reserves were 300,000 men of the 1900 class called up in June, the American army in France had risen to 1,473,190. It was not the present that was impossible; it was the future. The British and the French had won the battles of 1918, but it was the Americans who won the war. The German army was never "stabbed in the back." By the beginning of 1918, because of the growth of American military and technological strength, and because of the British blockade, Germany and her allies were steadily, ineluctably losing the war, with consequent effects of moral disintegration at home and in the forces. This was after all why Ludendorff had decided on *Michael.* Now the German army had been decisively beaten in the field; there was nothing left. Germany had lost a total war totally—by defeat in every sphere of national effort and last of all in the military sphere.

August to November 1918 was a dragging anticlimax as the sound troops of the German army fought dogged and skilled rear-guard actions back through France and Belgium and behind them the rest of the army, the nation and its allies dissolved. Because Ludendorff had refused to take Lossberg's advice on July 19, the retreat was conducted not voluntarily and in good time, but under the pressure of continual allied strokes. The Siegfried line, occupied too late and in haste by insufficient troops in poor heart, was broken into by the British on September 28. This followed a Franco-American success in the Argonne two days beforehand. These defeats started another urgent wave of panic in Ludendorff; this time it was not just the general idea of peace negotiations he recommended, but an immediate armistice. At a time of national calamity, when France found Clemenceau and in another war the British found Churchill, Germany was led only by this broken, hysterical soldier searching for ways and means to off-load his responsibilities now that he no longer took pleasure in them. In the hope that parliamentary government would induce the now powerful left-wing parties to take over the war, Ludendorff even on September 29 blessed the granting of a democratic constitution. In the words of Professor A. J. P. Taylor: "Constitutional monarchy, the highest ambition even of the Social Democrats, was achieved without the effort, almost without the knowledge of the German people; it was a manoeuvre on the battlefield, not an event in domestic history." [22]

On the same day, according to some witnesses, cumulative strain caused Ludendorff a fit of hysterical paralysis.

The alliance of the central powers was now like a great mansion in the last stages of a disastrous fire—a massive, hollow shell filled with the glowing embers of social unrest and the leaping flame of revolution. From time to time some great piece of the structure would collapse before the gaze of the watching democracies.

The allied forces round Salonika which had so far done little in the war except die of various diseases launched a major offensive on September 15 against the Bulgarian army. The German troops that had stiffened the Bulgarians had been withdrawn to shore up the western front; left to themselves and depressed by the German disasters in France, the Bulgarians were quickly smashed. After a racing pursuit northward over ground to be traversed in the opposite direction by panzer divisions in Operation *Marita* in April 1941 against Yugoslavia and Greece, the Bulgarians concluded an armistice on September 30. This first collapse among Germany's allies, and of one of her stoutest, drawn out over more than a fortnight of rout and disintegration, was in Ludendorff's own estimation an even worse experience for him than Haig's offensive of August 8.

Meanwhile on September 19 the final British offensive in Palestine swept the Turks away towards Damascus; Turkey could not last much longer either.

Under the cumulative bad news, military and political, that rolled like dark smoke across the scene of ultimate disintegration, Ludendorff deteriorated further into panic and incoherence. An armistice was now wanted, he urged the new government of Prince Max of Baden (who had replaced Hertling as Chancellor), with such desperate speed that, in the words of Ludendorff's representative, Major Freiherr von dem Busche, to Reichstag party leaders, "every twenty-four hours that pass may make our position worse." On October 4 the German and Austrian govern-

[22] Taylor, *The Course of German History*, 206.

ments despatched notes to President Wilson asking for armistice negotiations to be opened.

By now the average field strength of a German battalion in the west was down to 545 men—perhaps 250 rifles. More significant than waning numerical strength—German troops in weaker battalion strength fought stubborn defensive battles in 1944-5—was the moral disintegration of a thoroughly beaten army.

On October 9 the German government received Wilson's answer: acceptance of his Fourteen Points and the evacuation of all occupied territory by Germany must precede negotiations. On October 12 these terms were accepted. On October 16 the allies, realising the extent of German weakness in fighting power and in resolution, began to harden their bargaining; Wilson informed the German government that armistice conditions must be drafted by allied commanders.

On the western front the collapse that had threatened from September 28 till October 4 did not take place. The Siegfried line was lost, but the Germans retired to the line of the river Selle and to the Hunding-Brunhild defences, on which line they were not seriously attacked until October 14. On that day the Americans suffered heavy losses for small gains in the Argonne, and the allies' Flanders Army Group began a fresh offensive towards Courtrai. With the pace and pressure thus temporarily relaxed, Ludendorff veered wildly back from instant armistice towards continuation of the war and better peace terms. It hardly mattered. He was no longer in control of Germany's war. He was a nervous wreck, essentially ignored and on his way out. Power had passed to Prince Max of Baden, in whom at last and too late Germany had found a statesman of good sense and strong character. Even Hindenburg, whose close relationship with Ludendorff had survived the earlier quarrels unimpaired, was now drawing apart from the First Quartermaster-General. Max of Baden replied to Wilson, accepting his further conditions; U-boat warfare would be stopped.

Meanwhile the battle in the west lurched again towards disaster. On October 20 the allies reached the Lys and crossed the Selle, and the Germans evacuated the Belgian coast line. On the twenty-fourth a further note from Wilson further transformed the idea of a negotiated armistice into a surrender without conditions. The note included the threat that only the removal of the Hohenzollern monarchy and of German military rulers could lead to an offer of peace negotiations instead of capitulation. Ludendorff was more than ever expendable. By a final and characteristic stroke of miscalculation, Ludendorff now tried to sabotage Max of Baden's peace negotiations by sending a telegram on October 24, "For the Information of All Troops," over Hindenburg's name, which stated: "Wilson's answer is a demand for unconditional surrender. It is thus unacceptable to us soldiers." [23]

Next day the resulting indignation of the Reichstag, added to Wilson's demand, made it essential that Ludendorff should be discarded. Max of Baden accordingly informed the Kaiser so. Hindenburg and Ludendorff were in fact in Berlin to attend the conferences over Wilson's note. In the afternoon of October 26, 1918, a message came to the General Staff Office that both were wanted by the Kaiser at the Berliner Schloss. When the two soldiers were received by the Kaiser, it was Ludendorff alone who was the target of imperial hostility. ". . . he expressed himself," remembered Ludendorff, "particularly against the army order of the evening of the 24th. There followed some of the bitterest moments of my life. I said respectfully to His Majesty that I had gained the painful impression that I no longer enjoyed his confidence, and that I accordingly begged most humbly to be relieved of my office. His Majesty accepted my resignation." [24]

Although Hindenburg offered his resignation too, the Kaiser refused to accept it. Ludendorff left alone. He drove back to the General Staff Office a private man, his vast responsibilities, splendid victories and catastrophic defeats behind him, amid the closing scenes of a war that had opened with a similar journey to and from the Berliner Schloss on August 1, 1914, by another *de facto* supreme commander of the Field Army of the German Empire.

On November 11 the armistice ended hostilities, but not the blockade. Women and children went hungry, fell sick or died in Germany for a whole winter after the last soldier had been shot. Germany had been finally pulled down by the supreme exertions of the French, Russian and

[23] Ludendorff, 761.
[24] Ludendorff, 763.

British Empires together and the fresh and overwhelming weight of America. The allies controlled Europe and indeed most of the world. What would they do with it?

The war embraced infinitely complex elements and motives. The most important single one of those elements was the struggle for power in Europe, and the world. Between 1870 and 1914 Britain and France had been stagnant and declining in comparative industrial vigour. They nevertheless owned great territories and enjoyed vast traditional overseas markets. Germany, as Marshal Foch pointed out in his memoirs, had been comfortably and steadily taking over the markets before 1914; she would have liked the possessions as well. No wonder France and Britain had been so much in favour of defending the political status quo. Yet, as the endless surges and recessions of power throughout history indicate, a fixed status quo is an absurdity, because static. The problem of the world of nation states before 1914 was the eternal problem of continually adjusting political structure so that it always fits and expresses the reality of power. The reality of power before 1914 was that France and Britain were no longer growing and expanding vigorously, Germany was. While this process took place in purely industrial and economic terms France and Britain could not be bothered to resist it, although all that was needed to do so was industrial expansion equal to Germany's in relentless efficiency and single-minded purpose. When the process of German expansion took political forms, resistance followed. As the history of Turkey showed, the most moribund of powers hates to give up the territories or treaty rights that symbolise a no-longer-existing greatness. By allowing herself to be drawn into war in 1914 Germany made a capital mistake, for she now appeared to Britain and France as an armed threat. As in 1939, an armed threat was the one thing that could shake the British and the French out of their torpid complacency. Between 1914 and 1918 Britain displayed a creative vigour, driving energy and relentless purpose such as had not been seen there since the 1850's. Like France, she did in war what she had failed to do in peace: that is, oppose German power and expansion with her own.

Now in 1918 German power was broken. Instead of an economic *Mittel Europa*, there was a vacuum. Would the allies fill it? Would Europe now form a single technological unit under British and French domination? Would French and British industry here and in world markets replace the enormous inventiveness and dynamic expansion of pre-war German industry?

In fact the war in this respect changed nothing. Having smashed Germany, France and Britain returned happily to their dreams of the past, to a cosy stagnation. America was not the only nation that turned her back on the facts and responsibilities of power after 1918. The French and the British had endured the terrible losses of the war in order to try to achieve an impossibility, an absurdity—a permanent vacuum in place of German power, and a vacuum they were not prepared to fill themselves. To protect themselves against German revival they instead imposed stiffly restrictive peace terms they had not the moral courage or national vigour to enforce permanently. When Germany inevitably revived, the political status quo established by the Treaty of Versailles was therefore even more out of register with the facts of power in Europe and the world than the status quo existing before 1914. Out of the consequent distortions of the natural process of growth and decay were born Nazism and the Second World War.

Appendix

ORGANISATION OF ARMIES IN 1914

German

An army corps consisted of two infantry divisions each of 17,500 officers and men, 4,000 horses, 72 guns and 24 machine guns. In addition were corps troops, including heavy artillery, field hospitals, field bakeries, bridging trains and supply columns. A reserve corps lacked heavy artillery; and a reserve division had half the number of field guns.

A cavalry corps consisted of two or three cavalry divisions, each of 5,200 officers and men, 5,600 horses, motor transport, 12 guns, 6 machine guns and field radio.

French

A French corps consisted of two, but occasionally three, divisions, each of 15,000 officers and men, 36 guns and 24 machine guns. The French cavalry corps consisted of three divisions, each of 4,500 officers and men, and 8 guns.

British

A British corps consisted of two infantry divisions, each of 18,073 officers and men, 5,592 horses, 76 guns and 24 machine guns. The 76 guns included 54 field guns, 18 4.5-inch howitzers and 4 60-pounders; in a Continental corps, guns heavier than field were under corps command, not divisional.

A British cavalry division consisted of 9,269 officers and men, 9,815 horses, 24 guns and 24 machine guns.

Selected Bibliography

This bibliography is restricted to books either quoted in the course of the work or which the author found particularly useful. It is not intended to comprise all the books consulted by the author, nor to be a complete bibliography of the subject.

Sources referred to in the footnotes and quoted in the text are indicated by an asterisk. The name of the publisher is given in every case, and the author wishes to thank all those who have allowed him to quote from their books.

Angé-Laribé, Michel, and Pinot, Pierre, *Agriculture and Food Supply in France during the War.* Oxford University Press, 1927.

Bacon, Admiral Sir R. H., *Life of Earl Jellicoe of Scapa.* Cassell, 1936. *The Jutland Scandal.* Hutchinson, 1925.

Bauer, Colonel, *Der Grosse Krieg im Feld und Heimat.* Osiandersche Buchhandlung, 1921.

Baumgarten-Crusius, Major-General, *Le Haut Commandement Allemand Pendant la Campagne de la Marne en 1914.* Charles-Lavauzelle, 1924.

Behrend, Arthur, *As From Kemmel Hill.* Eyre and Spottiswoode, 1963.

Bell, A. C., *The Blockade of Germany, 1914-18.* HMSO, 1931.

Bellairs, Commander Carlyon, *The Battle of Jutland: the Sowing and the Reaping.* Hodder and Stoughton, 1920.

Bethmann-Hollweg, Theobald von, *Reflections on the World War.* Thornton Butterworth, 1921.

Binding, Rudolph, *A Fatalist at War.* Allen and Unwin, 1929.

Blake, Robert (Editor), *The Private Papers of Douglas Haig 1914-19.* Eyre and Spottiswoode, 1952.

Bloem, Walter, *The Advance from Mons.* Peter Davies, 1930.

Brassey's Naval Annual, 1911.

Bruchmüller, Colonel Georg, *Die Artillerie beim Angriff in Stellungskrieg.* Verlag "Offene Worte," 1926.

Bülow, Prince Bernhard von, *Memoirs.* Putnam 1931-32.

Bülow, Field-Marshal Karl von (see Koeltz).

Burnham, T. A., and Hoskins, G. O., *Iron and Steel in Britain 1870-1914.* Allen and Unwin, 1943.

Carré, Lieutenant-Colonel Henri, *Les Grandes Heures du Général Pétain.* Éditions du Conquistador, 1952.

Chalmers, Rear-Admiral W. S., *Life and Letters of David, Earl Beatty.* Hodder and Stoughton, 1951.

Chambers, F. P., *The War behind the War.* Faber and Faber, 1939.

Charteris, Brigadier-General John, *Field-Marshal Earl Haig.* Cassell, 1929.

Chatfield, Admiral of the Fleet Lord, *The Navy and Defence.* Heinemann, 1942.

Churchill, Winston S., *The World Crisis.* Thornton Butterworth, 1927.

Clapham, J. H., *Economic Development of France and Germany 1815-1914.* Cambridge University Press, 1923.

Clausewitz, Carl von, *On War.* Kegan Paul, 1908.

Clough, S. B., and Cole, C. W., *Economic History of Europe.* D. C. Heath and Co., 1952.

Colin, Colonel J., *Les Transformations de la Guerre.* Flammarion, 1911.

Contamine, Henri, *La Revanche, 1871-1914.* Berger-Levrault, 1957.

Dewar, Captain A. C., and Dewar, Captain K. G. B., *The Narrative of Jutland.* HMSO, 1924.

Dewar, Vice-Admiral K. G. B., *The Navy from Within.* Gollancz, 1939.

Dreyer, Admiral Sir Frederic, *The Sea Heritage.* Museum Press, 1955.

Dupont, General, *Le Haut Commandement Allemand en 1914.* Librairie Chapelot, 1922.

Edmonds, Sir James, *A Short History of the First World War.* Oxford University Press, 1951.

Encyclopaedia Britannica, 1911 Edition.

Falkenhayn, General Erich von, *General Headquarters, 1914-16, and Its Critical Decisions.* Hutchinson, 1919.

Falls, Cyril, *Marshal Foch.* Blackie, 1939. *The First World War.* Longmans, 1960.

Fawcett, H. W., and Hooper, G. W. W., *The Fighting at Jutland.* Hutchinson, 1920.

Foch, Marshal F., *The Memoirs of Marshal Foch.* Heinemann, 1931.

Förster, Lieutenant-Colonel Wolfgang, *Le Comte Schlieffen et la Guerre*

Mondiale: La Stratégie allemande pendant la Guerre de 1914-1918. Payot, 1930. *Der Feldherr Ludendorff in Unglück.* Limes Verlag, 1952.

French, Field-Marshal Viscount, *1914.* Constable, 1919.

Frost, Commander H. H., *The Battle of Jutland.* United States Naval Institute, 1936.

Gascouin, General, *L'Évolution de l'Artillerie Pendant la Guerre.* Flammarion, 1920.

Gaulle, General Charles de, *La France et Son Armée.* Berger-Levrault, 1945.

Gibson, Langhorne, and Harper, Vice-Admiral J. E. T., *The Riddle of Jutland: an Authentic History.* Cassell, 1934.

Girardet, Raoul, *La Société Militaire dans la France Contemporaine.* Plon, 1953.

Gooch, G. P., *History of Modern Europe.* Cassell, 1923. *Studies in German History.* Longmans, 1948. *Before the War: Studies in Diplomacy.* Longmans, 1936-38.

Görlitz, Walter, *The German General Staff.* Hollis and Carter, 1935.

Gough, General Sir Hubert, *The Fifth Army.* Hodder and Stoughton, 1931.

Grouard, Lieutenant-Colonel A., *France et Allemagne: Guerre Eventuelle.* Chapelot, 1913.

Haig Papers (document cited).

Hankey, Lord, *The Supreme Command 1914-1918.* Allen and Unwin, 1961.

Hanotaux, Gabriel, *Histoires Illustrées de la Guerre de 1914,* Tome 8. Gounouilhou, 1918.

Harper, Captain J. E. T., *Reproduction of the Record of the Battle of Jutland.* HMSO, 1927.

Harper, Vice-Admiral J. E. T., *The Truth about Jutland.* Murray 1927.

Hase, Captain Georg von, *Kiel and Jutland.* Skeffington, 1920.

Helfferich, Karl, *Der Weltkrieg.* Ullstein, 1919.

Henaffe, General le, *Le Rôle Militaire des Chemins de Fer.* Berger-Levrault, 1923.

Herbillion, Colonel, *Souvenirs d'un Officier de Liaison pendant la Guerre Mondiale,* Vol. 2. Tallandier, 1930.

Hindenburg, Field-Marshal Paul von, *Out of My Life.* Cassell, 1920.

H.M. Inspectors of Education, Report of, 1908-9. HMSO.

Hoffmann, General Max, *My War Diaries.* Secker, 1929.

Jane's Fighting Ships, 1914.

Jellicoe Papers (British Museum).

* *Jellicoe Private Papers.*

Jellicoe, Admiral of the Fleet, Earl, *The Grand Fleet 1914-16: its Creation, Development and Work.* Cassell, 1919.

Kluck, Colonel-General Alexander von, *The March on Paris.* Edward Arnold, 1920.

Koeltz, Lieûtenant-Colonel L. (Editor and translator), *Documents Allemands sur la Bataille de la Marne.* Payot, 1930.

> NOTE: This contains three works otherwise published separately:
>
> > Bülow, Field-Marshal Karl von, *Mon Rapport sur la Bataille de la Marne.*
> >
> > Tappen, General, *Jusqu'à la Marne en 1914.*
> >
> > Muller Loebnitz, Lieutenant-Colonel W. *La Mission du Lieutenant-Colonel Hentsch.*

Kuhl, General H. von, *La Campagne de la Marne.* Payot, 1927.

Laure, General, *Le Commandement en chef des Armées Françaises du 15 Mai 1917 à l'Armistice.* Berger-Levrault, 1937.

Liddell Hart, Captain B. H., *Foch: The Man of Orleans.* Eyre and Spottiswoode, 1931. *A History of the World War, 1914-18.* Faber and Faber, 1934. *The Real War, 1914-18.* Faber and Faber, 1930. *Reputations.* John Murray, 1928. *The Tanks,* Vol. I. Cassell, 1959. *French Military Thought before the First World War* (lecture notes).

Lloyd George, David, *War Memoirs.* Ivor Nicolson and Watson, 1933-36.

Lossberg, General von, *Meine Tätigkeit im Weltkriege 1914-18.* Mittler, 1939.

Ludendorff, General Erich, *My War Memoirs 1914-18.* Hutchinson, 1919. *Mein Militärischer Werdegang.* Ludendorffs Verlag, 1935. *Der Totale Krieg.* Ludendorffs Verlag, 1936. *Kriegfuhrung und Politik.* Mittler, 1922.

Ludendorff, Frau Mathilde, *My Married Life with Ludendorff.* Hutchinson, 1929.

Lutz, R. H., *The Causes of the German Collapse.* Stanford University Press, 1934.

Macpherson, Major-General Sir W. G., *Official History of the War, Medical Services, General History,* Vols. I-III, *Medical Services, Diseases of the War,* Vols. I-II.

Mansergh, Nicholas, *The Coming of the First World War; European Balance, 1878-1914.* Longmans, 1949.

Marder, Professor A. J., *From the Dreadnought to Scapa Flow: The Royal Navy in the Fisher Era,* Vol. I, *The Road to War, 1904-1914.* Oxford University Press, 1961. *Fear God and Dreadnought: the correspondence* of *Admiral Lord Fisher of Kilverstone.* Three volumes, 1952, 1956, 1959, Jonathan Cape. *British Naval Policy 1880-1905.* Putnam, 1941.

Max, Prince of Baden, *Memoirs.* Putnam, 1931-2.

Mead, Margaret and Wolfenstein, Martha (Editors), *Childhood in Contemporary Cultures.* Chicago University Press, 1955.

Mermeix, *Fragments d'histoire, 1914-19,* Tome 2: *Nivelle et Painlevé: La Deuxième Crise du Commandement, Decembre 1916-Mai 1917.* Librairie Paul Ollendorff, 1919.

Moltke, Colonel-General Helmuth Graf von, *Erinnerungen, Briefe, Dokumente 1877-1916.* Der Kommende Tag A. G. Verlag, 1922.

Müller, Admiral George von, *The Kaiser and His Court.* Macdonald, 1961.

Niemann, Alfred, *Kaiser und Revolution. Ereignisse im Grossen Hauptquartier.* Scherl, 1922.

Official Histories

 British. *The Official History of the War: Military Operations in France and Belgium, 1914-18.* All volumes. *Naval Operations,* Volumes III (1940 edition) and IV. *History of the Ministry of Munitions.* (For *Medical Services* see Macpherson above.)

 French. *Les Armées Françaises dans la Grande Guerre,* Tome I, I-III and annexes, Tome VI, I-II, and annexes.

 German. *Der Weltkrieg,* Band 1-3, Band 14; *Der Krieg Zur See,* Band 5; *Die Schlacht bei Mons* (General Staff Monograph).

Painlevé, Paul, *Comme J'ai Nommé Foch et Pétain.* Alcan, 1923.

Palat, General, *La Grande Guerre sur le Front Occidental:* Tome 12, *L'Année d'Angosse.* Berger-Levrault, 1927.

Pétain, Marshal Philippe, *La Bataille de Verdun.* Payot, 1929. *Le Devoir des Élites dans la Défense Nationale.* Berger-Levrault, 1936.

Pierrefeu, Jean de, *GQG—secteur 1.* Editions Françaises Illustrées, 1920.

Pitt, Barrie, *Coronel and the Falkland Isles.* Cassell, 1960.

Poincaré, Raymond, *Au Service de la France;* Volume VIII, *La Ruée sur Verdun;* Volume IX, *L'Année Troublée,* 1917; Volume X, *Victoire et Armistice, 1918.* Plon, 1933 and 1932.

Projectile Committee, Final Report of President of, 1917. HMSO.

Repington, Lieutenant-Colonel A. C., *The First World War, 1914-1918, Personal Experiences.* Constable, 1920.

Réquin, Lieutenant-Colonel E., *America's Race to Victory.* Stokes, 1919.

Ritter, Professor Gerhard, *The Schlieffen Plan.* Oswalf Wolff, 1958.

Rupprecht, Crown Prince of Bavaria, *Mein Kriegstagebuch.* Deutscher National Verlag, 1929.

Scheer, Admiral Reinhard, *Germany's High Sea Fleet in the World War*, Cassell, 1920.

Seely, Major-General J. E. B., *Adventure*. Heinemann, 1930.

Serrigny, General, *Trente Ans avec Pétain*. Plon, 1959.

Ship Design, Report of Committee on, 1905. HMSO.

Statesmen's Yearbook, editions of 1918, 1919 and 1920; *Statistics of the Military Effort of the British Empire during the Great War 1914-1920.* HMSO.

Sulzbach, Herbert, *Zwei Lebende Mauern*. Bernard and Graefe, 1935.

Tappen, General A. (see Koeltz).

Taylor, A. J. P., *The Course of German History*. University Paperbacks. *The Struggle for Mastery in Europe*. Oxford University Press, 1954.

Terraine, John, *Mons: the Retreat to Victory*. Batsford, 1960. *Haig: The Educated Soldier*. Hutchinson, 1963.

Tirpitz, Grand Admiral von, *My Memoirs*. Hurst and Blackett, 1919.

Trading in Arms, Report of Royal Commission on, 1936. HMSO.

University Grants Committee, Report of, 1908-9. HMSO

Waldeyer-Hartz, Hugo von, *Admiral von Hipper*. Rich and Cowan, 1933.

Watts, Sir Philip (Director of Naval Construction 1902-12), *Paper in the Transactions of the Institution of Naval Architects*, 1919.

Wheeler-Bennett, John, *Hindenburg: The Wooden Titan*. Macmillan, 1936.

Wryall, Everard, *The History of the 17th Battalion, Royal Fusiliers, 1914-19*. Methuen 1930.

Wynne, Captain G. C., *Pattern for Limited (Nuclear) War; The Riddle of the Schlieffen Plan* (Articles in the *Journal of the Royal United Services Institution*, 1957 and 1959).

Acknowledgements

In the first place, the author wishes to express his gratitude to the Dowager Countess Jellicoe for her kindness in granting him access to her husband's private papers and to the present Earl Jellicoe and Lady Gwendoline Latham for their advice and encouragement.

Secondly, the author's thanks are due to Mr. Herbert Sulzbach for permission to reproduce passages from his First World War diary; to Brigadier Desmond Young for the use of the signal book kept by him during the March Retreat, 1918; and to Sir Robert Chance and Brigadier-General S. V. P. Weston for background information on conditions of fighting on the western front.

For help, advice and research on British, French and German sources the author wishes to thank:

The librarians and staff of the War Office Library, the London Library, the Imperial War Museum Library, the Admiralty Library, the Library of the Royal United Services Institution, the Norwich City Library.

Commander P. K. Kemp, R.N., of the Admiralty Historical Section, General de Cossé-Brissac of the *Service Historique de l'Armée* at Vincennes, M. Pelissier, Librarian of the *Ecole Supérieure de Guerre,* Dr. J. Rohwer of the *Bibliothek für Zeitgeschichte* at Stuttgart, the *Militärgeschichtliches Forshungsamt* at Freiburg, as well as to the German Federal Ministry of Defence.

Colonel von Schroetter, Colonel Kraus, Commander Lechtenfield and Major Holtorff of the German Embassy in London.

The author also wishes to thank:

Mr. Gordon Fielden, for translating all the German source material.
Dr. Hugh l'Etang for information on Colonel-General von Moltke's health.
Mr. A. W. Tarsey, late of the Cabinet Office Historical Section, for advice over British sources,
Mr. William Bromage for drawing the maps.

The author's gratitude is owed to the following who were kind enough to read the book in typescript or proof and enable him to avoid many solecisms of fact or style: Major-General J. F. C. Fuller, Professor Norman Gibbs, Dr. Calvin Wells, Major-General E. Dorman O'Gowan, Captain S. W. Roskill, R.N., Captain D. A. Barnett, Mr. John Terraine and Mr. L. S. Brooks.

To Captain B. H. Liddell Hart, the author wishes to record his very special gratitude for the great care and trouble he has taken to help him by reading the typescript and making detailed suggestions and comments.

The errors of fact and interpretation that remain are the author's own.

Finally the author must again thank his wife for tolerating three years of acute absent-mindedness.

Index

Aachen, 17, 20, 25, 32, 60
Abbeville, 59, 60, 289, 315, 320, 322
Abdiel, 171
Admiralty, 103, 106, 109, 113, 114, 117, 124, 127, 152, 157, 160, 163, 173, 175, 179, 184, 185, 194, 237
Agincourt, 164
Ailette, 254
Airaines, 328
Aisne, 22, 63, 70, 193, 217, 307, 333, 334, 346
Albert, 292, 323, 325
Albrecht, Duke of Württemberg, 27, 40, 68
Alexander-Sinclair, Commodore, 129, 135, 136, 141
Allen, Captain, 128
Allenby, Major General, 48
Almereyda, Monsieur, 221, 259
Alsace, 36, 83
Alsace-Lorraine, 24, 36, 43, 46, 49, 60, 63, 72, 222, 226
  German annexation of, 11
  German victory in, 43
Amade, General d', 41
America, *see* under United States of America
Amiens, 16, 60, 294, 300, 313, 314, 315, 319, 321, 324, 325, 327, 328, 329, 330, 332, 347, 349

Amrum, 123
Ancre, 323, 324, 349
André, General, 226
Anthoine, General, 253, 261
  replaces Debeny, 261
Antwerp, 21, 32, 33, 39, 343
Arbuthnot, Rear-Admiral Sir Robert, Bart., 133, 158-59
Arcis-sur-Aube, 70
Ardennes, 40, 46, 49, 50, 56, 68, 246
Argonne, 72, 80, 295, 356
Armentières, 299, 305, 322, 330
1st Army (British), 299, 301, 309
2nd Army (British), 299, 301, 309
3rd Army (British), 293, 298, 299-300, 305, 307, 308, 309, 310, 311, 313, 314, 319, 323, 324
4th Army (British), 347
5th Army (British), 293, 294, 295, 298-299, 299-300, 301, 305, 306, 307, 308, 309, 310, 311, 312, 313, 314, 319, 322, 323
1st Army (French), 27, 43, 77, 253, 261, 321, 347, 349-50
2nd Army (French), 27, 43, 77, 190, 193, 253
3rd Army (French), 27, 41, 46, 47, 68, 77, 265, 294, 313, 321, 335
4th Army (French), 27, 41, 46, 47, 68, 77, 80, 337, 349

« 375 »

5th Army (French), 17, 27, 31, 41, 44, 53, 65, 76, 77, 78, 81, 82, 92, 199-200, 337

6th Army (French), 60, 66, 76, 80, 84, 87, 90, 199-200, 250, 254, 333, 337

9th Army (French), 76, 77, 80, 301, 314

10th Army (French), 199-200, 212

1st Army (German), 18, 25, 26, 31-32, 39, 40-41, 45, 48, 49, 52, 54-56, 62, 63, 64, 66, 67, 71, 72, 74, 75, 78, 79, 81, 85, 86, 88, 89, 90-91, 292

2nd Army (German), 17, 26, 32, 40-41, 44, 45, 47, 48, 57, 62, 63, 71, 72, 74, 75, 78, 85, 86, 88, 89, 90-91, 293, 311, 312, 315, 318-19, 321, 322, 323, 325, 328, 339, 350, 351, 353-54

3rd Army (German Saxon), 26, 40-41, 44, 47, 57, 59, 62, 63, 64, 74-75, 89, 293, 337

4th Army (German), 27, 37, 40, 59, 62, 63, 64, 68, 70, 72, 74, 89, 315, 330, 342

5th Army (German), 27, 37, 40, 59, 62, 63, 64, 70, 72, 74, 89

6th Army (German), 27, 36, 44, 51, 63, 74, 292, 315, 322, 330

7th Army (German), 27, 44, 51, 63, 74, 336, 344

8th Army (German), 37, 255, 272

9th Army (German), 336, 344

17th Army (German), 292, 311, 312, 315, 318, 321, 322, 323, 325, 328

18th Army (German), 289, 292, 311, 312, 315, 317, 318, 321, 322, 323, 325, 328, 335, 344, 353

Army Group "A" (German), 289, 292

Army Group Centre, 190, 194, 197, 248

Army Group East, 248, 321-22

Army Group North, 248, 260

Arras, 271, 283, 284, 285, 289, 291, 300, 315, 322, 323, 330

Artois, 96

Asquith, Herbert Henry, 273

Auchinleck, General Sir Claude, 236

Aufmarsch, 25

Austerlitz, 29

Australia, 349

Austria, 11, 12-13, 14, 15, 17, 18, 20, 37, 42, 96, 122, 207, 233, 255-56, 278, 355, 357-58

demands participation in Serbian investigations, 13

declares war, 19

attack by Serbs, 42

situation, Moltke's analysis, 13

1866 campaign, 96

Emperor Charles visits Spa, 355

Austria-Hungary, 11, 12, 20, 178, 279

Avesnes, 303, 312, 315, 322, 333, 339, 346, 351, 353, 354

Avre, 66, 238, 349

Avricourt, 347

Bacon, Admiral Sir R. H., 122

Baden, Prince Max of, 357, 359

Balkan Army Group, 346

Balkans, 11, 15, 205, 294

Balkan War, 29, 31

Baltic, 118, 121, 156, 177

Bapaume, 292, 309, 311, 315, 319, 325

Barescut, General de, 195-96, 250, 260

Barham, 136, 144, 147, 149

Barisis, 299, 305

Bar-le-Duc, 70

Basle, 20

Bassée, la, 282, 322

Battle Cruiser Fleet, 122, 125, 131

1st Battle Cruiser Squadron (British), 137

2nd Battle Cruiser Squadron (British), 127, 130, 137

3rd Battle Cruiser Squadron (British), 125, 126, 128, 158

2nd Battle Squadron (British), 125, 126, 127, 175

4th Battle Squadron (British), 128

5th Battle Squadron (British), 125, 126, 131, 135, 137, 138, 154

Battle Squadron 1 (German), 123, 131, 146, 159, 165

Battle Squadron 2 (German), 123, 124, 169

Battle Squadron 3 (German), 123, 165

1st Battleship Division, 168, 169

Bauer, Colonel, 26, 36, 50, 276, 337

Bavaria, 17

Bavaria, Crown Prince Rupprecht, *see* under Rupprecht

Bavay, 45

Beatty, Vice-Admiral Sir David, 119, 122, 123, 125, 126, 128-29, 130, 131, 132, 133, 134-41, 142, 143, 144, 145, 146, 147, 148, 149, 150, 151, 154, 155, 158, 162, 163, 164, 165, 167, 168, 169, 170, 172, 176, 180, 184, 189

    force at Rosyth, 122

    action against Hipper, 130-31, 143

    flees from Scheer, 134

    character and background, 134-35

    steers for Horn Reef, 135

    fails to signal intention, 135

    orders action stations, 136

    sights Hipper, 136

    heads for Grand Fleet, 147

    sends no reply to Jellicoe, 148, 149

    fails to chase Scheer, 168

    famous signal to Jellicoe, 168

    dispute over Jutland blame, 176

    made C-in-C Grand Fleet, 189

Beauvais, 319, 324

Belfort, 4, 21, 27, 60, 70, 74, 259

Belgian Congo, 207

Belgium, 4, 16, 17, 18-19, 20, 21, 22, 23, 24, 25, 26, 27, 32, 33, 37, 38-39, 41, 44, 51, 60, 95, 199, 207, 237, 245, 259, 277, 289, 295, 299, 301, 358

    Germany declares war, 18

Below, Otto von, 292, 310, 315

Beneckendorff und von Hindenburg, *see* Hindenburg

Berchtold, Count, 13, 15

Beresford, Admiral Lord Charles, 112

Berlin, 4, 8, 13, 18, 25, 31, 95, 277, 303, 359

Bethmann-Hollweg, Theobold von, 5, 6, 7, 8, 209, 270, 272, 273, 276, 277

    opposes restricted submarine warfare, 273

    submits peace proposals, 273

    proposals rejected, 273

Binche, 53

Bismarck, 110

Bismarck, Otto von, 4, 10, 11

Black Prince, 133, 173, 175

Blücher, 128

Blücher, Field-Marshal Prince, 317

Bödicker, Rear-Admiral, 141, 158

Boer War, 31, 54, 244

Bois Grenier, 300

Bolo Pasha, 221, 259

Bombon Conference, 347

Bonnal, General, 245

Bordeaux, 326

Borkum, 171

Boulogne, 40, 285, 322

Bourges, 70

Boxer Rebellion, 108

Brandenburg Grenadiers, 49

Bray, 326

Bremen, 303

Brest-Litovsk, 262, 275

Bridgeman, Admiral, 113

Brimont, 199

British Empire, 209, 275

British Expeditionary Force, 21, 31, 41, 44, 45, 46, 53, 55, 58, 64, 66, 76, 77, 82, 83, 85, 92, 106, 110

Broodseinde, 255

Bruchmüller, Colonel, 292, 306, 311, 328, 330, 333, 349

Brusilov, General, 235

Brussels, 32, 39, 40, 84

Buchanan, Sir George, 234, 235

Bucharest, fall of, 273

Bulgaria, 207, 278, 279, 351, 357

Bülow, Prince Bernard von, 4

Bülow, Colonel-General Karl von, 26, 31, 32, 40, 41, 44, 45, 47-48, 51, 52, 56, 57-58, 59, 60, 64, 65-66, 68, 70-72, 74, 76, 77, 78, 81, 82-83, 84, 85, 86, 87, 89, 90, 91, 92-93

    attacks Lanrezac along Sambre, 48

    omits to advise Hausen of plans, 48

    calls for Hausen's help, 57

    sheds corps to mask Maubeuge, 58

    orders pursuit in SW direction, 59

    calls for Kluck's help, 65

    impressions of French dissolution, 76

    crowded by Kluck, 78

Moltke's orders arrive too late, 78
  not told of Kluck's swing, 82-83
  excessive caution, 85
  split from Kluck by BEF, 85
  takes la Fère-Champenoise, 89
  discussion with Hentsch, 89
  orders retirement of his army, 91
Burney, Vice-Admiral Sir Cecil, 133, 161
Busche, Major Freiherr von dem, 357
Byng, General Sir Julian, 23, 299, 301, 323, 324, 325

Calais, 285
Callaghan, Admiral Sir George, 103, 105, 106, 107, 119
Calliope, 133, 169
Cambrai, 59, 256, 263, 292, 295, 300, 309, 311, 312, 349
Campania, 132
Canada, 326, 349
Canterbury, 125
Caporetto, 255, 256, 259, 260, 349
Cardot, Colonel, 242, 243, 244, 246
Cassel, 25
Casteau, 48
Castelnau, General de, 27, 84, 248
Castor, 130
Cateau, le, 58, 64
Cavalry Corps (British), 349-50
2nd Cavalry Corps (German), 32
Cerny, 251
Chagny, 70
Chalmers, Rear-Admiral, 139
Châlons, 63, 72, 74, 89
Châlons-sur-Marne, 248
Champagne, 96, 265, 295, 313, 319, 324
Champion, 131
Channel Fleet, 102, 113
Chantilly, 189, 324
Charteris, Brigadier-General, 236
Château de Montmort, le, 89
Château-Thierry, 63, 74, 90, 335, 347
Chatfield, Lord, 145
Chatham, 109
Chaulnes, 315, 318, 321
Chauny, 66, 313, 328
Chemin des Dames, 199, 202, 251, 254, 332, 338

Chester, 125
Chiers, 47, 50
Churchill, Winston S., 102, 103-7, 112, 117, 139, 153, 155, 180, 182, 261, 273, 354, 356
  telescopes Fisher's plans for Jellicoe, 102
  telegrams from Jellicoe, 105-7
  replies to Jellicoe, 105-7
  Haig's confidential paper, 112
  writes about Beatty, 139
  criticism of Jellicoe's deployment, 153
Clapham, Professor J. H., 186-87
Clausewitz, Carl von, 10, 55, 77, 204, 241, 276
Clemenceau, Georges, 209, 259, 260, 261, 264, 277, 281, 282, 324, 326, 327, 335, 356
  interferes in Petain's command, 261
  stops "Bulletin of the Armies," 261
  accepts Foch's ideas; rejects Pétain's, 264
Clermont, 72
Coastal Patrol, 122
Coblenz, 31, 36, 42, 44, 49, 50, 51, 61, 67, 69
Colin, General, 245, 247
Cologne, 25, 309
2nd Colonial Infantry Division (French), 202
Colossus, 129
Combles, 325
Commercy, 27
Compiègne, 65, 80, 86, 193, 215, 230, 239, 258, 260, 263, 324, 328
Comus, 170
Conchy, 354
Condé en Brie, 72
Conquest, 184
Conrad von Hotzendorff, Field-Marshal, 3
Corap, General, 301, 314
1st Corps (British), 58
2nd Corps (British), 55, 58
3rd Corps (British), 324, 349
18th Corps (British), 323, 324
19th Corps (British), 323, 324
2nd Corps (French), 212
18th Corps (French), 57

32nd Corps (French), 211
Coulommiers, 78
Courcelette, 323
Crécy, 178
Crépy, 70
Croisilles, 292, 312
Cromarty, 109, 122, 123, 125, 127
Crozart, 292, 309, 312, 313
1st Cruiser Squadron (British), 133
2nd Cruiser Squadron (British), 126
3rd Cruiser Squadron (British), 133

Damascus, 357
Debeney, General, 195, 215, 237, 260, 261, 321, 348, 350
Defence, 159
Denmark, 123, 135
Derfflinger, 140, 142, 143, 144, 160, 164, 165, 166, 169
Déroulède, Paul, 241
Destroyer Flotilla 1 (German), 123
Destroyer Flotilla 2 (German), 122-23
Destroyer Flotilla 3 (German), 123
Destroyer Flotilla 5 (German), 123
Destroyer Flotilla 7 (German), 122-23
Destroyer Flotilla 8 (German), 123
Destroyer Flotilla 9 (German), 122-23
Diest, 32
Digby Bell, Surgeon Commander, 108
Dijon, 70
Dinant, 57
5th Division (British), 166
6th Division (British), 161, 166
5th Division (French), 214
9th Division (French), 214
16th Division (German), 7, 8, 18
Dogger Bank, battle of, 128, 135, 184, 185
Dormans, 337, 343
Doullens, 315, 321, 322, 323, 324, 326, 327, 328
Doumergue, Paul, 234
Dover, 122, 123
Dover Patrol, 122
Drake, Sir Francis, 120
Dreadnought, 102, 182
Dresden, 25

Dreyer, Captain, later Admiral Sir Frederick, 119-20, 149, 154, 159, 185
Dreyfus, Captain Alfred, 30, 225, 226
Drina, 42, 255
Dubail, General, 27
Dublin, 170
Duchêne, General, 196, 333
Duke of Edinburgh, 163
Dunkirk, 16, 21, 41, 299, 320
Dury, 319, 320, 324
Duval, Colonel, 250

Echelle, l', 354
Edmonds, Sir James, 350
Einem, General von, 337
Elbing, 135, 136
Emmich, General von, 26
Ems, 171, 172
Engadine, 132
Enghien, 48
England, *see* under Great Britain
Entente (1904), 14
Epernay, 63, 72
Epinal, 21, 27, 63, 70, 74
Espérey, Franchet d', 76, 81, 82, 92, 215-216, 248, 333, 337
Essen, 303
Esternay, 77
Etalle, 40
Ethe, 47
Evan-Thomas, Vice-Admiral, 125, 126, 131, 135, 136, 137, 138, 139, 141, 144, 146-47, 149, 150, 151, 154, 158, 165, 168
uninformed by Beatty, 146
heavily shelled by Scheer, 146
running battle with Hipper, 147

Falkenhayn, General Erich von, 5, 95, 121, 189, 251, 253, 270, 271, 274, 280
to replace Moltke, 95
holds back Germany, 270
replaced, 270
Falkland Islands, 128
Falmouth, 130, 133
Farie, Captain, 131

Fayolle, Commandant, 198, 248, 249, 319, 320, 322, 324
Fère, la, 63, 65, 92, 288
Fère Champenoise, la, 89
Fère-en-Tardenois, 89, 91, 213, 335, 344
Ferté-sous Jouarre, la, 90
Ferté-Milon, la, 78, 84
Festubert, 284, 347
Festung Europa, 280, 281
Field, Marshall, 134
Fisher, Sir John, 101, 102, 108, 109, 112, 114, 178, 180, 182
  impressions of Jellicoe, 101, 102
  defines Jellicoe's proposed role, 102
  plans for Jellicoe telescoped, 102
  prejudiced plans, 109
  quarrel with Beresford, 112
  criticises Royal Navy system, 180, 182
Fismes, 88
N. J. Fjord, 135
Flanders, 92, 122, 123, 189, 200, 234, 237, 240, 250, 253, 257, 258, 282, 283, 284, 295, 296, 297, 300, 325, 334, 335, 336, 339, 340, 343, 344
Flesquières, 309, 311, 314
Foch, Marshal F., 43, 76, 80, 81, 82, 239, 243, 252, 257, 260-61, 263-264, 265, 269, 294, 295, 321, 324, 326, 327, 328, 333, 335, 348, 356, 360
  quarrel with Pétain over Italian support, 260-61
  leaves for Italy, 261
  opposes Pétain again, 263-64, 265
  heads executive committee of Supreme War Council, 264
  appointed allied supreme commander, 327-28
Fontaine les Croiselles, 309
Fort Douaumont, 201
France
  Germany declares war, 18
  modifies deployment, 27
  tactical doctrine, criticism, 27-30
  artillery strength, 29-30
  battle of, 36, 95
  defeat at Ardennes, 46
  government leaves Paris, 70
  battle crisis, 86
  attacks, 190
  inadequate weapons, 201
  army casualties, 202
  army in state of collapse, 205
  open mutiny in army, 210, 211-15
  women strikers riot in Paris, 223
  reasons for sense of defeat, 223-27
  troops' conditions improved, 217-18, 229-30
  army re-equips and reorganizes, 239-52
  Cardot's role in army failure, 242
  military ideas in 1911, 245-46
  army liaison improvement plan, 247
  new artillery plans, 248
  air power plans, 249
  army victories, 253-55
  plan to help Italy, 260
  strength and ability of army, 265
  similarities with Germany, 352
  effects of victory, 360-61
Francis Ferdinand, Archduke, 13
Frankfurt am Main, 25
Frauenlob, 170
Frederick II, 4
Frederick the Great, 10, 12
Frelinghien, 284
French, Sir John, 53, 54, 57, 58, 60, 76, 92
  Haig's opinion of, 54
  retreats southwards, 58
  gives up campaign, 76
Friedrich der Grosse, 123, 127, 158, 160, 165

Galatea, 129, 130, 135, 136, 141
Galicia, 289
Gallieni, Joseph S., 76, 93
Gallipoli, 97, 205
Gamelin, General, 301
Gascouin, General, 248-49
Gaulle, General Charles de, 44, 93
Gavrelle, 299
Gembloux, 40
George, 285, 322
George Two, 285
George V, King, 9, 108, 261
  denies British guarantee, 9

friendship with Haig, 261
Georgette, 322, 330-31
German High Seas Fleet, 98, 101, 108, 110, 114, 116, 118, 121, 122, 123, 125, 127, 132, 145, 146, 155, 160, 161, 164, 165, 167, 171, 173, 176, 180, 194, 262
German-Russo Armistice, 275
Germany
    expiry of ultimatum to Russia, 3
    declares war on France, 18
    declares war on Belgium, 18
    artillery strength, 29-30
    field tactics, 30-31
    first failure, 39
    victory at Ardennes, 46
    accuracy of howitzers at Mons, 55
    reasons for 1914 failure, 76
    crisis brings recriminations, 78
    battle and OHL crisis, 86
    command failure loses battle of Marne, 91-93
    needlessness of failure, 96
    commanding position, 96
    advances on Liége, 106
    superiority of navy, 114, 115
    naval strategy revised by Scheer, 121
    claims victory at Jutland, 176
    effects of Jutland, 176, 177
    comparison of tactics with Britain, 291
    secrecy of *St. Michael* operation, 293
    defence methods copied by Britain, 297-98
    civilian conditions in 1918, 302-3
    physical and moral state of troops, 318
    captures Bapaume, 319
    reasons for failure of *St. Michael,* 328-329
    advance towards Hazebrouck, 331
    failure of offensive, 335
    equipment comparison with Britain, 182-84
    army development, 243
    new army techniques, 251
    attacks Russian bridgehead, 255
    bombards Caporetto, 255-56
    victory at Riga, 255-56
    victory at Caporetto, 255-56

High Seas Fleet near mutiny, 262
handicapped by Falkenhayn, 270
effects of British blockade, 272-73
geographical disadvantages, 274
USA declares war, 274
armistice at Brest-Litovsk, 275
faces war on two fronts, 275
national strategy conference, 275
war planned by professional soldiers, 275-76
contrast between industry and technology, 277-78
moral cohesion begins to disintegrate, 278
state of national morale, 279-80, 302-303
war tactics and organization, 291-93
attacks around Reims, 336-37
defeat becomes fact, 340
Marwitz army collapses, 351
similarities with France, 352
effect of collapse of Bulgarian army, 357
effects of armistice, 359-61
Gette, 26, 39
Girardet, Raoul, 227
Givet, 40, 44, 57
Gneisenau, August Wilhelm Anton, 247
Gneisenau, 177
Göben, 128
Goodenough, Commodore, 131-32, 133, 134, 136, 142, 146, 150, 151, 164, 180
    sends Jellicoe incorrect report, 131
    scouts ahead of *Lion,* 142
    intelligence and resource praised, 164, 180
Gough, General Sir Hubert, 293, 294, 295, 299-300, 301, 309, 312, 314, 320, 323, 331, 350, 351
    ambiguity of instructions, 300
    orders retreat, 309, 312
Gouraud, General, 337
Gouzeaucourt, 299
Graf Spee, 177
Grand Couronné, 72
Grandmaison, Colonel de, 30, 244, 245
Grand Morin, 81, 82, 84

Grautoff, Lieutenant-Colonel, 79
Great Britain
    guarantee for France, 6
    declaration of war, 19
    general mobilisation order, 19
    first battle in N. Europe since Waterloo, 53
    weaknesses in navy, 111-12, 114-16
    restricts neutral sea-borne imports, 119
    superiority of British ships, 122
    claims victory at Jutland, 176
    equipment comparisons with Germany, 182-84
    industrial weaknesses, 185-88
    doubts over French plan, 199
    success at Messines and Broodseinde, 255
    blockade affects Germany, 272-73
    comparison of tactics with Germany, 291
    state of army in France in March 1918, 296
    copies German defence methods, 297-298
    modification of trench system, 298
    weakness of defences in France, 300
    5th Army begins to disintegrate, 312
    5th Army disintegrates, 323
    effects of victory, 360-61
Greece, 357
Greenland, 110
Grey, Sir Edward, 6, 9, 14, 17, 18-19
    promises naval support for France, 18
Gronau, General von, 79, 81
Grosser Kurfürst, 146, 167
Grouard, Captain A., 245, 247
2nd Guards Division, 45
Guignicourt, 63
Guillaumat, General, 253
Guise, 65, 66, 68
Gumbinnen, 42

Hagen, 339, 343
Haig, General Sir Douglas, 54, 58, 98, 112, 189, 199, 202, 204, 209, 234-235, 236-40, 252, 253, 255, 256, 257, 258, 261, 263, 264, 269, 271, 279, 282, 284, 291, 292, 294, 295,

296, 297, 299, 300-1, 308, 309, 310, 312, 313, 319-21, 322, 323, 324, 325-327, 331, 332, 333, 347, 348, 353, 356, 357
    confidential paper to Churchill, 112
    meeting with Pétain, 199
    optimism over Russian Revolution, 234-35
    wrongly assumes French support, 237
    orders further attack towards Passchendaele, 258
    comparison of defence measures with Pétain, 294
    forced to revise original plans, 296
    comparison with Gamelin, 301
    learns of *St. Michael* attack, 308
    extreme alarm, 320-21
    pleads for French reserves, 331
    issues Order of the Day, 331
    Amiens suggestion accepted, 347
Ham, 283, 299, 315
Hamburg, 289, 303
Hamburg, 123
Hamilton, Admiral Sir Frederick, 106
Hankey, Lord, 207
Hanover, 25
Hartog, Captain, 163, 166, 168, 169
Harvey, Major, 142-43
Harwich, 122, 123, 125, 157
Harwich Force, 122, 125
Hausen, Baron von, 26-27, 40, 41, 44, 51, 57-58, 68, 70
Havrincourt, 199
Hazebrouck, 282, 284, 285, 299, 331
Heeringen, General von, 27
Helfferich, Karl, 73
Helgoland, 158, 182
Heligoland, 109, 123, 127, 172, 177
Hentsch, Lieutenant-Colonel, 40, 41, 46, 48, 79, 87-92, 93
    error over BEF, 40, 41
    conference with Kluck, 79
    sent round army headquarters, 87, 88
    dispute over instructions and powers, 87-88, 91
    decides on general retreat, 90-91
    opinions of, 91
Herbillon, Colonel, 258

Hermann, Doctor, 36
Herstal, 32
Hertling, Graf, 354, 357
Heudicourt, 309
Hill 304, 253
Hindenburg, Field-Marshal Paul von, 50
    69, 94, 122, 189, 209, 251, 270-71,
    272, 274, 275, 276, 279, 280, 281,
    291-92, 303, 317, 330, 333-34, 339-
    340, 344-45, 346, 350, 351, 355,
    359
    succeeds Prittwitz, 50
    victory at Ortelsburg-Neidenburg, 69
    victory at Masurian Lakes, 94
    replaces Falkenhayn as leader, 189
    becomes Chief of General Staff, 270
    background and character, 271
    comparison with Ludendorff, 271
    tribute to Ludendorff, 272
    sums up results of possible success, 279
    discusses Festung Europa, 280
    issues operation order *St. Michael*, 291-
        292
    awarded Iron Cross with Golden Rays,
        317
    Ludendorff's display of rage, 339-40
    refuses Ludendorff's resignation, 355
    interview with Kaiser, 359
    resignation refused, 359
Hintze, Paul von, 355
Hipper, Vice-Admiral, 122-23, 127, 128-
    129, 132, 134, 135, 136-38, 139,
    140-41, 142, 143, 144, 145, 146,
    147, 158, 159, 164, 166, 168, 187
    sights Beatty, 136
    turns fleet round, 138
    accuracy of attack at Jutland, 142
    running battle with Evan-Thomas, 147
Hirson, 27, 57, 60
Hitler, Adolf, 4, 15, 206, 274, 275, 280,
    344, 353
Hoffmann, General Max, 50
Hohenzollern, 359
Holland, 16, 17, 25, 110, 119, 355
Home Fleet, 102, 106
Hood, Rear-Admiral Sir Horace, 126,
    130, 131, 133, 158, 160, 165
Horne, General Sir Henry, 325, 326

Horn Reef, 125, 135, 171, 172, 173, 176
Humbert, General, 265, 294, 313, 321,
    322, 335
Hunding-Brunnhild Line, 355
Hutier, General von, 255, 263, 292, 300,
    303, 310, 311, 312, 313, 317, 318,
    330, 335, 349, 353

Iceland, 110
Imperial Chancellor, *see* under Bethmann-
    Hollweg
Imperial Crown Prince, 27, 40
Indefatigable, 140, 143
Indomitable, 115, 169
18th Infantry (French), 213
128th Infantry (French), 212-13
158th Infantry (French), 213
Ingenohl, Admiral von, 118
Invergordon, 109
Invincible, 128, 160, 164
Ireland, 114, 189
Irles, 323
Iron Duke, 104, 105, 108, 115, 126,
    128, 129, 131, 134, 149, 150, 154,
    155, 157, 159, 164, 167, 171, 180
Italy, 14, 18, 207, 233, 255-56, 260, 263,
    283, 284, 289, 294, 337
    declares neutrality, 18
    Caporetto bombarded, 255-56
    army collapses, 256

Jade, 123, 125, 127, 164
Jagow, Gottlieb von, 5
Japan, 112, 189, 244
Jellicoe, Admiral Sir John, 17, 19, 49,
    91, 98, 101-8, 109, 110-11, 113-17,
    119-20, 122, 123, 125-26, 127-28,
    129, 130, 131-34, 135, 140, 144,
    146, 147-54, 155, 156, 157-58, 159,
    160, 161-63, 164, 165, 166, 167,
    168-69, 170-73, 175, 176, 179, 183,
    184, 189, 194-95, 237, 269
    arrives in Scapa Flow, 17
    takes Grand Fleet to sea, 19
    Fisher's impression of, 101, 102
    qualities and qualifications, 102, 103,
        108, 110-12, 119-20

Naval Controller, 102
proposed role in new navy, 102
appointed C-in-C designate of Home
Fleet, 102
reactions to new responsibility, 103-6
secret letter of appointment, 104
attempts to postpone appointment,
103-6
painful interview with Callaghan, 107
comparisons with Moltke, 107, 110-11
improvisation of equipment, 109
explanation of German failure, 109
extemporises naval strategy, 110
organises Grand Fleet staff, 113
shortcomings, 113-14
technical expertise, 114
knowledge of German fleet, 114
organisation skill, 125
plan for fighting Scheer, 128
orders action stations, 129
coolness under strain, 149, 150
orders "hoist equal speed pendant SE,"
150
comparison with Nelson, 151
new deployment plan, 150-54
Churchill's criticism, 153
refusal to chase Scheer, 162, 163
Beatty's famous signal, 168
dispute over Jutland blame, 176
criticises British ballistics, 183
made First Sea Lord, 189
reluctant to introduce convoy system,
195
Jena, 247
Jerram, Vice-Admiral Sir Martyn, 125,
126, 127-28, 163, 168, 169, 170
Joffre, General, later Marshal, 34, 41, 45-
46, 53, 55, 60, 65, 70, 72, 75, 76,
79, 80, 84, 85, 91, 93, 97, 155, 189-
190, 196, 198, 204, 245, 252, 257,
259, 263, 265, 270, 284
orders 3rd and 4th Armies into Ardennes, 46
surprised by German deployment, 46
orders BEF north of Mons, 53
informs French of formation of new
6th Army, 60
orders retreat, 70

details of plan, 80
orders BEF to advance between 1st and
2nd Armies, 85
competition with Moltke, 85
wins battle of the Marne, 91
dismissed, 189-90
replaced by Nivelle, 190
Junker, 271
Jura, 21
Jutland, battle of, 135-76, 262, 270, 303
its effects, 177-90, 262

Kaiser, *see* under Wilhelm II
Kaiserin, 146, 158
Kattegat, 156
Kent, 128, 184
11th King's (British), 308
Kinnaird's Head, 126
Kitchener, Field-Marshal Lord, 98
Klewitz, Lieutenant-Colonel W. J. von,
337-38, 353
Kluck, Colonel-General Alexander von,
18, 25, 26, 31-33, 39, 40, 41, 44-45,
48-49, 51, 52, 55, 56, 58, 59, 60,
64-68, 70-72, 73, 74, 75, 76, 77-79,
81, 82-83, 84, 85, 87, 88, 89, 90, 91,
92, 93, 96
protests at Bülow's command, 45
fails to penetrate Allenby screen, 48
decision to continue Mons attack, 56
released by Moltke, 59
bypasses Moltke, 66
disobeys Moltke's orders, 71
countermands Moltke's instructions, 78
conference with Hentsch, 79
brilliant performance, 81
moves HQ to la Ferté-Milon, 84
König, 146, 158, 159, 161, 165, 167
Königsberg, 17
Kraewel, General, 82, 84, 85, 92
Kronprinz, 146
Krupp, 185
Kruszewnia, 271
Kuhl, General H. von, 18, 79, 90-91, 92,
275, 282-84, 285, 289, 299, 302,
315, 322, 330, 332, 338-39, 352,
353-54

Langle de Cary, General de, 27, 41, 56, 57, 80
Lanrezac, General, 17, 27, 31, 41, 44, 45, 47, 48, 53, 56, 57, 58, 60, 65, 66, 76
Laon, 60, 62, 63, 92, 216
Lauenstein, General von, 89
Lawrence, General, 326
Leeb, Major von, 353
Leipzig, 303
Leningrad, 205
Lens, 53, 300, 322
Lichnowsky, Prince, 6, 9, 10
Liége, 17, 21, 25, 26, 27, 31, 50, 51, 75, 106, 272, 328
    fall of, 25, 26, 31
1st Light Cruiser Squadron (British), 135, 136, 146
2nd Light Cruiser Squadron (British), 136
3rd Light Cruiser Squadron (British), 136, 142, 146
4th Light Cruiser Squadron (British), 169
Lihons, 315
Lille, 21, 40, 41, 45
Lindesnes, 123
Lion, 128, 129, 136, 138, 140, 141, 142-43, 144, 145, 146, 148, 149, 150, 159, 169, 185
Lissa, 25
Liverpool, 115
Lloyd George, David, 208, 236, 261, 264, 270, 273, 277, 281, 282, 294
    replaces Asquith, 208, 273
    distrusts Flanders operation, 236
    persuades allies to set up Supreme War Council, 261
    plot against Haig, 261
    resolutions for allied central reserve, 294
London, 108
Longpont, 70
Lorette, 299
Lorraine, 24, 27, 37, 38, 41, 52, 73, 246
Lossberg, General von, 339, 342, 343, 346, 347, 353, 356
    conference with Ludendorff, 342

reports Marne situation to Ludendorff, 343
Loucheur, Louis, 326
Lough Swilly, 114
Louvain, 39
Ludendorff, General Erich, 17, 20, 24, 25, 45, 50, 69, 75, 94, 122, 189, 209, 234, 246, 251, 252, 255, 265, 269-272, 273, 274, 275, 276-82, 283, 284, 285, 289-90, 291, 293, 295, 303-4, 309, 311, 312, 314-17, 318, 321, 324, 325, 328, 330, 331-33, 334-35, 336-41, 324-47, 350, 351, 353-55, 356-57, 358, 359
    joins 2nd Army, 17
    appointed chief for east, 50
    victory at Ortelsburg-Neidenburg, 69
    victory at Masurian Lakes, 94
    replaces Falkenhayn, 189
    comments on effects of Russian Revolution, 234
    reorganises techniques, 251
    comparison with enemy counterparts, 269
    description and character, 269-72
    becomes 1st Quartermaster General, 270
    comparison with Hindenburg, 271
    plans Germany's grand strategy, 274
    chairman of strategy conference, 275, 278
    plans offensive in France, 278
    sums up Mons conference, 283
    holds second conference, 285
    tour of staff conferences, 285
    orders start of operation *St. Michael*, 304
    issues new *St. Michael* orders, 315
    conference with Kuhl and Schulenberg, 315
    orders capture of Amiens, 330
    orders operation *Georgette*, 330
    stops battle, 335
    resumes battle on Marne, 337
    turns rage on Hindenburg, 340
    reaction to Lossberg's Marne report, 342
    plans retreat, 344

issues secret order to OHL staff, 347
explains situation to Kaiser, 354-55
accepts national defeat, 354
defeatism due to US strength, 356
attempts to sabotage peace negotiations, 359
interview with Kaiser, 359
resignation accepted, 359
Lunéville, 27, 51
Lusitania, 119
Lützow, 137, 140, 142, 143, 144, 146, 160, 164, 166, 176, 184
Luxembourg, 4, 7, 8, 16, 17, 32, 69, 70, 79, 83, 88, 93, 106
Lyncker, General Freiherr von, 5, 94
Lyon, 70, 77
Lys, 283, 285, 296, 299, 330, 331, 358

Madden, Rear-Admiral Sir Charles, 106, 113, 171
Mafeking, 208
Maistre, General, 254, 337
takes Malmaison, 254
Malaya, 144, 147, 175
Malmaison, 199, 254-55, 349
Malmédy, 27, 301
Malvy, Monsieur, 221, 231, 258-59
Mangin, General, 339, 342
Manstein, General von, 289
Marengo, 29, 199, 241
Mareuil, 90
Margny-le-Thoult, 85
Marita, 357
Markgraf, 147, 160
Marlborough, 133, 147, 161, 163
Marlborough, First Duke of, 12
Marne, 63, 64, 66, 71, 72, 74, 77, 80, 84-85, 86, 87, 89, 90, 91, 92, 93, 94, 95, 155, 202, 258, 335, 336, 337, 342, 343, 344, 345, 346, 347
battle of, 64, 66, 76, 91, 93, 95, 202, 258
Mars, 285, 289, 322, 328, 330
Mars North, 322
Mars South, 322
Marson, 72
Marwitz, General von der, 32, 41, 48, 58,

81, 82, 84, 85, 92, 292, 310, 315, 323, 350, 351, 353, 354
Matz, 354
Matthes, Lieutenant-Colonel, 89
Maubeuge, 14, 21, 34, 41, 45, 48, 54, 57, 58, 81, 92
Maud'huy, Colonel de, 243-44
Maunoury, General, 60, 64, 66, 76, 80, 81, 82, 84, 85, 87, 90, 91, 92
Mauve, Rear-Admiral, 124, 169
Mayer, Captain, 243, 245, 247
May Island, 126
Meaux, 81
Melun, 70, 77
Merrheim, Monsieur, 221
Méry, 74
Messines, 255
Mesurier, Commodore le, 133, 169-70
Metternich, Prince, 11, 12
Metz, 17, 23, 24, 27, 32, 36, 37, 62, 68, 243
Meuse, 27, 32, 40, 41, 44, 45, 46, 47, 48, 49, 50, 52, 57, 58, 59, 63, 68, 192, 253, 314, 343
Mézières, 21, 27, 40, 56
Mirecourt, 248
Michael, see under *St. Michael*
Milford Haven, Marquis of, 103
Milner, Lord, 321, 324, 326
Miramont, 315
Moltke, Colonel-General Helmuth Graf von, 3, 4-9, 13, 16-17, 18, 19, 20, 21, 22, 23-25, 26, 31, 32, 33, 34-38, 40, 41, 42-43, 44, 45, 49, 50, 51, 52, 53, 57, 58, 59, 60-61, 62-64, 66, 68, 69, 70-71, 73-78, 79, 83-84, 85-87, 88, 91, 93, 94-96, 107, 110, 189, 195, 270, 271, 274, 290, 317
refuses responsibility, 8
refuses to sign order, 8
analyses Austrian situation, 13
defends Dutch neutrality, 16-17
ultimatum presented in Brussels, 18
open mind about Schlieffen Plan, 25
plan to seize Liége, 25
orders for advance north of Meuse, 32
personal details, 34-36
physical constitution, 35-36

effect of victory in Alsace-Lorraine, 44
backs Prittwitz decision to abandon E. Prussia, 50
backs Rupprecht's decision to advance, 51
problems of poor communications, 52, 67
wrong assessments of BEF and French 5th Army, 53
plans for consummation of victory, 61
General Directive, 63
modifies Schlieffen Plan, 62-64
moves to Luxembourg, 69
interview with Helfferich, 73
issues memo which loses campaign, 74-75
lack of real war experience, 75
effects of strain, 75-76, 83
confides terror to wife, 83-84, 86
competition with Joffre, 85
deterioration of morale, 86
staff conference on battle crisis, 86
confidence in Hentsch, 91
private comments on Marne defeat, 93
breaks down, 94
replaced, 94-95
comparisons with Jellicoe, 107
death, 189
Moltke, 140, 142, 143, 144, 165, 175
Mons, 45, 48-49, 53, 54, 55, 56, 59, 275, 279, 283
battle of, 48-49, 54-56
Montdidier, 294, 315, 319, 321, 325, 328, 329, 330, 335, 353
Montgomery, General, 326
Montmédy, 56
Montmirail, 78, 89
Mont Spin, 212
Moreuil, 328
Morhange-Sarrebourg, 43, 46
Mormal, Forest of, 58
Morocco, 40
Moronvilliers, 84
Mort Homme, 253
Moscow, 205
Moselle, 21, 63, 74
Mount Kemmel, 331
Mulhouse, 36

Müller, Admiral Georg von, 5, 52, 70, 317
Munich, 4

Namur, 21, 32, 40, 44, 45, 49, 52, 289
fall of, 49, 52
Nancy, 27, 70, 72, 73, 77-78, 84
Napoleon, 4, 29, 47, 77, 204, 245, 252
Nelson, Horatio Nelson, Viscount, 102, 108, 113, 116, 129, 132, 151, 177, 179, 181, 186
Neptune, 129-30, 164
Nesle, 325
Netherlands, 16
Neuchâteau, 63
Neufchâteau, 47, 70
Neuilly-St. Front, 90
Neumünster, 127
Neuve Chapelle, 96, 300
Nevers, 70
New Zealand, 136, 140, 143, 144, 145
Nied, 37
Niemann, Major, 354
Nietzsche, Friedrich, 35
Nivelle, General, 190, 193-94, 195, 196, 197, 199, 201, 203, 212, 216-17, 221, 222, 225, 246, 250, 253, 257, 258, 265, 284, 302, 351
replaced by Pétain, 194
Nogent, 70, 74
Normandy, 205
North Sea, 49, 108, 110, 116, 118, 121, 124, 126, 132, 156, 163, 177, 182, 273, 274, 282, 301
Norway, 49, 123
Nottingham, 130
Noyon, 294, 313, 315, 318, 321, 322, 328, 335

Oise, 22, 62, 63, 65, 70, 74, 263, 265, 300, 307, 322, 324, 328
Oldershausen, General von, 346
Omignon, 292, 309, 311, 318
Orléans, 70
Ortelsburg-Neidenburg, 69
Ory (French controller general), 245
Ostend, 236
Ostfriesland, 158, 176

Ourcq, 81, 82, 83, 84, 89

Painlevé, Paul, 198, 216, 217, 221, 222, 228, 239, 259, 261
  Pétain's first report, 216, 217
  refuses to take action against Malvy, 221
  becomes Prime Minister, 259
  ceases to be Prime Minister, 259
Pakenham, Rear-Admiral, 137
Palestine, 357
Paléologue, Maurice, 234
Paris, 16, 22, 33, 59, 60, 62, 63, 64, 66, 69, 70, 71, 73, 74, 75, 77, 78, 80, 82, 83, 86, 93, 94, 194, 198, 201, 209, 214, 221, 223, 239, 247, 260, 294, 295, 319, 335, 347
Pas de Calais, 325
Passchendaele, 205, 237, 256, 258, 282, 296, 298, 299, 310, 348, 349
Pearl Harbor, 155
Pentland Skerries, 125, 126
Péronne, 263, 283, 285, 288, 289, 292, 300, 312, 313, 315
Pershing, General John J., 294, 324
Pétain, General Henri Philippe Benoni Omer, 17, 58, 81, 116, 122, 189, 190, 193, 194-99, 202-3, 204, 209, 210, 213, 214, 215-22, 226, 227-28, 229-32, 234, 235, 236, 237, 239, 240-41, 246, 247-50, 252, 253, 254, 255, 256-57, 258, 259-63, 264-65, 269, 270, 272, 294-95, 299, 301, 309, 312, 313, 319, 320, 321-22, 324, 326, 327, 330, 331, 333, 335, 337
  joins 5th Army, 17
  skilful action against Hausen, 58
  commands 6th Infantry Division, 81
  assumes command of Army Group Centre, 122
  victory at Verdun, 189
  replaces Nivelle, 194
  holds first staff meeting, 195
  some impressions by his colleagues, 197-98
  revolutionary strategy, 198-99
  meeting with Haig, 199

Haig's opinion of, 199
  issues Directive No. 1, 202-3
  faces imminent disintegration of army, 209
  understanding of soldiers' hardships, 217
  criticises the press, 318-19
  makes charge against Malvy, 221
  moral authority, 227
  punishes mutiny ringleaders, 228
  given right to confirm death sentences, 228
  inaugurates new leave system, 229
  improves troop conditions, 229-30
  condemns Haig's Flanders plan, 236
  advocates waiting for US support, 239
  reorganises army, 240-41
  issues Directives Nos. 2 and 3, 247-49
  forms large general reserve, 248
  new artillery plans, 248
  air power plans, 249
  problems of Painlevé's accession, 259
  meets new government, 259
  reports strategic balance, 259
  criticised by presidents, 259
  quarrel with Foch over Italian support, 260-61
  prestige with Clemenceau declines, 261
  issues Directive No. 4, 262-63
  more opposition from Foch, 264
  ideas overruled by Clemenceau, 264
  assesses proposed German offensive, 265
  extent of efforts to prepare French army, 265
  meeting with Haig, 312-13
Petit Morin, 71, 82
Phaeton, 136
Picard, Captain, 196
Picardy, 60, 98
Pierrefeu, Lieutenant Jean de, 197
Plessen, General von, 7, 336
Plumer, Sir Herbert, 255, 325
Pohl, Admiral von, 118, 120
Poincaré, Raymond, 223, 228, 261, 326
Poland, 96, 280
Pommern, 169, 173
Pontavert, 70
Portugal, 203, 301, 331

Posen, 25, 271
Princess Royal, 138, 140, 142, 143, 145, 169
Prittwitz und Gaffron, General von, 37, 43, 50, 272
  decision to abandon E. Prussia, 50
  succeeded by Hindenburg, 50
Provins, 78
Prussia, 4, 10, 37, 42, 43, 49, 50, 52, 53, 113, 179, 241, 272
Pys, 323

Queen Elizabeth, 115, 146
Queen Mary, 140, 142, 144, 145, 182
Quirnheim, Colonel Mertz von, 337, 339, 340, 344, 351, 353

Rapallo, 261
Rarécourt, 72
Rawlinson, General, 326, 349-50, 351
Rebais, 78
Red Army, 205
Regensburg, 122, 141
162nd Regiment of Infantry (French), 211
Reichsland, 36
Reims, 63, 70, 88, 199, 335, 336, 337, 344
Repington, Lieutenant-Colonel A. C., 197
Reserve Army Group (French), 319
3rd Reserve Corps (German), 39
4th Reserve Corps (German), 39, 79, 81
7th Reserve Corps (German), 81, 92
9th Reserve Corps (German), 20
Revenge, 164
Ribot, Alexandre Felix Joseph, 259
Riga, 255, 256, 263, 292, 349
Riquenberg, 354
Rocroi, 57
Roques, General, 264
Roshdeshventsky, Admiral, 101
Rossignol, 47
Rostock, 123
Rosyth, 108, 122, 123, 125, 126
Royal Fusiliers, 323
Royal Marine Light Infantry, 142-43
Royal Navy, 98, 101, 103, 109, 111-15,

118, 128, 134, 147, 149, 156, 177, 178-86, 241, 303
  gunnery condition, 101
  weaknesses, 111-15, 178-86
  mistakes, 128-29
  Fisher's criticisms, 179-80, 182
  lack of research facilities, 185
Royal Navy Grand Fleet, 98, 104, 108, 109-10, 113-14, 118, 119, 122, 125-126, 127, 128, 134, 147, 150, 151, 154, 156, 157, 160, 164, 167, 171, 173, 175, 176, 177, 180
  battle orders, 113-14
  prepares for battle, 125-26
  results of battle of Jutland, 176-78
Roye, 322, 328, 349
Ruffey, 27
Rumania, 262, 273, 280
Rundstedt, General von, 289
Rupprecht, Crown Prince of Bavaria, 27, 36, 37, 43, 50-51, 62, 63, 72, 73, 74, 85, 87, 275, 289, 292, 311, 312, 321, 328, 335, 344, 353
  victory in Alsace-Lorraine, 43
  victory in Morhange-Sarrebourg, 50
Russia, 3, 6, 8, 11, 13, 14, 15, 16, 17, 18, 20, 35, 37, 42-43, 62, 69, 101, 122, 156, 177, 189, 195, 203, 211, 215, 218, 219, 223, 225, 233, 234-35, 236, 237, 244, 250, 255, 262, 263, 264, 270, 274, 275, 279, 280, 283, 294, 296, 299, 352, 360
  expiry of German ultimatum, 3
  action at Stallupönen, 37
  invasion of Prussia, 42-43
  defeat at Ortelsburg-Neidenburg, 69
  beginnings of failure, 156
  bridgehead attacked at Riga, 258
  defences collapse, 255
Russian Revolution, 195, 219
  memoranda on, 234-35
  importance in First World War, 274-75
Russo-German Armistice, 275
Russo-Japanese War, 31, 243

Saar, 207
St. Cyr, 227
St. Gond, 81

St. Michael, 285-93, 301-5, 306-26, 328-331, 356
St. Mihiel, 347
St. Omer, 257
St. Petersburg, 234
St. Pol, 294, 315, 321, 328
St. Quentin, 94, 263, 283, 284, 285, 300
St. Simon, 313
St. Soupplets, 79
St. Vincent, battle of, 102, 116, 151
St. Vincent, 164
Ste. Etienne, 229
Ste. Ménéhould, 27, 72, 88
Salonika, 337, 357
Sambre, 41, 45, 52, 55
3rd Saxon Army, *see* under 3rd Army
Scandinavia, 119, 156
Scapa Flow, 17, 103, 105, 108, 109, 110, 114, 122, 123, 125, 127, 131
Scarpe, 265, 322
Scharnhorst, Gerhard Johann David von, 247
Scharnhorst, 177
Scheer, Admiral Reinhard, 120, 121, 122, 123, 124, 125, 127, 128, 130, 131, 132, 133, 134, 135, 136, 137, 144, 146, 147, 150, 151, 152, 154, 156, 157, 158, 159, 160, 162-64, 165, 166, 167, 168, 169, 170, 171, 173-176, 177, 180, 189
  replaces von Pohl, 120
  persuades Kaiser to use aggression, 121
  extent of High Seas Fleet, 122
  orders fleet to sail for Skagerrak, 123
  misled by radio reports, 126
  arrives at battle of Jutland, 146
  battle and personal crises, 160
  saves his fleet, 162-63
  orders "Charge," 165
  escape plan, 171
  wins through, 173
Schlesien, 169
Schleswig-Holstein, 17, 20
Schleswig-Holstein, 169
Schlieffen, Count, 3, 4, 10, 15-17, 21-25, 34, 37, 38, 50, 59, 60, 62, 64, 72, 77, 81-82, 245, 271, 274, 311
Schlieffen Plan, 15-17, 18, 21-25, 27, 51,

59, 60, 64, 66, 68, 72, 76, 81-82, 96, 97, 245, 278
Schmaus, Lieutenant Dr., 304
Schneidemühl, 25
Schröder, Admiral, 122
Schulenberg, Colonel von der, 275, 282, 283, 284, 315
Schwerin, Graf, 346
Scotland, 110
Scouting Group 1 (German), 122-23, 127, 136, 143-44, 146, 164, 165, 166, 167
Scouting Group 2 (German), 122-23, 137, 141, 146
Scouting Group 4 (German), 123, 158
Sedan, 27, 56, 178, 226, 241, 289
Seely, Colonel J. E. B., 81
Seine, 74, 75, 78
Selle, 358
Sens, 70
Serbia, 12-13
Séré de Rivière, Colonel, 242
Serret, Colonel, 31
Serrigny, General de, 196, 197, 198, 199, 203, 204, 215, 237, 239, 248, 257, 259, 260, 261
Seydlitz, 128, 140, 142, 144, 146, 165, 166, 168, 169, 176, 182, 184, 185
Seymour, Ralph, 134-35, 136
Sichelsnitt Plan, 288, 301
Siegfried Line, 216, 318, 343, 347, 353, 355, 356
Singapore, 309, 354
Skagerrak, 123, 156
Smith-Dorrien, General Sir H. L., 55, 58
Soissons, 70, 89, 91, 295, 335, 340
Solthomer Watt, 127
Somme, 43, 189, 203, 205, 217, 257, 283, 292, 300, 309, 310, 312, 313, 314, 315, 317, 318, 320, 321, 323, 324, 326, 327, 328, 329, 349, 353, 354
  battle of the, 189, 205, 217, 257, 260
Spa Conference, 355
Spithead Review, 108
Stalingrad, 211, 354
Stallupönen, 37
Stein, General von, 44, 50, 87, 88, 94

Stettin, 18, 25
Stockholm conference, 219
Strasbourg, 17, 25
Sulzbach, Lieutenant Herbert, 302, 312,
    318, 325
Sunderland, 122
Supreme War Council, 261, 264, 294
Switzerland, 16, 21, 60, 63, 74, 116, 282,
    295

Talleyrand, Charles-Maurice de, 12
Von der Tann, 140, 141, 143, 144, 147,
    157, 165-66
Tappen, Lieutenant-Colonel A. von, 8, 51,
    52, 87, 88, 89
Tartigny, 328
Task Force, 77, 189
Taylor, Professor A. J. P., 357
Tergnier, 313
Terraine, John, 237, 300
Tertry, 311
Thames, 122, 123
Third Bureau (French), 196
Thionville, 25, 32, 40, 62
Thunderer, 164
Thuringen, 158, 175
Tieschowitz, Lieutenant-General von, 304,
    345
Tiger, 115, 128, 140, 142, 143, 146
Tirlemont, 32
Tirpitz, Grand Admiral von, 5
Tobruk, 309
Tocsani, Armistice of, 262
Tortille, 318
Toul, 21, 63, 74
Tournai, 54
Trafalgar, 102, 151, 166, 176, 177, 180
Trident, 126
Trier (16th) Division, 7
Troyes, 74, 78
Tschischwitz, Colonel von, 353
Tsushima, 101
Turkey, 128, 205, 278, 279, 360
Tyrwhitt, Admiral Sir Reginald, 122, 157
    force at Harwich, 122
    criticises Royal Navy gunnery, 179

United Nations, 97

United States of America, 5, 119, 155,
    177, 181, 186, 189, 195, 207, 209,
    232, 233-34, 235, 239, 253, 256,
    262, 273, 274, 275, 278, 282, 283,
    294, 301, 332, 335, 347, 356, 360,
    361
    enters war, 195
    landings in France, 262
    declares war on Germany, 274
    responsible for Ludendorff's defeatism,
    356
1st US Corps, 324
United States Pacific Fleet, 189

Valabrègue, General, 27
Valiant, 144
Valkyrie, 322, 328
Valmy, 72
Vendeuvre, 74
Verberie, 70, 84, 92
Verdun, 4, 21, 27, 59, 60, 62, 63, 70, 73,
    74, 80, 81, 86, 121, 122, 155, 189,
    190, 194, 195, 196, 197, 198, 201,
    202, 205, 226, 227, 248, 253, 255,
    257, 258, 265, 270, 279, 282, 283,
    284, 285, 293, 295, 326, 347
Versailles, Treaty of, 207, 361
Vertus, 78
Vervins, 27
Vesle, 70, 87, 334, 344, 346
Vezouse, 51
Vic-sur-Aisne, 248
Vienna, 13, 207
Vigo, 171
Ville-en-Tardenois, 344
Villeneuve, Pierre de, 108, 129
Villers-Bretonneux, 330
Villers-Cotterets, 70, 335, 339
Villiers St. Georges, 78
Vimy, 299
Virton, 47
Vise, 32
Vistula, 43
Vitry-le-François, 63, 70
Vosges, 24, 37, 285, 295
Voslapp Watt, 127

Wagram, 29

Warspite, 144, 147, 158
Washington, 119
Washington Treaty, 189
Waterloo, 244, 317
Wavell, General Sir A., 236
Wavre, 32
Wellington, Arthur Wellesley, 1st Duke of, 120
Westfalen, 175
Weston, Colonel, 323
Wetzell, Lieutenant-Colonel, 275, 281, 284, 285, 288, 330, 339, 342, 346, 354
  memo on attitude of Supreme Command, 281-82
  brilliant analysis of German and allied strength, 284
  attack by Ludendorff, 342
Weygand, General, 263, 324
Wick, 105
Wiesbaden, 158, 159, 163
Wilhelm II, 4, 5, 6-9, 10, 13, 22, 26, 31, 33, 34, 43, 52, 61, 69, 75, 94-95, 119, 121, 177, 206, 270, 274, 289, 303, 317, 354-55
  attack on Moltke, 7
  summons Moltke, 8
  reactions to results of war, 69
  accepts Bethmann-Hollweg's resignation, 274
  celebrates *St. Michael* victory too soon, 317
  Ludendorff explains situation, 354-55
Wilhelmshaven, 127
Wilson, General Henry, 236, 261, 264, 294, 321, 326
Wilson, President Woodrow, 273, 358
Woods, Commander A. R. W., 150, 154
Württemberg, Duke Albrecht of, 27, 40, 68

Ypres, 282, 285, 299
Ytres, 311, 314
Yugoslavia, 357

Zeebrugge, 136